W9-AWU-326

Family Circle
Christmas Treasury
1991

EDITORIAL

Editorial Director, Family Circle Books— Carol A. Guasti
Associate Editor— Kim E. Gayton
Project Editors— Leslie Gilbert Elman & Ceri Hadda
Copy Editor— Laura Crocker
Book Design— Bessen, Tully & Lee
Cover Photo— Elyse Lewin
Clip Art-1,001 Advertising Cuts from the 20's and 30's, copyright© 1987 by Dover Publications, Inc; Ready-To-Use Old Fashioned Christmas Illustrations, copyright© 1989 by Dover Publications, Inc.
Editorial Production Coordinator— Celeste Bantz
Editorial Assistant— Sherieann Holder
Senior Typesetter— Alison Chandler
Typesetting— Maureen Harrington, Cheryl Aden
Indexer— Candace Gylgayton

MARKETING

Director, Family Circle Books & Licensing— Margaret Chan-Yip
Direct Marketing Manager— Jill E. Schiffman
Associate Business Manager— Carrie Meyerhoff
Administrative Assistant— Laura Berkowitz

Published by The Family Circle, Inc.
110 Fifth Avenue, New York, NY 10011

Copyright® 1991 by The Family Circle, Inc.

All rights reserved. No part of this book may be reproduced in any form or by any electronic means, including information storage and retrieval systems, without permission in writing from the publisher, except by a reviewer who may quote brief passages in a review.

Manufactured in the United States of America

10 9 8 7 6 5 4 3 2 1

Library of Congress Cataloging in Publication Data
Main entry under title:

Family circle christmas treasury.
Includes index.
1.Christmas decorations. 2.Christmas cookery.
I.Family Circle, Inc. II.Title: Christmas Treasury.

1991 88-644807

ISBN 0-933585-21-7
ISSN 0892-3604

Other Books By Family Circle

BEST-EVER RECIPES

BEST-EVER RECIPES, VOLUME II

THE BEST OF FAMILY CIRCLE COOKBOOK SERIES
(Pub. Dates: 1985 – 1989)

BUSY COOK'S BOOK

GOOD HEALTH COOKBOOK

MAKE IT COUNTRY

THE COUNTRY KITCHEN

COUNTRY CRAFTS

THE FAMILY CIRCLE CHRISTMAS TREASURY SERIES
(Pub. Dates: 1986 – 1990)

TREASURY OF CHRISTMAS CRAFTS

FAVORITE NEEDLECRAFTS

HINTS, TIPS & SMART ADVICE

To order **FamilyCircle** books, write to Family Circle Books, 110 Fifth Avenue, New York, NY 10011.

To order **FamilyCircle** magazine, write to Family Circle Subscriptions, 110 Fifth Avenue, New York, NY 10011.

TABLE OF CONTENTS

OVERNIGHT SENSATIONS **88**

PRESENTS, PRESENTS, PRESENTS! **104**

CHRISTMAS COOKING **158**

INTRODUCTION

It's the most glorious season of the year. A time for celebrating all that is good, generous and loving. A time to gather together with family and friends, to cherish the joy in your lives and the love you share.

Family Circle has been helping you to "make the season bright" for almost 60 years. This year we welcome Christmas with beautiful door trims and twinkling lights, delightful table settings and wonderful ornaments. Each chapter brings another facet of the Yuletide season into your home. From decorating magnificent trees to adding lovely accents, there's something within these pages that will help make this Christmas especially wonderful.

Because one of the greatest joys of Christmas is giving something to your loved ones, we provide you with gifts for the home, for her, for him, and for those special children in your life. Nothing can compare with a present lovingly crafted by hand.

And what would Christmas be without the feasting and fun? In Chapter VI, we've created a holiday cookbook in miniature to bring the delicious tastes of the season into your home.

As always, there are hints to help make crafting decorations and gifts simple and easy. But this year we've also included some very special, ecologically sound "Tips for a Green Christmas" to insure bright holidays for our children and our children's children.

WELCOME CHRISTMAS

Be
merry all,
Be merry all,
With holly dress the festive hall;
Prepare the song,
the feast, the ball,
To welcome merry Christmas.
—W. R. Spencer

From the fragrant wreath on your front door to the tiny lights that sparkle around your windows at night, your holiday home can greet and cheer all who pass by.

We offer a splendid selection of wreaths to suit any style, from a sumptuous Victorian-style wreath to a spicy cinnamon stick wreath to a quaint felt teddy bear and holly wreath. Trim a fresh evergreen wreath with herbs, flowers or fruit, or craft a door plaque and matching transom decorations inspired by a Colonial Christmas.

Make your Christmas light display extra-special this year with an old-fashioned village scene in your window. Or create the illusion of stars falling through tree branches.

Let the beauty of your Yuletide home give all who pass by a greeting of love, peace and welcome.

HOLIDAY DOOR TRIMS

Adorn your front door
and entryway with holiday splendor
to greet the season.

ANTIQUE DOLL WREATH

(photo, page 3 and at left)
This beautiful, Victorian-style wreath may look ornate, but actually it is very easy to make.

Easy: Achievable by anyone.

Materials: Ceramic doll head (available at craft supply and hobby stores); antique-look decals; dried baby's breath; 1¼-inch-wide double-edged ecru lace; 2-inch-wide double-edged ecru lace; ⅛-inch-wide pink, red and green velvet ribbons; 1-inch-wide pink, red and green velvet ribbons; roll of gold metallic wrapping paper; sheets of lightweight poster board; floral foam; floral wire; stapler; glue stick; rubber cement; carbon paper; paper for pattern.

Directions:

1. Trace the full-size cornucopia pattern in Fig. I, 1 *(page 6)* onto paper. Using the carbon paper, trace the pattern onto the poster board 30 times. Repeat on the gold paper. Cut out all the cornucopias. Also draw and cut out a 15-inch-diameter circle from the poster board.

2. Roll each poster board cornucopia into a cone, lapping the edges ¼ inch. Secure the edges with the glue stick, and staple them together along the top edge.

3. Spread rubber cement on the backs of the gold paper cornucopias, and cover each poster board cornucopia with a gold cornucopia. Trim all the gold-covered cornucopias with the ribbons and laces; add the decals to 10 of the cornucopias *(see photo, page 3)*.

4. Fill each cornucopia with floral foam, and insert bunches of baby's breath into the foam.

5. Cover the poster board circle with gold wrapping paper, gluing down the paper edges securely in the back. Glue the 20 cornucopias without decals evenly spaced around the gold circle like the spokes of a wheel. Glue the 10 cornucopias with decals on top of the plain gold cornucopias, placing them between and on top of the first layer *(see photo)*.

6. Gather the ⅛-inch-wide velvet ribbons into loops to make a bow with 30-inch-long streamers, and wire the loops together. Wire the bow and streamers to the center of the wreath *(see photo)*. Wire the doll head to the center of the wreath above the bow.

TIPS FOR A "GREEN" CHRISTMAS

Feed the Birds!

A bird feeder makes a wonderful "family gift." Watching the birds that flock to eat, and helping your children learn to identify them, is a great way for kids to learn about nature and the world they live in. And, depending upon the area in which you live, putting out feed for the birds is necessary to help them live through the barren winter months. Even in more temperate climates, the extra feed will help keep your feathered friends happy and healthy during the winter.

You'll find a great selection of bird feeders at garden centers and home centers. Buy bird seed, or put together your own combinations of crumbs, seeds and nuts. Add a book on local birds, and you have a great "green" gift. (Be sure you wrap everything in recyclable wrapping paper!)

FIG. I, 1 ANTIQUE DOLL WREATH 1 SQ. = 1″

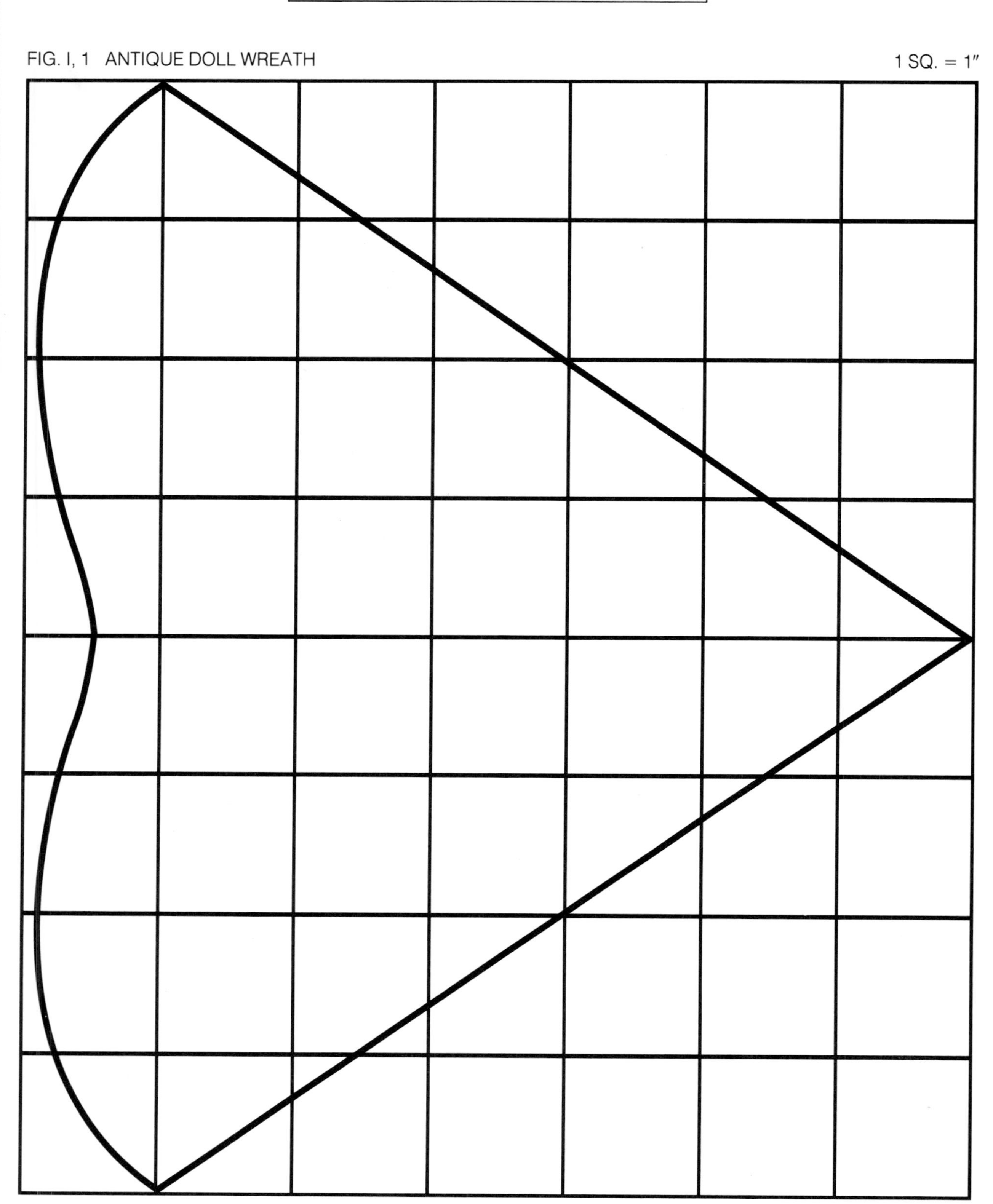

FOLK ART GOOSE

Hang this inviting folk art plaque on the front door to provide a special welcome to holiday guests.

Challenging: Requires more experience in painting.

Materials: 10 x 12 inches of plywood; graphite paper; stylus, or dry ballpoint pen; fine garnet sandpaper; tack cloth; oil paints: titanium white, ivory black, burnt umber, burnt sienna, Prussian blue, cadmium yellow light, cadmium yellow medium, cadmium red pale or light, cadmium red medium, and alizarin crimson; acrylic paints: white and black; clear matte-finish acrylic spray; polyurethane *(optional)*; paintbrushes: No. 2 flat, No. 6 flat, and small round brush or No. 1 liner; 1-inch sponge brush; palette paper; palette knife; odorless mineral spirits; paper toweling; jigsaw or sabre saw; tracing paper for pattern.

Directions:

1. Enlarge the goose pattern in FIG. I, 2 *(page 8)* onto tracing paper, following the directions on page 271. Using the graphite paper and stylus or dry ballpoint pen, trace the goose shape onto the plywood. Cut out the goose shape, and sand the edges smooth. Remove all the sawdust with the tack cloth.

2. Stain the back of the goose with burnt umber oil paint thinned with mineral spirits. Let the stain dry for 30 minutes.

3. Using the sponge brush, apply a coat of white acrylic paint to the front of the goose. Let the paint dry for 15 minutes. Sand the paint lightly, and remove all the sawdust with the tack cloth. Apply a second coat of white paint. Let the paint dry thoroughly.

4. Using the graphite paper and stylus or dry ballpoint pen, trace the detail lines onto the painted goose front.

5. Using the round or liner brush and black acrylic paint, paint the eye oval and eyelashes. Let the paint dry. Mist the eye with the clear acrylic to seal it.

6. Use the oil paints as they come from the tube; use only enough paint to cover an area. To clean the brushes between colors, wipe them well with paper toweling; do not use mineral spirits on the brushes while painting. Mix a soft bluish, blackish-gray using Prussian blue, a small amount of ivory black and a very small amount of titanium white. Shade around the eye, under the cheek, the wing, and the feathers with a dry No. 2 flat brush; apply a small amount of gray, and stretch it to cover. Soften the shading with the No. 6 flat brush to create a shadow effect; the darkest area should be where the holly shades the body. Mist the shading with the clear acrylic spray to seal it. Add a dot of titanium white to highlight the eye.

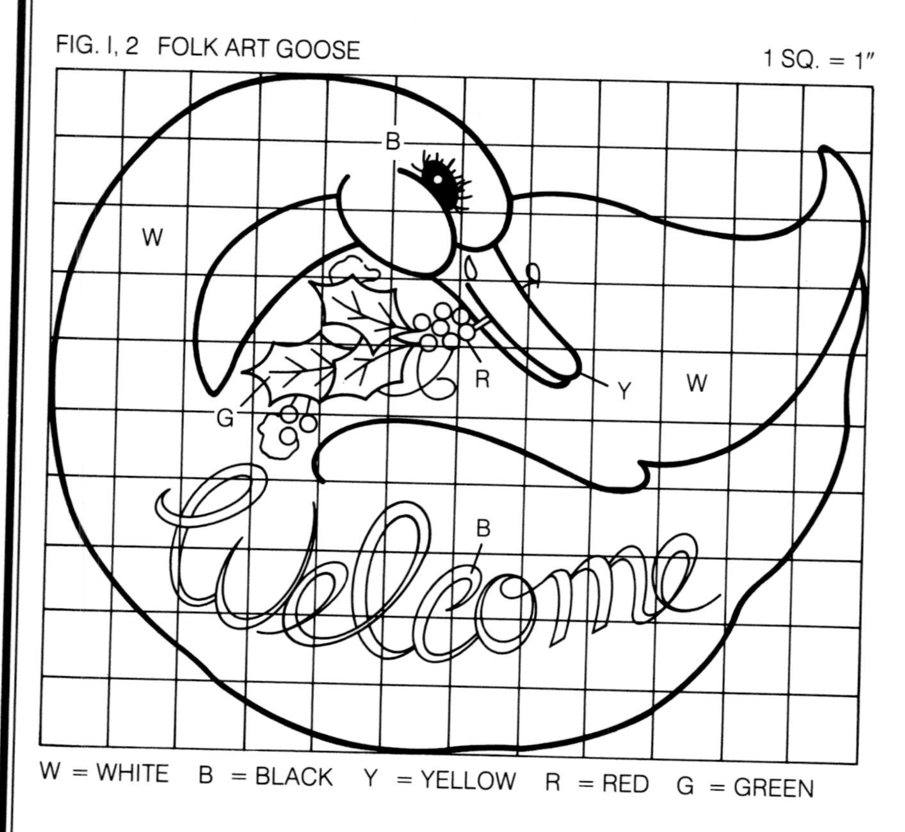

FIG. I, 2 FOLK ART GOOSE

W = WHITE B = BLACK Y = YELLOW R = RED G = GREEN

CLEVER CRAFTING

Easy Evergreen Wreath

It's not very difficult to make your own evergreen wreath. You'll need a wire wreath form, floral wire, and plenty of evergreen branches (all available at garden centers).

Simply wire the branches, or bunches of branches, to the form so that they all face in the same direction. Keep on adding branches, working around the ring, until the wreath is lush and full.

7. Using the No. 2 flat brush, paint the beak cadmium yellow medium. Pat on a touch of cadmium red pale or light to shade the beak where it joins the head, and at the division between the upper and lower beak. Tone with a touch of burnt sienna, if necessary. Highlight the division with titanium white. Using the round brush, paint the nostril ivory black.

8. Mix a medium dark green using cadmium yellow light and a small amount of ivory black. Use the dark green on the leaf vein lines, and where one leaf overlaps another. Add just a little Prussian blue to the dark green on the palette paper to brighten the color. Apply the brighter green around the outside edges of the leaves, letting the background show through as a highlight. Paint the berries with the round brush, using cadmium red medium as the basic color. Using burnt sienna, paint the holly stems with rather broken lines to look like branches.

9. Paint the letters with the small round or No. 2 flat brush and the gray paint used for the shading; thin the paint with one or two drops of mineral spirits. Make the edges of the letters clean and crisp.

10. Mist the painted goose very carefully and lightly with the clear acrylic spray, holding the can at least 12 inches away from the plaque and keeping the can moving continuously. If the clear acrylic is applied too heavily, it will crack and craze the paint. Mist the goose two or three times, letting the acrylic dry between coats. The acrylic spray finish is sufficient protection if the plaque is hung indoors, or in a protected outdoor area. If you wish to hang the plaque in an unprotected outdoor area, apply two or three coats of polyurethane to both sides of the plaque, sanding lightly between coats.

CLEVER CRAFTING

Forever Flowers

Yarrow, statice and baby's breath, the flowers called for in the Field of Flowers Wreath at right, all can be air dried. Air drying is the easiest way to dry fresh flowers.

- Tie six to ten stems together with string or a rubber band. Hang the bunches of flowers upside down in a dark, dry spot where air circulates freely—an attic, spare room, shady kitchen corner, or closet with the door left open a crack. Flowers dried in the dark last longer and maintain a truer color.
- The dried stems of some flowers, such as strawflowers and globe amaranth, are too brittle to work well, so replace them with wire before drying the flower heads. Pinch off each stem close to the bottom of the fresh bud or flower. Push a length of 16-gauge wire midway into the flower head. Place the flowers upright in a container. As they dry, the flowers will open and adhere to the wires.
- Most flowers will air dry in two to three weeks unless the weather is very humid.
- Leave bunches of air dried flowers hanging until you are ready to use them, or untie and store them, loosely packed, in a covered box.
- Some flowers, such as annual and perennial statice, baby's breath, yarrow, strawflowers, hydrangea, globe amaranth and oregano blossoms, can be dried upright; simply place them in a vase. Be sure to strip the leaves from yarrow after picking it.

FIELD OF FLOWERS WREATH

Trim a traditional evergreen wreath with summer's glory.

Easy: Achievable by anyone.

Materials: Pine or other evergreen wreath; fresh or dried flowers: golden yarrow, blue statice and baby's breath; floral wire.

Directions:
Attach short lengths of floral wire to the yarrow and statice about 2 inches below the flower heads. Trim the stems slightly below the wires so that when the flower heads are wired to the wreath, they will sit on the wreath with nothing of the stems showing through. Wire the yarrow to the wreath. Fill in with the statice. Tuck in the baby's breath as accents.

CLEVER CRAFTING

Sap Solution

Here's a quick way to remove pine cone "sap" from your hands: Put a few drops of vegetable oil on your hands, rub briskly then wash with soap and water.

CINNAMON STICK WREATH

Easy: Achievable by anyone.

Materials: Plywood or corrugated cardboard ring; several dozen cinnamon sticks; white glue; ¾ yard of 3-inch-wide velvet ribbon; dried or artificial flowers, or dried herbs; floral wire.

Directions:

1. Lay the plywood or cardboard ring on a flat surface. Using the photo as a guide, place the cinnamon sticks on top of the ring in a pleasing arrangement.

2. When you are satisfied with the arrangement, glue the sticks to the ring, a section at a time, by spreading glue over the entire width of the ring and replacing the cinnamon sticks on the ring carefully. Let the glue dry.

3. Fold in each end of the velvet ribbon to make two loops that cross in the center *(see photo)*. Hold the loops in place like a bow with a length of floral wire wrapped around the center. Glue some flowers or herbs over the wire to conceal it. Glue the bow over a sparse area of the wreath. Glue extra cinnamon sticks and flowers behind it.

4. Wire the flowers or herbs into small bunches. Evenly space the bunches around the wreath, and glue them in place. Let the glue dry thoroughly before hanging the wreath.

TIPS FOR A "GREEN" CHRISTMAS

Birdland Buffet

Decorate the outside of your home keeping your feathered friends in mind. String garlands of popcorn, orange sections, apple chunks, grapes, dried fruit, peanuts in the shell, cheese and bread. Drape the edible garlands around the trees and tall shrubs in your yard, tying the ends of the garlands with red ribbon bows. Don't have streamers on the bows as they frighten birds.

COLONIAL CHRISTMAS ENTRYWAY PLAQUES

Average: For those with some experience in crafting.

Materials: Floral oasis cage (block of oasis surrounded by chicken wire; available at nurseries and garden centers); pine or other evergreen branches; branches of dried white poplar leaves; bayberry, bittersweet or other branches with berries; pine cones; red apples; No. 22 or 24 floral wire; floral picks.

Directions:

1. Wrap a length of floral wire around the base of each pine cone. Wire each apple to a floral pick by cutting two 5-inch lengths of floral wire, and inserting one wire through the apple near the bottom. Insert the second wire at the same level at right angles to the first wire. Pull the four wire ends down, and twist them around a floral pick held against the bottom of the apple; do not puncture the apple with the pick.

2. Using the photo as a design guide, insert the pine or other evergreen branches into the oasis cage to define a pleasing outline for the plaque. Fill in the plaque's shape with the poplar leaf and berry-laden branches. Attach the pine cones and apples to the center of the plaque in a pleasing arrangement.

3. Make the transom decorations following Steps 1 and 2 above, using slightly smaller oasis cages.

TIPS FOR A "GREEN" CHRISTMAS

Apples Twice Over

The apples you use on your wreaths will look beautiful for a couple of weeks, but they'll eventually start to wither. Replace them with new apples to keep your decorations looking fresh. Cut up the old apples (seeds and all) and leave them out for the birds.

Directions:
1. Using the compass, draw a 5½-inch-diameter circle on the cardboard. Draw a 3½-inch-diameter circle inside the first circle to make a small wreath shape. Cut out the cardboard wreath shape with the craft knife. Using the cardboard shape as a pattern, cut out nine more small wreaths from the cardboard.
2. Glue the cardboard wreath shapes together in pairs to make five double-thickness small wreaths.
3. Trace the full-size holly leaf and bear patterns in Figs. I, 3A and 3B onto paper, and cut out the patterns.
4. Cut 80 holly leaves from the green felt. Glue the leaves together in pairs, placing a pipe cleaner between each pair to form a middle rib; let the excess pipe cleaner extend beyond the bottom point of the leaves to form the stem. Let the glue dry completely.
5. Attach eight double holly leaves to each small wreath by gluing their stems to the cardboard. Let the glue dry completely. Bend each leaf where it meets its stem to shape it.
6. Cut 30 green felt holly leaves. Glue six leaves to each small wreath to cover the cardboard and leaf stems completely. Let the glue dry.

HOLLY BEAR WREATH

Easy: Achievable by anyone.

Materials: 9 x 12-inch craft felt rectangles: 20 of green, 5 of old gold, and 1 each of white and black; 2½ yards of 1-inch-wide red ribbon; 1 yard of Red yarn; 41 pipe cleaners; corrugated cardboard; synthetic stuffing; craft knife; black fine-point permanent felt tip pen; small hole paper punch; compass; tacky white craft glue; paper for patterns.
Note: *Five small wreaths are assembled, and attached to form the large wreath.*

FIG. I, 3A HOLLY BEAR WREATH

FULL SIZE

7. Arrange the small wreaths, right side down, in a circle to form a large wreath. Cut out five 5½ x 1½-inch cardboard strips. Apply glue to one cardboard strip and place it, glue side down, on two adjacent small wreaths so that half the strip is on each wreath. Repeat to glue all the small wreaths together. Cut out additional green felt holly leaves, and glue them to the large wreath to cover any visible cardboard.

8. Cut out ten bears from the old gold felt. Glue a pair of bears together as close to the felt edges as possible, leaving an opening for stuffing. Repeat with the remaining bears. Let the glue dry completely. Stuff each double bear lightly, and glue the opening closed.

9. Cut out 30 small white felt circles for the bears' paw pads and inner ears. Cut out five white felt ovals for the bears' stomachs *(see photo)*. Glue the paw pads, inner ears, and stomachs in place. Cut out five 1¼-inch-diameter white felt circles. Cut into each circle's center along a radius, lap one cut edge over the other to form a slight cone shape, and glue the lapped edges together. Place a small amount of stuffing inside each cone, and glue a cone to each bear's face for a muzzle *(see photo)*. Cut out black felt eyes and noses with the paper punch. Using the photo as a placement guide, glue the eyes and noses to the bears. Draw a double curve mouth on each bear with the black felt tip pen. Divide the yarn into five equal lengths, and tie a length around each bear's neck.

10. Using the photo as a placement guide, glue each bear between two small wreaths. Cut five 18-inch lengths of ribbon. Tie each length into a bow, and glue the bow to a small wreath *(see photo)*. Shape the remaining pipe cleaner into a loop, and glue the loop to the back of the large wreath for a hanger.

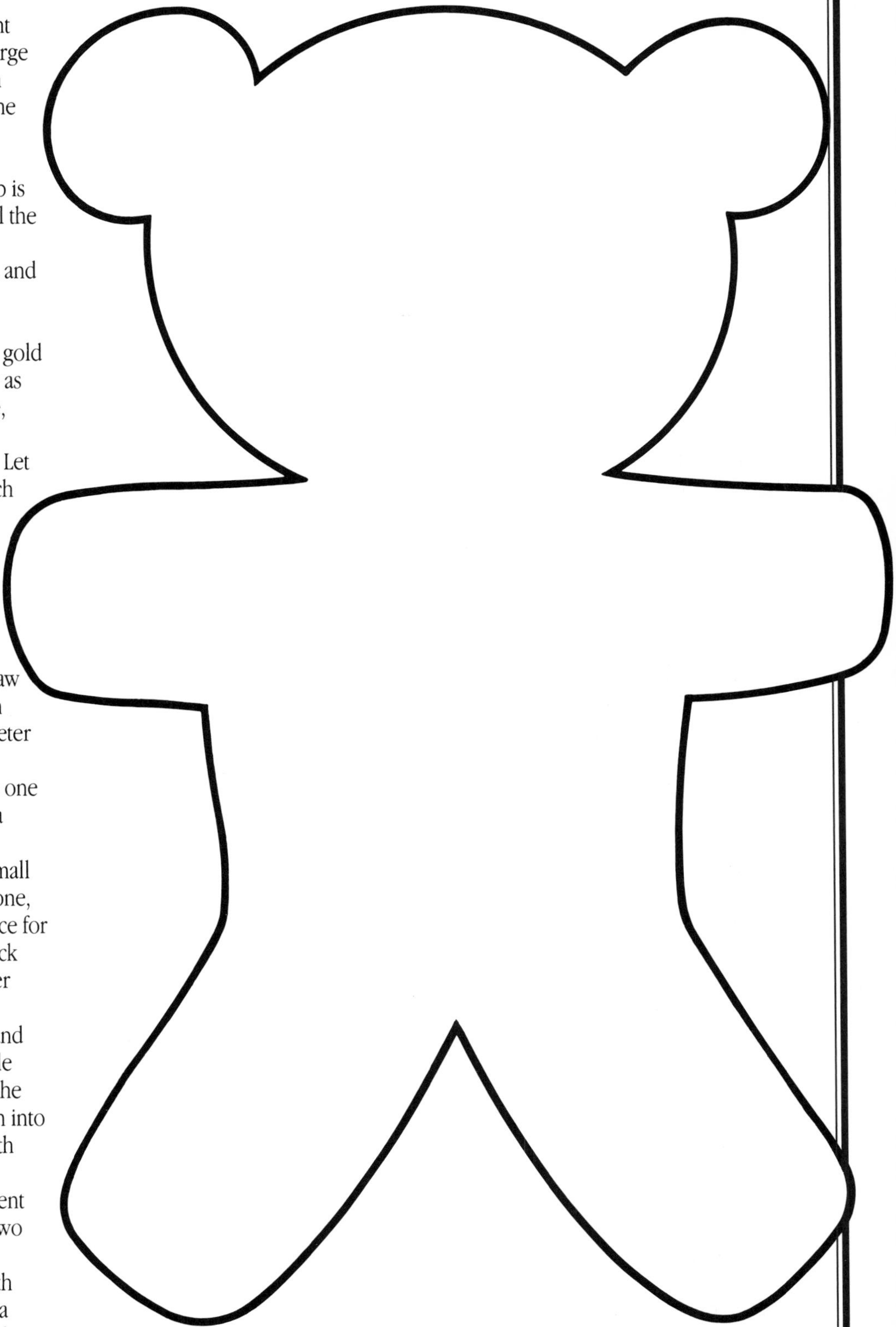

FIG. I, 3B HOLLY BEAR WREATH

FULL SIZE

LET THERE BE LIGHTS

Add a touch of Christmas magic
to your home with sparkling lights
that shine through the winter darkness.

CATCH A FALLING STAR

Average: For those with some experience in crafting.

Materials: Tall, sturdy, bare white birch branches; plastic icicles; strings of white- or green-corded clear, white miniature outdoor lights; strings of clear, white miniature indoor lights *(optional)*; survey stake for each outdoor tree; 2 hose clamps for each outdoor tree; 4 feet of 1 x 2 pine lumber for each indoor tree *(optional)*; 4-inch wood screw for each indoor tree *(optional)*; 1½-inch nails *(optional)*; No. 22 spool wire; wire cutter; saw; screwdriver *(optional)*; hammer *(optional)*.

Directions:

1. Cutting: Cut the birch branches to the desired height.

2. Outdoor Trees: Clamp the top of a survey stake to the bottom of each birch branch to make a "tree." Place the outdoor trees in front and on each side of the window, pushing their stakes firmly into the ground.

3. Indoor Trees (optional): For each indoor tree, cut the 1 x 2 pine lumber into two 18-inch-long legs and two 4-inch-long feet. Nail a foot under each end of one leg, outside edges even. Center the other leg on the upside down footed piece, and use a 4-inch wood screw to attach the legs where they cross. Continue screwing up into the bottom of a branch to make a "tree." Set the indoor trees in front of the window.

4. Attaching Lights: Work with the strings of lights turned on, so you can find the source easily if a problem arises. Starting at the top of each outdoor tree, wire a string of outdoor lights, plug end downward, to a single branch. Follow the shape of the branch closely; do not string the lights from side to side across the branch. Repeat on the other branches. If you are using indoor trees, repeat on them with strings of clear, white miniature indoor lights.

5. Icicles: Wire the plastic icicles into clusters. Wire the clusters to the outdoor trees to create the look of real icicles hanging from the branches *(see photo)*.

TIPS FOR A "GREEN" CHRISTMAS

Givin' of the Green

We need forests to help produce oxygen, to absorb airborne pollutants, to counteract global warming and to provide homes for thousands of woodland creatures. But for years we've been cutting down trees faster than we can grow them.

Now you can contribute to the "reforestation" of America without ever getting your hands dirty. For a donation of $1 per tree (a minimum of 10 trees per order) the American Forestry Association will plant trees in any name you choose . . . plant a group of trees in honor of your cousin's new baby or your son and daughter-in-law's first Christmas together. If you request it, the AFA will send a certificate to commemorate the planting. What a wonderful idea for that hard-to-buy-for person on your gift list!

Contact the American Forestry Association, Global ReLeaf Heritage Forest Program, P.O. Box 2000, Washington, DC 20013. Make checks payable to the American Forestry Association. In order to receive a certificate you must request it. With your check, enclose a letter with your name and address, the purpose of the gift and the address to which the certificate should be mailed.

WINTER VILLAGE WINDOW SCENE

Easy: Achievable by anyone.

Materials: Electric train set; scale model village with snow-covered trees; white bed sheet; books of varying thicknesses; mirror; strings of clear, white miniature lights; evergreen garlands; several yards of white tulle netting.

Directions:

1. Select a sturdy table that is large enough to hold the train set and village. Place the table in front of the window. Cover the table with the bed sheet, and place the books under the sheet to make plateaus on which to set the village buildings.

2. Assemble the train set, and lay out the village. If the village does not contain lights, you may be able to run a string of lights over the surface of the table, and place a building over each light. Place the mirror in the center of the village as a lake.

3. Drape the garlands around the outside of the window. Twist the light strings around the garlands.

4. Drape the tulle netting over the window's curtain rod so the netting gives the appearance of puffy clouds over the village scene. Run a string of lights behind the netting.

RUSTIC TIN LANTERNS

Make several of these lovely, Mexican-inspired lanterns, and use them to light the front walk when guests are expected. After the party gets started, bring the lanterns indoors as room decorations; don't leave them burning outdoors unattended.

Average: For those with some experience in crafting.

Materials: Coffee, juice, large vegetable or other heavy duty cans; medium-size chunky candles; tin snips; awl; pencil; manila folder *(optional)*; craft knife *(optional)*; silver, red or green spray paint *(optional)*.

Directions:

1. Select a cut out design that will let the candlelight shine through, but allows the can to keep its shape; simple slanted line patterns work well. Pencil the design on the can. If the design is fairly complicated, use a craft knife to cut a stencil of the design on a manila folder. Trace the design onto the can with a pencil.

2. Cut out the design on the can with the tin snips, using the awl to make starter holes. Or use the awl to punch out the entire design. When you have finished cutting the design, press down on the top of the can until it bulges slightly *(see photo)*.

3. If you wish, spray paint the lantern.

4. Melt the bottom of the candle slightly, and place the candle so it sits securely on the bottom of the lantern.

TIPS FOR A "GREEN" CHRISTMAS

Outdoor Lights

To help conserve energy, use mini-lights instead of standard-size outdoor Christmas bulbs.

CLEVER CRAFTING

The Light Fantastic

- Set up your display while it's still light outside, then check the effect after dark; you can't get an accurate picture in daylight. Note whatever adjustments you want to make, and wait until it's light again to change the display. Be careful when using a ladder outside; have a helper steady the ladder while you work.
- Every year, before setting up your illumination display, check light sets for cracked insulation, frayed wires or damaged sockets; all of these can cause short circuits.
- Don't overload string sets. Read the manufacturer's directions on each package to find out how many sets can be connected together.
- Avoid overloading circuits. Most home circuits can take 15 amps, or 1,800 watts. If you don't know your circuit capacity, play it safe and scale down your lighting display.
- Cover each outdoor plug and connector joint with plastic wrap to protect it from rain, sleet and snow; seal the wrapped joint carefully with electrical tape.
- If you use staples instead of tape to secure lights, be sure they're insulated staples.
- Make sure your decorations pose no danger to children or pets: Don't leave cords dangling, loose on the floor, or on the stairs.
- If you have questions about using decorative lights outdoors, you can call the GE Answer Center® information service 24 hours a day: 1-800-626-2000.
- Icicle lights are a pleasant change from the standard round or "flame" bulbs, but why stop there? There are strings of lights in all sorts of wild and whimsical shapes: carriage lamps, candles, even frogs and jalapeño peppers. Read the manufacturer's directions carefully before hanging light strings. If your novelty light set is not recommended for outdoor use, hang it indoors to frame a window.
- For a dramatic look to your outside lighting display, try floodlighting evergreens. Use blue, green, clear, or deluxe white mercury lamps—these colors enhance the colors of evergreens. Avoid using red, yellow, amber or pink lamps, which turn the trees a muddy brown color.
- Illuminate deciduous trees as well as evergreens. Flood a tree with a single spotlight to highlight its shape and pattern. Or place shiny ornaments on the tree, and light it from below with several smaller spotlights. If the tree is close enough to the house, use small lights for a festive look.
- Get more sparkle and glitter by using transparent bulbs. These, unlike color-coated bulbs, allow the filaments to show through.
- Use light bulb colors that are in the same color family. Blue and green are "cool colors." Red, orange, yellow and white are "warm colors."

GRAND ENTRANCE

This lovely lighting treatment makes the most of the unique architectural details of a house. You can adapt the same principles to your own home.

Easy: Achievable by anyone.

Materials: 2 small potted evergreen trees; evergreen garland; strings of clear, white medium-size lights; strings of blue miniature lights; green satin ribbon in widest width available.

Directions:
Using the photo as a guide, accent selected areas of the portico with the medium-size lights, spacing them widely. String medium-size lights on the potted trees, and place the trees on either side of the portico. String the miniature lights on larger shrubs in front of the house. Drape the evergreen garland over the entryway staircase banister, and tie the garland in place with green ribbon bows.

CHAPTER 2

YULETIDE TABLE MAGIC

Greetings,
good master, mistress, children
Greetings, good health to one and all!
Once more we come to you with singing;
Open your door, we've come to call!
Let us now to your heart draw near
and with warmth and with food be welcomed!
—"Carol of the Mistletoe Singers"

At Christmas time the dining table becomes the center of activity—after all, no celebration is complete without a feast! Set a holiday table with lovely linens and festive centerpieces. Since holiday entertaining can range from buffet breakfasts to elegant sit-down dinners, we've included table-trimming ideas for a variety of occasions. Some are as simple as a gathering of potted herbs, glass ball ornaments, candles and napkins to make a homey centerpiece. Others involve fancy cutwork or counted cross stitch techniques to create lovely table linens. Don't wait until Christmas Eve to set your holiday table. These festive table toppers will delight your family and friends at any meal of the season.

SET THE TABLE, SET THE MOOD

Greet your Christmas dinner guests with a table as festive as the rest of your home. From Victorian elegance to natural simplicity, our table settings will help you set the perfect tone for your feasting.

VICTORIAN SPARKLE TABLE SETTING

Easy: Achievable by anyone.

Materials: Green satin tablecloth; white lace-edged napkins; glass tabletop to fit dinner table; assorted antique or replica Christmas cards, postcards and paper ornaments; small gift boxes; gold doilies; gold metallic ribbon; little party favor gifts.

Directions:

1. Spread the tablecloth on the table. Place the Christmas cards, postcards, paper ornaments and doilies on top of the cloth in a pleasing arrangement *(see photo)*. Lay the glass top on the table to hold the decorations in place.

2. Tuck a little gift inside each box. Tie the boxes with the gold ribbon. Place a gold doily on top of each plate, and a gift box on each doily.

3. Fold the napkins in small squares and place them on the table so they hide as little of the decorations as possible *(see photo)*.

COLOR IT CHRISTMAS TABLE SETTING

Easy: Achievable by anyone.

Materials: Flower Ornaments (directions, at right); Christmas stocking; artificial red and white flowers; potted poinsettias; red candles in white candleholders; white lace table runner.

Directions:

Hang the ornaments from a chandelier or in front of a window. Spread the table runner across the table. Group the flowers in the stocking in a pleasing arrangement, and lay the stocking in the center of the table. Arrange the candles around the stocking. Place the poinsettias around the room.

FLOWER ORNAMENTS

Easy: Achievable by anyone.

Materials: Styrofoam® balls; white artificial flowers and green leaves; red strawflowers; white glue; ¼-inch-wide red satin ribbon for hangers; T-pins or hairpins.

Directions:

1. Glue the flowers and leaves all over the surface of the foam ball.

2. Cut the ribbon twice as long as the hanging length desired. With a T-pin or hairpin, fasten the center of the ribbon to the top of the ball and suspend the ornament.

HARVEST HOME TABLE SETTING

Easy: Achievable by anyone.

Materials: Hurricane lamp; wheat wreath; cranberries; twine; small wood cutting boards.

Directions:

Place the wreath around the hurricane lamp in the center of the table. Fill in the spaces with loose cranberries. Tie each napkin with a length of twine for a napkin ring. Use small cutting boards instead of individual dessert plates to serve a simple dessert of cheese and fruit.

TIPS FOR A "GREEN" CHRISTMAS

Dine by Candlelight

Set the most wonderful of moods and dine by candlelight. This adds intimacy, romance and instant beauty to any meal, and is especially nice during the holiday season. Best of all, it conserves a little energy during a time of year when you tend to use a lot of electricity.

SWEET CEDAR TABLE SETTING

Easy: Achievable by anyone.

Materials: Cuttings of fresh cedar; country-style place mats and matching napkins; stoneware plates; wooden napkin rings; chunky candles of various heights and colors.

Directions:
Set the place mats on the table and center a plate on each mat. Roll the napkins, place them in the napkin rings and set a ring with napkin on top of each plate. Spread the cedar cuttings around the place mats in a pleasing arrangement. Allow the cuttings to drape slightly across the place mats and over the table's edges. Place the candles among the cuttings.

CLEVER CRAFTING

Conversation Piece

A low centerpiece allows for a good flow of conversation across the table. The centerpiece should add to the overall look of the table, but it should never dominate. The stars of any meal should be taste-tempting food and cheerful company.

SIMPLE ELEGANCE HOLIDAY TABLE

Easy: Achievable by anyone.

Materials: Evergreen wreath; solid white tablecloth; white thread; sewing needle; wide red satin ribbon, or purchased large red satin bows with streamers; tall red candles; candleholders of various heights.

Directions:

1. If you are using red satin ribbon, make four large bows with long streamers. Place the tablecloth on the table. Gather the tablecloth at the center of one long side, and sew through the gathers to hold them in place *(see photo)*. Tack a bow over the stitches. If the table is long, gather the tablecloth twice along the side, and tack a bow over each set of gathers. Repeat on the other long side and two short ends of the table.

2. Place the wreath in the center of the table. Place the candles in the candleholders, and group them inside the wreath for a centerpiece.

TIPS FOR A "GREEN" CHRISTMAS

Natural Napkins

Changing over to reusable cloth napkins can dramatically cut down on your use of paper products. They're also more attractive and less expensive than paper napkins — a nice touch for family meals! Use them yourself, and give them as a "green" gift to neighbors and friends.

Here are some of our thoughts on how to turn ordinary cloth napkins into a beautiful Christmas gift; you'll probably come up with some creative ideas on your own.

- Buy a family-sized set of napkins and embroider the initials of each family member in the corner of "their" napkin.
- Give enough napkins for a week's worth of meals, so they all can be thrown in with the weekly laundry. Choose varying shades of a single color to match the recipient's decor, or offer a rainbow of different colors.
- Buy a set of napkins in a light color, and stencil a design on the corner of each napkin.
- Make napkins by hemming squares of fabric. Colorful floral prints, plaids or solids all make good choices. Or make a set of holiday napkins from fabrics for Easter, Valentine's Day, St. Patrick's Day, Halloween, Thanksgiving and, of course, Christmas!
- Roll the napkins and tie them with ribbons. Then group them in a pretty basket for giving.
- Accompany your gift of napkins with place mats, napkin rings or a book on napkin folding.

CENTERPIECES AND ACCENTS

Whether you revel in nature's bounty or "go for the gilt," you can create a lovely focal point for your holiday table. Or add Christmas cheer to any corner of the house with just the right accent.

POINSETTIA BASKET

(photos, page 21 and at left)

Easy: Achievable by anyone.

Materials: Basket with handle; potted red poinsettia; 2 to 4 gladioli; white lace-edged napkin; red satin ribbon; 2 small jars; floral foam; thin floral wire.

Directions:

1. Place the napkin in the basket, draping napkin corners over the basket's front and back edges. Place the poinsettia in the basket.

2. Wire an upright small jar on the inside of the basket at the bottom of each end of the basket handle. Fill the jars with floral foam.

3. Place one or two gladioli in each jar. Wire the gladiolus stems to the basket handle to cover it. Tie a red ribbon bow at each end of the handle.

CLEVER CRAFTING

Poinsettias

The following "holiday" schedule will make caring for a poinsettia very easy.

- Christmas season: As long as the plant is in bloom, keep it in a well-lighted spot (direct sunlight isn't necessary once it is past blooming), with evenly moist, not soggy, soil. Feed the poinsettia every two weeks, year-round, with a complete fertilizer, such as 10-15-10.
- St. Patrick's Day: Cut back the bracts. These are the large, brightly colored, modified leaves that are often mistakenly called flowers.
- Memorial Day: Repot the plant into a larger container and put the plant outdoors for the summer.
- Fourth of July: Cut the stems back by six inches.
- Labor Day: Move the plant indoors to a sunny window.
- Columbus Day: Begin giving the plant 14 hours of darkness daily. Poinsettias are photoperiodic — producing colorful bracts and blooms (the yellow berries in the center of the bracts) in response to shorter periods of daylight. Cover the plant with a box or place it in a closet; it must have absolute darkness.

Continue this treatment for 8 to 10 weeks. During the day, place the plant in a window where it will receive 4 to 6 hours of direct sun; water and feed as usual. As soon as the poinsettia comes into bloom, discontinue the treatment.

By following this schedule, you should have a colorful poinsettia again for Christmas.

CLEVER CRAFTING

Handy Arrangements

If you have these items on hand, you'll always be able to create "instant arrangements" for your table.

- Candles: A selection of tapers, chunk candles and votive candles in red, green and white with holders to match.
- Pretty bowls and baskets: They can give your table a theme — baskets say "country," a pewter bowl is distinctly Colonial, ornate china or crystal bowls are elegant, stoneware adds a homey touch.
- Pine cones: Large and small, paint them, wire them, glue them, roll them in glitter, tie them with bows or simply toss them in a pretty container.
- Fruit: Fill a bowl or basket with bright green apples, red apples or citrus for a pretty and fragrant centerpiece.
- Ball ornaments: Use them as you would fresh fruit. They make a simple, sparkling centerpiece.
- Mirror: Lay it flat on the table and place your arrangement on top, the mirror will reflect candlelight or give a simple arrangement more presence.

HERB GARDEN CENTERPIECE

Easy: Achievable by anyone.

Materials: Large wooden salad bowl; variety of potted herbs, such as parsley, sage, dwarf sage, rosemary, oregano and scented geranium; additional fresh parsley; red striped or checked dishtowel; 3 red striped or checked napkins; red glass ball ornaments in assorted sizes; three 10-inch-tall dripless red candles; 3 candle pins *(metal disc with spike in middle; optional)*; 6 wooden napkin rings; empty medicine bottles; heavy-duty aluminum foil.

Directions:

1. Centerpiece: Line the salad bowl with a piece of aluminum foil. Cover the foil with the dishtowel, draping the corners of the towel over the edge of the bowl.

2. Arrange the potted herbs in the bowl. Fill the medicine bottles with water, and place a clump of fresh parsley in each bottle. Fill in the spaces around the potted herbs with the bottled parsley; the parsley will last for 2 to 3 days. Place the bowl in the center of the table. Group the ball ornaments into clusters around the bowl to imitate fruit.

3. Candleholders: Stack two napkin rings. Place a candle in the center of a napkin, and push them both into the stacked rings so the napkin gathers into petals. Separate the stacked rings slightly. Repeat with the remaining candles, napkins and napkin rings. If a candle needs to be steadied, press its bottom onto a candle pin. Arrange the candles around the centerpiece.

GOLDEN ANGEL

Average: For those with some experience in crafting.

Materials: ½ yard of 36-inch-wide solid white or pastel cotton fabric; matching thread; 14 x 8 inches of scrim or stiff cotton tulle; 1 yard of narrow lace trim; ½ yard of ¼-inch-wide ribbon; 2-inch-long Styrofoam® egg; scraps of 4-ply yarn; 1 pair of long false eyelashes; 12-inch square of heavy cardboard; 12-inch-wide manila folder or other lightweight cardboard; wire coat hanger; gold spray paint; gold glitter; liquid starch; sewing needle; ¾-inch-wide plastic strapping tape; stapler; all-purpose glue; wax paper; paper for pattern.

Directions:

1. Cover the heavy cardboard square with wax paper, and use it as a working surface. From the manila folder or other lightweight cardboard, make a 12-inch-long cone with a 4-inch-diameter base for the angel body. Staple and tape the overlapping edges together. Impale and glue the Styrofoam egg on the point of the cone for the angel head.

2. Cut a 14-inch length from the straight section of the wire hanger. Bend and shape the wire to form the angel shoulders, bent arms, and hands *(see photo)*. Holding the shoulder piece at the base of the head, secure the piece very firmly in place by winding strapping tape several times over and around the wire and body, and around the base of the head.

3. Enlarge the pattern in Fig. II, 1 *(page 34)* onto paper, following the directions on page 271. Place the dotted line of the Dress pattern along a folded edge of paper, cut out and open for a full pattern. Cut out the Wings and Collar pattern pieces. Fold the cotton fabric into an 18-inch square. Place the top edge of the Dress pattern on the fabric fold, and cut out the Dress through the double thickness fabric. Cut out the Collar from a single thickness of the same fabric. Cut a 2-inch-long opening down the center back of the Dress. Cut a 1¼-inch-long opening down the center back of the Collar. Turn in the hems. Sew lengths of lace trim around the sleeve edges and the bottom edge of the Collar. Right sides in, sew the Dress side/sleeve seams; turn the Dress right side out.

4. Pour some undiluted liquid starch into a bowl. Saturate the Dress in the starch, and squeeze out the excess starch. Place the Dress carefully on the angel, threading the wire arms through the sleeves. Drape the Dress into graceful folds, and turn under about 1 inch at the Dress bottom. Place the Collar around the neck, with the opening at the back, and secure the Collar at the back of the neck with small stitches. Tie the ribbon firmly around the angel's waist for a sash.

5. Cut approximately fifty 6-inch-long strands of yarn. Dip the strands into the starch, and arrange them on the angel's head to resemble hair. Trim the strand ends neatly around the angel's face and forehead to make rounded bangs.

6. Soak a 6-inch length of lace trim in the starch, and arrange the lace upright on top of the angel head as a coronet.

7. Cut each false eyelash into two ¼-inch sections. Glue the sections to the face as eyes *(see photo)*.

8. Let the angel dry completely; it may take several days. When the angel is completely dry, cut the Wings from the scrim or tulle. Clip, overlap, and staple each Wing in place to make a graceful curving shape *(see Wings pattern piece in* Fig. II, 1*)*. Lift the hair away from the angel's back gently but firmly, and insert the Wings underneath the hair so the Wings' flat center section is just below the top of the angel's shoulder blades. Glue the Wings in place securely.

9. Make a 4-inch-long cone with a 1-inch-diameter base from the manila folder for the trumpet. Staple and tape the overlapping edges together. Wrap tape around the ends of the angel's wire arms to form the hands. Glue the trumpet to the angel's hands, and to the angel's face at the mouth.

10. Spray several coats of gold paint over the completed angel to cover every crack and crevice, letting the paint dry between coats. After the last coat, sprinkle the trumpet with gold glitter before the paint dries.

FIG. II, 1 GOLDEN ANGEL

1 SQ. = 1″

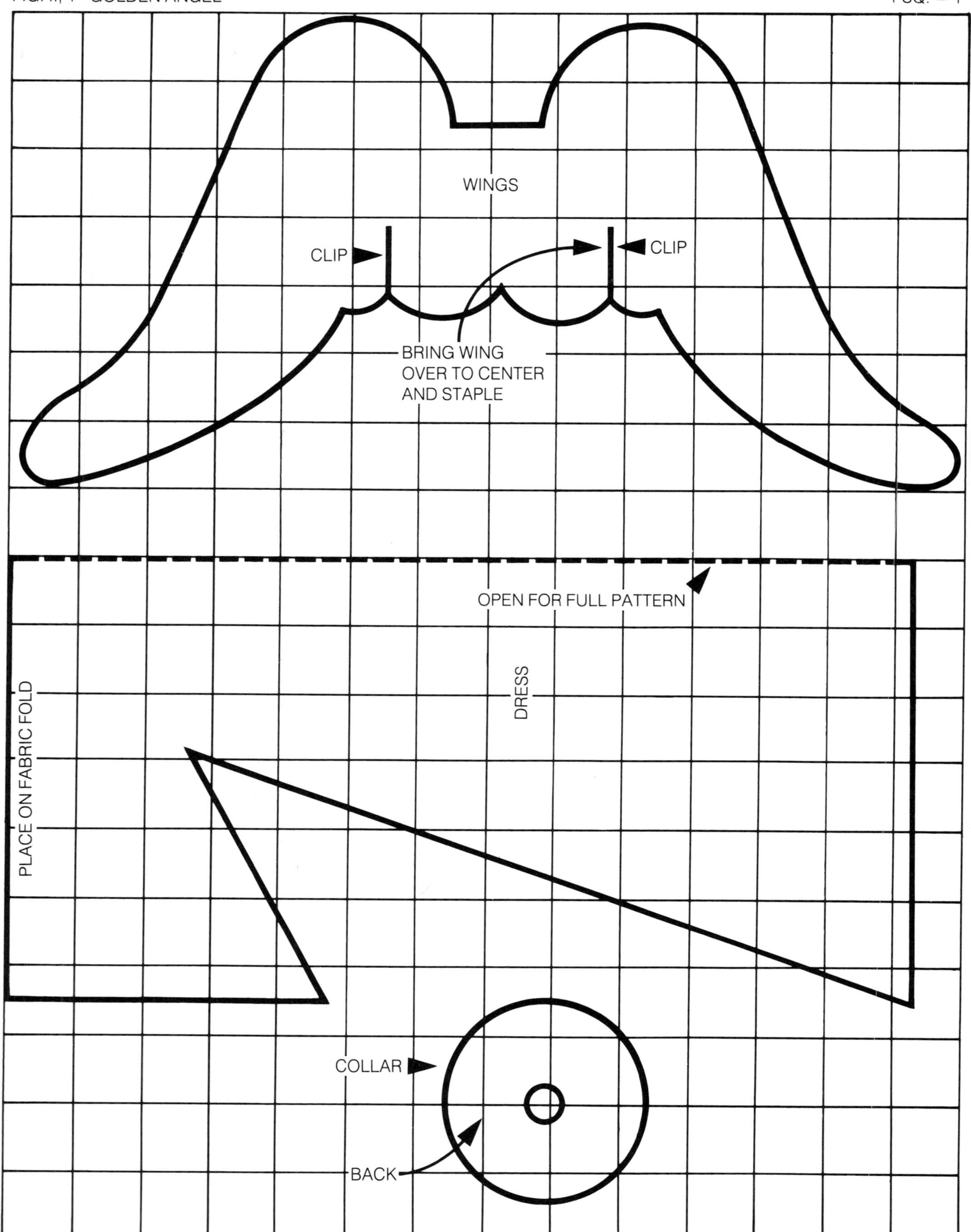

GOLDEN VINES WREATH

Without the candleholders, this also makes a lovely door decoration.

Easy: Achievable by anyone.

Materials: Plain grapevine wreath; artificial ivy; pine cones; clip-on candleholders with red candles; gold paint or spray paint; floral wire.

Directions:

1. Spray paint the ivy gold. Or pour gold paint into a dish, and dip the ivy leaves into the paint. Let the paint dry.

2. Wire the ivy around the wreath. Wrap a length of floral wire around the base of each pine cone. Then wire the pine cones, evenly spaced, around the wreath.

3. Space the candleholders evenly around the wreath, and clip them to the wreath securely. Make sure the candleholders sit straight on the wreath, so they can catch the wax drippings from the burning candles.

4. Place the wreath in the center of the table, and light the candles. Do not leave the centerpiece unattended while the candles are burning.

CLEVER CRAFTING

Pine Cone Pointer

Before using pine cones for wreaths or other Christmas decorations, place them in a warm oven for about an hour. The heat makes them open up.

HOLIDAY TABLE LINENS

Whether you're having a family breakfast on Christmas morning or a lavish Christmas Eve supper, dress your table beautifully with special holiday table linens.

FANCY CUTWORK TABLECLOTH

(about 54 inches square)

Challenging: Requires more experience in sewing or embroidering.

General Materials: 1½ yards of 54-inch-wide linen; washable or disappearing fabric marker; black fine-point permanent felt tip pen; sharp-point embroidery scissors; white paper; tracing paper for pattern.

General Directions:

1. The tablecloth can be embroidered by machine *(see photo)*, or by hand. Directions are given for both hand and machine methods.

2. Straighten the raw edges of the linen to form a perfect 54-inch square. Enlarge the corner motif half pattern in FIG. II, 2A *(page 38)* onto folded tracing paper, following the directions on page 271. Trace the motif onto the other half of the paper, and open the paper for the full motif. Enlarge the center motif quarter pattern in FIG. II, 2B *(page 39)* onto tracing paper folded into quarters; place the paper folds on the pattern center lines. Trace the motif onto the remaining quarters, and open the paper for the full motif. Go over the lines of the full motifs with the black felt tip pen.

3. Place white paper under the center motif. Center the linen square over the center motif; the motif should show through the linen clearly. Trace the motif onto the linen with the washable or disappearing fabric marker. Repeat with the corner motif on the linen corners.

4. If you use a washable fabric marker, when you have finished embroidering the tablecloth, remove remaining motif tracings following the washable fabric marker manufacturer's instructions. Dry the tablecloth, and press it.

MACHINE-SEWN TABLECLOTH

Materials: General Materials; 2 yards of tear-away stabilizer; 15 spools of red machine embroidery thread; 1 pack of size 90 Schmetz universal needles; pins.

Directions:

1. Prepare the linen following General Directions, Steps 2 and 3.

2. Place a large square of tear-away stabilizer under the center motif, and pin it in place. Repeat at each corner, extending the stabilizer 1 inch beyond the edges of the linen for ease of stitching.

3. Use a new needle in the sewing machine. Wind several bobbins with the red thread. Select a 2-mm-wide, 2-mm-long zigzag stitch. Decrease the presser foot pressure two to three notches. Decrease the upper thread tension two to three notches.

4. Zigzag stitch over all the design lines of the center motif except the richelieu lines, which are the connecting threads between the open spaces. Plan a stitching route, rather than jumping from spot to spot. When jumping is unavoidable, lift the presser foot, slide the linen to the new location without cutting the threads, and continue stitching. Clip the needle and bobbin threads last.

5. Cut out the linen cutwork areas with the embroidery scissors, leaving the richelieu lines in place; do not cut the tear-away stabilizer.

6. Decrease the stitch length and width to 1 mm. Start the richelieu stitching 1 mm to 2 mm in from the linen cutwork edges to secure the stitching. Stitch on the richelieu lines across the cutwork areas, stitching through the tear-away stabilizer. Press the reverse button on the machine, and stitch back over the first layer of richelieu stitching.

7. Work the vein lines on the leaves in buttonhole stitch *(see* FIGS. II, 2A *and* 2B, *and photo)*. Work the flower centers in tapered satin stitch *(see* FIGS. II, 2A *and* 2B, *and photo)*. Then decrease the stitch length to 4/10 mm, increase the stitch width to 3 mm, and check the bobbin thread. Satin stitch around all the cutwork areas; the left swing of the needle will fall off the linen into the tear-away stabilizer, and the right swing of the needle will fall into the linen, covering the previous stitching completely. For a more natural look, stitch the background areas first, then the foreground areas. Use tapered satin stitch to stitch into angles and corners. When the embroidering is completed, pull the tear-away stabilizer carefully away from the linen, then from the cutwork, being careful not to tear the delicate richelieu lines. Trim stray threads.

8. Dust the bobbin and feed teeth area. Change the needle. Repeat Steps 3 through 7 on each corner.

9. Insert a buttonhole presser foot. Select a 3-mm-wide, 4/10-mm-long zigzag stitch. With each edge of the linen square following the center of the foot, stitch to form a rolled satin stitch hem. Stitch twice. Remove remaining motif tracings following General Directions, Step 4.

EMBROIDERED TABLECLOTH

Materials: General Materials; red pearl cotton or embroidery floss; embroidery hoop; embroidery needle.

Directions:

1. Prepare the linen following General Directions, Steps 2 and 3, using a washable fabric marker.

2. Place the linen square in the embroidery hoop. Using the embroidery needle and pearl cotton or 3 strands of embroidery floss, outline the design lines of the center and corner motifs with a running stitch *(see Stitch Guide, page 270)*. As you come to one of the richelieu lines, which are the connecting threads between the open spaces,

Continued on page 39

FIG. II, 2A FANCY CUTWORK TABLECLOTH CORNER MOTIF — HALF PATTERN 1 SQ. = 1″

FIG. II, 2B CENTER MOTIF—QUARTER PATTERN 1 SQ. = 1″

carry the floss across the space to the opposite side, take a stitch, carry the floss back, take another stitch in the same place on the first side, and repeat to stretch three threads across the area.

3. When the motifs have been outlined, complete the richelieu lines by working buttonhole stitches over the three threads of each line, being careful not to catch the linen underneath the threads that will be cut away *(see Stitch Guide, page 270)*. When the richelieu lines are completed, work buttonhole stitches over the design outlining stitches so the ridge formed by each buttonhole stitch lies along the edge to be cut.

4. Work the vein lines on the leaves in blanket stitch. Work the flower centers in satin stitch *(see Stitch Guide, and* FIGS. II, 2A *and* 2B*)*.

5. Make an X in all the linen areas to be cut away. Turn over the linen square, and cut out the areas from the wrong side with the embroidery scissors. Be careful not to cut into the buttonhole stitches.

6. Hem the edges of the linen square with buttonhole stitches. Remove remaining motif tracings following General Directions, Step 4 *(page 37)*.

WINTER VILLAGE STENCILED TABLECLOTH & NAPKINS

Easy: Achievable by anyone.

Materials: Purchased solid white or ivory tablecloth and napkins untreated for soil resistance; Stencil-Ease® "Miniature Township" and "Sleigh Ride" stencils, or Mylar® (available at craft supply stores) or acetate sheets (available at art supply stores), black fine-point permanent felt tip pen, craft or utility knife, cardboard, piece of glass with taped edges, or piece of acrylic (available at home centers), masking tape, transparent tape, and artist's flat paintbrush; Fab-Tex® fabric stenciling paints: Barn Red, Country Blue, Slate Blue, Telemark Green, Colonial Gold and Historic Brown, or the colors of your choice; six No. 10 or 12 stencil brushes; paper toweling; paper; newspaper *(optional)*; cotton rags *(optional)*; rubbing alcohol *(optional)*.

Directions:

1. If you are making your own stencils, use the photo as a design guide to draw a simple sleigh, horse, tree and three or four different houses on paper. Cut a piece of Mylar or acetate an inch larger than each shape. Tape the acetate over the shape with masking tape. Trace the shape onto the acetate with the black felt tip pen. Using the cardboard, piece of glass with taped edges, or piece of acrylic as a cutting board, cut out the traced stencil shapes with the craft or utility knife. Pull the knife toward you, and cut in a continuous motion. If a stencil shape needs to be turned, turn the acetate rather than the knife. Once the knife tip pierces the acetate, do not lift the tip again until you have finished cutting the line or curve. If you make a mistake or the acetate tears, repair the spot with a piece of transparent tape.

2. Wash the tablecloth and napkins to remove sizing, and iron them.

3. Place the tablecloth on a hard surface. Place several layers of paper toweling underneath the tablecloth where you will start stenciling. Using your own or the purchased stencils, and the photo as a color and placement guide, stencil houses, trees, and a horse and sleigh around the tablecloth to resemble an old-fashioned village scene. If you are using the "Miniature Township" stencil, use the evergreen trees, and stencil the mountains lightly in Country Blue to suggest a winter scene. If you are using your own stencils, paint the mountains freehand with an artist's flat paintbrush.

4. Tape the top of the first stencil in place with masking tape. If the shape uses more than one color, mask off all the cut outs except for the first color by taping paper under them. Holding a stencil brush like a pencil, dip it into the first color stencil paint. Using an up-and-down pouncing motion, pounce the brush on folded paper toweling or newspaper until the brush is almost dry. Pounce the brush on the open stencil cut outs, starting at the cut edges. Stencil the cut outs from the outside in so the center of the shape is lighter colored than the edges. Let the paint dry. Mask off those cut outs. Repeat with the remaining colors for the shape. Use a different stencil brush for each color used. Repeat with the other stencils, changing the paper toweling padding under the tablecloth each time you start a different shape. Wrap the stencil brushes in plastic wrap, or self-sealing plastic bags, to prevent the paint from drying on the brushes before you are finished stenciling. Clean the stencils when the paint starts to build up on them, to prevent paint build-up from distorting the stencil shapes.

5. Stencil a house, with evergreen trees on either side of it, in a corner of each napkin; use a different house for each napkin.

6. Clean the stencils with paper toweling or cotton rags soaked in soapy water or rubbing alcohol. Pat the stencils dry. Store the stencils flat or between layers of cardboard. Clean the stencil brushes with soap and water until the rinse water runs clear. Let the brushes dry completely before using them again.

7. Allow the stenciling to cure overnight. Set the stenciling with heat following the stencil paint manufacturer's instructions.

CROSS STITCH COUNTRY MAT

Average: For those with some experience in counted cross stitch.

Materials: 12-inch square of green 14-count Aida cloth; embroidery floss: 2 skeins of White, and 1 skein each of Medium Pink, Red, Coral, Dark Orange, Royal Blue, Gold and Dark Brown; tapestry needle; sewing needle; embroidery hoop.

Directions:

1. Find and pin mark the center lines of the cloth. Place the cloth in the hoop. Using two strands of floss in the tapestry needle, cross stitch the design in Fig. II, 3 centered on the cloth *(see Stitch Guide, page 270).* Each symbol in Fig. II, 3 represents one cross stitch in the color indicated. The row outside the border is 1 inch in from the edge of the cloth. Begin and end each floss length by running it through stitches on the back.

2. When the stitching is completed, block the mat, right side down, using a pressing cloth and steam iron.

3. Trim the edges of the mat 1 inch beyond the row outside the border. Turn under the edges of the mat 1 inch all around, press, and hem them.

FIG. II, 3 CROSS STITCH COUNTRY MAT

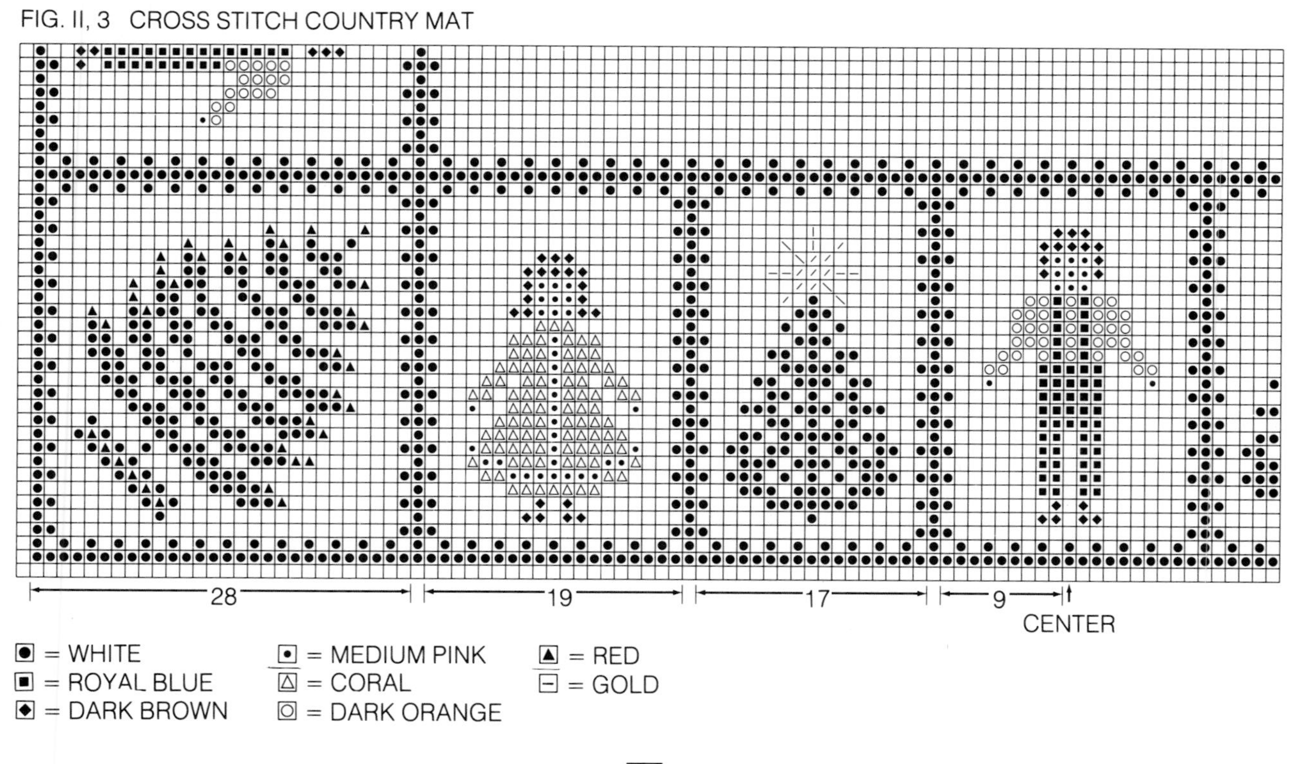

"HAPPY HOLIDAYS" CROSS STITCH TABLE RUNNER

(13 x 26⅜ inches)

Average: For those with some experience in counted cross stitch.

Materials: 18 x 32 inches of white 14-count Aida cloth; matching sewing thread; embroidery floss: 6 skeins of Red, 4 skeins of Light Green, 2 skeins each of Medium Green and Dark Green, and 1 skein each of Pink, Dark Red, Blue, Yellow and Brown; tapestry needle; sewing needle; embroidery hoop.

Directions:

1. The outer dimensions of the embroidered area are 12½ x 25¾ inches. Find the center lines of the Aida cloth, and pin mark them. Place the Aida cloth in the embroidery hoop. Using three strands of floss in the tapestry needle, cross stitch a motif of your choice in Fig. II, 4 *(page 44)* centered on the Aida cloth *(see Stitch Guide, page 270)*. Each symbol in Fig. II, 4 represents one cross stitch in the color indicated. Then cross stitch the other motifs, arranging and repeating the motifs on the grid as you like and alternating them with empty grid squares *(see photo)*. Work the straight dark grid lines in Red backstitch. Work the straight lines around the lights on the corner Christmas trees in Yellow backstitch *(see Stitch Guide)*. Begin and end each length of floss by running it through stitches on the back of the work.

2. When the cross stitching is completed, press the runner, right side down, with a damp cloth to block it. Hem the runner to the finished size, and press it again.

FIG. II, 4 "HAPPY HOLIDAYS" CROSS STITCH TABLE RUNNER

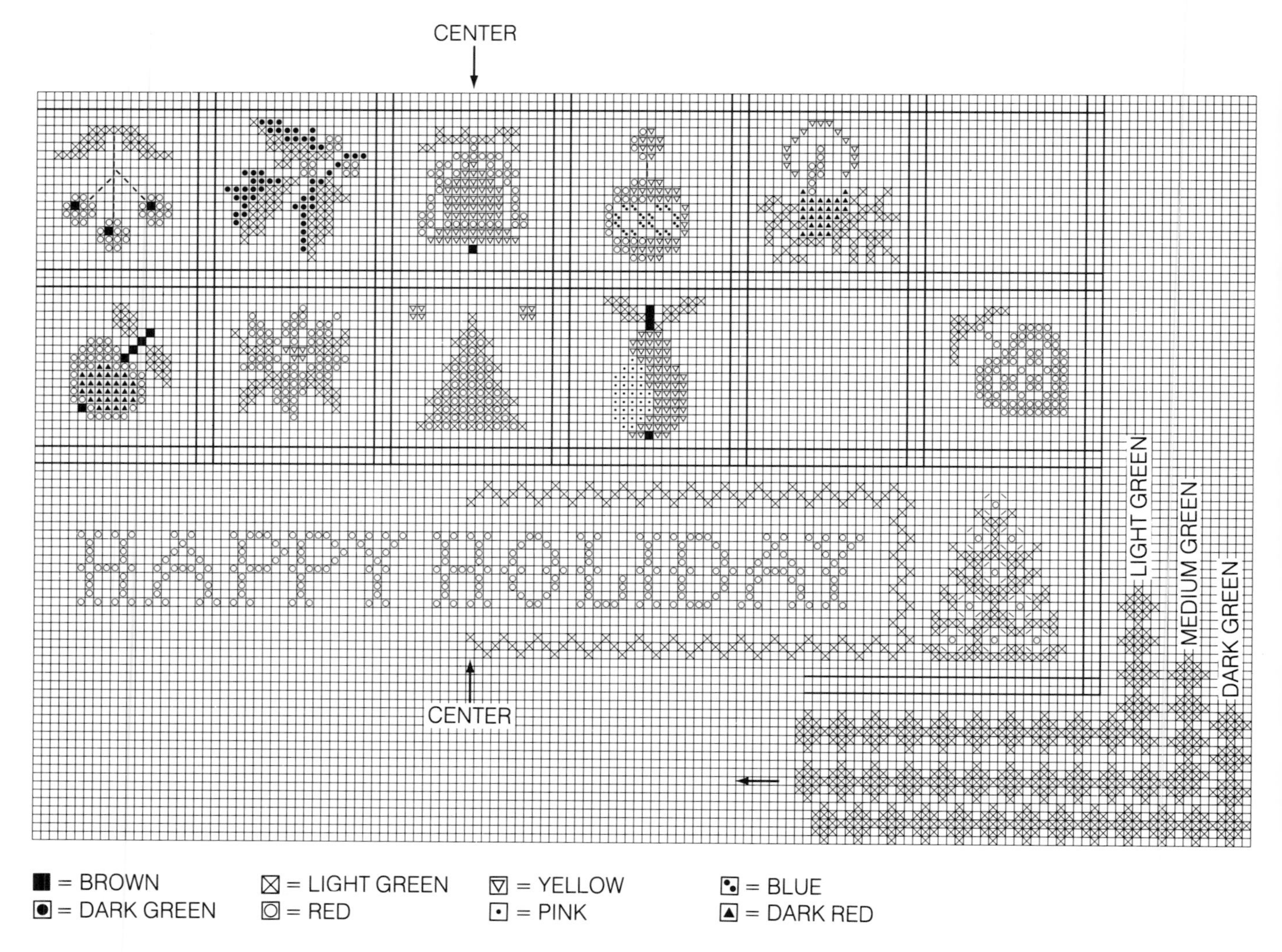

CHRISTMAS MORNING PLACE SETTINGS

Average: For those with some experience in sewing.

Materials for Each Place Mat: 24 x 17 inches of fabric for mat top; 21½ x 14½ inches of coordinating fabric for mat back; 60 inches of ½-inch-wide red braid; 60 inches of ½-inch-wide green braid; matching threads; sewing needle. ***For Each Napkin:*** 22½ x 21½ inches of place mat back fabric. ***For Each Napkin Ring:*** 18 inches of 1½-inch-wide red grosgrain ribbon; 4-inch dark green frog closure.

Directions:

1. Place Mat: Turn under the edges of the place mat top ¼ inch all around, then 1 inch, and press. Place the place mat back on the place mat top, wrong sides together, and tuck the back's raw edges underneath the top's folded edge. Topstitch through all the layers using the inside folded edge as a stitch guide. Turn over the place mat. Place the red braid on the place mat top, using the stitchline as a guide. Slipstitch the braid in place. Repeat with the green braid, lapping it slightly over the red braid's inside edge *(see photo)*.

2. Napkin: Turn under the edges of the fabric ¼ inch all around, then 1 inch, and press. Stitch, mitering the corners.

3. Napkin Ring: Knot the ribbon, leaving a loop for the napkin to fit through. Cut the ribbon ends into fish tails. Stitch the frog closure over the ribbon knot.

CLEVER CRAFTING

Handy Sewing

To keep polyester sewing thread from snarling and knotting while you hand sew, run the thread over a candle end before threading it through the needle. It makes hand-sewing much easier!

ALL THROUGH THE HOUSE

Mistletoe
hung from the gas brackets
in all the front parlors;
there was sherry and walnuts
and bottled beer and crackers
by the dessertspoons;
and cats in their fur-abouts watched the fires;
and the high-heaped fire spat,
all ready for the chestnuts
and the mulling pokers.
—Dylan Thomas

Whether you prefer
Victorian finery or the sweet simplicity of Americana, you'll find a wealth of holiday trims and decorations in this chapter. You can carry a theme throughout the house, or select your favorite elements to mix with your family treasures.

Fill your home with Victorian splendor: there are dainty crepe flowers for piling in pretty bowls or trimming your tree to rich velvet stockings and floppy velveteen rabbits. If your heart is "in country," try our cheery peppermint-striped ornaments, down-home stockings or lovely balsa wood nativity scene.

There's also a wonderful selection of Santa ornaments and wooden figures for your tree.

Let the spirit of Christmas spill into every room and corner of your home!

GRAND VICTORIANA

Enchant your family and friends with the opulence of a Victorian-style Christmas. Dazzle the eye with delicate crepe paper flowers brightened by leaves of green satin and holiday plaid taffeta ribbons. Bedeck your tree with these pretties, adorn a wreath or pile the flowers in a beautiful porcelain bowl. Create sumptuous stockings from chintz and velvet, or stitch up a velveteen rabbit to make this Christmas just grand!

CREPE PAPER FLOWERS WITH BOWS

Average: For those with some experience in crafting.

Materials: 1 package of off-white extra-strength crepe paper (enough to make 8 to 9 flowers); red and medium green regular crepe paper; 1 yard of plaid taffeta; matching thread; 1½-inch-wide apple green satin ribbon; small red sequins; No. 26 green covered wire; No. 19 stem wire; green floral tape; clear acrylic spray varnish; small watercolor paintbrush; red wide felt tip marker; black fine-point permanent felt tip pen; rubbing alcohol; extra-large cotton cosmetic puffs; waxed dental floss; toothpicks; needlenose pliers; wire cutters; scissors; white glue; newspapers.

Directions:

1. Flower Center: Make a small hook at one end of a 6-inch length of stem wire. Pull the wire through a cotton puff, catching the hook inside the puff. Cut a 4-inch square of red crepe paper, and cover the cotton puff with it. Wind a 6-inch length of dental floss tightly around the base of the covered puff to secure the crepe paper. Make dots on the crepe paper with the black fine-point pen.

2. Cutting across the grain, cut a 2 x 8-inch strip of medium green crepe paper. Fringe the strip's long edges with the scissors. Fasten one short end of the strip to the base of the flower center with a dot of glue. Wind the strip around the base, and glue the loose end to the base.

3. Petals: Cut the package of extra-strength crepe paper crosswise into five equal parts. Cut each part in half lengthwise *(see* Fig. III, 1A*)*. Round off the corners at one short end of each paper bundle to make petals *(see* Fig. III, 1B*)*. Color each rounded petal edge with the red marker. Touch the colored area with the watercolor brush dipped in the alcohol, so the color will run and soften. Let the petals dry. Ripple the rounded petal edges by stretching them gently between your fingers.

4. Double Petal Flower: Space four petals evenly around the flower center, and wind a 12-inch length of dental floss around the base of the flower to secure them. Space four more petals evenly around the flower center. Pulling tightly, wind all the floss around the base; it isn't necessary to tie the floss. Cup the base of each outside petal slightly by stretching it gently between your thumbs and forefingers. Using a toothpick, glue six to eight sequins to the flower center.

5. Single Petal Flower: Assemble the flower following Step 4, using only four petals.

6. Green Bow: Using an 18-inch length of satin ribbon, make 2¼-inch-long double ribbon loops, and crimp the loops in the center. Using the pliers, twist a 5-inch length of covered wire tightly around the crimped center. Attach the bow to the base of the flower with the covered wire, and wrap the excess covered wire around the flower stem.

7. Plaid Bow: Place the taffeta on a sheet of newspaper. Size the taffeta by spraying it with two light coats of acrylic, letting the acrylic dry briefly between coats. Let the sized taffeta dry completely. Cut 1¾-inch-wide taffeta bias strips, and sew their ends together. Cut a 48-inch length from the pieced strip. Leaving a 5-inch-long tail, make a 3-inch-long plaid loop and crimp the base between your fingers. Wrap a 12-inch length of covered wire once around the base. Make a second loop, and wrap the base with the wire. Repeat until there are five loops. Attach the plaid bow to the base of the flower, opposite the green bow, and wrap the excess covered wire around the flower stem. Wrap the flower stem with floral tape. Use the stem to attach the flower to a tree or wreath.

FIG. III, 1A CREPE PAPER FLOWERS WITH BOWS

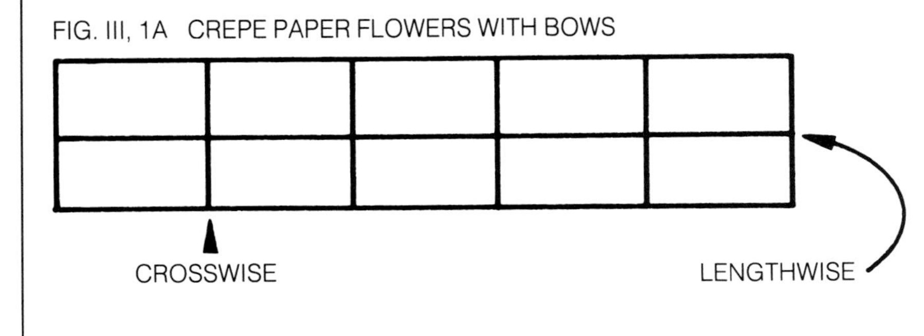

FIG. III, 1B

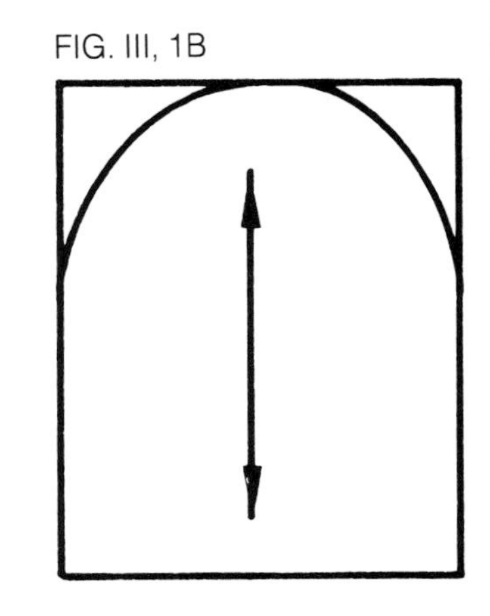

VICTORIANA WREATH

Average: For those with some experience in crafting.

Materials: 3 Crepe Paper Flowers with Bows *(directions, page 49)*; grapevine or straw wreath; dried baby's breath; 1¾-inch-wide plaid taffeta ribbon; floral wire; wire cutters.

Directions:

1. Divide the baby's breath into small bunches. Tie each bunch with floral wire, leaving the wire ends free.

2. Make plaid bows following Crepe Paper Flowers with Bows, Step 7 *(page 49)*, using the plaid taffeta ribbon and floral wire in place of the fabric and covered wire, and omitting the sizing. Wire several of the bows together into a cluster, leaving the wire ends free. Repeat with the remaining bows.

3. Using the wire ends, attach the plaid bow clusters around the outside edge of the grapevine or straw wreath. Attach the baby's breath to the front of the wreath to cover it completely *(see photo)*.

4. Using the photo as a placement guide, attach the Crepe Paper Flowers with Bows to one side of the wreath.

A PRETTY BOWL OF POSIES

Average: For those with some experience in crafting.

Materials: Porcelain bowl; Crepe Paper Flowers with Bows *(Directions, page 49)*; baby's breath; narrow red satin ribbon.

Directions:
Divide the baby's breath into small bunches, and tie each bunch with a long length of ribbon to make a nosegay. Arrange the Crepe Paper Flowers with Bows in the bowl, mounding them in the center. Fill in with the nosegays, letting their ribbon ends hang over the edge of the bowl.

TIPS FOR A "GREEN" CHRISTMAS

Recyclable Arts and Crafts

When the kids are home for Christmas vacation, you can be sure of having at least one foul-weather day. Be prepared! Collect various throwaway items that can be turned into arts and crafts. This way, you'll not only be ready for rainy-day activities, you'll be recycling as well.

Here are some throwaways that can be recycled into works of art.

- Plastic foam meat trays
- Plastic foam egg cartons
- Spools
- Old magazines
- Yarn scraps
- Buttons
- Beads and sequins

FIG. III, 2 DAINTY MINI-STOCKING

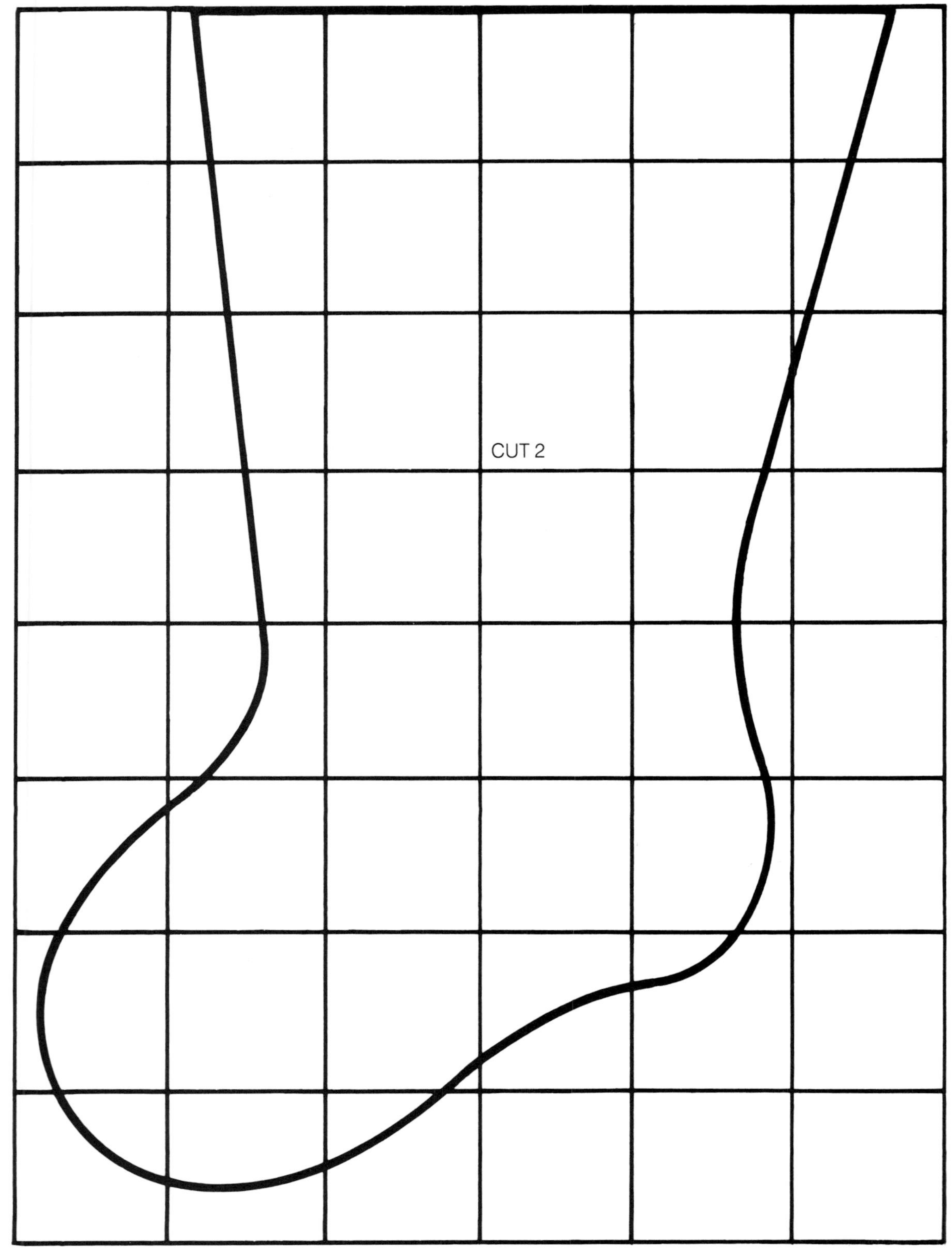

DAINTY MINI-STOCKING

Average: For those with some experience in sewing.

Materials: ⅓ yard of floral print fabric; matching thread; coordinating color ribbon; old or purchased crocheted round doily; old or purchased lace; fusible interfacing; tracing paper for pattern.

Directions (¼-inch seams allowed):

1. Trace the full-size stocking pattern in FIG. III, 2 onto paper.

2. Cut out two stockings each from the floral print fabric and interfacing. Fuse each interfacing stocking to the wrong side of a fabric stocking. Stitch the fabric stockings right sides together, leaving the top edge open. Clip the curves, and turn the stocking right side out.

3. Fold the doily in half twice, and pin mark the center point. Open the doily halfway. Pin mark on the fold 2 inches on either side of the center. Remove the center pin. Cut along the fold between the pins.

4. With right sides together and edges matching, pin the cut edge of the doily to the top edge of the stocking. Using a ½-inch seam allowance, stitch around the top edge of the stocking. Turn the seam allowance to the inside, and stitch ¼ inch from the raw edges through all thicknesses except the doily.

5. Tack the ribbon and lace bows around the front top edge of the stocking *(see photo)*. Fold a length of ribbon in half, and tack the raw ends to the stocking's inside back seam for a hanger loop.

VELVETEEN RABBITS

(small rabbit: 6 inches tall, seated; large rabbit: 12 inches tall, seated)

Average: For those with some experience in sewing.

Materials: 45-inch-wide velveteen: 3/8 yard for small rabbit, and 3/4 yard for large rabbit; matching sewing thread; heavy duty button thread; gold cording; small jingle bells; artificial pine sprigs; synthetic stuffing; sewing needle; paper for patterns.

FIG. III, 3 VELVETEEN RABBITS

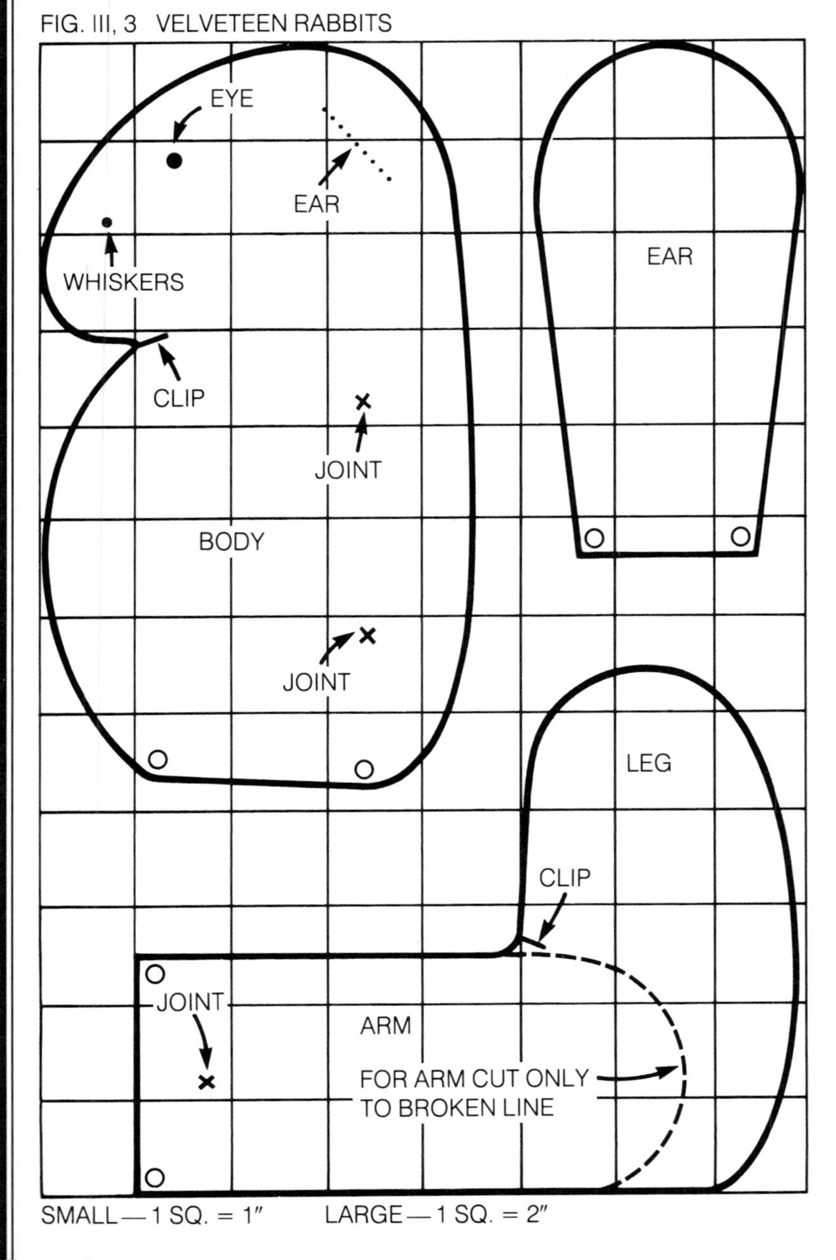

Directions
(1/4-inch seams allowed):

1. Patterns: Enlarge the small rabbit pattern in Fig. III, 3 onto paper following the directions on page 271, and using the ratio given. Enlarge the large rabbit pattern onto a separate sheet of paper using the larger ratio.

2. Cutting: For each rabbit, cut one pair of Body pieces and two pairs each of Arm, Leg and Ear pieces from the velveteen.

3. Stitching: Sew each pair of Body, Arm, Leg and Ear pieces right sides together, leaving an opening for turning between the circles. Clip the curves where indicated. Turn the Body, Arms and Legs right side out, and stuff them. Turn in their open edges, and slipstitch the openings closed *(see Stitch Guide, page 270).*

4. Ears: Turn the Ears right side out. Gather their open edges slightly, and slipstitch them to the Body at the ear positions *(see dotted line on Body pattern in* Fig. III, 3*).*

5. Assembling: Using the heavy duty button thread, sew the Arms and Legs to the Body, matching X's; take several stitches from each Arm or Leg to the Body so the limbs can move.

6. Face: Using the heavy duty thread, make a French knot for each eye as indicated on the pattern *(see Stitch Guide).* Thread the needle with three lengths of heavy duty thread. Push the needle into the whiskers mark on one side of the head, and out at the whiskers mark on the other side of the head *(see Body pattern).* Knot the threads against each side of the head, and cut the thread ends to 3 inches.

7. Trims: For each rabbit, cut a length of gold cording and sew a jingle bell to each end. Tie the cording around the rabbit's neck, and tuck a pine sprig under the cording.

VELVET STOCKINGS

(9, 13½ and 18 inches long)

Average: For those with some experience in sewing.

Materials: 44-inch-wide fabric: ¾ yard each of velvet and lining; selection of woven and metallic braids in various widths, including enough 2-inch-wide or wider woven braid to fit around top edge of each stocking for a cuff; matching threads; sewing needle; paper for patterns.

Directions (¼-inch seams allowed):

1. Enlarge the pattern in Fig. III, 4 onto paper following the directions on page 271, making a pattern for each size stocking using the ratios given. For each stocking, cut a pair of pieces from the velvet and the lining.

2. Using the photo as a guide, arrange the woven and metallic braids on the right side of each velvet stocking. Topstitch the braids in place.

3. Stitch each pair of velvet stockings, right sides together, leaving the top edges open. Repeat with the lining pieces. Clip the curves, and turn the velvet stockings right side out. If you wish, hand-sew narrow braid along the velvet stockings' outside seams.

4. Cut the cuff braid 1 inch longer than the stocking's top edge. Stitch the short ends together ½ inch from their raw edges. If you wish, stitch narrow braids to the cuff's edges. Pin the right side of the cuff to the wrong side of the velvet stocking, back seams matching. Stitch the cuff to the stocking. Turn the cuff to the outside.

5. Fold a 7-inch length of braid in half; stitch the ends to the stocking's inside back seam for a hanger.

6. Insert a lining into each stocking, seams matching. Turn under the raw top edge; slipstitch the lining to the stocking *(see Stitch Guide, page 270).*

FIG. III, 4 VICTORIAN VELVET STOCKINGS

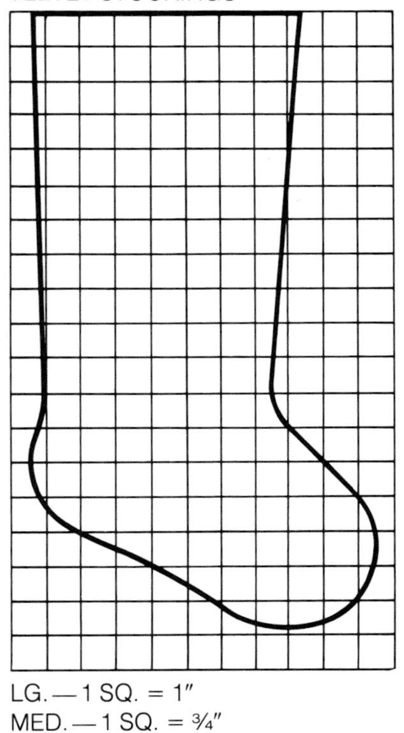

LG.—1 SQ. = 1″
MED.—1 SQ. = ¾″
SM.—1 SQ. = ½″

A CONTEMPORARY COUNTRY CHRISTMAS

Blend old and new by creating a country-warm holiday in a modern setting. Just adding a few simple touches can turn a contemporary room into a cozy, old-fashioned retreat. Quilts, old or new, quilted pillows, afghans or blankets all add Christmas cheer, particularly when they are brightly colored. Use lots of red and white and pick up the colors of the room in your tree ornaments.

PEPPERMINT-STRIPED ORNAMENTS

Easy: Achievable by anyone.

Materials: Balsa wood; craft knife; fine sandpaper; variety of Christmas cookie cutters; red and white acrylic paints; masking tape; narrow red velvet ribbon; metallic thread; white glue; artificial cherries with leaves.

Directions:

1. Using the craft knife and the cookie cutters as patterns, cut out as many ornaments from the balsa wood as desired. Sand the edges of each shape smooth. Cut a small hole about ½ inch from the top of each ornament.

2. Paint all the shapes white on one side and let the paint dry completely. Turn over the ornaments, and paint the other side and the edges white. Let the paint dry completely.

3. When the white paint has dried, carefully place pieces of the tape on the shape to form stripes. Try to space the stripes evenly. Paint the stripes without tape red. Let the paint dry, turn over the shape and repeat the taping and painting on the opposite side. Paint the edges of each ornament to match the red and white striping on the front and back sides.

4. For each ornament, cut a length of red velvet ribbon and tie the ribbon into a bow. Glue a double cherry with leaves on top of the bow and let the glue dry. Glue the bow and cherries to the top of the ornament directly above the hole.

5. Cut a longer length of gold metallic thread. Insert one end of the thread through the hole in the top of the ornament. Wrap the thread around the bow with the cherries. Repeat two times to further secure the bow and cherries to the ornament. Knot the ends of the thread to make a hanger.

TIPS FOR A "GREEN" CHRISTMAS

Giving Back

At holiday time, it is important to remember those in need with donations of clothing and usable household goods. Putting useful items that you no longer need back into circulation not only is valuable in terms of recycling, it also can help bring back the spirit of giving into your Christmas celebration. Get the whole family to make up a care package of clothes, dishware, appliances, toys — even books and records. Call the Salvation Army, Goodwill Industries or charitable organization of choice for a drop location near you.

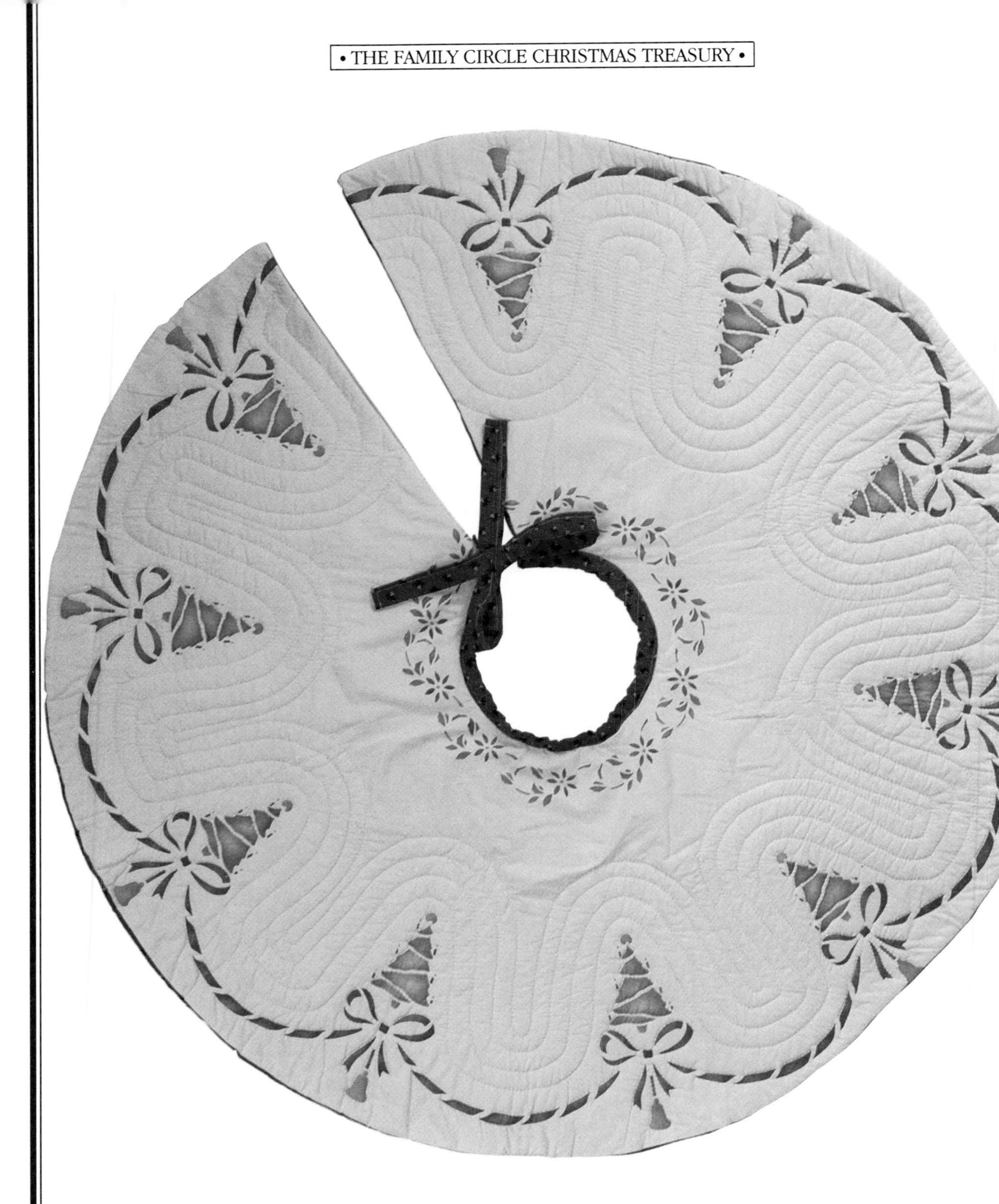

O TANNENBAUM TREE SKIRT

Average: For those with some experience in stenciling and quilting.

Materials: 1¼ yards of 45-inch-wide bleached muslin; 1½ yards of red calico fabric; 1¼ yards of 45-inch-wide synthetic batting; red sewing thread; white quilting thread; Stencil-Ease® "New England Bows" and "Christmas Designs" stencils; Fab-Tex™ fabric stenciling paints: Dark Red, Bright Green, and Colonial Golde; three No. 10 or 12 stencil brushes; between needle *(optional)*; quilting hoop *(optional)*; washable fabric marker; measuring tape; thumbtack; string; yardstick; masking tape; paper toweling; paper; iron; newspaper *(optional)*; cotton rags *(optional)*; rubbing alcohol *(optional)*.

Directions:

1. Wash and iron the fabrics. Tape the muslin square to a flat surface. Locate the center of the muslin, and use the thumbtack to secure one end of the string to the center. Attach the fabric marker to the other end of the string, positioning the marker at the edge of the muslin. Keeping the string taut, swing the marker around to mark a 45-inch-diameter circle. Shorten the string to 4½ inches, and mark a 9-inch-diameter circle in the center of the muslin. Draw a straight line from the smaller to the larger circle for the skirt opening.

2. Place the skirt on a hard surface. Place several layers of paper toweling underneath the skirt where you will start stenciling. Dampen a piece of paper toweling with water. Wipe the bristles of a stencil brush across the damp paper to pick up a slight amount of moisture on the bristles. Following Winter Village Stenciled Tablecloth & Napkins, Step 4 *(page 41)*, and using the photo as a color guide, stencil a bow on one side of the skirt opening 4¼ inches from the outer edge of the skirt. Stencil nine more bows evenly spaced around the outer edge. Retape the stencil to block off the bow, and stencil a rope swag between each bow, adjusting the stencil as necessary. Stencil a Christmas tree above and a bell below each bow. Stencil poinsettias around the center of the skirt, leaving a ½-inch seam allowance. Clean the stencils and brushes following Winter Village Stenciled Tablecloth & Napkins, Step 6.

3. Let the stenciled skirt dry overnight. Set an iron on dry and press directly over each stenciled area for 25 to 30 seconds.

4. Cut out the stenciled skirt on the marked lines. Using the skirt as a pattern, cut the batting and a calico skirt back to the same size. Place the calico back on the stenciled skirt, right sides together, and the batting on top of the calico. Stitch all the layers together ½ inch from the edges, leaving one straight edge open. Turn the skirt right side out and slipstitch the open edge closed *(see Stitch Guide, page 270)*.

5. If hand-quilting, place the skirt in the hoop. Using the between needle and quilting thread, quilt a line around the stenciled trees and swags *(see Stitch Guide)*. Repeat 1 inch inside the first line three times *(see photo)*. Or quilt by machine.

6. Make bias binding, pieced as needed, from the remaining calico. Leaving enough binding extending beyond the skirt opening edges for ties, sew the binding to the front center edge of the skirt using a ½-inch seam *(see photo)*. Turn the binding to the back, and slipstitch the binding to the skirt back *(see Stitch Guide)*. Turn in the ties' raw edges. Slipstitch each tie closed along its long edge and short end.

TIPS FOR A "GREEN" CHRISTMAS

Hot News from the Fireplace

It's particularly nice to make a roaring fire in the fireplace during the holidays. And, aside from the visual benefits, it can help lower those winter-high heating bills. A wood fire usually produces enough heat to warm a good size room, so turn down the thermostat when you light a fire.

If you're using three hour logs, check the packaging: Some are more environment-friendly than others.

When the fireplace is not in use, be sure to keep the damper tightly closed to prevent heat from escaping up the chimney.

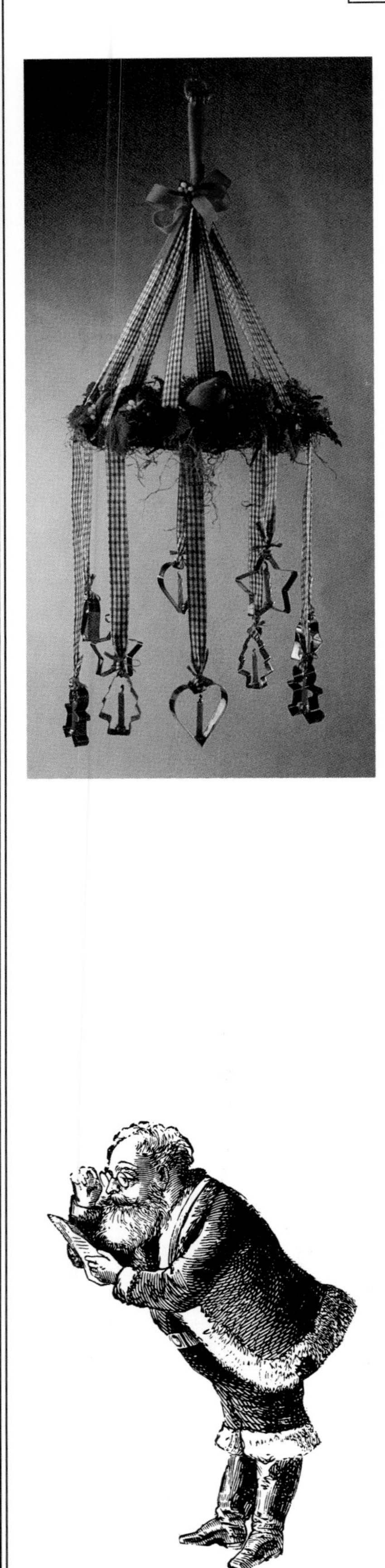

CHRISTMAS KITCHEN CHANDELIER

(12 inches in diameter)

Average: For those with some experience in crafting.

Materials: 12-inch-diameter grapevine wreath; cookie cutters: 2 each of star, heart, gingerbread man, bell and Christmas tree, or shapes desired; ten ¼-inch-diameter red candles; 13 yards of 1-inch-wide red, green and white checked ribbon; 2 yards of 1-inch-wide red grosgrain ribbon; 2¼ yards of ⅛-inch-wide red grosgrain ribbon; 1 yard of ⅛-inch-wide gold cording; gold glitter; artificial bird; 10 stems each of artificial holly and mistletoe; sphagnum moss; floral wire; red wide felt tip marker; plastic coffee can lid; white craft glue; hot glue gun, or thick craft glue.

Directions:

1. Cut off the candle bottoms so the candles are 2 inches long. Dip the wicks into the white glue, and then into the glitter. Let the glue dry.

2. Wrap gold cording twice around the base of each candle. Cut the cording, and glue it to the base.

3. Using the glue gun or thick glue, glue a candle to the inside bottom of each cookie cutter *(see photo).*

4. Cut the checked ribbon into ten 46-inch lengths. Thread about 4 inches of one ribbon length through the top of a cookie cutter. Make a single knot, and trim the short end of the ribbon to 1 inch. Repeat with the remaining ribbon lengths and cookie cutters.

5. Cut ten 8-inch lengths of ⅛-inch-wide grosgrain ribbon. Wrap a length above each checked ribbon knot, and tie the ends in a bow.

6. Separate the moss, and cover the wreath completely with it. Place the wreath on a flat surface. Leaving the cookie cutter and about 12 inches of ribbon hanging below the wreath, wrap the long end of one checked ribbon around the wreath from the outside over the top to the inside, under the bottom to the outside, and up to the top again. Repeat with the remaining checked ribbons, varying the lengths of the cookie cutter ends and spacing the ribbons evenly around the wreath *(see photo).*

7. Gather the checked ribbons' short ends above the wreath; the ribbons' lengths will be uneven. Make sure the ribbons' edges are even and straight. Starting 14 inches above the wreath, wrap about 5 inches of floral wire around the ribbons. Leave 3 inches of the ribbon ends free at the top, and cut off the excess ribbon.

8. Cut a 1½-inch-diameter circle from the plastic coffee can lid. Color the circle with the red marker. Cut an X in the center of the circle, and insert the free ends of the checked ribbons through the opening. Secure the ribbon ends above the plastic circle by wrapping them with wire.

9. Wrap a length of 1-inch-wide grosgrain ribbon around the wire above the circle. Glue the grosgrain ribbon in place, securing the ends. Cut another length of 1-inch-wide grosgrain ribbon, and fold it in half to make a loop for a hanger. Glue and wire the hanger ends to the top of the chandelier just above the plastic circle. Make a bow with the remaining 1-inch-wide grosgrain ribbon, and attach it to the top of the chandelier to cover the hanger ends.

10. Decorate the wreath with the holly, mistletoe and bird *(see photo).*

TIPS FOR A "GREEN" CHRISTMAS

Environment-Smart Sparkle

When you want to give your Christmas tree extra sparkle, you probably trim it with tinsel, then throw the tinsel away. Besides producing waste, most places that recycle Christmas trees won't accept any with tinsel on them. But there are alternatives to add glitter without waste.

- Strings of sequins. Use these as garlands, or cut the strings into smaller strips and hang the strips from branches to look like icicles.
- Metallic ribbons. Either tie the ribbons in bows and wire them to branches, or curl lengths of ribbons and use them as streamers.
- Strings of faceted beads, gold or silver beads, or fake pearls.
- Tiny mirrors. Hang them like ornaments.
- Glass ball ornaments. To add extra sparkle, spray glue on the balls and roll them in glitter, or glue sequins to the balls in a pleasing design.
- Tin or metallic paper ornaments.
- Chandelier crystals.

GIFTS OF NATURE KISSING BALL

All the natural trims you need for this lovely ornament can be found on a walk through the autumn woods.

Easy: Achievable by anyone.

Materials: 6- to 8-inch diameter Styrofoam® ball, or large ball ornament; tiny pine cones; acorns; gumballs; nuts; 1-inch-wide metallic gold ribbon; hot glue gun.

Directions:
Glue the pine cones, acorns, gumballs and nuts to the Styrofoam ball or large ball ornament to cover it completely. Glue a ribbon loop to the top of the ball for a hanger.

ABC

RIBBON PATCHWORK STOCKING

(photo, pages 62-63)

Average: For those with some experience in sewing.

Materials: ½ yard of solid color fabric; ¼ yard each of assorted ribbons, laces, eyelet laces, cluny laces and fringes in various widths; extra-wide double fold bias tape; matching threads; purchased appliqué; assorted fabric scraps; synthetic batting; 4 buttons; sewing needle; paper for pattern.

Directions:

(¼-inch seams allowed):

1. Using the photo on pages 62-63 as a guide, draw a stocking pattern on paper. Add a ¼-inch seam allowance to all but the top edge. Cut out four stockings from the solid color fabric, and two stockings from the batting.

2. Arrange the fabric scraps and appliqué on the right side of one fabric stocking. Cover the scraps' raw edges with the assorted trims. Sew the buttons to a wide ribbon *(see photo)*. Topstitch the trims in place.

3. Place a fabric stocking wrong side up. Place a batting stocking and then the patchwork stocking, right side up, on top. Stitch the stockings together along the outside edges to make the stocking front. Repeat with the remaining batting and fabric stockings for the stocking back.

4. Stitch the stocking front and back right sides together, leaving the top edge open. Turn the stocking right side out. Starting at the back seam and with raw edges even, stitch one long edge of the bias tape to the stocking top edge. Leaving enough tape at the back seam for a hanger, fold the tape to the inside of the stocking and slipstitch it in place *(see Stitch Guide, page 270)*. Make a loop for a hanger with the extra tape, and stitch the hanger to the inside back seam.

WHITE QUILTED STOCKING

(photo, pages 62-63)

Average: For those with some experience in sewing.

Materials: ½ yard of quilted satin fabric; ½ yard of lining fabric; matching threads; 2½ yards of ³⁄₁₆-inch-wide lurex-edge velvet ribbon; 2¼ yards of ⅜-inch-wide metallic grosgrain ribbon; ½ yard of synthetic batting; white glue; paper for pattern.

Directions:

1. Using the photo on pages 62-63 as a guide, draw a stocking pattern on paper. Cut out two stockings from the batting. Add a ⅝-inch seam allowance to the pattern, and cut out two stockings each from the quilted fabric and lining.

2. Using the photo as a placement guide, glue lengths of the velvet and metallic ribbons to the right side of each quilted stocking.

3. Working from the right side, pin a batting stocking to the wrong side of each quilted stocking. Stitch the quilted stockings right sides together, leaving the top edge open. Clip the curves, and turn the stocking right side out. Do not remove the pins yet.

4. Stitch the lining stockings together the same way, but do not turn them. Slip the lining into the quilted stocking. Turn in the stocking and lining seam allowances at the top edge, and pin them in place. Fold a 6-inch length of metallic ribbon into a loop, and tack the loop ends together. Slip the loop ends between the lining and stocking at the stocking's back seam, and tack the loop in place for a hanger. Slipstitch the stocking and lining together, reinforcing the hanger while stitching *(see Stitch Guide, page 270)*. Remove the pins.

SAMPLER STOCKING

(photo, pages 62-63)

Average: For those with some experience in sewing and counted cross stitch.

Materials: 23 x 12 inches of 6-mesh natural burlap; 23 x 12 inches of fabric for stocking back; two 23 x 12-inch pieces of lining fabric; matching threads; 4-ply worsted knitting yarn: 20 yards of Red, 12 yards of Green, 3 yards of Brown, 1 yard of Yellow, and ½ yard of Blue; tapestry needle; embroidery hoop.

Directions:

1. The stocking is 19½ inches long from top to bottom. Using this dimension, and those marked on the chart in Fig. III, 5, pencil an outline of the stocking on the burlap. Staystitch the edges of the burlap by machine to prevent raveling.

2. The Red cross stitches at the top and bottom of the stocking are worked over 3 threads. The cross stitches for the design in Fig. III, 5 are worked over 2 threads. Place the burlap in the embroidery hoop. Using the yarn and tapestry needle, work eight rows of Red cross stitches across the top of the stocking, and four rows of cross stitches across the bottom of the stocking *(see Stitch Guide, page 270)*. Then cross stitch the design in Fig. III, 5 on the stocking; each symbol in Fig. III, 5 represents one cross stitch worked over 2 threads in the color indicated.

3. When the cross stitching is completed, baste around the stocking outline. Press the embroidered burlap, right side down, with a damp cloth to block it. Let the burlap dry.

4. With right sides together, stitch the embroidered burlap to the stocking back fabric over the basted outline, leaving the top edge open. Trim all edges to a ½-inch seam allowance.

5. Cut two stockings from the lining fabric to match the embroidered stocking, including the seam allowance. Stitch the lining stockings, right sides together, leaving the top edge and toe open.

6. Twist together four 10-inch lengths of Red yarn. Repeat. Wind the twisted yarns together in the opposite direction to make a cord. Fold the cord into a loop, and tack it to the top of the embroidered stocking's back seam for a hanger.

7. Clip the curves, and turn the stocking right side out. Do not turn the lining. Insert the stocking into the lining. Stitch the top of the stocking to the top of the lining. Pull out the stocking through the toe of the lining. Turn in the open toe edges, and slipstitch the opening closed *(see Stitch Guide)*. Insert the lining into the stocking and take a few stitches to secure it in place. Press the finished stocking lightly.

FIG. III, 5 SAMPLER STOCKING

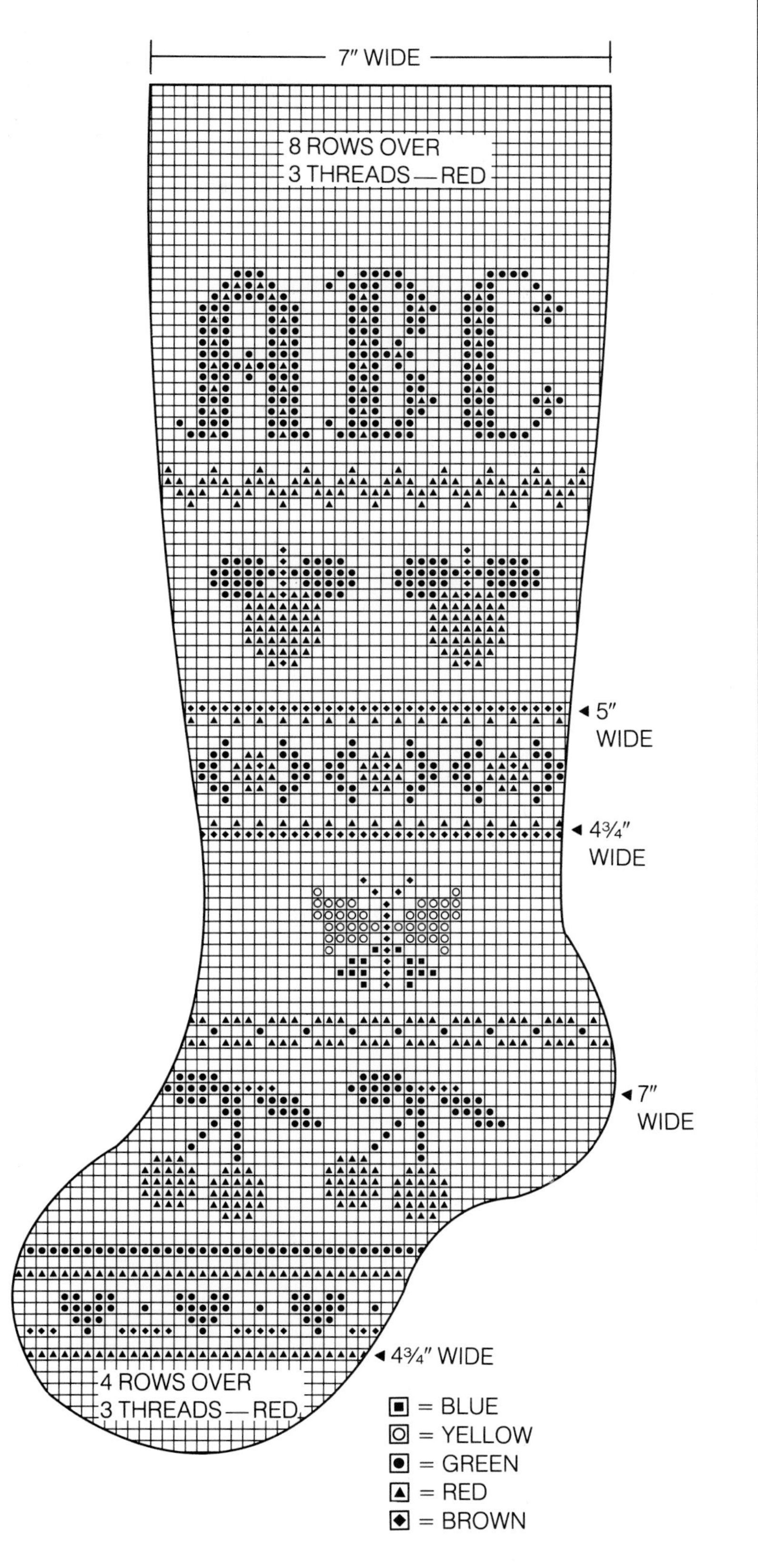

CHECKED STOCKING

(photo, pages 62-63)

Average: For those with some experience in knitting.

Materials: Aunt Lydia's Rug Yarn: 2 skeins of Emerald Green, and 1 skein each of White, Red and Gold; four size 10½ double-pointed knitting needles (dp); size G crochet hook.
Note: *Carry the unused colors loosely on the wrong side of the work. If you wish, twist the unused colors with the working yarn every 2 sts.*
Directions:
1. Stocking: With Emerald Green, cast on 56 sts, dividing them evenly among 3 dp needles. Close the circle, and k 2 rows. ***Check Pattern, Rows 1 to 4:*** *K 4 Green, k 4 Gold; rep from * around. ***Rows 5 to 8:*** *K 4 Red, k 4 Green; rep from * around. ***Rows 9 to 12:*** *K 4 Green, k 4 White; rep from * around. ***Rows 13 to 16:*** Rep Rows 1 to 4. Repeat Rows 5 to 16 twice. Drop all colors but Green. Work one row in Green.
2. Heel: K 14 sts on 1 dp needle, k 28 sts on 2nd dp needle, k 14 sts on 3rd needle and slip the first 14 sts onto the 3rd needle. Break off the yarn. Work only the 28 sts on the 2nd needle for the Heel. Join Green. Work 2 inches of k 1, p 1 ribbing; end on the right side. ***Row 1 (wrong side):*** P 16, p 2 tog, p 1, turn; sl 1, k 7, sl 1, k 1, psso, k 1, turn; sl 1, k 5, sl 1, k 1, psso, k 1, turn; sl 1, p 6, p 2 tog, p 1, turn; sl 1, p 8, p 2 tog, p 1, turn. Continue in this way, working 1 more stitch on each row until all sts have been worked. End on the right side with 16 sts. Pick up and k 4 sts along the side of the Heel. On the 2nd needle, k across 28 sts of the instep. On the 3rd needle, pick up 4 sts along the side of the Heel and k 8 sts across the Heel. There should be 12 sts on each Heel needle.
3. Shaping, Rnd 1: On the 1st needle, k 9, k 2 tog, k 1; on the 2nd needle, k 28; on the 3rd needle, k 1, sl 1, k 1, psso, k 9. ***Rnd 2:*** K. Rep Rnds 1 and 2 until there are 6 sts on each Heel needle.
4. Foot: Work even for 4 inches. ***Toe, Row 1:*** K 2 tog, k 1; rep around. ***Row 2:*** K. ***Row 3:*** K 2 tog; rep around. Rep Rows 2 and 3. Draw the yarn through the rem sts, and fasten off from the wrong side. With the crochet hook, work 1 row of sc around the top of the Stocking in Red.

FROSTY THE SNOWMAN & JOLLY ST. NICK KNITTED STOCKINGS

(photo, pages 62-63)

Average: For those with some experience in knitting.

General Materials: Four size 6 double-pointed knitting needles (dp), OR ANY SIZE NEEDLES TO OBTAIN GAUGE BELOW; stitch holder; crewel needle.
Gauge: 5 sts = 1 inch; 6 rows = 1 inch.
General Directions:
1. Stocking: With MC, cast on 64 sts, dividing them among 3 dp needles 22-21-21. Close the circle. ***Rows 1 to 18:*** P each row. ***Rows 19 to 38:*** K each row. ***Row 39:*** Dec 1 st at beg of each needle (61 sts). Rep Rows 19 to 39 three times (52 sts). K next row.
2. Heel: Divide the sts between 2 needles. Slip 26 sts onto the stitch holder, and work the remaining 26 sts. ***Rows 1 to 26:*** K each row. ***Row 27:*** K 13, sl 1, k 1, psso, k 1, turn. ***Row 28:*** P 2, p 2 tog, p 1, turn. ***Row 29:*** K 4, sl 1, k 1, psso, k 1, turn. ***Row 30:*** P 6, p 2 tog, p 1, turn. Continue this way until 1 st remains after the space. K tog with the next st. P across until last 2 sts, p 2 tog (16 sts). Break off the yarn.
3. Shaping: With the right side facing, tie the yarn at the beginning of the top of the Heel; pick up and k 13 sts. Work across 16 sts on the Heel needle. Pick up and k 13 sts on the other side of the Heel. Divide the 42 sts between the 2 needles. K and return the 26 sts on the stitch holder to the third needle. ***Rows 1 to 7:*** K each row, dec 1 st at the beginning of the first Heel needle and the end of the second Heel needle (54 sts). ***Rows 8 to 36:*** K each row.
4. Toe, Row 1: K 1 row, dec 1 st at the beginning of the first Heel needle

and at the end of the second Heel needle. ***Row 2:*** Dec 1 st at each end of the front needle, at the beginning of the first Heel needle and at the end of the second Heel needle. ***Row 3:*** K 1 row. Rep Rows 2 and 3 seven times (20 sts). Place 10 sts on each of 2 needles. Weave the Toe with the crewel needle, and run the end of the yarn into the knitting.
5. Top Trim: With White, cast on 65 sts. K 3 rows. Bind off.
6. Hanger: With MC, cast on 30 sts. K 3 rows. Bind off.
7. Figure: Make Frosty the Snowman or Jolly St. Nick following the individual directions below.
8. Finishing: Press all knitted pieces with a warm steam iron. Using the crewel needle and matching yarn, sew the Top Trim to the Stocking, joining the Trim's ends at the back. Fold the Hanger into a loop, and sew it to the inside back of the stocking. Attach Frosty the Snowman or Jolly St. Nick to the Stocking following the individual directions.

FROSTY THE SNOWMAN STOCKING

Materials: Lion Brand Pamela 4-ply knitting worsted yarn (3½-ounce skein): 1 skein of Scarlet (MC), and small amounts of White, Orange, Emerald and Black; General Materials.

Directions:

1. Make the Stocking following General Directions, Steps 1 to 6.
2. Snowman: With White, cast on 13 sts. ***Rows 1 to 3:*** K each row. ***Row 4:*** Inc 1 st each side (15 sts). ***Rows 5 to 13:*** K each row. ***Row 14:*** Inc 1 st each side. ***Rows 15 to 21:*** K each row. ***Row 22:*** Dec 1 st each side. ***Rows 23 and 24:*** K each row. ***Row 25:*** Dec 1 st each side. ***Row 26:*** K 1 row. ***Row 27:*** Inc 1 st each side. ***Rows 28 to 38:*** K each row. ***Row 39:*** Dec 1 st each side. ***Row 40:*** K 1 row. ***Rows 41 and 42:*** Dec 1 st each side. ***Row 43:*** K 1 row. ***Row 44:*** Inc 1 st each side. ***Rows 45 to 48:*** K each row. ***Row 49:*** Inc 1 st each side. ***Rows 50 to 57:*** K each row. Bind off.
3. Scarf: With Emerald, cast on 4 sts. K 14 rows. Bind off.
4. Scarf Ends: With Emerald, cast on 4 sts, k 15 rows, and bind off for 1 scarf end. With Emerald, cast on 4 sts, k 13 rows, and bind off for the other scarf end.
5. Button/Eye (make 5): With Black, cast on 4 sts. ***Row 1:*** K 1 row. ***Row 2:*** P 1 row. Gather the edges of the knitted strip, and add a few Black yarn scraps inside. Pull the gathered strip into a ball, and tie it.
6. Hat: With Black, cast on 11 sts. ***Row 1:*** K 1 row. ***Row 2:*** P 1 row. Rep Rows 1 and 2 six times. Bind off.
7. Hat Brim: With Black, cast on 18 sts. K 1 row. Bind off.
8. Nose: With Orange, cast on 3 sts. ***Row 1:*** K 1 row. ***Row 2:*** P 1 row. Bind off. Sew the knitted strip into a carrot shape.
9. Finishing: Press all knitted pieces and finish the Stocking following General Directions, Step 8. Using the crewel needle and matching yarn, sew the Snowman to the center of the Stocking. Sew the Hat and Hat Brim in place. Sew 2 Eyes and the Nose to the Snowman. Make the mouth with 2-ply Scarlet yarn. Sew 3 Buttons down the Snowman's front. Sew the Scarf and Scarf Ends around the neck *(see photo, pages 62-63)*.

JOLLY ST. NICK STOCKING

Materials: Lion Brand Pamela 4-ply knitting worsted yarn (3½-ounce skein): 1 skein of Emerald (MC), and small amounts of White, Light Pink and Scarlet; two ⅜-inch-diameter blue shank buttons; General Materials.

Directions:

1. Stocking: Make the Stocking following General Directions, Steps 1 to 6.
2. Face: With Light Pink, cast on 15 sts. ***Row 1:*** K 1 row. ***Row 2:*** P 1 row. Rep Rows 1 and 2 eight times. Bind off.
3. Nose: With Light Pink, cast on 4 sts. ***Row 1:*** K 1 row. ***Row 2:*** P 1 row. Rep Rows 1 and 2 twice. Bind off. Gather the edges of the knitted strip, and add a few Light Pink yarn scraps inside. Pull the strip into a ball, and tie it.
4. Beard: With White, cast on 15 sts. ***Rows 1 to 4:*** K each row. ***Row 5:*** K 1 row, inc 1 st each side. ***Rows 6 to 20:*** K each row. ***Row 21:*** K 3 sts; bind off the middle 11 sts; slip the last 3 sts onto the stitch holder. ***Rows 22 to 35:*** K each row. Bind off. Pick up the 3 sts on the stitch holder, and k 14 rows. Bind off.
5. Cap: With White, cast on 17 sts. ***Rows 1 to 4:*** K each row. Change to Scarlet. ***Row 5:*** K 1 row. ***Row 6:*** P 1 row. ***Row 7:*** K 1 row, dec 1 st each side. ***Row 8:*** P 1 row. ***Row 9:*** K 1 row. ***Row 10:*** P 1 row. ***Row 11:*** K 1 row, dec 1 st each side. Rep Rows 8 to 11 six times. K 1 row. P 5 rows on the remaining 5 sts. Bind off.
6. Pompon: With White, cast on 9 sts. Knit 12 rows. Bind off. Gather the edges of the knitted strip, and add a few White yarn scraps inside. Pull the gathered strip into a ball, and tie it.
7. Finishing: Press all knitted pieces and finish the Stocking following General Directions, Step 8. Using the crewel needle and matching yarn, sew the Face to the Stocking. Sew the Beard over the Face. Sew the Cap over the top of the Face, leaving the Cap tip loose. Sew the Pompon to the tip of the Cap. Sew the blue buttons to the Face for eyes. Using 2-ply White yarn, make a few stitches over the eyes for eyebrows *(see photo, pages 62-63)*. Sew the Nose in place. Make the mouth with 2-ply Scarlet yarn.

TIPS FOR A "GREEN" CHRISTMAS

Rag Time

Use cotton cloth rags instead of paper towels for cleaning chores. Washable, reusable rags cut down on paper waste, are cheaper to use and are sturdier than paper for scrubbing, polishing, washing mirrors and windows, and general cleaning.

Just pop the rags in the washing machine when you're finished cleaning, and they'll be fresh and ready to use again.

BALSA WOOD NATIVITY SCENE

(photo, pages 68-69)
The beauty of the crèche recreated in balsa wood. The layering of the wood pieces gives this lovely project its three-dimensional quality.

Average: For those with some experience in woodworking.

Materials: 3 x 36-inch balsa wood planks: one 1/32 inch thick, two 1/16 inch thick, and three 1/8 inch thick; two 16½ x 11-inch illustration boards; graphite paper; stylus or dry ballpoint pen; sandpaper; tack cloth; clear varnish; 1-inch foam brushes; straight edge metal ruler; utility knife; craft knife with No. 11 blade; white craft glue; newspapers; sawtooth hanger *(optional)*; tracing paper for patterns.

Directions:

1. Manger Window: The photo *(pages 68-69)* is the actual size of the project, and can be used as the pattern for the manger and all the figures. Using the photo as the pattern, trace the location and shape of the manger window opening onto tracing paper. Cover a flat surface with a thickness of newspapers, and place one illustration board on it. Using graphite paper and the stylus or dry ballpoint pen, transfer the window opening to the illustration board. Cut out the window opening with the utility knife. Place the board with the window opening on top of the remaining illustration board, and mark the window opening on the second background board.

2. Window Scene: Cut a 4½-inch length from the 1/32-inch-thick balsa plank. Glue the length to the upper part of background board's marked window opening as the sky that is seen through the window. Cut several curved lengths from the 1/16-inch-thick balsa as hills. Using the photo as a placement guide, glue the hills to the wood sky piece and the background board to fill in the remaining space in the window opening.

3. Manger Floor, Wall and Window Frame: Using the straight edge ruler and utility knife, and the photo as the pattern, measure and cut the pieces for the manger floor, wall, and window frame from the 1/8-inch-thick balsa; the manger wall and floor extend ½ inch beyond the photo's top, bottom and sides. Glue the floor and wall pieces flush with the window opening. Glue the window frame around the window opening over the wall pieces.

4. Cutting the Figures: Using the photo as the pattern, trace each piece of each figure separately onto tracing paper, filling in the lines of any covered edges. Using the graphite paper and stylus or dry ballpoint pen, transfer each figure piece to the balsa indicated. Cut out each figure piece with the craft knife. Keep all the pieces for each figure together.

5. Mary: From the 1/16-inch-thick balsa, cut out the head and left sleeve as one piece, the body, and the left hand. From the 1/32-inch-thick balsa, cut out the veil.

6. Joseph: From the 1/16-inch-thick balsa, cut out the head and robe as one piece, the left sleeve, and the left hand. From the 1/32-inch-thick balsa, cut out the beard, moustache, headcloth, and headband.

7. Christ Child and Crib: From the 1/16-inch-thick balsa, cut out the head, halo, crib rim, four horizontal crib pieces, and four crib legs.

8. Three Wise Men: For the wise men on the left and in the middle, cut out the head and robe as one piece, the right sleeve, right hand, and gift from the 1/16-inch-thick balsa. Repeat for the wise man on the right, but make the head and robe separate pieces. Also cut the collar for the wise man in the middle from the 1/16-inch-thick balsa. From the 1/32-inch-thick balsa, cut out the hair/beards, moustaches, and crowns.

9. Shepherd on the Left: From the 1/16-inch-thick balsa, cut out the head and tunic as one piece, the upper right arm, lower right arm, right hand, and two legs. From the 1/32-inch-thick balsa, cut out the crook, headcloth, and headband.

10. Shepherd on the Right: From the 1/16-inch-thick balsa, cut out the head and robe as one piece, the left sleeve, and the left hand. From the 1/32-inch-thick balsa, cut out the beard, headcloth, headband, and moustache.

11. Shepherd Boy: From the 1/16-inch-thick balsa, cut out the head and tunic as one piece, the left, and the left arm. From the 1/32-inch-thick balsa, cut out the headcloth and headband.

12. Sheep: The body piece includes the head, tail, and two legs. For each sheep, cut out the body piece, the ear, and the two partially hidden legs from the 1/16-inch-thick balsa.

13. Donkey: The body piece includes the head, right ear, and tail. From the 1/16-inch-thick balsa, cut out the body piece, left ear, and four legs.

14. Assembling the Figures: When all the pieces for each figure have been cut out, sand their edges lightly to round the edges and remove any roughness. Wipe off all the sawdust with the tack cloth. Using the foam brushes, varnish the manger floor, wall, window frame, window scene, and the pieces for each figure. Let the varnish dry completely. Using the craft glue, assemble each figure. Let the glue dry completely.

15. Attaching the Figures: Using the photo as a placement guide, arrange the figures on the manger wall. Glue Mary and Joseph together where they overlap, and glue the pair to the manger wall. Glue the wise men together where they overlap. Cut four 1 x 4-inch lengths from the 1/16-inch-thick balsa for supports. Glue two of the supports together. Glue the double-thickness support to the center back of the wise man on the left. Glue a single-thickness support to the back of the wise man in the middle. Glue the remaining single-thickness support to the back of the shepherd on the left. Glue the wise men and shepherd on the left to the manger wall. Cut another double-thickness support, and glue it to the back of the shepherd on the right. Glue the shepherd boy to him, and glue the pair to the manger wall. Glue the left-facing sheep to the shepherd boy. Glue the right-facing sheep to the donkey. Cut and glue a 2 x 1-inch double-thickness support to the back of the donkey. Glue the donkey to the wise man on the left. Glue the Child to the crib. Cut and glue a 1 x 1-inch support to the crib's left side on the back. Glue the crib to Mary. Let the glue dry completely.

16. Completing the Manger: Cut one 12-inch, two 10-inch, and one 8-inch length from the 1/8-inch-thick balsa. Glue a 10-inch length to each side of the background board. Glue the 12-inch length to the bottom, and the 8-inch length to the top left of the background board. Let the glue dry completely. Place the manger board over the background board, outer edges flush, and glue the boards together along the wood strips. If you wish, make a thin frame from the 1/8-inch-thick balsa, and glue the frame to the manger's outside edges. If you wish to hang the nativity scene, glue a sawtooth hanger to the back.

TIPS FOR A "GREEN" CHRISTMAS

Buy in Bulk

When you buy products in bulk, you give up only the fancy packaging. What you get is what you want, minus the throwaway wrappings. That means less paper and plastic waste.

Bulk buying is a good idea at any time of year, but it's truly beneficial at Christmas. You're likely to have a full house during the holidays, and having bulk products on hand will help to insure you against running out of necessities.

As a bonus, bulk buying often gives consumers a price discount. During the holiday season, it's always nice to find a smart way to cut costs.

You'll find food, paper goods, cleaning supplies and toiletries available in bulk at supermarkets, warehouse clubs, and some general merchandise stores.

P.S. Check the package labels for the three-arrow symbol indicating recycled goods. Many cleaning products now are sold in recycled plastic, and you can find napkins, tissues, toilet paper and paper towels made from recycled paper.

ORNAMENTS TO TREASURE

Make any or all of these festive ornaments to delight young and old. Celebrate the season with a bevy of St. Nick ornaments. Or give a country-style look to your tree with balsa wood ornaments.

PAPER SANTA ORNAMENT

Easy: Achievable by anyone.

Materials: 1 sheet each of pink, white and red construction paper; 1½-inch-diameter cardboard tube; metallic gold thread; craft knife; scissors; ruler; pins; rubber cement; pencil; manila folder, or other lightweight cardboard, for pattern.

Note: *It is easier to cut the construction paper with the craft knife and ruler than with scissors. When covering the cardboard tube with the construction paper, keep the overlapping ends of the paper in a vertical line at the back of the ornament unless otherwise noted. If necessary, pin the paper pieces in place until the glue sets.*

Directions:

1. Cut a 4-inch length of cardboard tube. Cover the outer side and one open end of the tube with red paper; the uncovered end is the bottom of the ornament.

2. Cut a 1-inch-wide pink paper strip. Glue the strip around the tube, with the strip's bottom edge 2¼ inches above the ornament's bottom edge.

3. Enlarge the Hat pattern in Fig. III, 6 onto the manila folder or other lightweight cardboard, following the directions on page 271. Cut out the manila pattern. Enlarge the Beard half-pattern onto folded manila, cut the folded manila around the outside pattern lines, and open the manila for the full pattern.

4. Cut a Hat from red paper. Glue the Hat around the tube, with the Hat's bottom edge 3¼ inches above the ornament's bottom edge, and the Hat's overlapping edges above the ornament's left ear *(see photo)*. Cut a ½-inch-wide white paper strip for a hatband. Glue the hatband around the ornament, with the hatband's bottom edge 2⅞ inches above the ornament's bottom edge. Bend the tip of the Hat over to the opposite side of the ornament, and glue the tip in place *(see photo)*. Cut a ⅜-inch-wide white paper strip, and roll it around the pencil. Glue the roll to the tip of the Hat for a pompon.

5. Cut a Beard from white paper, and cut along the marked pattern lines to make fringes. Curl the end of each fringe and each Beard side strip by running it over a sharp scissor edge. Glue the Beard to the face. Extend the Beard fringes in varying lengths *(see photo)*, and hold each fringe in place with a dab of glue.

6. Cut and roll a ½-inch-wide pink paper strip for a nose. Glue the nose in place. Run a length of gold thread through the top of the Hat, and tie the thread ends to make a hanger loop.

CLEVER CRAFTING

The Cutting Edge

A craft knife is an indispensable tool when you're working with cardboard, balsa wood or paper, but the knife should be used carefully!

- Always cut on a padded surface, such as an old magazine, a piece of cardboard, or several layers of newspaper.
- Cut in a slow, smooth motion to avoid creating bumps or rough edges. When you're cutting thick material, score it first by cutting a slight indentation along the entire cutting edge before slicing through. To cut a straight edge, hold a ruler firmly along the cutting edge, and keep the knife blade against the ruler while you cut.
- Keep the open blade away from curious youngsters. Store the craft knife in a tool kit or other closed box where kids can't get to it.

FIG. III, 6 PAPER SANTA ORNAMENT 1 SQ. = 1″

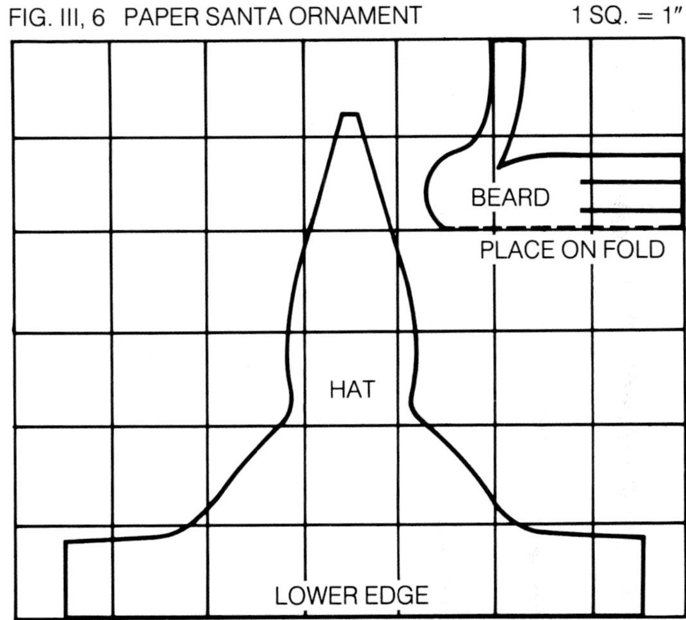

PEEK-A-BOO SANTA

Easy: Achievable by anyone.

Materials: 31 x 24-mesh plastic canvas rectangle; felt for ornament back; 3-ply tapestry yarn: White, Peach, Bright Red, Brick Red, Blue, Black, and Golden Brown; tapestry needle; ½-inch-diameter white pompon; glue.

Directions:

1. Using three strands of yarn in the needle, and following the chart in FIG. III, 7 for stitch placement and colors, work the bricks in continental stitch over two meshes. Fill in the corners, and work the rest of the ornament except the eyes, in continental stitch over one mesh. Work each eye in Blue smyrna stitch. Work a single strand Black French knot in the center of each eye. Outline the bricks in single strand Black straight stitch *(see Stitch Guide, page 270).*

2. When the embroidering is complete, cut out the ornament *(see* FIG. III, 7*).* Using the embroidered ornament as a pattern, cut a felt ornament back.

3. Using corresponding color yarn, whipstitch around the edges of the ornament *(see Stitch Guide).* Glue the pompon to the top of the hat. Glue the felt back to the ornament, catching in the ends of a length of yarn to make a loop for a hanger.

CLEVER CRAFTING

Kid-Proof Hangers

If you have toddlers, or are making ornaments for folks who have small children, use yarn or ribbon to make hanger loops. Soft hangers are safer than metal hooks or metallic threads when inquisitive little ones are around.

FIG. III, 7 PEEK-A-BOO SANTA

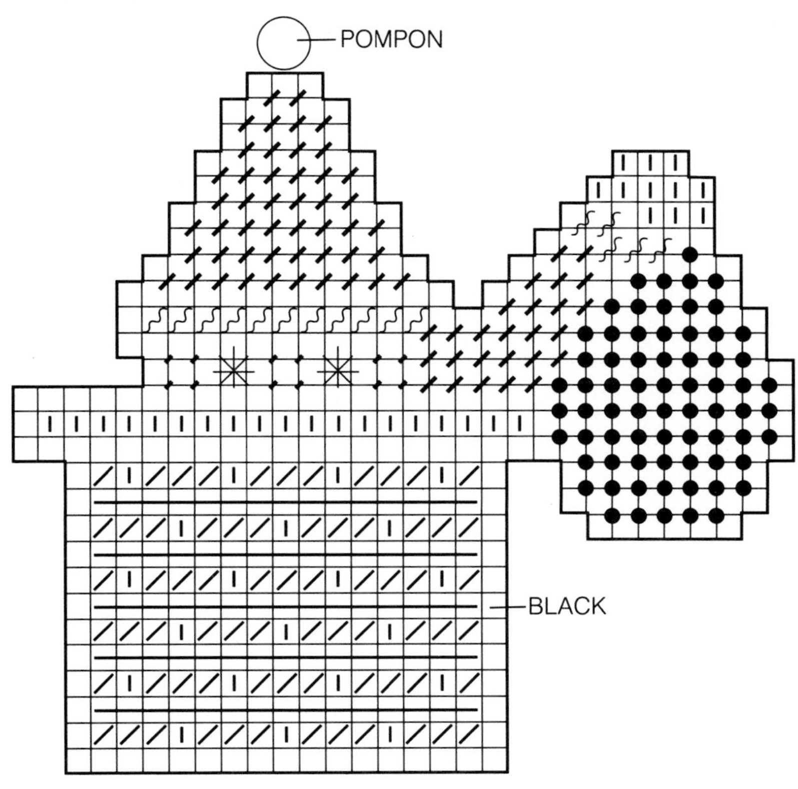

CLEVER CRAFTING

Canvas with a Twist

Plastic canvas is a great material for needlepoint beginners to use. It's easy to handle and doesn't distort, even when stitch tension isn't entirely even. Plus, the large holes make it easy and fast to finish a stitched piece.

If you've got budding young crafters at home, let them try stitching plastic canvas ornaments of their own.

SANTA SACK

(6½ x 5 inches)

Easy: Achievable by anyone.

Materials: Two 7¾ x 6-inch rectangles of loose-weave white fabric, or cut from dishcloth; matching thread; felt: 3 x 4 inches of white, 2½ x 3 inches of red, 1½ x 1¼ inches of pale pink, and 1 square inch of dark pink; 16 inches of ⅛-inch-wide red ribbon; ½-inch-diameter white pompon; ¼-inch-diameter red pompon; two ¼-inch-diameter plastic eyes; glue.

Directions (½-inch seams allowed):

1. Sack: Stitch the white fabric or dishcloth rectangles, right sides together, along the long edges and one short end. Turn the sack right side out. Turn the open edges to the wrong side, and stitch a ½-inch casing. Insert the ribbon in the casing, and tie the ribbon ends together.

2. Santa: Cut 1 inch off the white felt to make a 3-inch square and a 1 x 3-inch rectangle. Cut two 1-inch-wide, 1½-inch-long curved moustaches from the white rectangle. Cut a ½-inch square off each top corner of the white square. Beginning below the cut out squares, scallop three sides of the square to make a beard. Using the photo as a guide, cut out a 1 x ¾-inch face. Glue the pale pink felt to the white felt behind the face. Cut two ⅜-inch-diameter circles from the dark pink felt. Curve the edges of the red felt for the hat *(see photo).*

3. Assembling: Glue the hat to the center of the sack. Glue the beard over the hat *(see photo).* Glue the white pompon to the longer end of the hat. Glue the dark pink circles to the pale pink face. Glue the plastic eyes to the dark pink circles. Glue the moustaches just below the eyes *(see photo).* Glue the red pompon over the moustaches for a nose.

SECRET SANTA

(6 x 3 inches)

Easy: Achievable by anyone.

Materials: Nylon stocking; 5 x 2½ inches of red ribbed top from anklet sock; 8 yards of 4-ply white yarn; matching threads; 2-inch square of green felt; 6 inches of ⅛-inch-wide green ribbon; 1-inch-diameter white pompon; ¼-inch-diameter red pompon; synthetic stuffing; tapestry needle; glue; paper for pattern.

Directions:

1. Cut 3½ inches off the nylon stocking toe to make a pouch. Stuff the pouch to make a 2-inch-wide, 2½-inch-long oval for a head. Gather the open top of the head, and tie it with thread. Pinch up a small ball of stuffing in the center of the head, and form a flat, ½-inch-diameter round nose. Wrap the nose with thread, and stitch to secure it.

2. Gather and stitch one end of the red sock top to form the peak of the cap *(see photo).* Glue the center of the ribbon to the peak. Glue the white pompon over the ribbon. Tie the ribbon ends together to form a loop for a hanger.

3. Stuff the top half of the cap. Turn up the cap's lower edge ½ inch, and pull the cap down over the head *(see photo).* Stitch the cap to the head through all layers.

4. Using the photo as a design guide, draw a holly leaf on paper. Using the paper pattern, cut out two holly leaves from the felt. Glue the holly leaves to the cap, along with the red pompon for a berry *(see photo).*

5. Wind the white yarn around your thumb to cover 2 inches, slide the wound yarn off, and topstitch it by machine. Repeat until all the yarn is wound and stitched for the beard. Sew the beard to the face all around the bottom of the head *(see photo).*

SANTA STOCKING

(6½ inches long)

Easy: Achievable by anyone.

Materials: Felt: 4½ x 6½ inches of red, and 2 x 4 inches of pink; thread; two ½-inch-diameter plastic eyes; 1½-inch-diameter white pompon; 1-inch-diameter red pompon; 11-inch giant-loop chenille; pinking shears; glue; paper for pattern.

Directions:

1. Cut a 4½ x 7-inch paper rectangle. Holding the rectangle so the short ends are at the top and bottom, cut off a 1½ x 4-inch strip from the upper left side. Round the bottom corners to create a stocking shape. Using the paper pattern and the pinking shears, cut two stockings from the red felt. Topstitch the stockings together ¼ inch from the raw edges, leaving the top edge open.

2. Glue the pink felt strip to the front of the stocking across the instep area for a face. Glue the plastic eyes to the face. Glue the red pompon to the face for a nose, and the chenille to the top and bottom of the face for hair and a beard. Glue the white pompon to the top right-hand corner of the stocking *(see photo).*

TIPS FOR A "GREEN" CHRISTMAS

Ornamental Recycling

Don't throw away ball ornaments that are past their prime. Cover them with ribbons or sequins, paint them or decorate them with stickers.

For a fast, easy and beautiful "recycled" ornament, cut a square of fabric large enough to cover the ornament, plus about 1½ inches. Place the ornament in the center of the square, gather the edges of the square at the top and tie with yarn, twine or ribbon.

DANCING SANTA TREE TOPPER

(about 7½ inches tall)

Average: For those with some experience in woodworking.

Materials: Balsa wood: 1/32-, 1/16- and 3/16-inch-thick planks, and 1/4-inch-thick scrap; brass brads; scrap of brass wire; graphite paper; stylus or dry ballpoint pen; red and white flat paints; gold and black glossy paints; paintbrushes; craft knife; tack hammer; glue; paper for pattern.

Directions:

1. Trace the full-size pattern in Fig. III, 8 onto paper. Using the graphite paper and stylus or dry ballpoint pen, trace the Head/Hat, Left and Right Legs, Left and Right Arms, and Left and Right Boots onto the 1/16-inch-thick balsa. Trace the Body onto the 3/16-inch-thick balsa. Trace the Pompon, Hatband, Nose, Moustache, Beard, Belt, Buckle, Suit Trim, two Sleeve Cuffs, and two Boot Cuffs onto the 1/32-inch-thick balsa. Cut out the wood pieces with the craft knife.

2. Using the photo and Head/Hat pattern as color guides, paint the front and sides of the wood pieces, mixing red and white paint to make pink paint. Let the paint dry completely.

3. Using the photo as a placement guide, glue the Pompon, Hatband, Beard, Moustache and Nose to the Head/Hat. Glue the Suit Trim, Belt and Buckle to the Body. Glue the Sleeve Cuffs to the Left and Right Arms, and the Boot Cuffs to the Left and Right Boots.

4. Nail two brass brads for eyes to the Head/Hat where indicated on the pattern. Using the photo as a placement guide, glue the Left Boot to the Left Leg, and the Head/Hat to the Body. Nail the Right Boot to the Right Leg, and both Legs and Arms to the Body where indicated on the pattern.

5. Glue the 1/4-inch-thick balsa scrap to the back of the Left Leg, and push the brass wire into the scrap. Twist the extending end of the wire into a loop. Attach the Santa to the top of the tree with the loop.

FIG. III, 8 DANCING SANTA TREE TOPPER FULL SIZE PATTERN

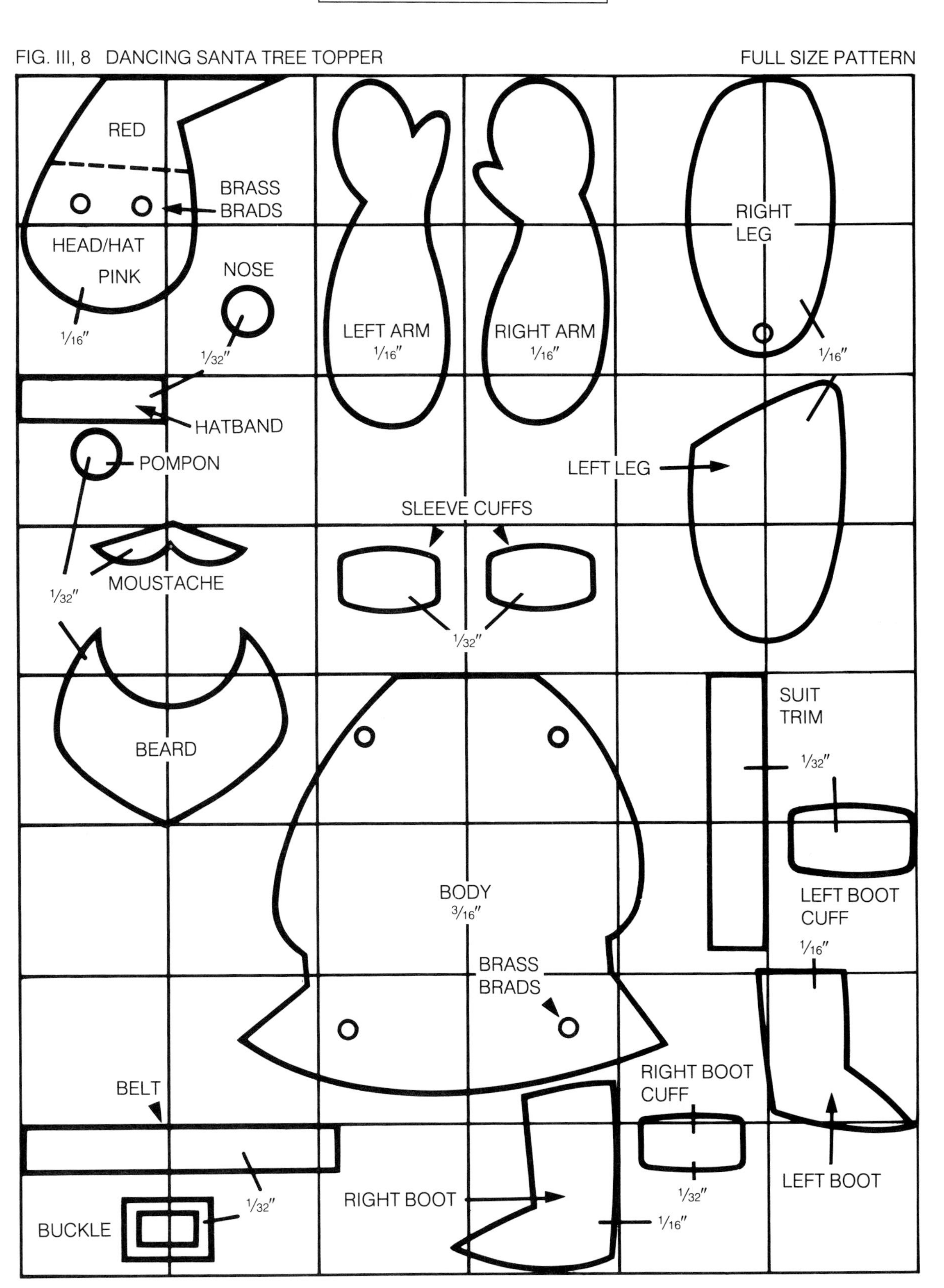

WOODEN WONDERLAND ORNAMENTS

(photos, pages 80-84)

Average: For those with some experience in woodworking.

Materials: Balsa wood planks; larger and smaller brass brads; brass wire; graphite paper; stylus or dry ballpoint pen; fine sandpaper; tack cloth; varnish; 1-inch foam brushes; craft knife; tack hammer; wire cutters; string; white glue; paper for patterns.

Directions:

1. Trace the full-size patterns in FIGS. III, 9A-9F *(pages 80-85)* onto paper. Cut out the paper patterns. Using the graphite paper and stylus or dry ballpoint pen, trace each pattern piece separately onto the balsa wood.

2. Cut out the wood pieces with the craft knife. Sand the wood pieces smooth, removing any graphite marks. Wipe off all the sawdust with the tack cloth.

3. Using the patterns and photos as placement guides, glue the wood pieces together, bottom layers first. Nail the smaller brass brads where indicated by dots on the patterns. Nail larger brass brads where indicated by circles on the patterns. For each ornament, glue a piece of balsa to the top back of the ornament, and push one end of a 2-inch length of brass wire into the balsa piece. Bend the other wire end into a hanger loop.

4. Using the foam brushes, varnish the ornaments; let dry completely.

5. Fold three 5-inch lengths of string in half, and glue them to the horse for a tail. Repeat with three 2-inch lengths of string for the horse's forelock. Wrap and glue a length of string around the bugle handle; fray the back end of the string, and let it hang below the bugle *(see photo, page 84)*.

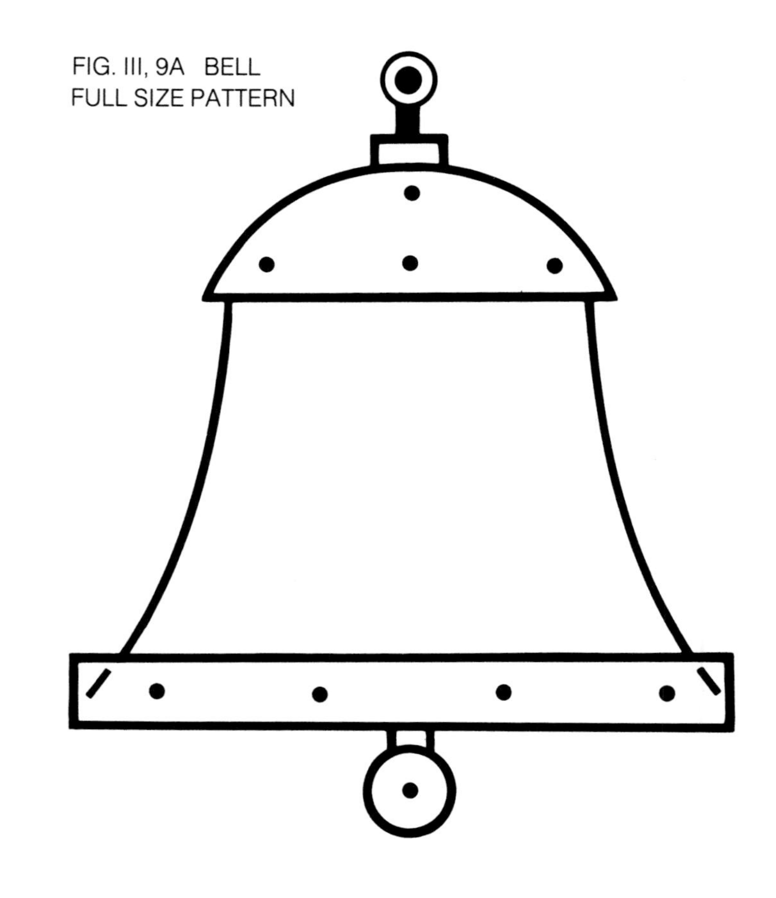

FIG. III, 9B HORSE
FULL SIZE PATTERN

FIG. III, 9C DOVE OF PEACE
FULL SIZE PATTERN

FIG. III, 9D LITTLE BROWN CHURCH

FULL SIZE PATTERN

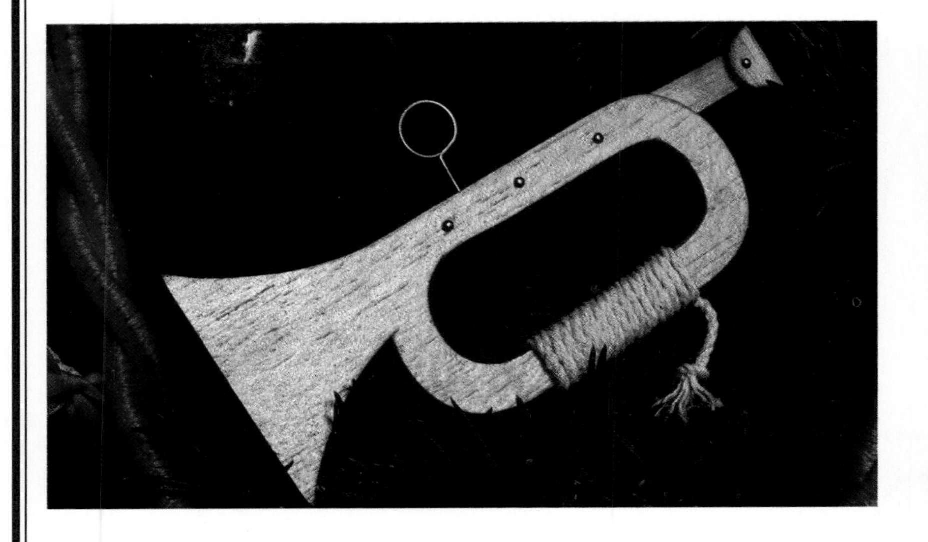

TIPS FOR A "GREEN" CHRISTMAS

A Christmas Tree with Roots!

This year, choose a Christmas tree that keeps on giving—and living! Small evergreens come in pots; larger trees have rootballs wrapped in burlap; both are available at nurseries or garden centers. After the holidays, plant the tree in your yard.

Before the ground freezes, dig a hole that is 2 feet across and at least 1½ feet deep. Cover the hole with insulating material, such as straw or leaves.

Place the soil dug out of the hole in a plastic bucket or trash can, and store it in the basement or garage to keep the soil from freezing.

Choose a tree that is no more than 4 feet tall and has fresh, not brittle, needles with signs of new growth. Have a pot or sturdy box at home in which to put the tree.

Water the tree well while it is in the house; keep the rootball moist. Set the tree in the coolest part of the room, away from heating vents, radiators or the fireplace.

Keep a live tree indoors for no more than 10 days; 4 to 5 days is best. Before planting, place the tree in a garage or basement for a few days to accustom it to the cold.

Before planting the tree, adjust the hole to be twice the size of the rootball and slightly deeper. If the tree is potted, remove it from its pot and place it in the hole. If the tree's rootball is wrapped in burlap, loosen the ties, and plant the tree as is; the burlap will disintegrate over time.

Hold the tree straight while the hole is filled in, packing soil around the rootball; the rootball top should be left slightly exposed. Then cover the planted area with a 3-inch-thick layer of mulch.

If the tree cannot be planted because the ground is frozen, keep the tree outdoors near the house or other trees. Cover its rootball or container with a 6- to 12-inch-thick layer of mulch. Plant the tree as soon as the ground thaws.

FIG. III, 9E TOY SOLDIER

FULL SIZE PATTERN

FIG. III, 9F BUGLE

FULL SIZE PATTERN

HERALD ANGEL TREE TOPPER

Hark! This herald angel sounds his trumpet gloriously from the top of your Christmas tree.

Average: For those with some experience in woodworking.

Materials: Balsa wood: ¼ x 4 x 8 inches, and 3⁄32 x 4 x 36 inches; brass brads; spool wire; graphite paper; stylus or dry ballpoint pen; varnish; 1-inch foam brush; craft knife; tack hammer; wire cutters; white glue; sharpened pencil; paper for pattern.

Directions:

1. Enlarge the pattern in Fig. III, 10A onto paper, following the directions on page 271. Using the graphite paper and stylus or dry ballpoint pen, transfer the pattern pieces to the balsa wood; transfer the A body piece to the ¼-inch-thick balsa, and the other pattern pieces to the 3⁄32-inch-thick balsa. Cut out the wood pieces with the craft knife. Also cut a ½ x 1-inch block from the ¼-inch-thick balsa.

2. Following the assembly diagrams in Figs. III, 10B and 10C, glue the B hair, C cheek, D eye, and E left arm to the front of the A body. Glue the G leg and F right arm to the back of the A body. Glue the H horn to the mouth between the E and F arms.

3. Glue the J, K, L, M and N feathers to the I wing. Glue the O feather to the I wing on top of the J/K/L/M/N feathers. Glue the Q feather to the P wing. Glue P/Q to the I/O assembly. Let the glue dry completely. Glue the wing assembly to the A body.

4. Cut the brass brads to ¼-inch lengths. Using the pencil, make starter holes for the brads where indicated by the black dots in Fig. III, 10B. Nail the brads to the angel. Notch the balsa block to hold a piece of wire *(see* Fig. III, 10C*)*, and glue the block to the back of the angel.

5. Varnish the angel, and let the varnish dry completely. Run a 6-inch length of wire through the notch in the back block. Attach the angel to the top of the tree with the wire.

FIG. III, 10A HERALD ANGEL PATTERN 1 SQ. = 1″

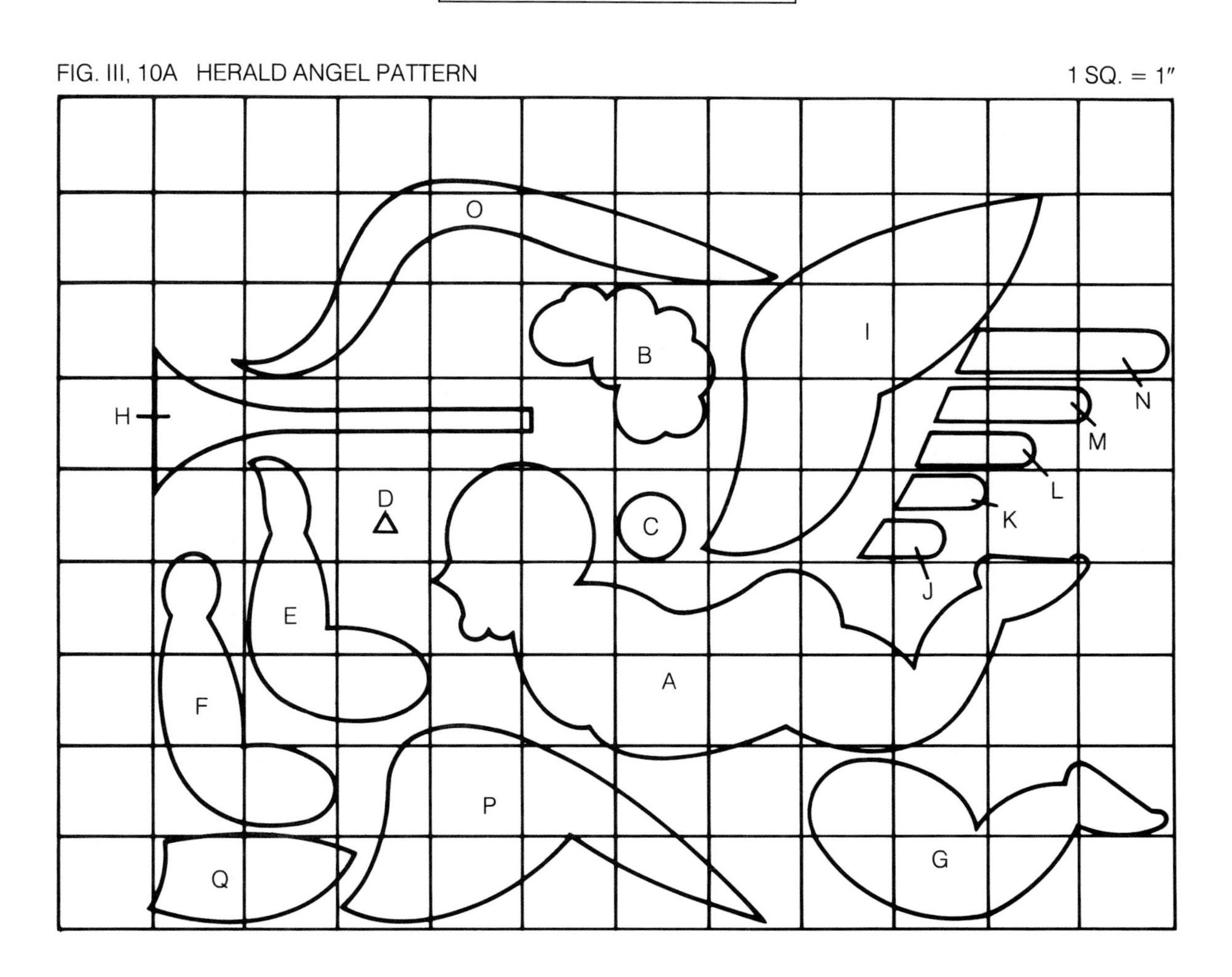

FIG. III, 10B FRONT VIEW ASSEMBLY DIAGRAM

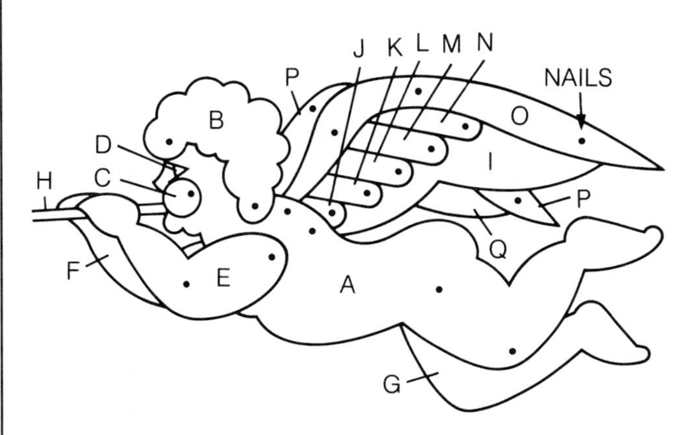

FIG. III, 10C BACK VIEW ASSEMBLY DIAGRAM

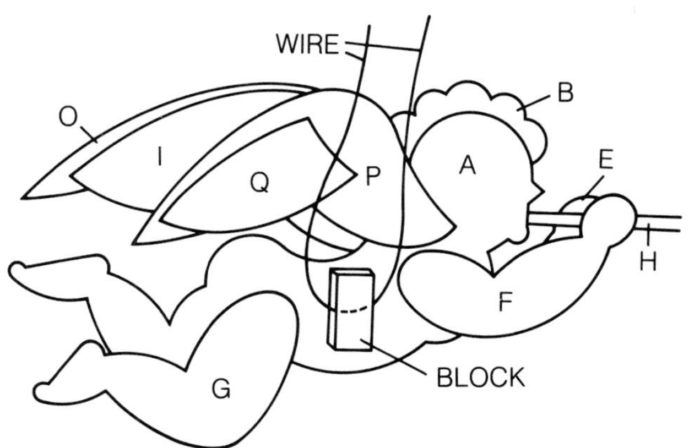

OVERNIGHT SENSATIONS

The
holly's up,
the house is all bright,
The tree is ready,
The candle alight;
Rejoice and be glad,
all children tonight!
—Carl August Peter Cornelius

What do you do when
you need a gift at the last minute? Or your holiday feast is planned and prepared, but the house still doesn't have that beautiful Yuletide glow?

In this chapter, we've collected our quickest and easiest trims and gifts to help you through the hectic holidays. Many of our table or mantel arrangements can be made by simply grouping together a few easy-to-find items. Just add a dab of glue, a sprinkle of glitter or a twist of wire and you have instant Christmas cheer!

Simple gifts can be the nicest, especially when they're hand-crafted with love by you. These timely presents will easily fill those last-minute holes in your gift list.

Every holiday season has its crazy moments, but these bright ideas and pretty projects can help...even if you wait until Christmas Eve to use them!

TERRIFIC TRIMS

Lovely, down-to-the-wire decorating projects to add Christmas cheer to any room in the house.

A COOKIE CUTTER CHRISTMAS

Use these jolly decorations as festive accents all through your home, or to add a special touch to gifts for your friends and family.

Easy: Achievable by anyone.

COOKIE CUTTER TIES

Materials for One Tie: Holiday print fabric; 18 inches of metallic gold or silver ribbon, or satin ribbon to match or complement fabric; cookie cutter in shape desired; fusible interfacing; iron; glue *(optional)*; three small red pompons *(optional)*.

Directions:

1. Place a piece of fabric right side down with two layers of fusible interfacing over it. Place a second piece of fabric, right side up, on top of the interfacing. Fuse the layers following the fusible interfacing package directions.

2. Place the cookie cutter on the fused fabric, and trace carefully around the outer edge of the cookie cutter. Cut out the fabric shape. Repeat to make a second fabric shape.

3. At the center top of one fabric shape, pull the interfacing layers apart about ½ inch. Insert one end of the ribbon between the layers, press the layers together, and iron to fuse them again. Repeat with the second fabric shape on the opposite end of the ribbon. If you are using a holly leaf or gingerbread man cookie cutter, glue the pompons to the leaves for berries *(see photo, at left)* or to the gingerbread man for buttons.

4. Fasten the tie to a gift package, or around the neck of a jar *(see photo, above right)*. Or make a holiday wreath by fastening several ties to a grapevine or straw wreath, and adding a bow of coordinating print ribbons *(see photo, at left)*.

COOKIE CUTTER APPLIQUÉS

Materials: Holiday print fabrics; cookie cutters in shapes desired. ***For Fabric Appliqués:*** Matching threads; fusible interfacing; iron; sewing machine. ***For Wood Appliqués:*** Glue; clear acrylic spray varnish.

Directions:

1. Fabric Appliqué: Place a piece of fabric right side up. Place a cookie cutter on the fabric, and trace lightly around the outer edge of the cookie cutter. Place the fabric with the tracing on top of a piece of fusible interfacing, and cut out the cookie cutter shape through both layers.

2. Place the fabric shape on the fabric object to be decorated, with the interfacing in between. Fuse the layers together following the fusible interfacing package directions.

3. Satin stitch by machine around the edges of the fabric shape.

4. Wood Appliqué: Make a fabric shape following the directions in Step 1, omitting the fusible webbing.

5. Apply a thin layer of glue evenly to the wrong side of the cookie cutter fabric shape. Place the shape carefully on the wooden object to be decorated *(see photo, above)*, and press the fabric shape lightly but firmly to make sure it adheres properly. Let the glue dry completely.

6. Spray several light coats of acrylic over both the fabric shape and the surrounding wood, letting the acrylic dry between coats.

SWEET 'N SIMPLE

Easy: Achievable by anyone.

Materials: Ceramic pot; contrasting color saucer; candy canes; sprigs of fresh juniper.

Directions:

Turn the saucer upside down, and set the ceramic pot on top of it. Hang the candy canes around the edge of the pot. Arrange the juniper sprigs around the pot, placing them in the same direction.

HOLIDAY POMANDERS

To make the fragrant centerpiece below, pile clove-studded pomanders and pine cones in a wooden bucket. Tuck in pine sprays, cinnamon sticks and a quaint ornament.

Easy: Achievable by anyone.

Materials for Five Pomanders: 5 medium-size sturdy fruits, such as apples or citrus fruits; box of whole cloves *(see Note, below)*; awl; tack hammer; pencil; ground cinnamon; orris root powder; paper bag; ribbon for hanging pomanders; straight pins for hanging pomanders.

Note: *The clove designs on the fruits in the photo let a good amount of rind show through. If you wish to cover five fruits completely, you may need more than one box of cloves.*

Directions:

1. Clove-Studded Pomanders: Using the pencil, outline a design on each fruit rind. Make starter holes with the awl along the designs on thick-skinned fruits. Hammer the cloves in place gently. These pomanders can be used immediately.

2. Cinnamon-Coated Pomanders: Place equal amounts of ground cinnamon and orris root powder in the paper bag. Place a clove-studded pomander in the bag, and shake to coat the pomander. Repeat to coat the remaining pomanders. Place the coated pomanders in a loosely covered container for 3 to 4 weeks to allow them to dry.

3. Hanging Pomanders: Plan the clove designs on the pomanders to leave room for ribbon hangers. For each pomander, cut a length of ribbon to go completely around it once. Cut a second length of ribbon 6 inches longer than the first. Wrap the shorter length around the pomander, and pin it in place at the top and bottom. Wrap the longer length around the pomander at right angles to the first, and pin it to the bottom of the pomander. Knot the longer ribbon at the top of the pomander, and pin the knot in place. Knot the ends of the ribbon to make a loop for a hanger. Cut a third length of ribbon, tie it in a bow and pin the bow to the pomander over the knot.

HOLIDAY HAND TOWEL

For an extra-special holiday touch in the bathroom, wrap guest soaps in colored cellophane, and display them in a bowl or basket.

Easy: Achievable by anyone.

Materials: Hand towel in solid holiday color; colorfast holiday print or color ribbon with same fabric content as towel; matching thread.

Directions:
Cut a length of ribbon ½ inch longer than the width of the towel. Pin the ribbon to the towel over the towel's woven band, turning under the ribbon's raw edges ¼ inch. Edgestitch the ribbon in place, making sure the folded ribbon ends are flush with the towel's long edges.

TIPS FOR A "GREEN" CHRISTMAS

Merry Mugs

Using a mug for hot beverages in the office instead of a disposable cup cuts down tremendously on the use of paper and plastic foam. A ceramic mug makes a great gift for a co-worker. And a spill-proof mug is perfect for your favorite commuter!

Mugs come in every color imaginable, with decorations to suit every taste. Look for them in card stores, gift shops, gourmet and housewares departments, and even the grocery store.

A SYMPHONY IN SILVER

Easy: Achievable by anyone.

Materials: 7-inch-diameter twig basket with handle; 6- to 12-inch-long birch twigs; sphagnum moss; artificial mistletoe with berries; 1 yard of ¾-inch-wide silver ribbon; 1-inch-diameter silver balls with attached wires; white glitter; silver glitter; gloss Mod Podge®; 1½-inch foam brush; floral foam; floral pick; floral wire; wax paper.

Directions:

1. Cut the floral foam to fit inside the basket just below the rim. Set the foam aside.

2. Cover your work surface with wax paper. Using the foam brush, coat areas of the basket with Mod Podge. Sprinkle the wet areas with the white glitter. To achieve a more natural look, leave some basket areas unfrosted. Repeat on the basket handle, and on the birch twigs. Coat areas of the mistletoe with Mod Podge, and dust them lightly with the silver glitter.

3. Make a silver ribbon bow with streamers. Wire the floral pick to the back of the bow.

4. Place the foam in the basket, and cover the foam with the moss. Using the photo as a guide, insert the birch twigs, mistletoe, silver balls, and silver ribbon bow into the foam in a pleasing arrangement.

BY CANDLELIGHT

Easy: Achievable by anyone.

Materials: Brass candleholder; large glass hurricane shade; tall white candle; spruce branches; pine cones in assorted sizes.

Directions:

1. Set the candle in the candleholder in the center of the table. Place the glass hurricane shade over the candle and candleholder.

2. Arrange the spruce branches around the glass hurricane shade; if necessary, trim the branches to create a full-looking arrangement.

3. Set the pine cones on top of the branches in a pleasing arrangement.

RUSTIC BIRCH CANDLEHOLDERS

Tuck pine sprays around the birch candleholders for a simple and lovely centerpiece. These country-style candleholders make great gifts.

Easy: Achievable by anyone.

Materials: 2½-inch-diameter white birch logs in various lengths; tall red candles in various widths and heights; saw; drill with assorted bits.

Directions:

1. Long Candleholder: Select the longest log, and leave bits of branches on it to keep it from rolling. Steady the log on a flat surface. Drill ⅝-inch-deep holes 2 inches apart across the log. Insert different-height candles in the holes *(see photo)*.

2. Tall Candleholders: If necessary, make a straight cut on one end of each log so the log stands straight. Center and drill a ⅝-inch-deep hole in the opposite end of each log, and insert a candle. Vary the widths of the holes and candles for visual interest.

CLEVER CRAFTING

Candle Light Care

The birch candleholders shown in the photo above have a lovely rustic quality, but be careful when using them. Never leave candles burning unattended, and never let candles burn down to the ends. If you wish, place a glass bobèche, or drip catcher, at the base of each candle.

EASY MINI-WREATHS

Easy: Achievable by anyone.

Materials: Six 4-inch-diameter twig wreaths; miniature pine cones; dried rosebuds; bunches of artificial small berries with leaves; 3 miniature snow-covered evergreen trees; 3 miniature glass ball ornaments; multi-colored miniature bead ornaments; miniature mallard duck; Spanish moss; metallic-edged dark green ribbon; metallic-edged gold ribbon; loose-weave gold ribbon; gold and red satin cording; metallic gold cording; gold braid; gold star sequins; gold spray paint; floral wire; hot glue gun.

Directions:

1. Glue the miniature evergreen trees to the bottom of a wreath's center opening. Glue the gold star sequins around the wreath. Glue a metallic gold cording bow below the trees.

2. Cut short lengths of floral wire. Attach two or three bunches of berries with leaves to each wire, and wind the wires around a wreath. Wire a dark green ribbon bow with streamers to the top of the wreath.

3. Glue the multi-colored miniature bead ornaments in a cluster to the bottom of a wreath. Cut a short length of gold braid, knot it, and glue it underneath the bead ornaments. Glue the miniature glass ball ornaments around the braid knot.

4. Glue a loose-weave gold bow to the top of a wreath. Make a "nest" from the Spanish moss, and glue it to the wreath's center opening. Glue the miniature duck on top of the nest.

5. Spray paint a wreath gold, and let the paint dry. Wind gold and red satin cording around the wreath. Tie the cording ends into a bow at the top.

6. Glue miniature pine cones around a wreath. Glue dried rosebuds between the pine cones. Wire a metallic-edged gold ribbon bow with streamers to the top of the wreath.

GIFTS IN A FLASH

Great ways to take care of last-minute entries on your gift list.

BREAKFAST IN BED TRAY & NAPKIN RINGS

Easy: Achievable by anyone.

Materials: Wooden tray; self-sticking paper in 2 complementary holiday patterns; graphite paper; stylus or dry ballpoint pen; scissors.

Directions:

1. Tray: Measure the tray's inside edges. Cut a piece to these measurements from the first pattern self-sticking paper. Peel off the paper's backing. Lay the paper gently in position on the tray bottom, and press the paper in place.

2. Napkin Rings: Cut four 10-inch squares from the second pattern self-sticking paper. Peel the backing from the top edge of two squares. Holding the squares up to a light and matching their top corners exactly, press the squares together, wrong sides facing. If the paper's pattern is squares or plaid, match the pattern exactly. Pull off the rest of the backing carefully, smoothing the squares together from the center out as you pull. Repeat with the remaining paper squares.

3. Using the graphite paper and stylus or dry ballpoint pen, trace the full-size pattern in FIG. IV, 1 onto each double paper square. Cut out the shapes, and slash the slots where indicated on the pattern. Slide one slot through the other on each shape to close the napkin rings.

CLEVER CRAFTING

Quick Tile Trivet

Press a self-stick felt pad onto each bottom corner of a pretty tile and you have an instant trivet. Add an adhesive hanger loop centered on a back side edge so the tile can be displayed when not in use.

FIG. IV, 1 BREAKFAST IN BED TRAY AND NAPKIN RINGS

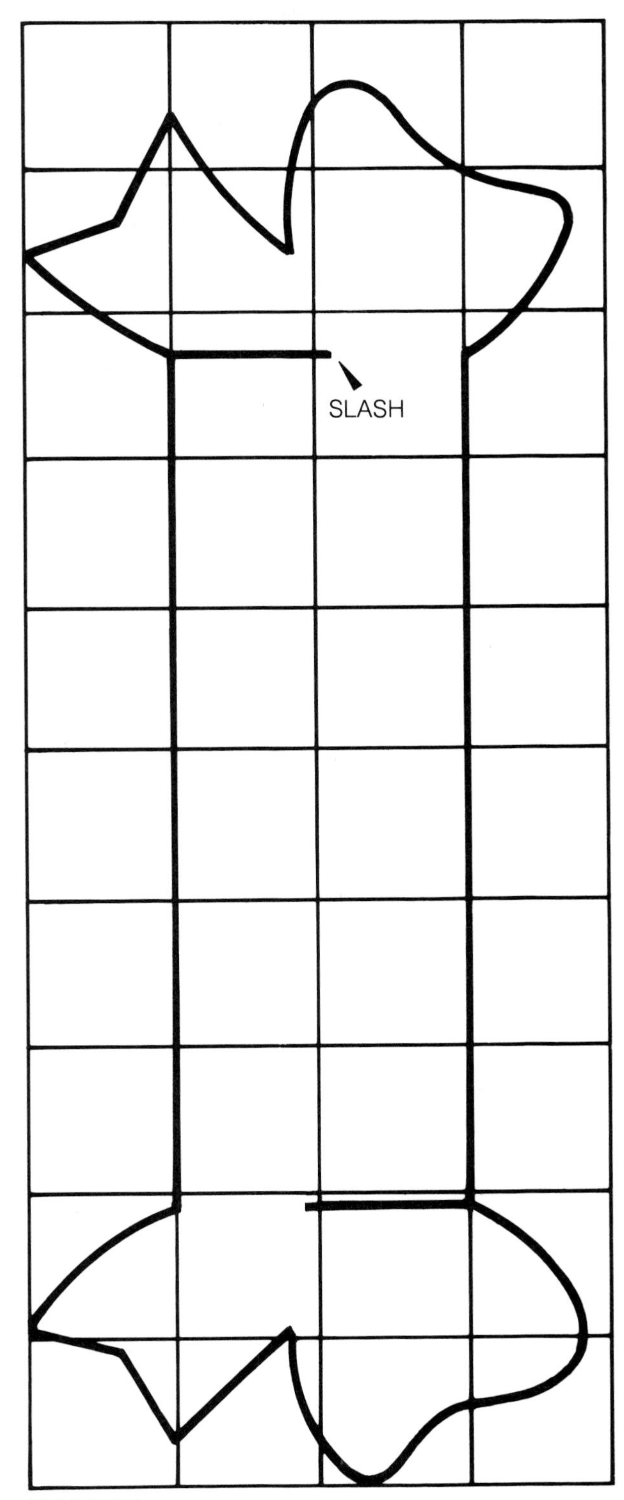

FULL SIZE

SWEET SACHETS

Make these sweet-smelling dainties with inexpensive embroidered handkerchiefs.

Easy: Achievable by anyone.

Materials: 4 purchased embroidered handkerchiefs, or print fabric; matching thread; solid white opaque fabric for backing (if using handkerchiefs); 1¼ yards of 1-inch-wide gathered lace; ⅔ yard of narrow satin ribbon; 2 ounces of potpourri; tracing paper for pattern.

Directions (¼-inch seams allowed):

1. Heart Sachet: Trace the heart half-pattern in Fig. IV, 2 onto folded tracing paper. Trace the half-pattern to the other side of the paper, and open the paper for the full pattern.

2. If using purchased embroidered handkerchiefs, pin a 7-inch backing fabric square to the wrong side of each handkerchief; treat each set as a single piece. Cut two heart shapes from the embroidered handkerchiefs or print fabric. With right sides together and edges even, machine-baste the lace to one fabric heart, overlapping the short ends of the lace at the top indentation. Stitch the fabric hearts right sides together, leaving an opening for turning. Turn the heart right side out, and fill it with potpourri. Turn in the open edges, and slipstitch the opening closed *(see Stitch Guide, page 270).* Cut a 12-inch length of ribbon, and make a bow. Sew the bow to the sachet at the top indentation *(see photo).*

3. Square Sachet: Make the square sachet following the directions in Step 2, using two 5½-inch squares cut from the embroidered handkerchiefs or print fabric. Attach the bow to one corner of the sachet.

FIG. IV, 2 SWEET SACHETS FULL SIZE

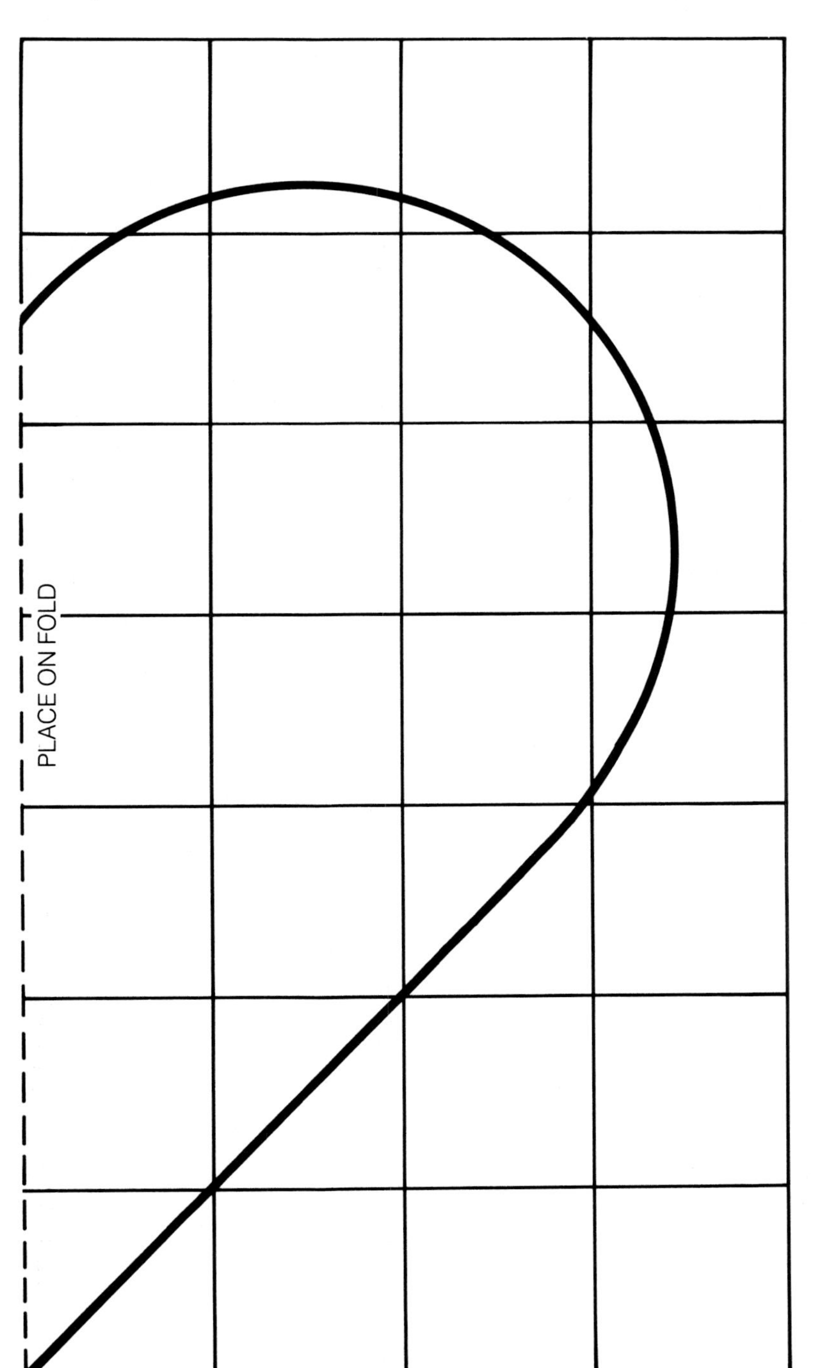

TIPS FOR A "GREEN" CHRISTMAS

Potpourri Power

Stop using aerosol room fresheners! Potpourri is an all-natural, very personal way to fill your home with a lovely, subtle scent. These aromatic mixtures of herbs, flowers, fruits and spices are easy to make, and are widely available in card and gift stores, and even in some supermarkets!

Fill pretty bowls or baskets with your favorite potpourri mixture, and place the containers in every room of your house. When the scent begins to fade, just add a drop or two of essential oil (available at craft shops and some natural food stores) to the potpourri to refresh it. For extra scent, place a drop of essential oil on a light bulb; as the bulb warms the oil, it becomes more fragrant.

TAKE A NOTE! BOOK

Easy: Achievable by anyone.

Materials: Two 3¼ x 5½-inch, and one ⅝ x 5½-inch mat boards; 5¼ x 6½ inches, and 1½ x 5 inches of book cloth; 3¼ x 6½ inches of decorative paper for front cover; sturdy paper for pockets; two 3 x 5-inch note pads; white glue; scissors.

Directions:

1. Lap the decorative paper ¼ inch over the larger book cloth rectangle along a 6½-inch edge. Glue the paper in place; let the glue dry completely.

2. Spread glue over the wrong side of the decorative paper and book cloth. Place the mat boards on the wrong side of the paper and cloth, with the narrow board strip centered for a spine between the wider board covers. Leave ⅛ inch between the strip and each cover, and a ½-inch border around the outside edges. Turn the border up and over the edges of the boards. Glue the border in place, mitering the corners.

3. Center the narrow book cloth strip over the inside of the spine, and glue the cloth in place.

4. Cut two 5 x 6-inch rectangles from the pocket paper. Fold each rectangle to make a flat tube, butting the rectangle's short ends at the center back. Spread glue on the backs of the paper tubes, and attach a tube to the inside of each cover for a pocket. Let the glue dry completely.

5. Slip the note pads into the pockets.

TIPS FOR A "GREEN" CHRISTMAS

Gifts From the Farm

A gift of local fruit, nuts or cheese, or a bottle of domestic wine is always welcome, and your purchases help support American farmers. Search the aisles of a supermarket for some great last-minute gifts.

- Red and green apples in a basket for your child's teacher.
- A decorative jar filled with red and white pistachios for your secretary.
- A chunk of Wisconsin or Vermont Cheddar cheese, or California Monterey Jack cheese for a neighbor.
- Your favorite wine from a local winery for a family member who lives out of town.
- A mixture of nuts, chopped dates and raisins you made yourself for a holiday hostess.

THE DESK SET

Easy: Achievable by anyone.

Materials: Beige imitation leather pencil holder, letter holder and ledger desk set; rust and dark blue acrylic paints; 2 natural sponges; old newspapers.

Directions:

1. Dip a sponge in the rust-colored paint. Dab the sponge on a sheet of newspaper to remove excess paint, and to check the effect created. Adjust the amount of paint on the sponge until you are satisfied with the effect. Dab the rust-colored paint on the imitation leather surfaces of the desk set, letting the beige color show through underneath. Let the paint dry completely.

2. Repeat with the dark blue paint and remaining sponge until you have achieved the desired effect. Let the paint dry completely.

"DESIGNER" BATH TOWELS

Easy: Achievable by anyone.

Materials: Set of solid color bath towels; contrasting print fabric from bed sheets or fabric scraps; matching thread; sewing machine.

Directions:

Cut a print fabric strip ½ inch longer than the width of one of the towels. Pin the strip to the towel along the towel's bottom edge, or 3 inches above the bottom edge, turning under the long raw edges ¼ inch as you pin. Turn under the strip's short ends ¼ inch. Edgestitch around all the strip edges. Repeat on the remaining towels.

PRESENTS PRESENTS PRESENTS!

"I
want some crackers,
And I want some candy;
I think a box of chocolates
Would come in handy;
I don't mind oranges,
I do like nuts!
And I should like a pocket-knife
That really cuts.
And, oh! Father Christmas, if you love me at all,
Bring me a big, red india-rubber ball!"
—A. A. Milne

Since that miraculous night when the Magi knelt to offer gold, frankincense and myrrh to the babe in the manger, Christmas has been celebrated by giving to those we love.

A gift created by hand is especially cherished. The time and effort spent to knit a sweater, craft a wooden toy, or stitch a pretty doll shows that special someone how much you care.

In this chapter you'll find presents for the home, for her, for him, and for the little ones in your life. Choose from projects such as a snuggly afghan, woolly sweaters, wonderful wooden toys, a marquetry box, a trio of pastel dollies, winter-warm mittens, and so much more. There's sure to be something here for everyone on your list!

Some of these crafts take time to finish. You'll probably want to start them early, so they'll be done before the holiday rush. Others can be done at the last minute, and tucked under the tree on Christmas Eve.

Giving a handmade gift is like giving a part of yourself—and there's no better way to make this Christmas special.

GIFTS FOR THE HOME

From your heart and hands
to a special someone's home—what better
way to say "I love you" at Christmas time?

PINEAPPLE AFGHAN

(60 x 56 inches)
The eternal symbol of hospitality decorates this extra-warm afghan.

Average: For those with some experience in knitting, crocheting and embroidery.

Materials: Reynolds Bulky Reynelle yarn (2-ounce skein): 29 skeins of Natural (A); Reynolds Reynelle yarn (4-ounce skein): 2 skeins each of Navy (B) and Light Gold (C), and 1 skein each of Cardinal (D), Loden (E) and Clay (F); 1 pair size 10 knitting needles, OR ANY SIZE NEEDLES TO OBTAIN GAUGE BELOW; size I crochet hook; No. 16 tapestry needle.
Gauge: In Stockinette Stitch (st st), 3 sts = 1 inch; 9 rows = 2 inches.
Note: *Use a single strand of Bulky Reynelle yarn, and a double strand of Reynelle yarn throughout.*
Directions:
1. *Pineapple Panel (make 3):* With the knitting needles and A, cast on 23 sts. Work in st st (k 1 row, p 1 row) for 240 rows. Bind off.
2. *Long Side Edging, Row 1:* With the right side facing and the crochet hook, join A in the right-hand corner of a long edge, and ch 1. Working into the sides of the knit rows and keeping the edge flat, sc in each of first 2 rows, * [sk 1 row, sc in next row] twice; sk 1 row, sc in next 2 rows; rep from * to the end of the long edge. ***Row 2:*** Ch 1, turn, sc in each sc across. Fasten off. Rep Rows 1 and 2 of the Long Side Edging along the opposite edge.
3. *Embroidery:* With yarn, mark off 4 sets of 60 rows on each Pineapple Panel for the beginning and end of the pineapple design. Using a double strand of yarn in the tapestry needle, and beginning at the lower edge of each Panel, work the pineapple design in FIG. V, 1A in duplicate stitch on each Pineapple Panel *(see Stitch Guide, page 270).*
4. *Motif Panel (make 4):* With the knitting needles and A, cast on 19 sts. Work in st st for 240 rows. Bind off. Work the Long Side Edgings on each Motif Panel following Step 2. Using a double strand of yarn in the tapestry needle, beginning at the lower edge of each Panel, and repeating Rows 1 to 11 to the upper edge, work the alternate design in FIG. V, 1B in duplicate stitch on each Motif Panel.
5. *Blocking:* Place each Panel wrong side up on a towel, pin to size, and cover with a damp towel. Run a warm, dry iron lightly over the towel; *do not press.* Let the Panels dry completely.
6. *Joining:* With the crochet hook or tapestry needle and A, alternating Pineapple Panels with Motif Panels, and working through both lps of the sc edges, sew or sl st the Panels tog, beginning and ending with a Motif Panel. From the right side with A, work 1 row sl st along each side edge of the afghan. Block the edges flat.
7. *Top Edging, Row 1:* With the right side facing and the crochet hook, join A in the upper right-hand corner, and ch 1. Keeping the edge flat, sc along the top edge, working a multiple of 9 sts plus 6. ***Rows 2 and 3:*** Ch 1, turn, sc in each sc across. Fasten off. Turn. ***Row 4 (wrong side):*** Join 2 strands of D in the first sc, ch 1, sc in same sc, ch 7, sk 4 sc, sc in next sc, * ch 3, sk 3 sc, sc in next sc, ch 7, sk 4 sc, sc in next sc; rep from * across. ***Row 5:*** Ch 1, turn, 9 sc in first ch-7 sp, * ch 3, sk ch-3 sp, 9 sc in next ch-7 sp; rep from * across. Fasten off. Turn. ***Row 6:*** Join A in first sc, ch 1, sc in same sc, ch 8, sk 7 sc, sc in last sc of same group, * ch 3, sc in first sc of next 9-sc group, ch 8, sc in last sc of same group; rep from * across. Turn. ***Row 7:*** Sl st in first ch-8 lp; ch 3, 9 dc in same lp, * sk ch-3, 10 dc in next ch-8 lp; rep from * across. Fasten off. Work the Top Edging along the bottom edge. Pin the afghan to the finished measurements, and block it following Step 5.

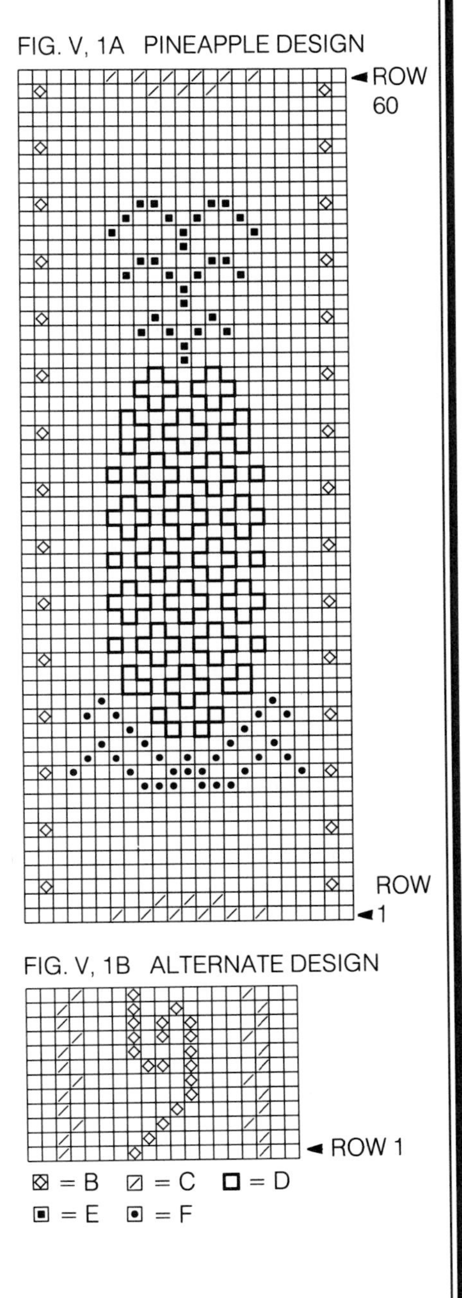

PENNSYLVANIA DUTCH FOOTSTOOL

Average: For those with some experience in decorative painting.

Materials: Purchased wooden footstool (available at craft supply stores); graphite paper; stylus or dry ballpoint pen; medium-fine sandpaper; tack cloth; white acrylic paint; cadmium red light, burnt alizarin, leaf green light, leaf green medium, leaf green dark, burnt umber, and black oil paints; clear oil-based antiquing glaze; wood sealer; clear acrylic spray varnish; oil-based varnish; odorless turpentine; artist's paintbrushes: No. 6 or 8 small PH Red Sable, No. 10 or 12 medium-size PH Red Sable, No. 14 or 16 large PH Red Sable, and No. 1 liner or scroll brush; sponge brushes; palette; palette knife; wide mouth container for turpentine; soft rags; masking tape; tracing paper for patterns.

Directions:

1. Mix burnt umber paint with turpentine to make a stain. Spread the stain on the footstool with a clean rag. Wipe off the stain with another clean rag, wiping off more stain in the design area on each long stool side *(see photo)*. If you wish, repeat to make the stain darker. Let the stain dry completely. Apply a coat of wood sealer, and let it dry. Sand the footstool lightly, and wipe off all the sawdust with the tack cloth.

2. Using a sponge brush and white acrylic paint, and the photo as a placement guide, paint the oval design area on the stool top. Let the paint dry. Seal the design area by spraying with several light coats of clear acrylic varnish.

3. Trace the full-size half pattern for the stool side design in FIG. V, 2A onto folded tracing paper. Trace the design onto the other half of the paper, and open the paper for the full design. Trace the full-size quarter pattern for the stool top design in FIG. V, 2B onto tracing paper folded into quarters. Trace the design onto the remaining quarters, and open the paper for the full design. Using the graphite paper and stylus or dry ballpoint pen, center and transfer the designs to the top and both long sides of the footstool.

4. Squeeze the oil paints onto the palette. Use the turpentine to thin the reds to the consistency of soft butter, and the greens to the consistency of heavy cream. Using the large paintbrush, paint the tulips cadmium red light. If you wish, wipe the brush and apply a little burnt alizarin to the left side of each tulip, blending the colors together where they meet.

5. Paint the comma strokes above the stool top tulips cadmium red light; mix in some burnt alizarin for the larger strokes. Paint the large green comma strokes with thinned leaf green dark, the medium-size strokes with leaf green medium, and the small strokes with leaf green light. Using the liner or scroll brush, outline the edge of the white oval design area with black *(see photo)*.

6. Let the paint dry completely; this will take several days depending on the temperature, humidity and air circulation. When the paint is completely dry, apply a coat of oil-based varnish to the entire footstool.

7. Mix a little burnt umber paint into a tablespoon of the antiquing glaze. Brush the antiquing mixture over the entire footstool. Use a clean rag to wipe off as much of the antiquing glaze as you wish. Let the glaze dry completely, and apply a final coat of oil-based varnish.

FIG. V, 2A PENNSYLVANIA DUTCH FOOTSTOOL SIDE

FULL SIZE

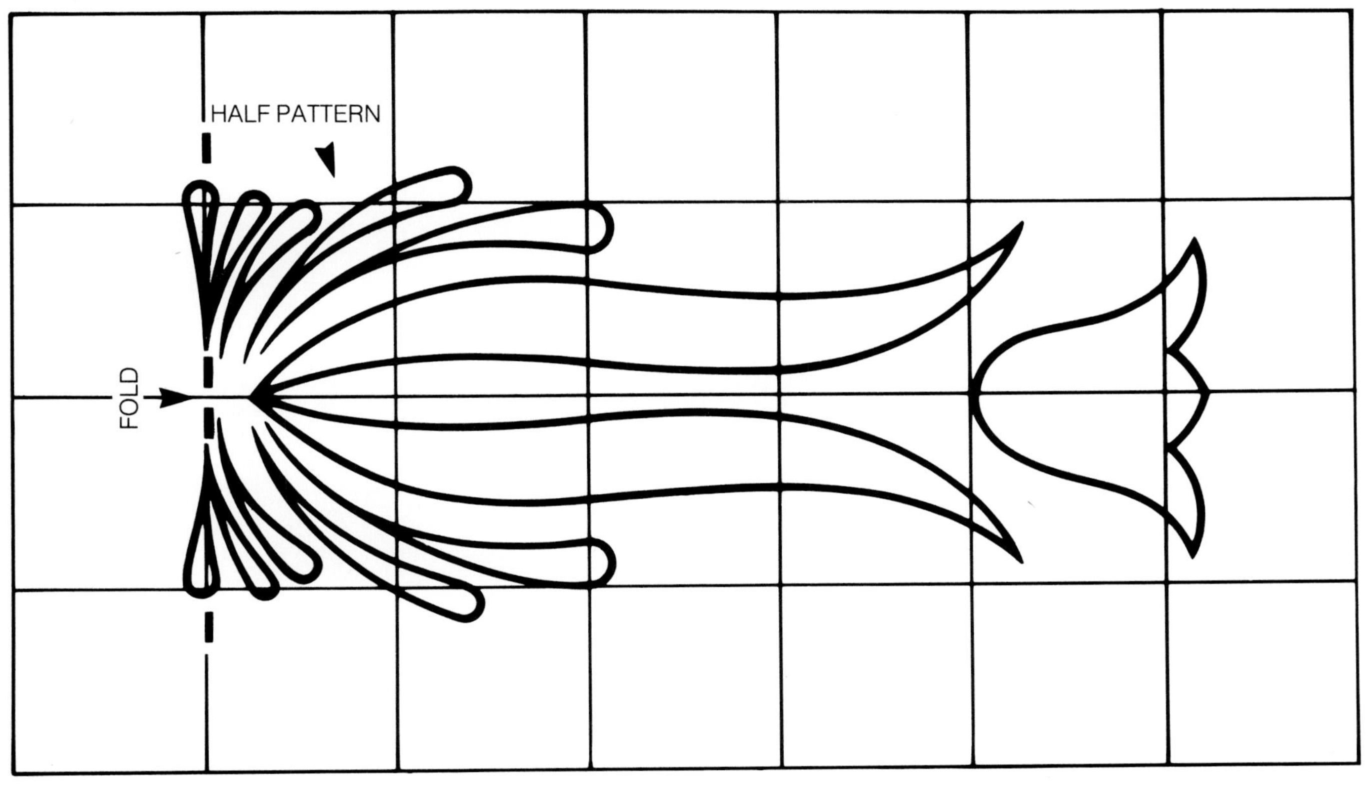

FIG. V, 2B STOOL TOP

FULL SIZE

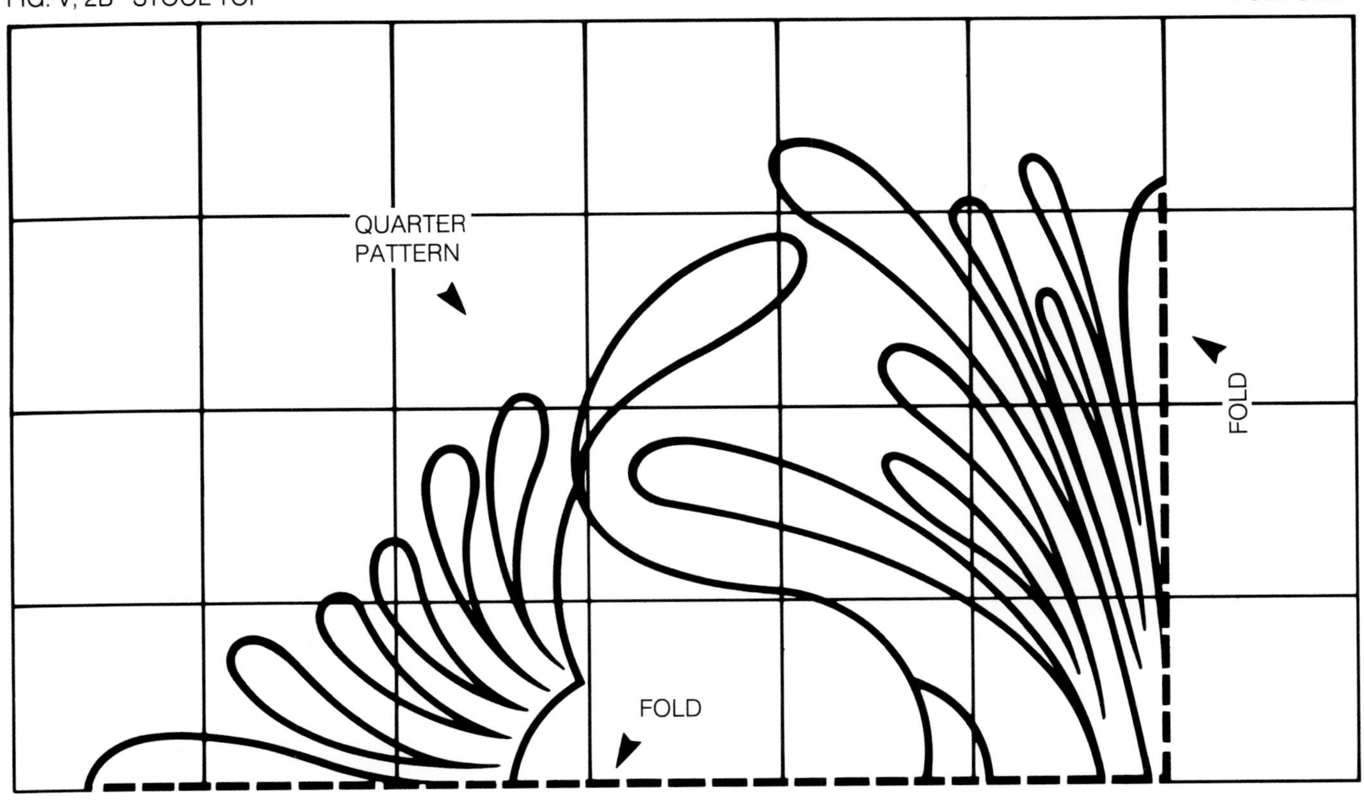

PUPPY PALACE

Average: For those with some experience in woodworking.

Materials: 4 x 8-foot panel of ⅜-inch APA 303 roughsawn plywood siding; galvanized nails; wood glue; graphite paper; stylus or dry ballpoint pen; sandpaper; tack cloth; exterior paint in color desired; paintbrush; table saw, band saw, or circular saw; sabre saw; hammer; paper for patterns.

Directions:

1. Draw the house pieces on the plywood panel following the measurements in Fig. V, 3A. If you are using a table or band saw, draw the house pieces on the face of the panel. If you are using a circular or sabre saw, draw the house pieces on the back of the panel. Leave space between the house pieces for kerf. Cut out the house pieces.

2. For the ramp and front opening, enlarge the patterns in Figs. V, 3B and 3C *(page 112)* onto paper, following the directions on page 271. Using the graphite paper and stylus or dry ballpoint pen, transfer the ramp pattern to the back of the plywood panel. Transfer the front opening pattern to the back of the front piece. Use the sabre saw with a fine blade to make the ragged cuts on the ramp and front opening. Set aside the front opening cutout.

3. Nail the floor support cleats to the sides, front and back. Nail the front and back to the sides. Drop in the floor, and glue and nail it to the floor support cleats.

4. Nail two 12-inch roof pieces to the front and back as the lower roof pieces. Overlap the remaining roof pieces 1 inch over the lower roof pieces, and glue and nail the upper pieces in place, butting them together at the roof peak. Fit trim pieces around the outside corners of the

house, and nail the trims in place *(see* Fig. V, 3D, *page 113).*

5. If you are making a chimney, glue and nail the chimney pieces to form an open box. Glue and nail trims around the chimney top. Glue and nail the chimney to the roof *(see* Fig. V, 3D, *and photo).*

6. Place the ramp in the front opening, and nail the ramp to the floor. Glue and nail the front opening cutout to the outside back.

7. Sand the rough edges of the house smooth, and wipe off all the sawdust with the tack cloth. Paint the house.

FIG. V, 3A PUPPY PALACE HOUSE PIECES

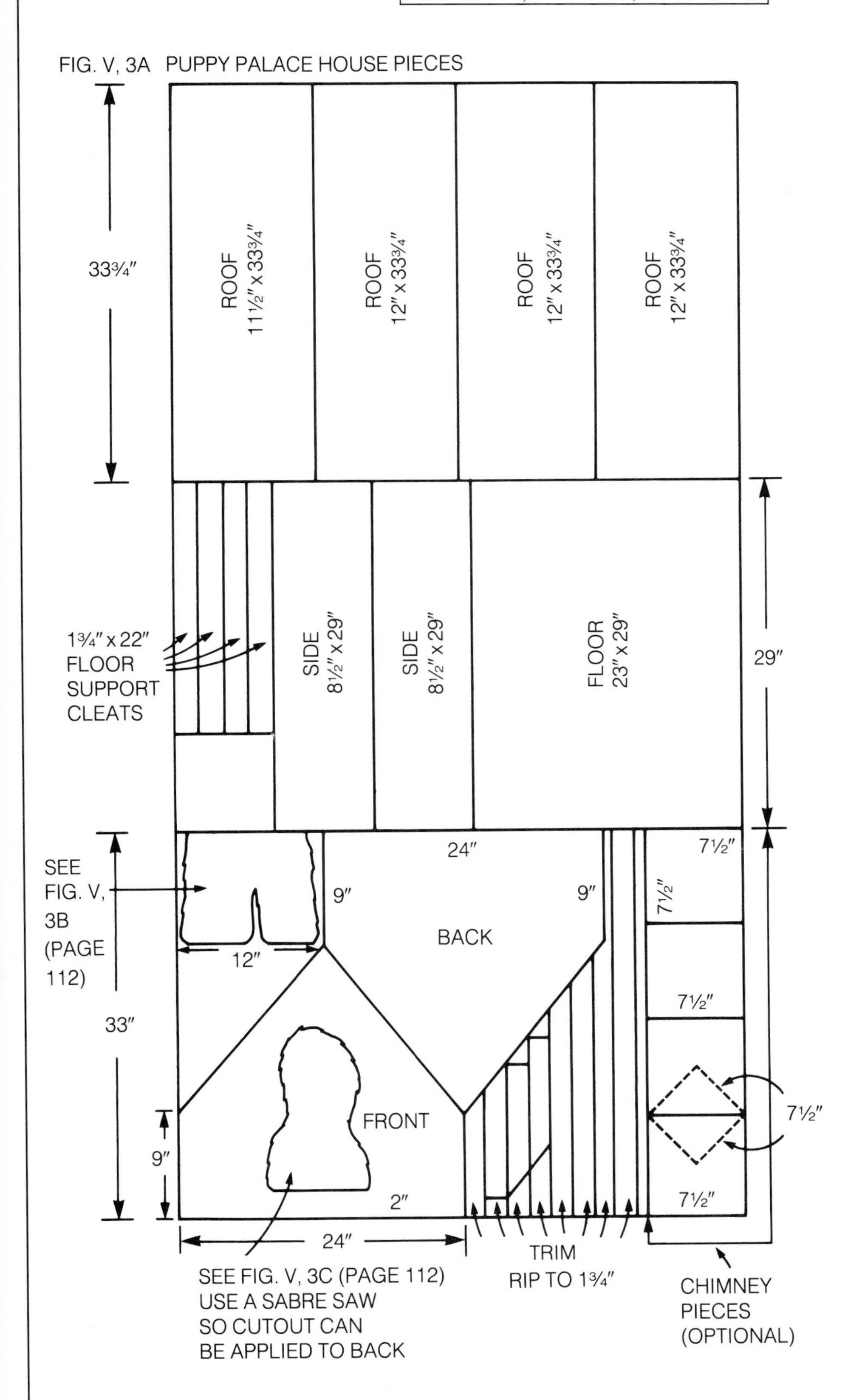

FIG. V, 3B RAMP 1 SQ. = 1″

FIG. V, 3C FRONT OPENING 1 SQ. = 1″

CENTER LINE OF FRONT

FLOOR REFERENCE

BOTTOM OF FRONT

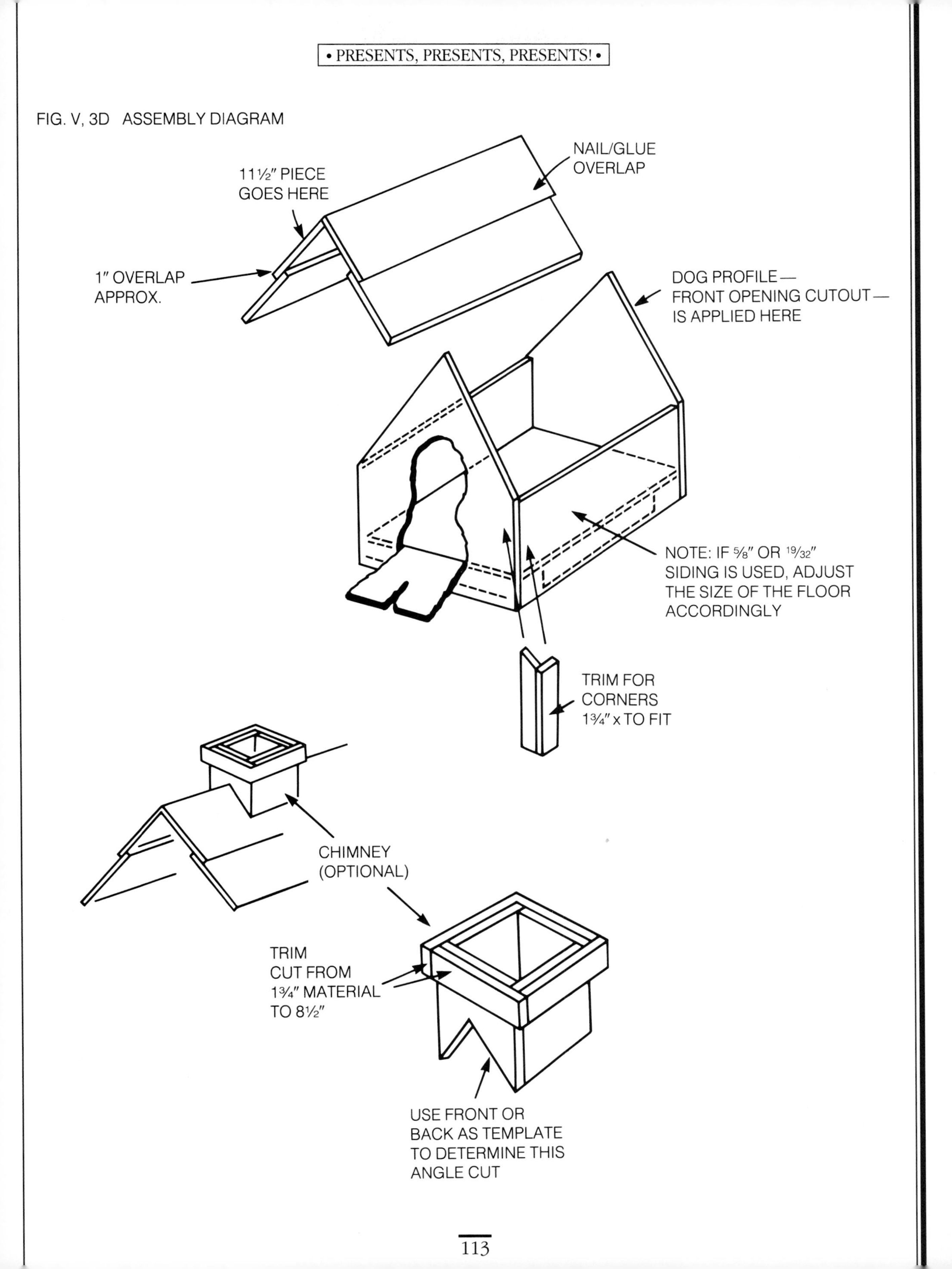

FIG. V, 3D ASSEMBLY DIAGRAM
NAIL/GLUE OVERLAP
11½″ PIECE GOES HERE
1″ OVERLAP APPROX.
DOG PROFILE— FRONT OPENING CUTOUT— IS APPLIED HERE
NOTE: IF ⅝″ OR 19/32″ SIDING IS USED, ADJUST THE SIZE OF THE FLOOR ACCORDINGLY
TRIM FOR CORNERS 1¾″ x TO FIT
CHIMNEY (OPTIONAL)
TRIM CUT FROM 1¾″ MATERIAL TO 8½″
USE FRONT OR BACK AS TEMPLATE TO DETERMINE THIS ANGLE CUT

ESPECIALLY FOR HER

Pretty and practical presents for mothers, daughters, sisters and best friends.

WOMAN'S ARAN KNIT SWEATER

Challenging: Requires more experience in knitting.

Directions are given for Size Petite (6). Changes for Sizes Small (8-10), Medium (12-14) and Large (16) are in parentheses.

Materials: Bernat Blarney Spun 100% wool (50-gram ball): 17 (18, 19, 20) balls of Natural; 1 pair each size 5 and size 8 knitting needles, OR ANY SIZE NEEDLES TO OBTAIN GAUGE BELOW; 1 double-pointed needle (dp); 4 stitch holders; stitch marker; tapestry needle.

Gauge: With size 8 needles in Stockinette Stitch (st st; k 1 row, p 1 row), 9 sts = 2 inches; 6 rows = 1 inch. In Aran Patterns over center sts, 68 sts = 12 inches.

Note: *The sweater is loose fitting.*

Aran Pattern I (worked over even number of sts), Rows 1 and 2: K across. ***Rows 3 and 4:*** * K 1, p 1; rep from * across. Rep Rows 1 to 4 for Pat I.

Aran Pattern II (worked over 5 sts), Row 1: * Through back lp knit 2nd st on needle, leave on needle, k first st, sl both sts off needle *, p 1; rep between * once. ***Row 2:*** *Sk 1 st, p 2nd st on left-hand needle, leave original st on needle, p skipped st, take 2 original sts off left-hand needle*—***PT made;*** k 1, PT. Rep Rows 1 and 2 for Pat II.

Aran Pattern III (worked over 11 sts), Row 1: P 2, k 7, p 2. ***Rows 2 and 4:*** K 2, p 7, k 2. ***Row 3:*** P 2, sl next 2 sts to dp needle, hold in back of work, k 1, k 2 off dp needle, k 1, sl next st to dp needle, hold in front of work, k 2, k 1 off dp needle, p 2. Rep Rows 1 to 4 for Pat III.

Aran Pattern IV (worked over 26 sts), Row 1: P 3, *sl next st to dp needle, hold in back of work, k 1, k 1 off dp needle*—***C2 made;*** [p 4, C2] 3 times; p 3. ***Row 2 and All Even Numbered Rows through 12:*** K the k sts, and p the p sts. ***Row 3:*** P 2, *sl next p st to dp needle, hold in back of work, k 1, p 1 off dp needle*—***RT made;*** *sl next k st to dp needle, hold in front of work, p 1, k 1 off dp needle*—***LT made;*** [p 2, RT, LT] 3 times; p 2. ***Row 5:*** P 1, [RT, p 2, LT] 4 times; p 1. ***Row 7:*** P 1, k 1, [p 4, C2] 3 times; p 4, k 1, p 1. ***Row 9:*** P 1, [LT, p 2, RT] 4 times; p 1. ***Row 11:*** P 2, [LT, RT, p 2] 4 times. Rep Rows 1 to 12 for Pat IV.

Measurements:

SIZES:	PETITE (6)	SMALL (8-10)	MEDIUM (12-14)	LARGE (16)
BODY BUST:	30½"	32½"	36"	38"

Finished Measurements:

BUST:	35"	38"	40½"	43½"
WIDTH ACROSS BACK OR FRONT AT UNDERARMS:	17½"	19"	20¼"	21¾"
WIDTH ACROSS SLEEVE AT UPPER ARM:	14½"	15¼"	16¼"	17"

Directions:

1. Back: Starting at the lower edge with size 5 needles, cast on 74 (80, 86, 92) sts. Work in twist ribbing as follows: ***Row 1:*** * P 1, through back lp k next st twisting st; rep from * across. Rep Row 1 for pat to 2½ inches, inc 20 sts evenly spaced across last row—94 (100, 106, 112) sts. Change to size 8 needles and Pats. ***Row 1 (right side):*** Following Row 1 of each Aran Pattern, work as follows: Pat I over 12 (14, 18, 20) sts; p 1 (2, 1, 2); * Pat II over 5 sts, Pat III over 11 sts, Pat II over 5 sts, * Pat IV over 26 sts; rep between * once; p 1 (2, 1, 2); Pat I over 12 (14, 18, 20) sts. ***Row 2:*** Following Row 2 of each Aran Pattern, work as follows: Pat I over 12 (14, 18, 20) sts; k 1 (2, 1, 2); * Pat II over 5 sts, Pat III over 11 sts, Pat II over 5 sts *, Pat IV over 26 sts; rep between * once; k 1 (2, 1, 2); Pat I over 12 (14, 18, 20) sts. Keeping to the Pats as established, work to 15½ inches from beg, or desired length, ending with a wrong side row.

2. Armhole Shaping: Keeping to Pats, bind off 5 (6, 7, 8) sts at beg of next 2 rows. Dec 1 st each end every other row 5 times—74 (78, 82, 86) sts. Work even in Pats until armholes measure 7½ (8, 8½, 9) inches, ending with a wrong side row.

3. Shoulder Shaping: Keeping to Pats, bind off 8 (8, 9, 9) sts at beg of next 4 (2, 6, 4) rows, then bind off 9 (9, 0, 10) sts at beg of next 2 (4, 0, 2) rows. Bind off remaining 24 (26, 28, 30) sts for the Back Neck edge.

4. Pocket Linings (make 2): With size 8 needles, cast on 24 sts. Beg with Row 1, work in Pat I for 12 rows. Sl these sts to a st holder.

5. Front: Work the same as the Back until 12 rows above the ribbing band.

6. Pocket Opening, Left Side: Keeping to Pats, work 15 (18, 21, 24) sts, sl remaining sts to another st holder to be worked later, sl 24 lining sts to free needle. Keeping to Pat I, work these 24 sts. These sts will be worked in Pat I until pocket opening is completed. Work 5 inches, ending with a right side row. ***Last Row:*** Bind off 24 lining sts, complete row. Leave yarn attached. Slip these sts to a st holder. Sl center 64 sts from holder to a size 8 needle. Work to the same length as the end of the Pocket Opening, ending with a wrong side row. Break off yarn. Sl these sts to a st holder. Work 24 lining sts, then the remaining 15 (18, 21, 24) sts from st holder. Work the same as the Left Side, reversing the shaping. ***Joining Row:*** Beg at the Left Side edge in Pats, work 15 (18, 21, 24) sts, 64 center sts, and 15 (18, 21, 24) Right Side sts. Work the same as the Back to 6 rows after the start of the Armhole Shaping—80 (84, 88, 92) sts.

7. Neck Shaping, Row 1: Dec 1 st at the Armhole edge, and work until 27 (28, 29, 30) sts are on needle; join a 2nd ball of yarn, bind off center 24 (26, 28, 30) sts; work to last 2 sts, dec 1 st—27 (28, 29, 30) sts each side of the Neck. Working both sides at once, dec 1 st at each Armhole edge every other row twice more—25 (26, 27, 28) sts each side of the Neck. Work until Armholes measure the same as the Back to the Shoulders. Shape the Shoulders the same as on the Back.
8. Sleeves: Starting at the lower edge of the Sleeve with size 5 needles, cast on 40 (44, 48, 52) sts. Work in twist ribbing following Step 1 to 3 inches, inc 15 sts evenly spaced across last row—55 (59, 63, 67) sts. Change to size 8 needles and Pats. ***Row 1 (right side):*** Following Row 1 of each Aran Pattern, work as follows: Pat I over 16 (18, 20, 22) sts; p 1; Pat II over 5 sts, Pat III over 11 sts, Pat II over 5 sts; p 1; Pat I over 16 (18, 20, 22) sts. Keeping to the Pats as established, inc 1 st each end every 12th row 6 times. Work the new sts into Pat I—67 (71, 75, 79) sts. Work to 17 inches from the beg, or the desired length, ending with a wrong side row (same Pat row as at the underarms of the Back).
9. Cap Shaping: Keeping to Pats, bind off 5 (6, 7, 8) sts at beg of next 2 rows. Dec 1 st each end every other row 16 (17, 18, 19) times. Bind off 5 sts at beg of next 5 rows.
10. Collar: With size 8 needles, cast on 25 (26, 27, 28) sts. Work in Pat I. Work 4 rows. Inc 1 st at beg of next row, then every 4th row 8 times more—34 (35, 36, 37) sts. Work even until the Collar is long enough to reach within ½ inch of the Back Neck edge, ending at the straight edge of the Collar. ***Short Rows:*** Keeping to Pat, work 28 (29, 30, 31) sts, ***turn,*** sl 1, work to end, ***turn,*** work 22 (23, 24, 25) sts, ***turn,*** sl 1, work to end, ***turn,*** work 16 (17, 18, 19) sts, ***turn,*** sl 1, work to end, ***turn,*** work 10 (11, 12, 13) sts, ***turn,*** sl 1, work to end. Work over all sts for 3 rows. Mark for the center back. Work 3 rows. Rep Short Rows. Continue as for the first side of the Collar, working decreases instead of increases.
11. Finishing: Sew the Shoulder, side and Sleeve seams. Sew the lower right edge of the Collar to the Front Neck edge. Sew the lower left edge of the Collar to the Front Neck edge under the right edge. Sew the Collar to the Front Neck edge. Sew in the Sleeves. Sew down the Pocket Linings. Block the sweater to the finished measurements following the directions on page 269.

TIPS FOR A "GREEN" CHRISTMAS

A Gift of Green

Houseplants are more than pretty; they are "clean machines," producing extra oxygen that can improve the atmosphere in the home. A plant makes an ideal gift for a friend, neighbor, co-worker, or any family member.

After buying a gift plant, repot it in a clay, ceramic or wooden pot, not a plastic one. Include the plant's care instructions on a plant marker, or handwritten on a decorative card. Add a simple watering can to the package, if you wish.

Choose a plant with a name to suit the holiday season, such as Christmas cactus, Star of Bethlehem, prayer plant, Christmas begonia, or angel-wing begonia.

SWEETHEART SWEATER

Average: For those with some experience in knitting.

Directions are given for Size Small. Changes for Sizes Medium and Large are in parentheses.

Materials: Patons Diana yarn (50-gram ball): 9 (9, 10) balls of Barley (MC), and 4 (4, 5) balls of Dusty Pink (CC); 1 pair each size 6 and size 9 knitting needles, OR ANY SIZE NEEDLES TO OBTAIN GAUGE BELOW; 2 stitch holders; stitch markers; tapestry needle.

Gauge: On size 9 needles in Stockinette Stitch (st st), 4 sts = 1 inch; 5 rows = 1 inch.

Measurements:

SIZES:	SMALL	MEDIUM	LARGE
BODY BUST:	32″-34″	36″-38″	40″-42″

Finished Measurements:

BUST:	36″	40″	44″

Directions:

1. Back: With size 6 needles and CC, cast on 73 (81, 89) sts. Work in k 1, p 1 ribbing for 2 inches. Change to size 9 needles. Join MC; do not cut CC. ***Row 1 (right side):*** Following FIG. V, 4A *(page 118)* as marked for Body, starting on Row 1 at size chosen (S, M, L), k through center st; starting at next st, read the chart back to S (M, L) to complete the row. ***Row 2:*** Reading FIG. V, 4A, Row 2 as above, p 1 row. Continue in st st (k 1 row, p 1 row) through Row 22. Work 2 rows of MC. Work Row 25 (snowflake row). Work 4 rows of MC. Work Row 30 (snowflake row). Repeat a snowflake row every 5th row, placing the snowflake sts between the snowflake sts of the row below. Work even in the established pat until 15 inches from beg, or desired length to the underarm. End on MC row.

2. Armhole: Mark each end of the last row for beg of the Armhole.

Beg FIG. V, 4B at size chosen for Body, reading it the same as FIG. V, 4A. Work Rows 1 to 26, then work Rows 25 to 1 in that order. If additional rows are needed to complete Armhole length, work MC rows and snowflake rows as for Body. When Armhole measures 10 (10½, 11) inches, end with a p row.

3. Shoulder Shaping: Bind off 23 (25, 27) sts at beg of next 2 rows. Place remaining 27 (31, 35) sts on a st holder for the Back Neck.

4. Front: Work same as the Back to 7 (7½, 8) inches above the Armhole markers, ending with a p row.

5. Neck Shaping: K 30 (34, 38) sts, sl 13 sts to another st holder for the Front Neck; attach a new ball of yarn, k 30 (34, 38) sts. Working both sides at the same time, dec 1 st at the Neck edge every row 7 (9, 11) times. Work even on 23 (25, 27) sts until the Armhole measures the same as the Back. Bind off all sts.

6. Sleeves: With size 6 needles and CC, cast on 37 (41, 43) sts. Work in k 1, p 1 ribbing for 2 inches. Inc 16 (16, 18) sts across last row—53 (57, 61) sts. Change to size 9 needles. Attach MC; do not cut CC. Following FIG. V, 4A as marked for Sleeve, starting on Row 1 at size chosen (S, M, L), work the same as the Back, and at the same time inc 1 st each side every 5th row 14 times—81 (85, 89) sts. Work even to 16 (16½, 17) inches from beg, ending on MC row. Work Rows 1 to 8 of FIG. V, 4B. Bind off all sts loosely.

7. Neckband: Sew the left Shoulder seam. With the right side facing you, size 6 needles and CC, k 27 (31, 35) sts from the Back holder, pick up 15 sts along the left Neck edge, k 13 sts from the Front holder, pick up 16 sts along the right Neck edge—71 (75, 79) sts. Work in k 1, p 1 ribbing for 1 inch. Bind off loosely in ribbing. Sew the right Shoulder seam and Neckband seam. Mark the center of the Sleeve, place it at the Shoulder seam, and sew in the Sleeve between markers. Sew side and Sleeve seams.

FIG. V, 4A SWEETHEART SWEATER BOTTOM OF BODY AND SLEEVE

FIG. V, 4B YOKE

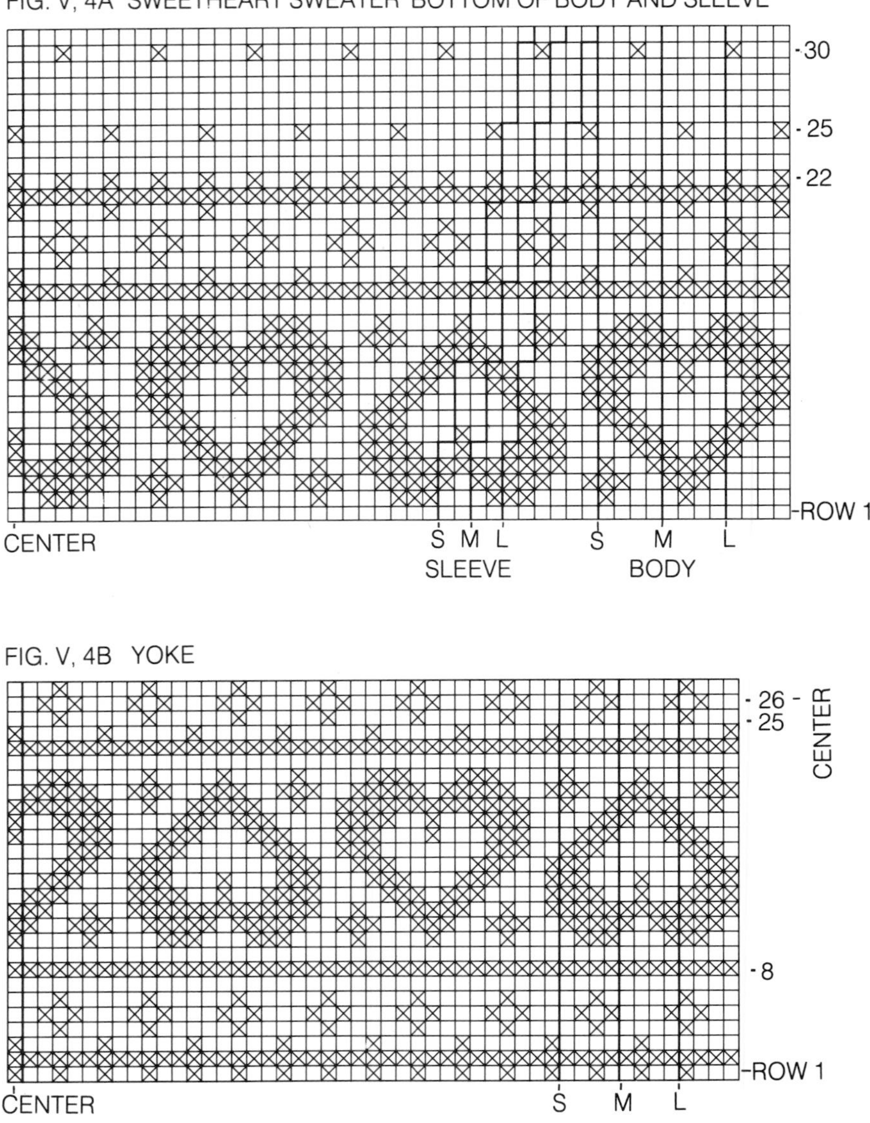

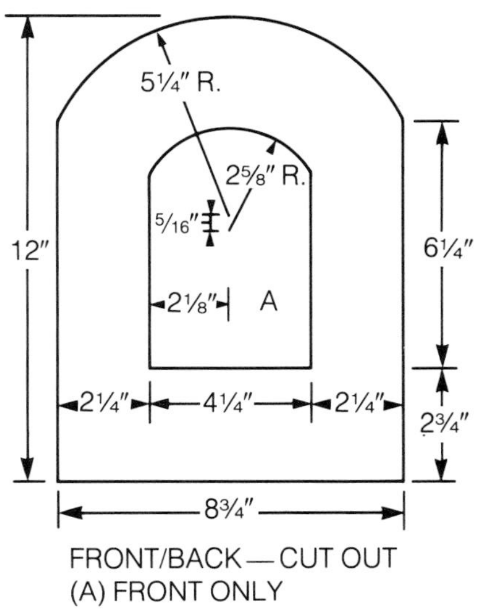

VICTORIAN DOUBLE FRAME

(holds two 5 x 7-inch photos)

Challenging: Requires more experience in crafting.

Materials: ½ yard of mauve moire taffeta; 1¼ yards of ecru cluny lace; 1¼ yards of 1½-inch-wide ecru ruffled lace; 1 yard of ¼-inch-wide mauve ribbon; ½ yard of ¼-inch-wide burgundy ribbon; lace appliqué; 3 large ribbon roses; synthetic stuffing; iron-on fusing tape; craft knife; very sharp scissors; straight pins; compass; ruler; white glue; corrugated cardboard.

Directions:

1. Using the compass and ruler, draw a frame front and frame back on the cardboard following the dimensions in Fig. V, 5. Cut out the frame front and back with the craft knife; cut out the center opening on the frame front only. Also cut two 9 x 2¼-inch cardboard spacer strips, and one 8¾ x 2¾-inch cardboard spacer strip. Cut two 9¾ x 13-inch pieces from the taffeta. Trim the top edge of each taffeta piece to match the frame top curve plus 1 inch; do not cut out the center opening in the taffeta. Repeat for the second frame.

2. For each frame, glue the spacer strips to the inside of the frame front, placing the longer strips on the sides and the shorter strip on the bottom. Let the glue dry.

3. Place each frame front face down on the wrong side of a taffeta piece. Fold the taffeta around the straight edges of each frame front, over the spacers, and glue the taffeta in place, mitering the corners. On the curved edge, slash the taffeta every ½ inch to within ¼ inch of the cardboard. Glue the tabs in place, keeping the taffeta smooth. Repeat on the frame backs.

4. On each frame front, push small pieces of stuffing between the cardboard and taffeta through the center opening in the cardboard. Be sure the stuffing is evenly distributed and smooth; lumps will spoil the look of the taffeta. Pack the stuffing tightly to the edges of the center opening.

5. On each frame front, use the scissors to cut out a center opening in the taffeta that is ½ to ¾ inch smaller than the cardboard opening. Slash the taffeta allowance every ½ inch all around. With the frame front facing you, pin the tabs securely to the cardboard behind the opening, pulling the taffeta taut. When the tabs are securely fastened and the taffeta lies smooth and even, turn over the frame front, and glue the tabs to the cardboard without removing the pins. Let the glue dry completely before removing the pins.

6. Glue cluny lace around each center opening *(see photo)*.

7. Cut a 4 x 9½-inch taffeta strip, and fold it in half lengthwise. Insert a same-length piece of fusing tape inside the folded strip. Press with an iron to fuse the taffeta layers together to make a frame hinge. Turn the two frame backs wrong side up, and place them side by side, ½ inch apart, with their bottom edges even. Glue the hinge lengthwise to the frame backs. Glue ruffled lace to each frame back from the bottom left corner up the side, across the top, and down the other side; do not glue lace across the bottom. Let the glue dry completely.

8. Glue each frame front to a frame back on the spacer strips, leaving the top edge open to insert a photo. Using the photo as a placement guide, trim the double frame with the lace appliqué, ribbon roses, and mauve and burgundy ribbons tied into bows with streamers.

TIPS FOR A "GREEN" CHRISTMAS

Terrific Ties!

Tie your Christmas gifts with yarn instead of ribbon. One skein of red, white or green yarn will trim many gifts at relatively little cost. Plus, your "crafty" friends will find a way to put the yarn to good use during the year.

LACY CROCHET TOTE BAG

Average: For those with some experience in crocheting.

Materials: J. & P. Coats Knit-Cro-Sheen (250-yard ball): 4 balls of Ecru; size 8 steel crochet hook, OR ANY SIZE HOOK TO OBTAIN GAUGE BELOW; stitch markers; tapestry needle.

Gauge: 4 spaces = 1 inch.

Note: *The tote bag is made in rounds. The bottom of the tote is made last, and stitched to the side and back panels. The shell trim and handles are added after the tote is finished.*

Directions:

1. Panels: Starting at the bottom, ch 272. ***Rnd 1:*** Ch 4 (counts as dc and ch-1), *skip 1-ch, dc in next ch-1 —* ***sp made*** (place a marker in this space); * ch 1, skip 1-ch, dc in next ch; rep from * 11 times more, place a marker; make 56 spaces, place a marker; make 12 spaces, place a marker; end ch 1, join with sl st in third ch of ch-4. You will have 13 spaces from marker to marker, and 55 spaces between — 136 spaces in all. ***Rnd 2:*** *Ch 4, dc in dc —* ***starting space made;*** ch 1, skip 1-ch, dc in next dc all around. End with sl st in third ch of ch-4. ***Rnds 3 to 62:*** Follow the chart in FIG. V, 6. To make a block, dc in ch-1 sp.

Rnd 63: Ch 1, * sc in dc, sc in ch-1 sp; rep from * around. ***Rnds 64 to 69:*** Rep Rnd 63. Break off and fasten.

2. Bottom: Attach the thread to the front panel marker, and work across 55 spaces only. Make 12 more rows of 55 spaces. Break the thread. Sew the Bottom to the side and back panels, being careful to sew space for space.

3. Shell Trim: With the bag upside down, starting at the upper left marker, * sc, ch 2, 3 dc, skip 1 sp; rep from * around the filet flower panel. Repeat for the other filet flower panel.

4. Handles (make 2), Row 1: Ch 101. Sc in 2nd ch from hook, sc in each ch across — 100 sc. Ch 1, turn. ***Rows 2 to 10:*** Sc in each sc across. Ch 1, turn; ***do not*** ch 1 at the end of Row 10. ***Row 11:*** Fold the handle in half lengthwise. Sl st into first sc on the other side of the fold. Ch 1, * sc through both sides; rep from * around — 100 sc. Fasten off.

5. Finishing: Using the photo *(page 120)* as a placement guide, center and sew the handles to the front and back flower panels.

FIG. V, 6 LACY CROCHET TOTE BAG

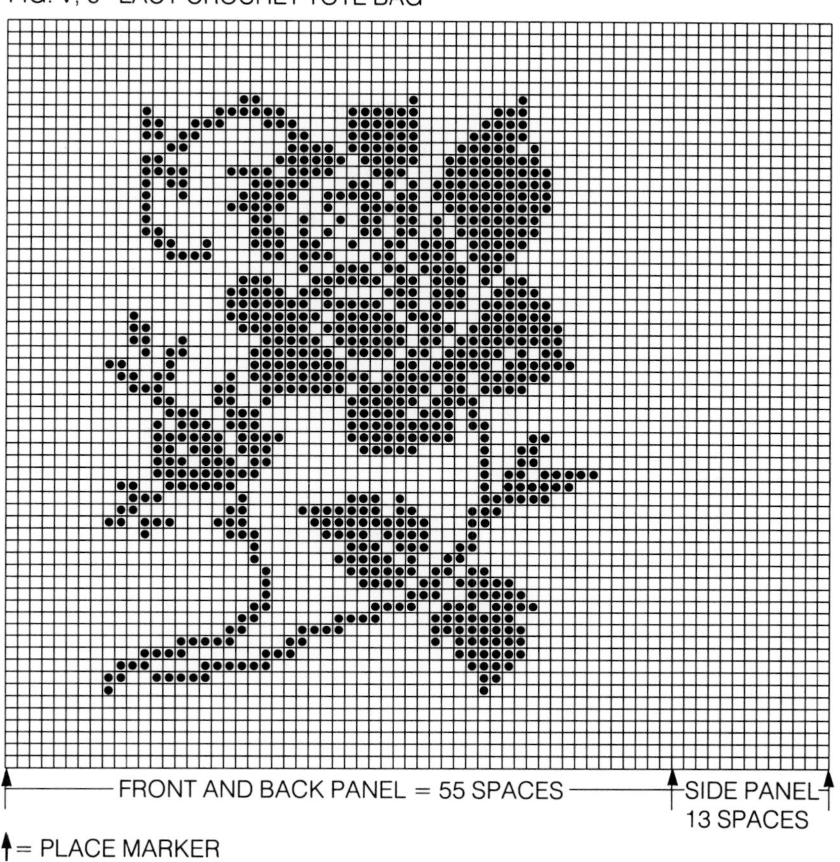

TIPS FOR A "GREEN" CHRISTMAS

Green Bagging It!

Some department stores, especially fancy ones, wrap purchases in tissue paper, pack them in a small bag, and put the bag in a handled shopping bag. That's a lot of paper wasted. Instead, ask the store clerk to put your purchase in a handled shopping bag without any other wrapping. Then use the large bag to hold your other purchases — no extra paper needed!

JUST FOR HIM

A choice selection of perfect presents for the special men in your life.

MOUNTAIN SCENE MARQUETRY BOX

(7 x 4½ x 3 inches)

Marquetry is the art of creating inlaid scenic pictures from wood veneers in the style of a jigsaw puzzle. The varieties of wood suggested below can be replaced with others that appeal to you more, or that you happen to have on hand. The grain, color, and feel of the wood varieties used are integral parts of the scene.

Challenging: Requires more experience in crafting.

Materials: ¼ x 36 x 4-inch walnut or other hardwood board; veneer sheets: cherry, Carpathian elm burl, ebony, mahogany, maple, oak, green poplar burl, purpleheart, satinwood, walnut and walnut butt; 6½ x 4 inches of velvet or felt; two ¾-inch brass butt hinges; wood glue; white glue; contact cement; rubber cement; rubber cement thinner *(optional)*; cotton swabs *(optional)*; 100, 150 and 220 grit sandpaper; sanding block; No. 0000 steel wool; tack cloth; fine sawdust; Deft Interior Satin Finish; paste wax *(optional)*; clean soft cloth *(optional)*; paintbrush; scissors; small putty knife; craft knife; straight edge; power saw, or handsaw; fret saw, or scroll saw; backsaw; No. 4/0 (jeweler's) saw blades; miter box; router; screwdriver; band clamp; parallel clamp or vise; 2 boards for clamping; corrugated cardboard; sheet of oaktag paper; wax paper; carbon paper; paper for patterns.

Note: *The veneer sheets can be ordered from: Craftman Wood Service Co., 1735 West Cortland Ct., Addison, IL 60101; Bob Morgan Woodworking Supplies, 1123 Bardstown Road, Louisville, KY 40204; Constantine's, 2050 Eastchester Rd., Bronx, NY 10461.*

Directions:

1. Trace the full-size inlay pattern in Fig. V, 7A *(page 125)* onto paper. Make three exact copies of the pattern. Spread out the veneers and two copies of the pattern, along with the scissors, craft knife and rubber cement. Use the key in Fig. V, 7A and the photo as guides to select the veneer to use for each scene part.

2. Starting with one of the smallest scene parts, such as a tree trunk or bush, cut out a piece of veneer slightly larger than the scene part. Cut the piece so the wood grain goes in a direction that enhances the scene; the arrows on the pattern in Fig. V, 7A suggest the direction of the grain for some scene parts. Glue the piece of veneer in place on one pattern sheet, making sure the scene part is covered completely. Continue to cover scene parts on the pattern sheet in this way, progressing from the smallest to the largest scene parts, and looking for interesting grains or patterns in the veneers to make the scene come alive. After a while, you will begin to cover the lines of other scene parts on the pattern sheet, making it difficult to work accurately. At that point, begin gluing veneer pieces onto the second pattern sheet. It doesn't matter which pattern sheet the veneer pieces are glued onto, as long as all the scene parts are covered completely.

3. When all the scene parts are covered with veneer pieces, cut a piece of corrugated cardboard the same size as the pattern sheets. Line up the two pattern sheets carefully, and place them on the cardboard. Place the third pattern sheet on top. Glue the cardboard and the pattern sheets together by spreading rubber cement over the entire surface of each sheet. Making sure the sheets are lined up exactly, clamp the pattern sandwich between the two clamping boards, and let the glue dry overnight.

4. Use the fret saw or scroll saw with a No. 4/0 blade for the final cutting of the veneer scene pieces. Cut out each scene piece carefully, one piece at a time, sawing through the entire sandwich at once as you work. Two or more veneer pieces are likely to have overlapped in the gluing process, so separate the papers of each scene part gently until you find the veneer piece cut in the correct shape. When you have cut and removed all the veneer scene pieces, discard the remainder of the sandwich.

5. To assemble the veneer pieces into the scene, spread a thin layer of rubber cement on the oaktag. Place the largest veneer piece, the oak sky, face down on the oaktag. Place an adjacent veneer piece, such as the purpleheart mountain, face down in place against the oak sky. Continue in this way until all the veneer pieces are assembled into the scene. Let the rubber cement dry for a few minutes. Using 100 grit sandpaper, sand off any excess rubber cement that is on the back of the veneer scene, which is the side facing up. Or, if you wish, use rubber cement thinner very sparingly on a cotton swab to remove the rubber cement.

6. Mix some fine sawdust with white glue to a putty-like consistency. Using the putty knife, push the sawdust putty into any gaps or imperfections in the veneer scene. Wipe off any excess putty.

7. Cut two 7 x 3-inch pieces, and two 4⅜ x 3-inch pieces from the walnut or other hardwood board for the box sides. Miter their ends 45°. Rabbet a ¼-inch groove on the inside top and bottom edges of each box side *(see Fig. V, 7B, page 125)*. Glue the sides together with wood glue, band clamp them, and let the glue dry overnight.

8. Cut two 6¾ x 4⅛-inch pieces from the walnut board for the box top and bottom. Glue the top and bottom into the rabbet joints in the box sides, clamp the top and bottom in place, and let the glue dry overnight. Progressing from 100 grit to 220 grit sandpaper, sand the box top and bottom smooth. Wipe off all the sawdust with the tack cloth.
9. Following the package directions, spread a thin layer of contact cement on the box top, and on the back of the veneer scene. Let the contact cement dry. Coat the box top and back of the scene again. Centering the veneer scene carefully on the box top, attach the scene to the box top by pressing hard and evenly on the scene to assure good contact and remove air bubbles. Peel off the oaktag.
10. Using the craft knife, cut the ebony veneer into 1/16-inch-wide strips to go around the perimeter of the veneer scene. Cut the Carpathian elm burl veneer into ½-inch-wide strips to go around the ebony strips *(see* FIG. V, 7A*)*. Coat the top edges of the box and one side of the veneer strips with contact cement. Let the contact cement dry. Coat the box top and veneer strips again. Place a small piece of wax paper on each corner of the box top, overlapping the box edges. Press the veneer strips in place; they will overlap each other at the corners. At one corner, use the straight edge and craft knife to cut down to the box top through all the veneer strip layers from the corner of the scene to the corner of the box, creating a 45° miter *(see photo, page 122)*. Peel off and discard the scrap veneer pieces. Slip out the wax paper, and press the mitered strips against the box top; they should fit together tightly. Repeat at the other corners.
11. Using 100 grit sandpaper on the sanding block, sand the veneered box top very carefully. Sand just until the scene and border seem level and smooth; the veneer is only 1/28 inch thick. Then sand carefully with 150 grit sandpaper, and finish with 220 grit sandpaper.
12. Brush the veneered box top with four very heavy coats of Satin Finish, allowing 1 day's drying time between coats. After the fourth coat, sand the box top with 150 grit sandpaper until the surface is level. Wipe off the dust with the tack cloth. Check that the finish has coated the veneered scene evenly. Touch up any uneven spots, and let them dry. Give the box top a final heavy coat of finish, and let it dry for at least 1 week.
13. While the veneered top is drying and hardening, complete the box. Measure down 1 inch from the top of the box, and cut through the entire box *(see* FIG. V, 7B*)*. Attach the brass hinges to the top and bottom sections of the box at the back. Sand the box sides smooth, progressing from 100 to 220 grit sandpaper, and wipe off all the sawdust with the tack cloth. Brush the box sides with three very thin coats of finish, allowing 1 day's drying time between coats.
14. When the box has dried completely, sand it lightly with 220 grit sandpaper. For a satin finish, rub the entire box lightly with the steel wool. For a gloss finish, apply a coat of paste wax with a clean soft cloth after rubbing with the steel wool. Attach the velvet or felt to the inside bottom of the box with rubber cement, rolling under the edges of the velvet as you glue.
15. Dust the box regularly, and rub it periodically with a soft cloth to remove fingerprints. To remove scratches or dirt stains, rub them with No. 0000 steel wool in the direction of the wood grain.

TIPS FOR A "GREEN" CHRISTMAS

Better than Boxes

Cut down on the number of gift boxes you use this Christmas; it's an easy way to save a tree.

Wrap gifts in reusable containers tied with ribbon. Use baskets, tin canisters, or fabric sacks in place of cardboard boxes. For a real old-fashioned touch, fold sweaters, afghans and other soft, heavy items neatly, and wrap them in tissue paper without boxes.

FIG. V, 7A MOUNTAIN SCENE MARQUETRY BOX INLAY

FULL SIZE

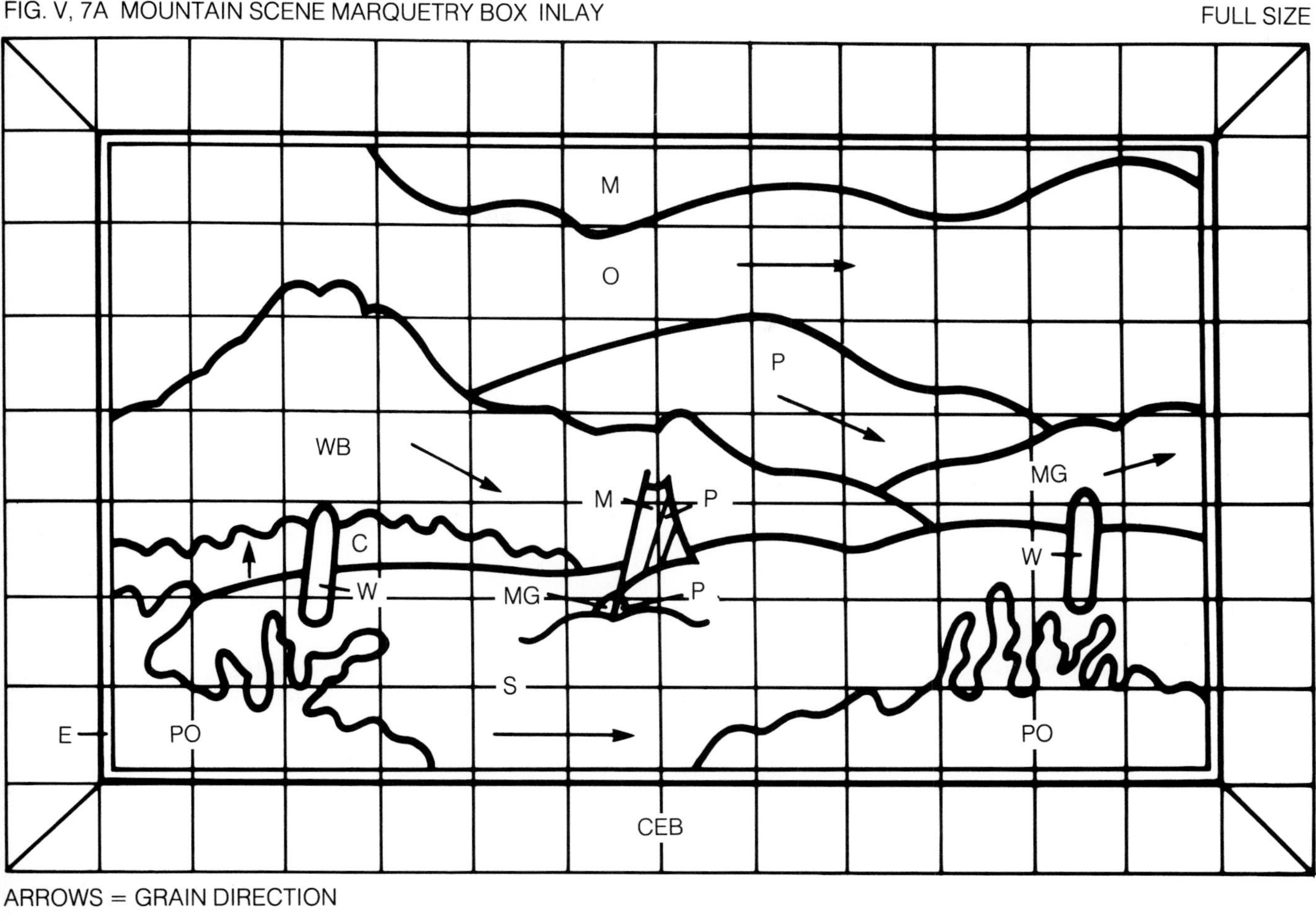

ARROWS = GRAIN DIRECTION

C = CHERRY
CEB = CARPATHIAN ELM BURL
E = EBONY
M = MAPLE
MG = MAHOGANY
O = OAK
P = PURPLEHEART
PO = POPLAR BURL
S = SATINWOOD
W = WALNUT
WB = WALNUT BUTT

FIG. V, 7B BOX

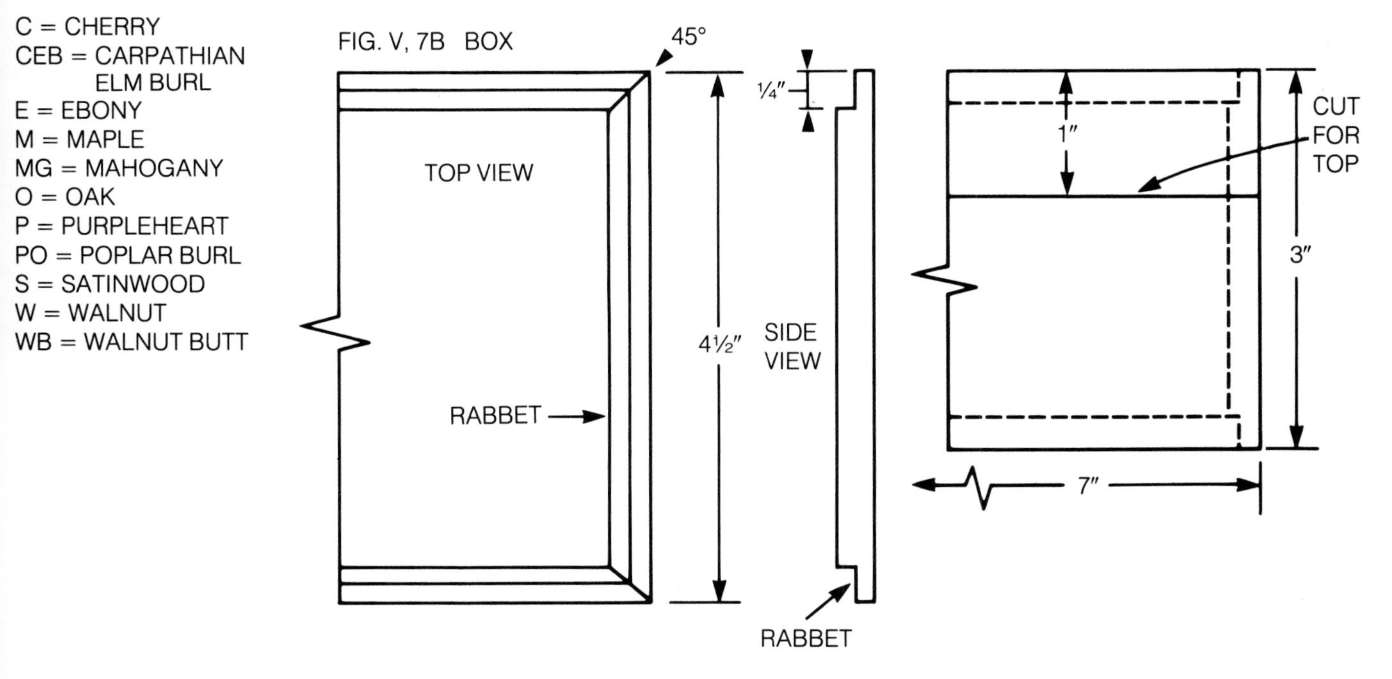

CLEVER CRAFTING

Dyed in the Wool

Check the dye lots on the yarn you use for sweaters, afghans and other large knitted or crocheted projects. Make sure all skeins of the same color come from the same dye lot. The slightest variation in color or shade will be noticeable in the finished project.

MAN'S V-NECK CARDIGAN

Challenging: Requires more experience in knitting.

Directions are given for Size Small. Changes for Sizes Medium and Large are in parentheses.

Materials: Knitting worsted weight yarn: 33 (36, 40) ounces of color desired; matching sewing thread; 6 decorative buttons in matching color; 1 pair each size 6, size 7, and size 9 knitting needles, OR ANY SIZE NEEDLES TO OBTAIN GAUGE BELOW; cable needle; stitch holder; stitch markers; tapestry needle; sewing needle.

Gauge: On size 9 needles in Pattern Stitch I, 14 sts = 2½ inches; 6 rows = 1 inch. On size 9 needles in Stockinette Stitch (st st), 3¾ sts = 1 inch; 5 rows = 1 inch. On size 7 needles in Pattern Stitch II, 9 sts = 2 inches; 8 rows = 1 inch.

Buttonhole, Row 1: Work first 4 sts of the Edge Band, bind off next 4 sts, work rem 4 sts. ***Row 2:*** Work first 4 sts, cast on 4 sts, work rem 4 sts.

Pattern Stitch I: Worked as a multiple of 7 sts plus 1 st, plus 1 selvage st at each edge. ***Rows 1, 3 and 5:*** K 1, p 1, * (**) slip next 2 sts to cable needle, hold in back of work, k 1, k 2 off cable needle, slip next st to cable needle, hold in front of work, k 2, k 1 off cable needle (**), p 1, k 6, p 1 *; rep from * to * (even multiples of 7) to last st, end k 1; (odd multiples of 7) to last 8 sts, end rep from (**) to (**) over 7 sts, k 1. ***Row 2 and all wrong side rows:*** K the knit sts and p the purl sts. ***Rows 7, 9 and 11:*** K 1, p 1, * k 6, p 1, work (**) to (**) of 1st row, p 1 *; rep from * to * (even multiples of 7) to last st, end k 1; (odd multiples of 7) to last 8 sts, end k 6, p 1, k 1. ***Row 12:*** Rep Row 2. Rep Rows 1 to 12 for pattern.

Pattern Stitch II (worked over odd number of sts), Row 1 (wrong side): Knit. ***Row 2:*** K 1, * p 1, k 1 *; rep from * to * to end. Rep Rows 1 and 2 for pattern.

Finished Measurements (Blocked):

SIZES:	SMALL	MEDIUM	LARGE
CHEST:	47″	50″	53″

Directions:

1. Back: With size 6 needles, loosely cast on 107 (115, 121) sts. Work in k 1, p 1 ribbing for 2 inches, ending with a right side row. Change to size 9 needles, and work the following foundation row on the wrong side, increasing 1 st for sizes S and L: P 1, k 1, * p 6, k 1 *; rep from * to * to last st, p 1. Start with Row 1 of Pattern Stitch I on the next row, and work even in Pat until total length measures 26 (26½, 27) inches. Bind off in Pat.

2. Left Front: The Left Front is worked with the Edge Band attached, and 6 buttonholes made in the Band at ¾ (1, 1) inch, 3¼ (3½, 3½) inches, 5¾ (6, 6) inches, 8 (8½, 8¾) inches, 10½ (11, 11¼) inches, and 13 (13½, 14) inches. With size 6 needles, loosely cast on 61 (63, 67) sts. Work in k 1, p 1 ribbing for 2 inches, making the first buttonhole at ¾ (1, 1) inch. End with a right side row. Change to size 9 needles, and work p 1, k 1 ribbing over the first 12 sts, then work the following foundation row over the remaining sts, increasing 1 st for sizes M and L: S and L (k 2, p 3, k 1); M (k 2); * p 6, k 1 *; rep from * to * to last st, p 1—61 (64, 68) sts. Start with Row 1 of Pattern Stitch I on the next row, working extra sts after Pat repeats in k or p as established, and working k 1, p 1 ribbing over the Edge Band sts. Continue to work Pat over Pat sts, and ribbing over ribbing sts while making buttonholes at the appropriate measurements, and skipping the Edge Band sts for 2 rows every 12 rows as follows: Work across Pat sts on right side row, bring yarn to front, slip next st to right needle, bring yarn to back, slip the slipped st on right needle back to the left needle, turn work and work across Pat sts on wrong side to end of row. Work until the total length measures 13½ (14, 14½) inches. Place a marker.

3. V-Neck Shaping: On the next row decrease 1 st over the 2 Pat sts that are just next to the 12 Edge Band sts. (The shaping is done over the Pat sts, not over the Edge Band sts.) Rep on the next row. Then decrease 1 st over these 2 sts every 5th row 13 (14, 14) times more. When the total length measures 26 (26½, 27) inches, bind off Pat sts in Pat, and place the Edge Band sts on the st holder.

4. Right Front: The Right Front is worked without an Edge Band. The Edge Band will be worked later from the sts on the Left Front holder and sewn to the Right Front. With size 6 needles, loosely cast on 49 (53, 57) sts. Work in k 1, p 1 ribbing for 2 inches, ending with a right side row. Change to size 9 needles and work the following foundation row, increasing 1 st for size S: P 1, k 1, * p 6, k 1 *; rep from * to * 5 (6, 6) times more, work S and L (p 3, k 3), M (k 3) over rem sts—50 (53, 57) sts. On the next row work Row 1 of Pat Stitch I as follows: S (p 3, k 3, p 1, * k 6, p 1, work cabling over next 6 sts, p 1 *; rep from * to * to last st, k 1); M (p 3, k 6, p 1, * work cabling over next 6 sts, p 1, k 6, p 1 *; rep from * to * to last st, k 1); L (p 3, k 3, p 1, work cabling over next 6 sts, p 1, * k 6, p 1, work cabling over next 6 sts, p 1 *; rep from * to * to last st, k 1). Continue working in Pat as established, working the extra sts after the Pat repeats in k or p as established. Work until the total length measures 13½ (14, 14½) inches—the same row as the marker on the Left Front.

5. V-Neck Shaping: On the next row, decrease 1 st over the 2 sts at the center edge. Rep on the next row. Then decrease these 2 sts every 5th row 13 (14, 14) times more. When the total length measures 26 (26½, 27) inches, the same as the Left Front, bind off in Pat.

6. Sleeves: With size 6 needles, loosely cast on 49 (51, 53) sts. Work in k 1, p 1 ribbing for 2 inches, ending with a right side row. Change to size 9 needles and work the following foundation row, increasing 22 (22, 24) sts evenly spaced: S (k 1); M (p 1, k 1); L (p 3, k 1); * p 6, k 1 *; rep from * to * to S (end); M (last st, p 1); L (last 3 sts, p 3). Work Row 1 of Pat Stitch I as follows: S (p 1); M (k 1, p 1); L (k 3, p 1), * k 6, p 1, work cabling over next 6 sts, p 1 *; rep from * to * to S (end); M (last st, k 1); L (last 3 sts, k 3). Continue working Pat as established, working the extra sts at the edges as established. When total length measures 2½ inches, increase 1 st at each edge every 5th row 15 (16, 16) times. When increasing, expand the Pat appropriately, working the cables in half or whole only when there are at least 2 edge sts. When the total length measures 15½ (16, 16) inches, end with a wrong side row. Change to size 7 needles, and k the knit sts and p the purl sts for 3 rows. Then work Pattern Stitch II for 3 (3, 3½) inches — the total length will measure 19 (19½, 20) inches. Bind off. Sew the Shoulder seams.

7. Edge Band: Count the number of ribbing rows worked on size 9 needles (the rows above the waistband). Place a marker on the last row worked. Continue in ribbing as established on size 9 needles. Work a length to loosely fit the back of the Neck, and place a marker. From the second marker, work the same number of rows that you counted on the Left Front. Change to size 6 needles, and work for 2 inches more — the number of rows worked for the waistband. Bind off loosely. Pin the Edge Band to the Right Front and back of the Neck, matching markers to the Shoulder seams. Lay the pieces flat, and sl st them together through half of each edge st.

8. Pockets: Pick up 30 sts evenly spaced over 7 inches of the Back side edge, starting 1 inch above the ribbing. Work in st st (k 1 row, p 1 row; the right side the same as the Back's right side) for 8 inches. Bind off.

9. Finishing: Block the pieces to the finished measurements, and help to shape the V-neck. Sew the side seams from the bottom edge to the beginning of the Pocket and above the Pocket upwards, leaving 11 (11½, 12) inches open for the Sleeve. Sew the Sleeve seams. Sew in the Sleeves. From the outside, pin the Left and Right Front edges in place over the Pockets. Open the Fronts to the inside, and pin the Pockets in place on the Fronts. Using the sewing needle and thread, slipstitch the edges of the Pockets to the Fronts *(see Stitch Guide, page 270)*. Sew the buttons in place.

TIPS FOR A "GREEN" CHRISTMAS

Shaving Saving

Disposable razors can be convenient, but using them every day only contributes to the plastic waste problem. Cans of shaving cream also end up on the garbage heap when they're empty.

Instead of using throwaway products, try an old-fashioned approach to shaving. Give an earth-wise shaving set: reusable razor, extra blades, shaving soap, shaving brush, and shaving mug.

You can find most of what you need in the drug store or supermarket. If you're looking for something extra special, head to an apothecary shop, natural cosmetics boutique, or the men's fragrance counter at your favorite department store.

TRAVELING SLIPPERS WITH CASE

Average: For those with some experience in sewing.

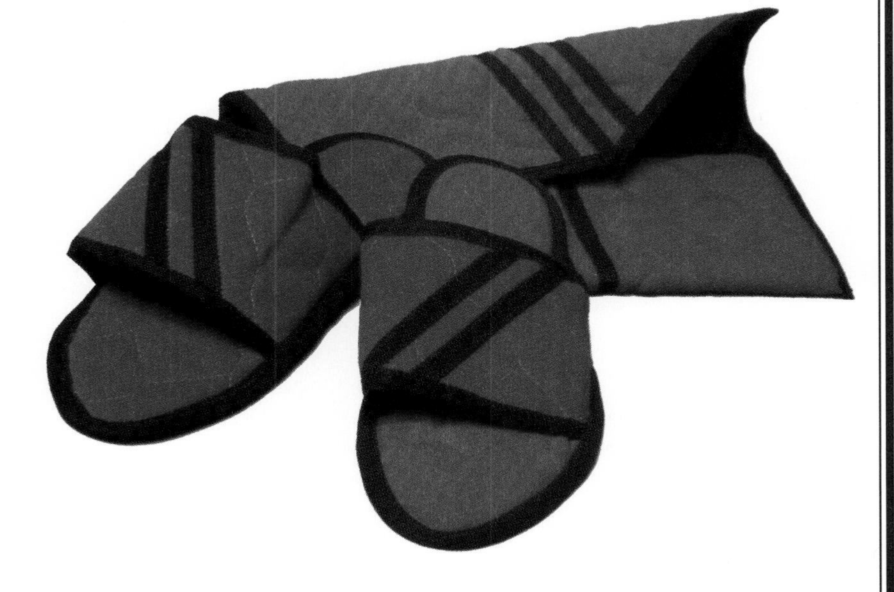

SLIPPERS

Materials: 1 pair of insoles in size required; ½ yard of 45-inch-wide quilted red corduroy fabric; 4 yards of extra-wide black bias tape; black thread; dressmaker's carbon; tracing wheel; tracing paper for pattern.

Directions:

1. Trace the full-size half pattern for the Slipper Top in Fig. V, 8 *(page 130)* onto folded tracing paper. Cut out the half pattern through the double-thickness paper. Open the paper for the full pattern.

2. Using the dressmaker's carbon and tracing wheel, trace two Slipper Tops onto a double thickness of the red corduroy, leaving at least 1 inch between the Tops. The traced lines are the sewing lines; cut ½ inch outside the traced lines to make two pairs of Slipper Tops. Using the insoles as patterns, repeat to cut out two pairs of Slipper Bottoms.

3. Using the photo as a design and placement guide, attach bias tape trim to two Slipper Tops with a machine zigzag stitch.

4. Baste one trimmed Slipper Top to a plain Slipper Top, wrong sides together and edges matching. Using a machine zigzag stitch, bind the two long edges of the double Slipper Top with bias tape. Repeat.

5. Place one pair of Slipper Bottoms wrong sides together, and place the matching insole between them. Machine baste all the layers together. Repeat to make a second complete Slipper Bottom.

6. Pin a Slipper Top to each Slipper Bottom, with the Top's shorter bound edge facing the Bottom's toe *(see photo).* Try on each Slipper, and adjust the Top's position for comfort if necessary. Machine baste the raw side edges of the Slipper Tops to the Slipper Bottoms.

7. Using a machine zigzag stitch, bind the edges of the Slipper Bottoms with bias tape, lapping the tape over the Slipper Tops' raw side edges.

CASE

Materials: 12½ x 18½ inches of quilted red corduroy fabric; 12½ x 18½ inches of black lining fabric; 3 yards of extra-wide black bias tape; black thread; large snap fastener.

Directions:

1. Fold the corduroy in half lengthwise, raw edges even. Mark the raw long edge 2 inches in from one short end. Draw a line from the mark to the end of the folded long edge on the same side. Cut along the drawn line through both layers of fabric to shape the case flap. Repeat on the lining fabric.

2. Pin a strip of bias tape across the lengthwise center of the case, and machine zigzag stitch along each edge of the tape. Pin and zigzag stitch a strip of bias tape ⅜ inch from each side of the center tape *(see photo).*

3. With wrong sides together, pin and machine baste the lining to the corduroy. Bind the straight end of the case with a 12½-inch-long strip of bias tape. Fold the bound end 5½ inches up, and pin the side edges together.

4. Bind the case side edges with bias tape, folding under the tape's raw ends. Repeat on the case flap edges, mitering the tape at the corners.

5. Sew half the snap fastener to the underside of the flap, and the other half to a corresponding position on the case front.

TIPS FOR A "GREEN" CHRISTMAS

Recycled Wrapping

Just about every kind of gift wrap, including aluminum foil gift wrap, can be recycled. However, some types of wrapping paper are more difficult and more costly to process than others. Before you invest in yards and yards of Christmas wrapping, ask your local paper recyclers what kinds of paper they process. Then you can choose your gift wraps accordingly.

According to Bob Patterson, spokesman for Automated Materials Handling, a Kensington, Connecticut recycler, most household paper is recycled into two forms: newsprint and boxboard. Newsprint, used for printing newspapers, is made almost exclusively from old newspapers. Boxboard — a lightweight cardboard used for such things as tissue boxes, pizza boxes and shirt cardboard — is made from old newspapers, magazines, junk mail, phone books, and other low-grade paper. Used wrapping paper can be processed into boxboard.

If you're still unsure about what kind of paper to use for your Christmas wrapping, try newspaper! With a little imagination, you can turn the daily paper into newsworthy gift wrap.

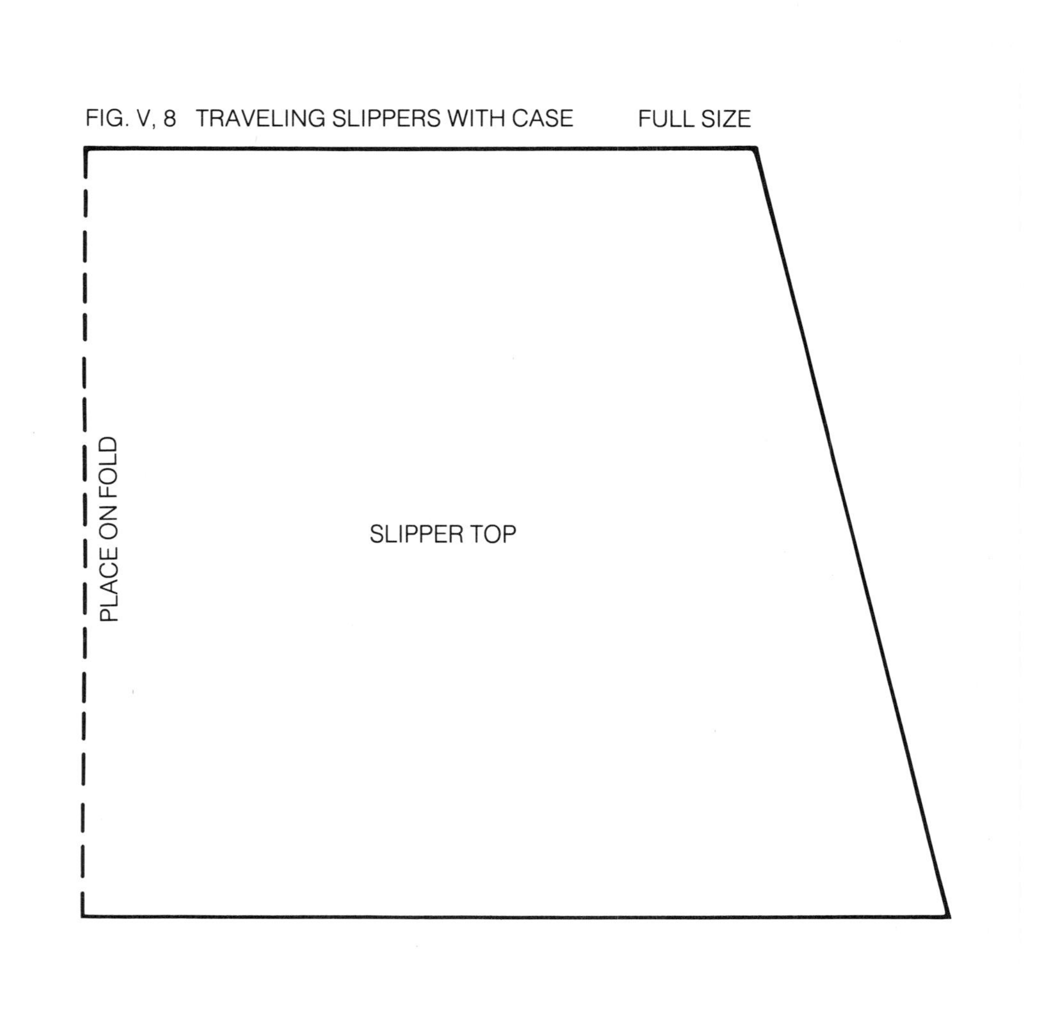

Toiletries Rack; Shower Shelf (directions, page 133)

TOILETRIES RACK

Average: For those with some experience in woodworking.

Materials: 6 feet of 1 x 4 clear pine lumber; 12 feet of ½ x ½-inch pine ballister; ¾-inch brads; wood glue; wood putty; sandpaper; tack cloth; satin polyurethane; paintbrush; saw; hammer; nail set.

Directions:

1. Cut, rabbet and notch the A top and bottom shelves, B long shelf, and C short shelves *(see Cutting Directions and* FIG. V, 9, *page 132).* Cut the D supports and E short supports to size.

2. Glue and nail the C short shelves and B long shelf to the D supports and E short supports. Glue and nail the A top and bottom shelves in place *(see* FIG. V, 9*).* Check that all is square.

3. Set the nails, and fill the nail holes with wood putty. When the putty is dry, sand it. Sand the rack smooth, and wipe off all the sawdust with the tack cloth. Apply three coats of polyurethane, sanding the rack lightly between coats.

TIPS FOR A "GREEN" CHRISTMAS

Twice as Nice Cards

Cut the front panels off old Christmas cards to make holiday postcards. It's a great way to reuse the cards you received last year, and a smart way to salvage cards when you've run out of envelopes or made a writing mistake. Your ingenuity will cut down on paper waste, and you'll save on holiday postage costs.

FIG. V, 9 TOILETRIES RACK

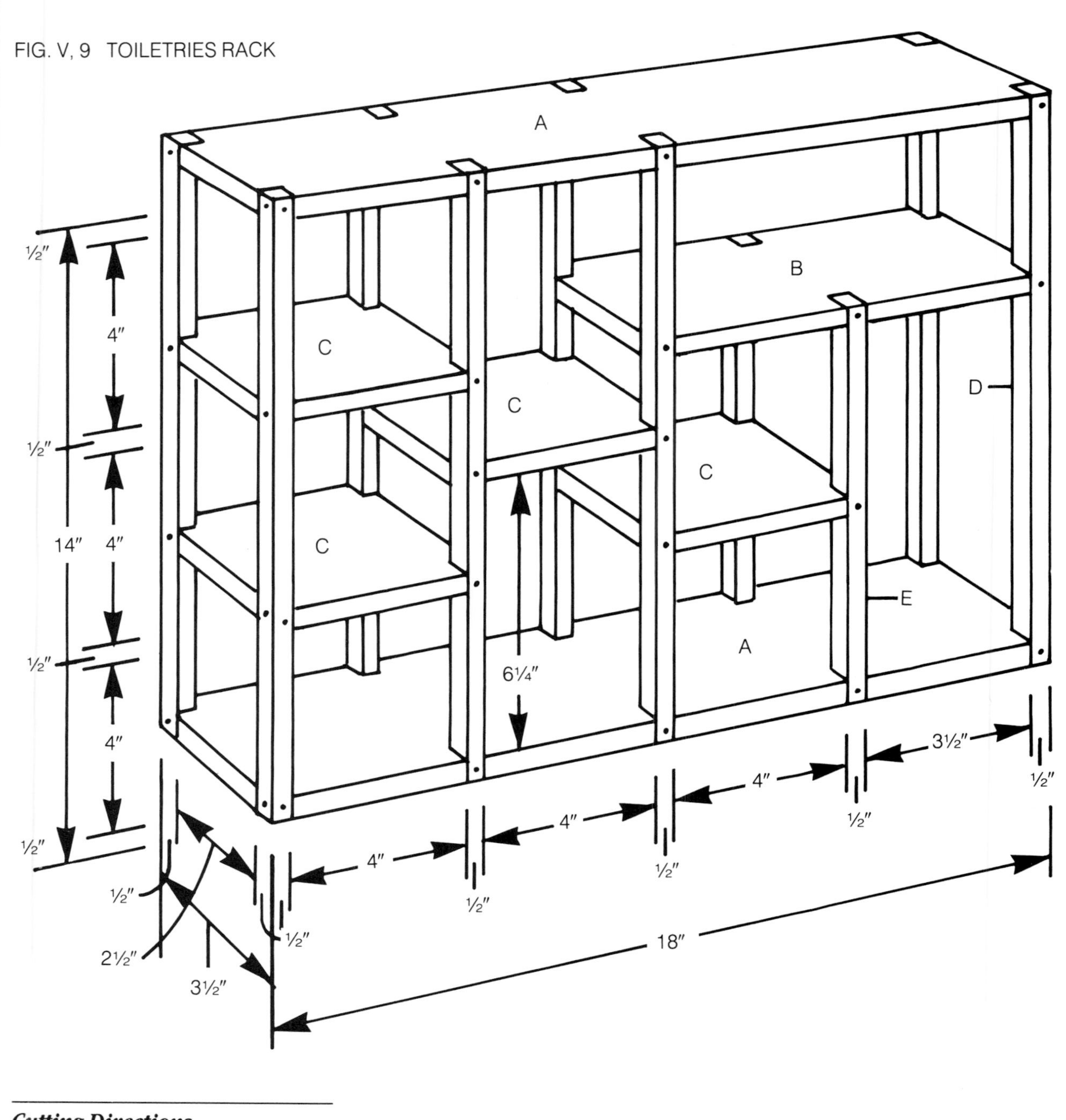

Cutting Directions

Code	*Pieces*	*Size*
A	2	½″ x 3½″ x 18″ Top and bottom shelves
B	1	½″ x 3½″ x 9″ Long shelf
C	4	½″ x 3½″ x 5″ Short shelves
D	8	½″ x ½″ x 14″ Supports
E	2	½″ x ½″ x 9½″ Short supports

SHOWER SHELF

(photo, page 131)

Average: For those with some experience in woodworking.

Materials: 1 x 5 clear pine lumber; ⅜-inch-diameter wooden dowels; ¼-inch-diameter nylon rope; sandpaper; tack cloth; exterior marine grade polyurethane; paintbrush; saw; power bore, or power drill.

Directions:

1. Cut two 8½-inch lengths from the pine lumber. On the long front edge of each length, mark 1½ inches up from the bottom. On the top edge, mark in 1½ inches from the back. Connect the marks, and cut on the line. Sand all the corners round to make the shelf sides.

2. On one shelf side, measure ¾ inch O.C. from the back edge, and mark the positions for four dowels 1 inch apart and ¾ inch from the bottom edge. Three inches O.C. above the lower positions, mark three more dowel positions to align with the back three lower marks.

3. Drill a ⅜-inch-diameter hole at each marked position; a power bore will work best. Also drill a ¼-inch-diameter rope hole 1 inch from the top and ¾ inch from the back edge of the shelf side.

4. Use the drilled shelf side to mark the hole positions on the second shelf side; drill the holes. Cut seven 6⅞-inch-long dowels, and insert them into the shelf sides flush with the sides' outer edges.

5. Sand the shelf smooth, and wipe off all the sawdust with the tack cloth. Apply three coats of polyurethane, sanding lightly between coats. Let the polyurethane dry completely.

6. Thread a 4-inch length of nylon rope through the rope holes from the inside to the outside of the shelf, and knot the ends of the rope *(see photo)*.

CLEVER CRAFTING

Potato-Stamp Wrap

Kids love to make potato-stamp gift wrap. Depending on the age of the child, you can cut the stamps for them or let them create their own stamps.

Cut a potato in half across the width. Pencil a simple shape on the cut surface of each potato half, or use Christmas cookie cutters for patterns. Use a kitchen paring knife to cut away the potato around each design, leaving a raised area that will be the stamp.

Test the potato stamps by pressing them on an ink stamp pad, and then on a piece of scrap paper. Adjust the stamp designs, if necessary. Try different combinations of shapes and colored inks, but use only one ink color on each stamp.

Spread plain brown paper on a flat surface (the unprinted sides of grocery bags work well for this), and let the kids stamp on the designs. Colored wide felt tip markers can be used to add zigzags, dotted lines, and stars around the stamped designs.

The kids also can make stamped ribbons for bows. Cut brown paper into strips of various lengths, and let the kids stamp them. Bend the ends of each strip to meet in the middle, and secure the ends with tape. Stack strip loops on top of each other in order of size, with the largest at the bottom. Wind a short brown paper strip around the loops in the middle, and secure the strip with tape.

TIPS FOR A "GREEN" CHRISTMAS

Set for Green Business

Anyone who works at a desk, including a college student, will appreciate receiving an attractive set of desk accessories as a Christmas gift. Make sure the set includes a refillable pen and pencil, and a desk-top adhesive tape dispenser. These reusable items reduce the need for disposable pens, wooden pencils, and throwaway plastic tape dispensers.

THE KIDS' CORNER

Surprise your special children with wondrous toys, snuggly sweaters, winter-warm mittens, or a hand-painted rocking chair just their size!

WINTER WONDERLAND SWEATERS & HATS

Average: For those with some experience in knitting.

Directions are given for Child's Size 2. Changes for Sizes 4 and 6 are in parentheses.

Materials: Melrose Woolympia yarn (2-ounce skein): 3 (3, 4) skeins of Navy for each sweater, and 1 skein of Navy for each hat; Lion Brand Molaine yarn (40-gram ball): 1 ball each of Red and White; Lion Brand Angora yarn (10-gram ball): 1 ball of Green; 1 pair each size 6 and size 8 knitting needles, OR ANY SIZE NEEDLES TO OBTAIN GAUGE BELOW; 4 stitch holders; stitch markers; tapestry needle; 3-inch cardboard square.

Gauge: On size 8 needles in Stockinette Stitch (st st), 4 sts = 1 inch; 6 rows = 1 inch.

Note: *The tree or snowman motif is worked in duplicate stitch when the sweater is completed.*

SWEATER

Measurements:

SIZES:	2	4	6
BODY CHEST:	21″	23″	25″

Finished Measurements:

CHEST:	23″	25″	27″
WIDTH ACROSS BACK OR FRONT AT UNDERARMS:	11½″	12½″	13½″
WIDTH ACROSS SLEEVE AT UPPER ARM:	8½″	9″	9½″

Directions:

1. Back: With size 6 needles and Navy, cast on 45 (49, 53) sts. ***Ribbing, Row 1 (wrong side):*** P 1, * k 1, p 1; rep from * across. ***Row 2:*** K 1, * p 1, k 1; rep from * across. Work even in ribbing for 2 inches, ending with Row 1; inc 1 st at end of last row. Continue in st st (k 1 row, p 1 row) with size 8 needles on 46 (50, 54) sts until 6 (6½, 7) inches above ribbing, or desired length to underarm, ending with a p row.

2. Raglan Armhole Shaping: Bind off 2 sts at beg of next 2 rows. ***Dec Row:*** K 1, sl 1, k 1, psso, k across until 3 sts rem, k 2 tog, k 1. P 1 row, k 1 row, p 1 row. Rep Dec Row on next row, then every other row until 20 sts remain. Sl sts to a st holder.

3. Front: Work as for the Back until 3 inches above beg of Armhole Shaping. Mark center 12 sts.

4. Neck Shaping: Continuing to work Raglan dec as for the Back, work to first marker, with 2nd strand of yarn, work to next marker, sl center 12 sts to another st holder, work to end. Working each side separately, dec 1 st at each Neck edge on next row, then every other row 3 times more. Continue Raglan dec until 1 st rem. Fasten off.

5. Sleeves: With size 6 needles and Navy, cast on 23 (25, 27) sts. Work in ribbing as for the Back, inc 1 st on last row—24 (26, 28) sts. Change to size 8 needles. Work even in st st for 1 inch. If desired, stripes can be knitted now for the Trees sweater as follows: Work 2 rows of Red, 6 rows of Navy, 2 rows of Red, working incs as indicated. Keeping in st st, inc 1 st each edge on next row, then every 1 inch 4 times more—34 (36, 38) sts. Work even until the Sleeves are 8½ (10½, 11½) inches from beg, or desired length to underarm.

6. Raglan Cap Shaping: Bind off 2 sts at beg of next 2 rows. Dec 1 st at each edge for Back on next row, then every other row 11 (13, 15) times more. Sl rem 6 (4, 2) sts to a st holder.

7. Finishing: Pin the pieces to the finished measurements, dampen the pieces, and let them dry. Sew the left Sleeve to the Back and Front. Sew the right Sleeve to the Front *only*.

8. Neckband: With the right side facing and size 6 needles, k across sts on the Back holder, k sts from the Sleeves, pick up and k 9 (13, 16) sts to the Front holder, k sts from the holder, pick up and k 10 (14, 17) sts to the end—63 (67, 69) sts. Work even in ribbing as for the Back for 4 rows. Bind off in ribbing.

9. Embroidery: Following the chart in FIG. V, 10A or 10B *(page 136)*, work the Trees or Snowman design in duplicate st *(see Stitch Guide, page 270)*. Using the photo as a placement guide, work snowflakes in White straight stitch, and flowers in Red straight stitch. Work the Snowman's mouth in Green straight stitch. Work Navy French knots for the Snowman's eyes and buttons *(see Stitch Guide)*.

10. Finishing: Sew side and Sleeve seams. Sew right Sleeve to the Back.

HAT

Directions:

1. With size 6 needles and Navy, cast on 67 sts. Work in k 1, p 1 ribbing as for the Back for 23 rows; if desired, beg stripe pat on 7th row and work following Step 5. Change to size 8 needles and st st, and work even until 6½ inches above ribbing. ***First Dec Row:*** K 1, * k 2 tog, k 8; rep from * across, end last rep with k 4. Work 1 row even. ***Second Dec Row:*** * K 2 tog, k 8; rep from * across. Work 1 row even. ***Third Dec Row:*** * K 2 tog, k 7; rep from * across. Work 1 row even. ***Fourth Dec Row:*** * K 2 tog, k 6; rep from * across. Work 1 row even. ***Fifth Dec Row:*** * K 2 tog, k 5; rep from * across. For the shorter Hat, work even on 36 sts for 3 inches. For the longer Hat, work even for 6 inches, work 2 rows of Red, work 2 inches of Navy. ***Last Row:*** K 2 tog across. Cut the yarn, leaving a 12-inch end. Thread the yarn through the remaining sts, and draw up tightly. Fasten securely. Sew the back seam, taking care to sew the seam at the cuff on the wrong side.

2. Pompon: Wrap yarn around the cardboard. Slip a separate strand under the yarn at one end, and knot the strand securely. Cut the yarn at the other end. Fasten the pompon to the top of the Hat.

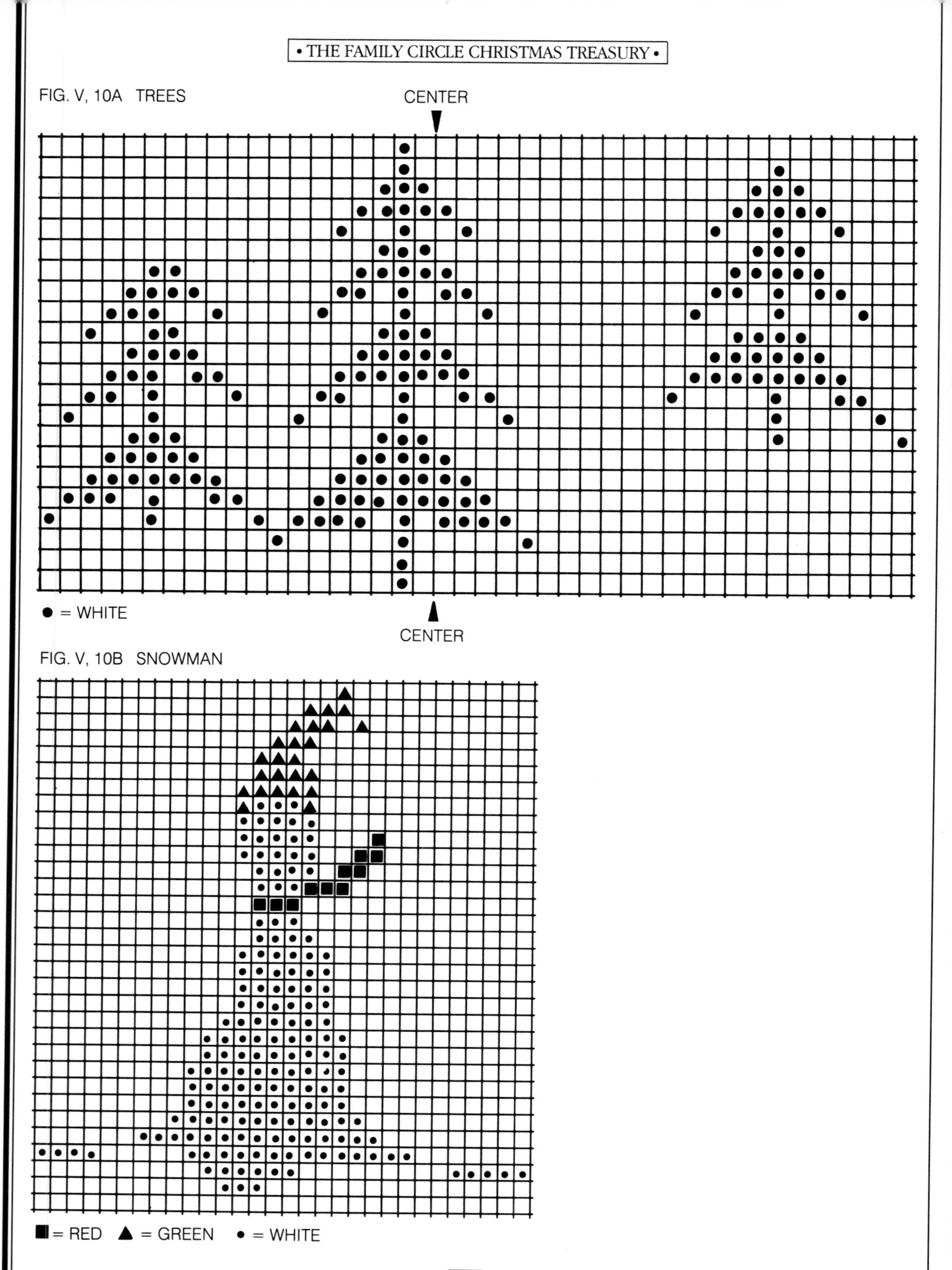

FIG. V, 10A TREES
CENTER
● = WHITE
CENTER
FIG. V, 10B SNOWMAN
■ = RED ▲ = GREEN • = WHITE

MITTEN MAGIC

Average: For those with some experience in knitting.

Directions given for Size 6-7 Years.
Materials: Worsted weight yarn: about 2 ounces of main color (MC), and scraps of other colors indicated for design of your choice in Fig. V, 11A or 11B *(page 138)*; four size 5 double-pointed knitting needles (dp), OR ANY SIZE NEEDLES TO OBTAIN GAUGE BELOW; 2 stitch holders; 4 bobbins; 4 stitch stoppers, or rubber bands; tapestry needle.
Gauge: In Stockinette Stitch (st st), 5 sts = 1 inch; 6½ rows = 1 inch.
Directions:
1. First Mitten: Begin the Mitten on 2 needles. Place the stitch stoppers or rubber bands on the ends of the needles to keep the stitches from falling off. With MC, cast on 30 sts, and work in k 1, p 1 ribbing for 14 rows. Start st st (k 1 row, p 1 row) and the design, following the chart in Fig. V, 11A or 11B, on ***Row 15,*** inc 4 sts evenly; odd numbers are knit rows. Work Santa's beard using 1 bobbin. Work each Reindeer leg with 1 piece of yarn without using a bobbin. Work through Row 20. ***Thumb Increase, Row 21:*** K 16, inc 1 in each of next 2 sts, k 16. ***Row 22:*** P. ***Row 23:*** K 16, inc 1 in next st, k 2, inc 1 in next st, k 16. ***Row 24:*** P. ***Row 25:*** K 16, inc 1 in next st, k 4, inc 1 in next st, k 16. ***Row 26:*** P. Keep inc in this manner, with 2 more sts between incs each time, and work a p row between inc rows. When you have 10 sts between incs, p one more row. ***Next Row:*** K 17, and put on a st holder, k across 12 sts for thumb, and put rem 17 sts on another st holder. Divide the thumb sts on 3 needles, remove the stoppers, and work around 9 rnds evenly. ***Next Rnd:*** * K 1, k 2 tog; rep from * around. ***Next Rnd:*** Work 2 tog across. Run yarn through sts, pull up and fasten off. Slip first sts from holder to right needle, last to left needle. Tie in yarn in front of left needle. Picking up 1 st at base of thumb, work with 2 needles across the last sts and continue to end of chart. ***Row 45:*** * K 1, k 2 tog, k 12, sl 1, k 1, psso; rep from * across. ***Row 46:*** P. ***Row 47:*** * K 1, k 2 tog, k 10, sl 1, k 1, psso; rep from * across. ***Row 48:*** P. Continue like this for 2 more dec rows and 2 more p rows. Divide rem sts equally between 2 needles, and weave top together.
2. Santa, Face: With pale pink, cast on 3 sts, work 2 rows st st, bind off, and sew into a ball. Sew the ball to

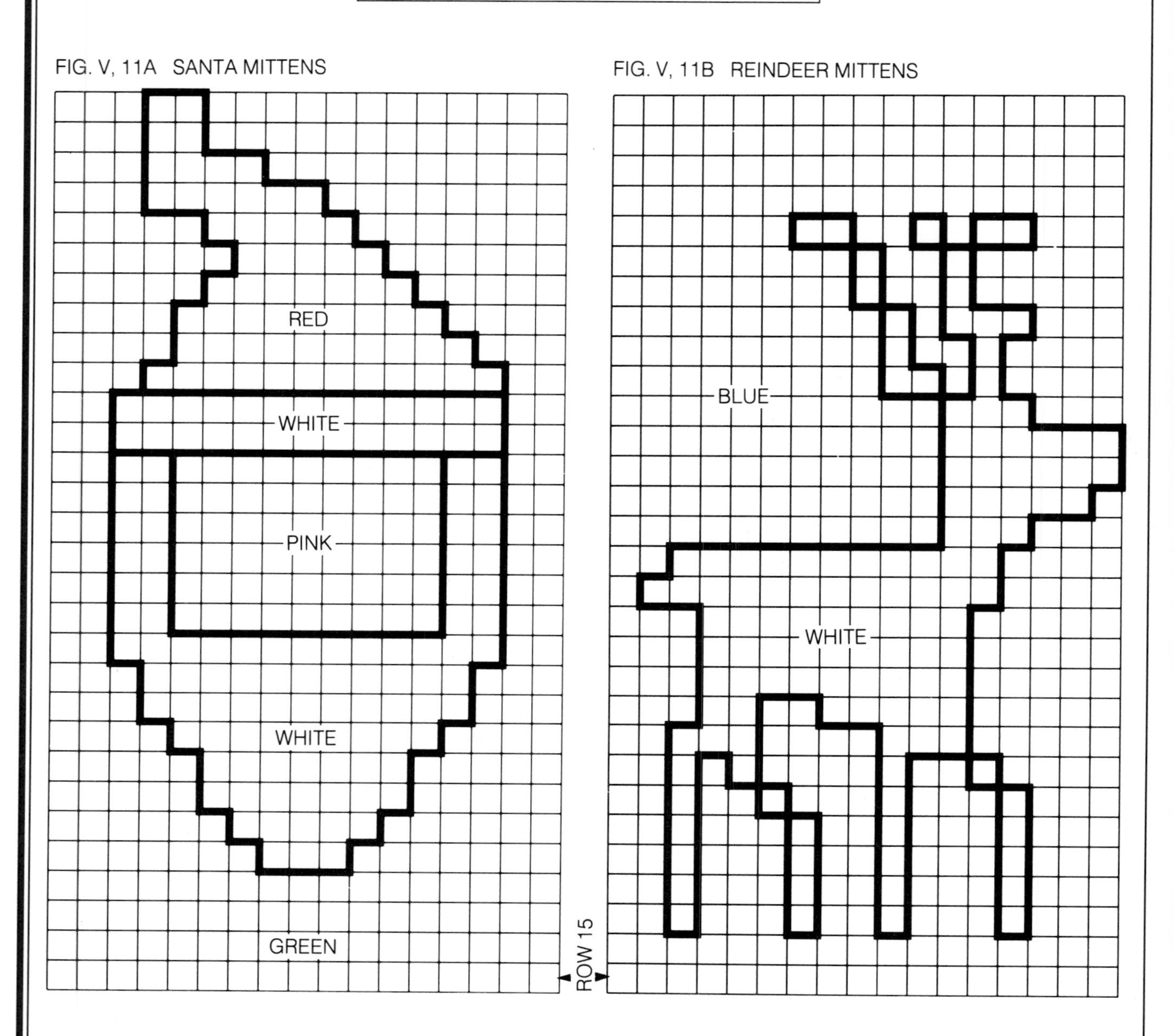

Santa's face for a nose. Work Santa's eyes in blue straight stitch *(see Stitch Guide, page 270, and photo, page 137)*. ***Pompon:*** With white, cast on 5 sts, work 4 rows st st, bind off, and sew into a ball. Sew the ball to the tip of Santa's hat for a pompon.

3. Reindeer: Work the Reindeer's eye with 1 blue French knot, and nose with 1 red French knot. Work 1 red straight stitch for the collar *(see photo and Stitch Guide)*.

4. Second Mitten: Reverse the design, and work it on the other side of the Mitten.

5. Finishing: Sew the side seams using a backstitch. Press the Mittens lightly with a warm steam iron.

FLOWER GIRLS

Make our trio of pretties—Bluebell, Daisy and Rose—to delight any special young girl.

Average: For those with some experience in sewing.

Materials for One Doll: One pastel pink, blue or yellow nylon anklet sock; ¼ yard of 36-inch-wide matching color nylon tulle; 2 yards of ¾-inch-wide matching color nylon lace; 2 ounces of matching color sport yarn; scraps of ⅛-inch-wide matching color ribbon; scraps of matching color embroidery floss, plus Blue and Pink if necessary; matching color and white sewing threads; matching color buttontwist thread; 1 Girls extra-large white cotton sock (shoe size 1-4½); sewing needle; long dollmaking needle; synthetic stuffing; blusher; white glue; strong cardboard.

Directions:

1. Body: Turn the white sock inside out, and lay it flat with the heel up. Pinch up the heel, and fold it toward the toe *(see* FIG. V, 12, *page 140).* Mark, pin and machine-stitch along the solid lines indicated in FIG. V, 12 for the Arms and Legs. Stitch again close to the first rows. Cut apart the Arms and Legs along the broken lines indicated in FIG. V, 12, and trim the seam allowances to ¼ inch. Slit the sock at the toe where indicated in FIG. V, 12, and turn the sock right side out. Stuff the Legs and Body firmly through the slit. Using buttontwist thread, stitch a gathering row around the slit. Pull up the gathers, and fasten the thread securely to close the top of the head.

2. Neck and Arms: Tie a length of buttontwist thread around the Body about 3½ inches from the top of the head to make the neck. Turn the Arms right side out, stuff them, and gather them across their open ends with buttontwist thread. Sew the Arms securely to the Body about ½ inch below the neck.

3. Leotard: Cut off the anklet sock cuff ¾ inch below the ribbing. Tack the front securely to the back at the center top edge of the cuff to make the leotard crotch. Put the leotard on the doll, and roll the leotard's raw edge down around the doll's neck. Tack the leotard to the doll at each shoulder. Cut a 14-inch length of lace, and sew a gathering row with buttontwist thread along the lace's straight long edge. Draw up the thread, wrap the lace twice around one doll shoulder, and sew the lace in place. Repeat on the other doll shoulder. Glue a ribbon choker around the doll's neck over the leotard. Tie a matching color embroidery floss bow around each wrist and ankle, and secure the bows with a drop of glue.

4. *Tutu:* Cut a 6 x 36-inch tulle strip, and stitch lace along one edge. Fold the strip in half lengthwise to 3 inches. Using buttontwist thread, sew long gathering stitches through both layers down the strip's long center. Gather the tutu, lace edge on top, to fit around the doll's waist. Knot the thread, and glue the knot in place.
5. *Braids:* Lightly mark a center "part" line on the head from the forehead to the nape of the neck. Cut the yarn into 18-inch-long strands. Center the strands on the head at the "part" line. Starting at the forehead, hand-sew the yarn hair, very close together, to the head along the "part" line. Tie thread around the hair at each side of the head, and tack the ties to the head. Braid the hair below each tie into three braids, and trim the ends evenly. Bend each set of braids upward into a loop, and tie the loop in place with a ribbon bow *(see Blue Doll in photo, page 139).*
6. *Short Curls:* Wrap the yarn around a 2 x 12-inch cardboard strip; do not cut the yarn. Slide the yarn carefully off the cardboard onto the sewing machine, and stitch down the middle of the yarn. Continue to wrap and stitch yarn until you have a 40-inch-long strip of loops. Lightly mark the hairline around the head. Starting at the back of the head, hand-sew the yarn hair, along its stitch line, across the head from side to side. Tie a ribbon bow around the head for a headband *(see Yellow Doll in photo).*
7. *Pony Tail:* Wrap the yarn closely around a 4½ x 10-inch cardboard rectangle; do not cut the yarn. Slide the yarn carefully off the cardboard onto the sewing machine, and stitch ⅜ inch from the folds on one side. Lightly mark the hairline around the head. Starting and ending at the nape of the neck, hand-sew the yarn hair along its stitch line to the hairline *(see Pink Doll in photo).* Cut twenty 18-inch-long strands of yarn, and braid or twist them together. Tack

FIG. V, 12 FLOWER GIRLS

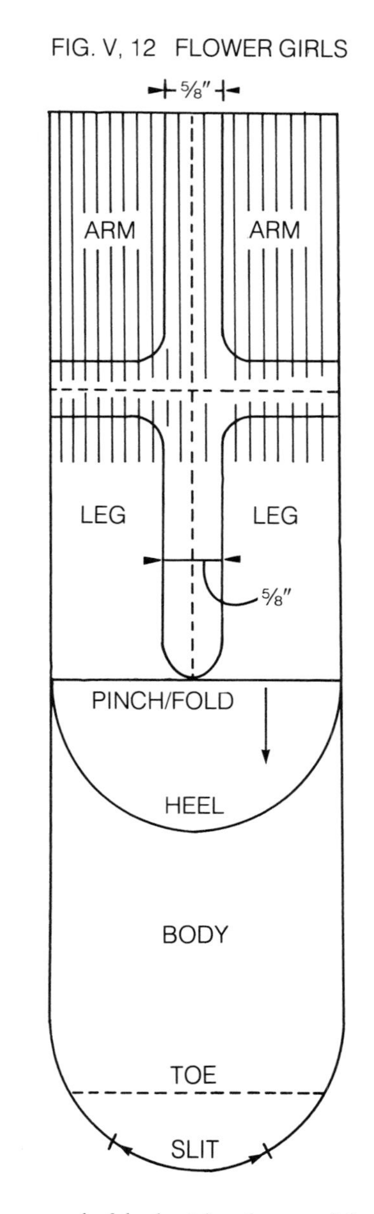

one end of the braid to the top of the head. Gather the yarn hair's loose folded edges around the tacked braid, wrap the loose edges with buttontwist thread, and tie the thread securely. Tie a ribbon bow around the thread.
8. *Face:* Pin mark the eyes and mouth. Using three strands of floss in the long needle, and entering and exiting through the side of the head to hide the starting and ending knots, work a Pink fly stitch for the mouth, and three Blue French knots for each eye *(see Stitch Guide, page 270).* Pat a little blusher on the doll's cheeks.

BUTTERCUP BABY SET

Average: For those with some experience in crocheting.

Directions given for Size 6 Months.
Materials: Coats & Clark Red Heart® Sofspun Baby Pompadour yarn: 8 ounces of Baby Yellow, and a few yards each of Light Pink, Baby Blue and White; size B crochet hook, OR ANY SIZE HOOK TO OBTAIN GAUGE BELOW; size 7 knitting needle; embroidery floss: ½ yard each of Green and Yellow; 3 yards of ¼-inch-wide yellow ribbon; safety pins; masking tape; tapestry needle; 2 small buttons.
Gauge: 11 ch st = 2 inches; 11 dc = 2 inches; 8 dc rows = 3 inches.

SACQUE
Directions:
1. *Right Front Section:* The Sacque is worked in one piece. Starting at the Right Front edge with Baby Yellow, ch 51. ***Row 1:*** Sc in 2nd ch from hook and in next 11 ch for yoke section; place a contrasting color thread between last and next st, and carry up on every row to separate yoke from lower section; dc in each remaining ch—50 sts. Mark this row for the right side. Ch 3, turn. ***Row 2:*** Dc in back lp of next dc and in back lp of each dc to thread marker, sc in back lp of each sc across. Ch 1, turn. ***Row 3:*** Sc in back lp of each sc to thread marker, dc in back lp of each dc to ch-3, dc in top of ch-3. Ch 3, turn. ***Rows 4 to 13:*** Rep Rows 2 and 3. ***Row 14:*** Dc in back lp of next 25 dc, do not work over remaining sts—26 dc counting ch-3 as 1 dc. Ch 3, turn. ***Row 15:*** Dc in back lp of each dc to ch-3, dc in top of ch-3. Mark last dc worked with a safety pin. Fasten off.
2. *Right Sleeve:* Starting at Sleeve seam, ch 28. ***Row 1 (right side):*** Dc in 4th ch from hook and in each ch across—26 dc counting ch-3 as 1 dc.

Ch 3, turn. ***Row 2:*** Dc in back lp of next 24 dc, dc in top of ch-3, with wrong side of previous section facing, dc in back lp of first free dc on last long row worked and in back lp of next 11 dc to thread marker, sc in back lp of each sc across — 50 sts counting ch-3 as 1 dc. Ch 1, turn. ***Row 3:*** Rep Row 3 of Right Front Section. ***Rows 4 to 17:*** Rep Rows 2 and 3 of Right Front Section. ***Row 18:*** Rep Row 14 of Right Front Section. Fasten off.

3. Back Section: With the wrong side of the Right Front Section facing, join yarn to dc marked with a safety pin. ***Joining Row:*** Ch 3, dc in back lp of next 25 dc, with wrong side of Sleeve facing, dc in back lp of first free dc on last long row worked and in back lp of each dc to thread marker, sc in back lp of each sc across — 50 sts counting ch-3 as 1 dc. Ch 1, turn. ***Row 1:*** Rep Row 3 of Right Front Section. ***Rows 2 to 27:*** Rep Rows 2 and 3 of Right Front Section. ***Rows 28 to 29:*** Rep Rows 14 and 15 of Right Front Section. Fasten off.

4. Left Sleeve: Work as for the Right Sleeve.

5. Left Front Section: With the wrong side of the Back Section facing, join the yarn to the dc marked with a safety pin. ***Joining Row:*** Work as for Joining Row of Back Section. ***Row 1:*** Rep Row 3 of Right Front Section. ***Rows 2 to 11:*** Rep Rows 2 and 3 of Right Front Section. ***Row 12:*** Rep Row 2 of Right Front Section. Fasten off. Sew the Sleeve and underarm seams.

6. Beading Row: With the right side facing, join the yarn to the Right Front neck corner. ***Row 1:*** Ch 3, dc in end st of next row and each row along neck edge — 86 dc counting ch-3 as 1 dc. Do not turn.

7. Scallop Edging, Rnd 1: Ch 3, dc in base of ch-3, skip ½ inch along Left Front edge, sl st in edge, * ch 3, dc in same place where sl st was made, skip ½ inch along edge, sl st in edge. Rep from * along Left Front edge, lower edge, Right Front edge, and neck edge. Fasten off. Sew the buttons on 1 Front edge to correspond to the first and third loop of the Scallop Edging on the opposite Front edge.

8. Sleeve Edging: With the right side of the Sleeve facing, join the yarn to the seam at the lower edge. ***Rnd 1:*** Ch 3, dc in same place where yarn was joined, skip ½ inch along edge, sl st in edge, * ch 3, dc in same place where sl st was made, skip ½ inch along edge, sl st in edge. Rep from * around. Fasten off. Cut a 30-inch length of ribbon, and lace it through the Beading Row, working over 2 dc and under 2 dc across.

9. Flowers: Make 2 Flowers each of Light Pink, Baby Blue and White. Cut a 36-inch length of yarn. Leaving a 3-inch end, tape the yarn lightly to the knitting needle just below the tip. With your left hand, hold the yarn on the needle 3 inches from the tape to form a 6-inch loop. Hold the loop in place with your left thumb. With your right hand, wind the remainder of the yarn 25 times around the needle to cover the taped loop, keeping the wound strand together. Holding the wound strand in place with your left forefinger, remove the tape. Grasp the strands of the taped loop firmly, slip them off the needle, pull them together, and tie them securely. Using the photo on page 141 as a placement guide, sew 1 Flower of each color to the Right Front Section below the yoke. Rep on the Left Front Section. Using the embroidery floss and tapestry needle, work a Yellow French knot at each Flower center. Work leaves around the outer edges of the Flowers in Green lazy daisy stitch *(see Stitch Guide, page 270).*

BOOTIES

Directions:

1. Cuff: Starting at the narrow edge with Baby Yellow, ch 15. ***Row 1:*** Sc in 2nd ch from hook and in each ch across — 14 sc. Ch 1, turn. ***Row 2:*** Sc in back lp of each sc across. Ch 1, turn. ***Rows 3 to 30:*** Rep Row 2. At the end of the last row, ch 1. Do not turn.

2. Lower Section, Rnd 1: Working along the next long edge, sc in end st of each row across. Join with sl st to first sc — 30 sc. ***Rnds 2 to 4:*** Ch 1, sc in joining and in each sc around. Join as before. ***Rnd 5:*** Ch 1, sc in joining, sc in next 12 sc, mark last st worked with a safety pin, 2 sc in next sc, sc in next 2 sc, 2 sc in next sc, sc in next sc, mark last st worked with a safety pin, sc in each remaining sc around, join — 32 sc. Move the safety pins up on every rnd. ***Rnd 6:*** Sc in joining and in each sc around. Join. ***Rnd 7:*** Sc in joining and in each sc to marked sc, sc in marked sc, 2 sc in next sc, sc in each sc to 1 sc before next marked sc, 2 sc in next sc, sc in marked sc and in each remaining sc around. Join. There are 2 sc more than on previous rnd. ***Rnds 8 to 13:*** Rep Rnds 6 and 7 — 40 sc on last rnd. ***Rnd 14:*** Ch 1, sc in joining and in each sc around. Join. Fasten off, leaving a 10-inch end for sewing. Fold the lower edge so marked sts are together; sew edges together. Remove safety pins. Sew narrow edges of the cuff together.

3. Tie: Cut two 16-inch lengths of ribbon. Lace a length through the sts on Rnd 2 of each Bootie, weaving over 1 sc and under 1 sc around.

BONNET

Directions:

1. Front Section: Starting at the front edge with Baby Yellow, ch 79. ***Row 1:*** Dc in 4th ch from hook and in each ch across — 76 dc counting ch-3 as 1 dc. Mark this row for the right side of the work. Ch 3, turn. ***Rows 2 to 12:*** Dc in back lp of next dc and in each dc to ch-3, dc in top of ch-3. Ch 3, turn. Fasten off.

2. Center Back Section, Row 1: With right side facing, skip first 25 dc on previous row, join yarn to next dc, ch 3, dc in back lp of next 25 dc; do not work over remaining sts — 26 dc.

Ch 3, turn. ***Row 2:*** Dc in back lp of next dc and in each dc to ch-3, dc in top of ch-3. Ch 3, turn. ***Row 3:*** *Holding back on the hook the last lp of each dc, dc in back lp of next 2 dc, yo and draw through all 3 lps on hook*—**dec made;** dc in back lp of next dc and in each dc to last dc and ch-3, dec over last dc and the ch-3—24 dc. Ch 3, turn. ***Rows 4 to 11:*** Rep Rows 2 and 3—16 dc on last row. ***Row 12:*** Rep Row 2. Fasten off. Sew the side edges of Center Back Section to adjacent free sts on Front Section.
3. Scallop Edging: With the right side facing, join the yarn to the lower left front corner of the Bonnet. Working along the neck and front edges, work the Scallop Edging following Sacque, Step 7.
4. Flowers: Make the Flowers following Sacque, Step 9. Sew 1 Flower of each color at each corner of the Bonnet. Embroider the Flower centers and leaves following Sacque, Step 9. Cut a 32-inch length of ribbon, and lace it through the Scallop Edging along the Bonnet neck edge.

RUFFLES & LACE LAYETTE

(photo, page 141; quilt: about 26 x 36 inches, plus ruffle; pillow: 11 inches square, plus ruffle)

Average: For those with some experience in sewing.

QUILT

Materials: 5 feet of 45-inch-wide ivory chintz cotton fabric; 1 yard of 45-inch-wide lace square fabric; 5 yards of 5-inch-wide white ruffled eyelet lace; 12 yards of ¼-inch-wide apricot satin ribbon; apricot and white sewing threads; white buttontwist thread; synthetic batting; large sewing needle; long needle with large eye.

Note: *The directions are based on a lace square fabric with 5¾-inch squares. If fabric with larger or smaller squares is used, the quilt's measurements change accordingly.*

Directions:

1. Cut the lace fabric into a 5-square by 6-square rectangle, or about 28 x 34 inches. Cut two chintz rectangles and two batting rectangles to match. Baste the wrong side of the lace rectangle to the right side of one chintz rectangle. Pin the ruffled eyelet to the lace rectangle right sides together, folding in an extra inch of ruffle at each corner, and having the ruffle's raw ends meet at the center bottom of the rectangle. Using a ¼-inch seam allowance, sew the ruffle's raw ends together. Press the seam open, and topstitch. Baste around the edges of the rectangle.
2. Pin the remaining chintz rectangle to the lace rectangle right sides together, with the ruffle in between. Using a ½-inch seam allowance, stitch around three sides and four corners, leaving a 12-inch opening at the bottom. Trim the seams, but do not turn the quilt right side out yet.
3. Place the batting rectangles underneath the quilt's bottom chintz rectangle. Sew the batting to the quilt along the stitching line, leaving the 12-inch opening at the bottom. Trim the seams, and turn the quilt right side out. Turn in the open edges, and slipstitch the opening closed *(see Stitch Guide, page 270).*
4. Thread the sewing needle with the buttontwist thread. Working from front to back so the knots will be on the front, tack together the quilt front and back at each corner of the lace squares; ribbon bows will cover the thread knots.
5. Cut the ribbon into eight 5-inch lengths, and twenty-four 16-inch lengths. Using the long needle, thread a 16-inch ribbon lengthwise through the lace between two squares *(see photo)*; leave about 5 inches of ribbon at each end. Repeat to complete the row. Repeat on the remaining lengthwise rows. There should be two 5-inch-long ribbon ends at each corner of the lace squares; tie the ribbon ends into bows. There should be an extra 5 inches of ribbon at each end of the ribbon rows. Sew one end of a 5-inch ribbon to the quilt where the quilt joins the ruffle at each end of the ribbon rows, and tie a bow. The completed quilt should have 28 bows.

PILLOW

Materials: 1 yard of ivory chintz cotton fabric used in Quilt; ½ yard of lace square fabric used in Quilt; 1½ yards of white ruffled eyelet lace used in Quilt; apricot and white sewing threads; 42 inches of ¼-inch-wide apricot satin ribbon; synthetic stuffing; long needle with large eye.

Directions:

1. Cut the lace fabric into a 12-inch square, or about 2 lace squares by 2 lace squares. Cut two chintz squares to match. Assemble the pillow following Quilt, Steps 1 and 2. Trim the seams, and clip the corners. Turn the pillow right side out, and stuff it. Turn in the open edges, and slipstitch the opening closed.
2. Finish the pillow following Quilt, Step 5; place the ribbons at right angles to each other down the center of the pillow *(see photo).*

PENNSYLVANIA DUTCH CHILD'S ROCKING CHAIR

Average: For those with some experience in woodworking and decorative painting.

Materials: ½-inch-thick birch plywood; 1-inch finishing nails; wood glue; graphite paper; stylus or dry ballpoint pen; fine sandpaper; tack cloth; yellow oxide, chromium green, red, blue and white acrylic paints; paintbrush; artist's paintbrushes; sabre saw, or scroll saw; hammer; tracing paper for patterns.

Directions:

1. Draw the chair back and seat on plywood following the measurements in FIG. V, 13A. Enlarge the chair side pattern in FIG. V, 13B onto tracing paper, following the directions on page 271. Enlarge the patterns for the chair back top and front seat brace designs in FIGS. V, 13C and 13D *(pages 146-147)* onto tracing paper, following the directions on page 271. Using the graphite paper and stylus or dry ballpoint pen, transfer the shape of the chair back top to the chair back. Transfer the chair side pattern and the front seat brace shape to the plywood.

2. Cut out the chair pieces. Using glue and nails, assemble the rocking chair following the diagram in FIG. V, 13A. Let the glue dry completely. Sand the chair smooth, and wipe off all the sawdust with the tack cloth.

3. Paint the chair with two coats of yellow oxide, letting the paint dry between coats.

4. Transfer the designs for the chair back and front seat brace to the chair parts. Using the artist's paintbrushes, and the photo as a color guide, paint the designs.

FIG. V, 13A ASSEMBLY DIAGRAM

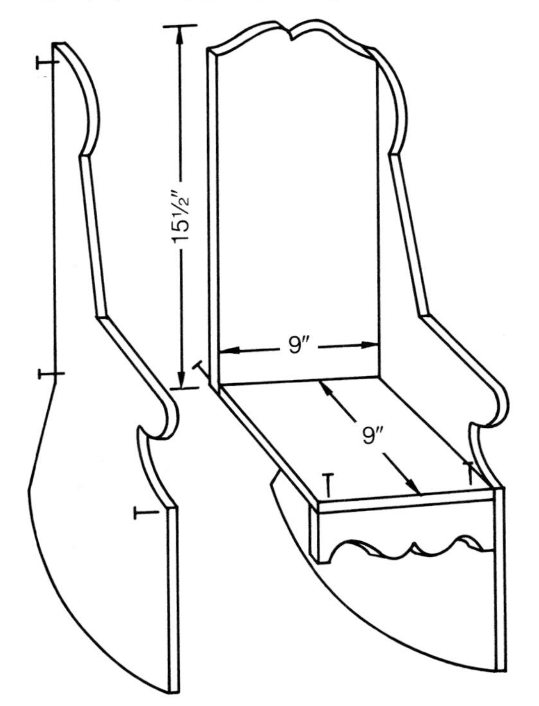

FIG. V, 13B PENNSYLVANIA DUTCH CHILD'S ROCKING CHAIR SIDE 1 SQ. = 1"

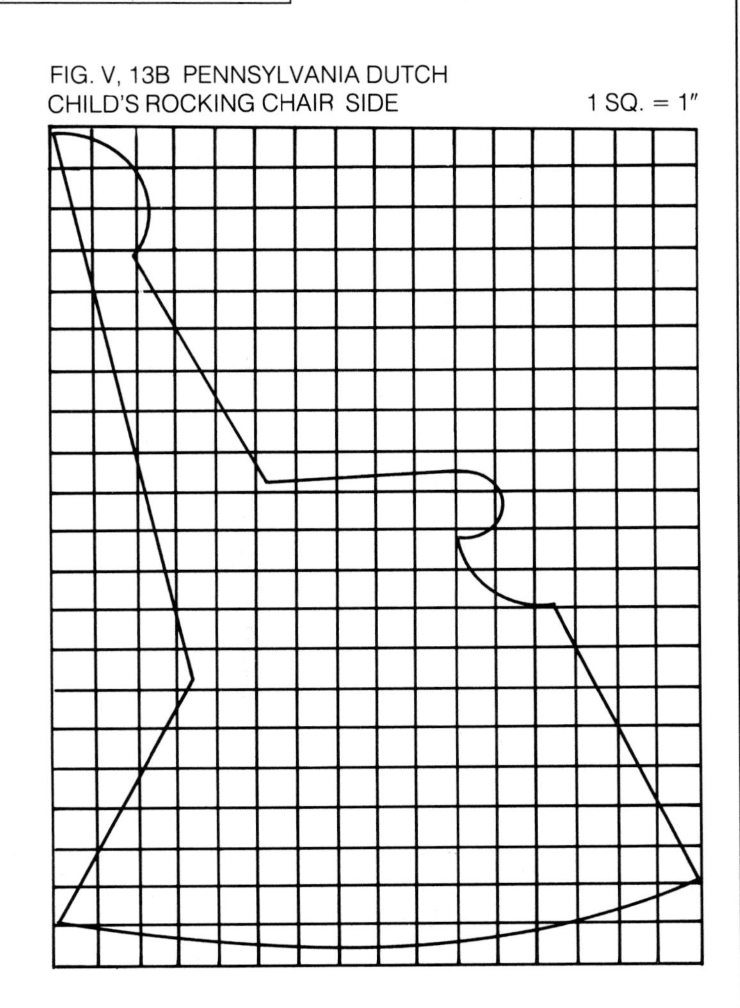

FIG. V, 13C CHAIR BACK TOP 1 SQ. = 1″

FIG. V, 13D FRONT SEAT BRACE 1 SQ. = 1″

THE BEAR NECESSITIES

A set of wonderful wooden bear toys to delight both girls and boys.

Average: For those with some experience in woodworking.

TEDDY PULL TOY

(4 x 7½ x 10 inches)

Materials: 12 inches of 1 x 12 pine lumber; ¼-inch-diameter wooden dowel; 1-inch-diameter round wooden knob; four 2-inch-diameter flat wooden knobs; 1 yard of red cord; wood glue; graphite paper; stylus or dry ballpoint pen; sandpaper; tack cloth; red, blue, beige and black acrylic paints; paintbrush; artist's paintbrush; jigsaw, or sabre saw; drill with ¼-inch bit; clamp; tracing paper for pattern.

Cutting Directions

Code	***Pieces***	***Size***
A (PINE)	1	¾" x 7" x 9" Bears
B (PINE)	2	¾" x 1¼" x 7½" Frames
C (DOW)	2	¼" dia. x 3¼" Axles
D	4	2" dia. Wheels

Directions:

1. Cut the toy parts to size. Enlarge the bears pattern in Fig. V, 14A onto tracing paper, following the directions on page 271. Using the graphite paper and stylus or dry ballpoint pen, transfer the solid pattern lines to the A bears wood piece. Cut out the bears along the outside line. Cut the inside line that separates the parent from the baby bear.

2. Drill a ¼-inch-diameter hole, centered, ⅝ inch in from each end of the B frames. Drill a ¼-inch-diameter hole in each D flat knob wheel to accommodate the C axles, and in the round knob to accommodate the cord *(see* Fig. V, 14B, *page 150).*

3. Sand all the wood pieces smooth, sanding the A bears' inside edges lightly for a snug fit. Wipe off all the sawdust with the tack cloth.

(Continued on page 150)

FIG. V, 14A TEDDY PULL TOY

1 SQ. = 1″

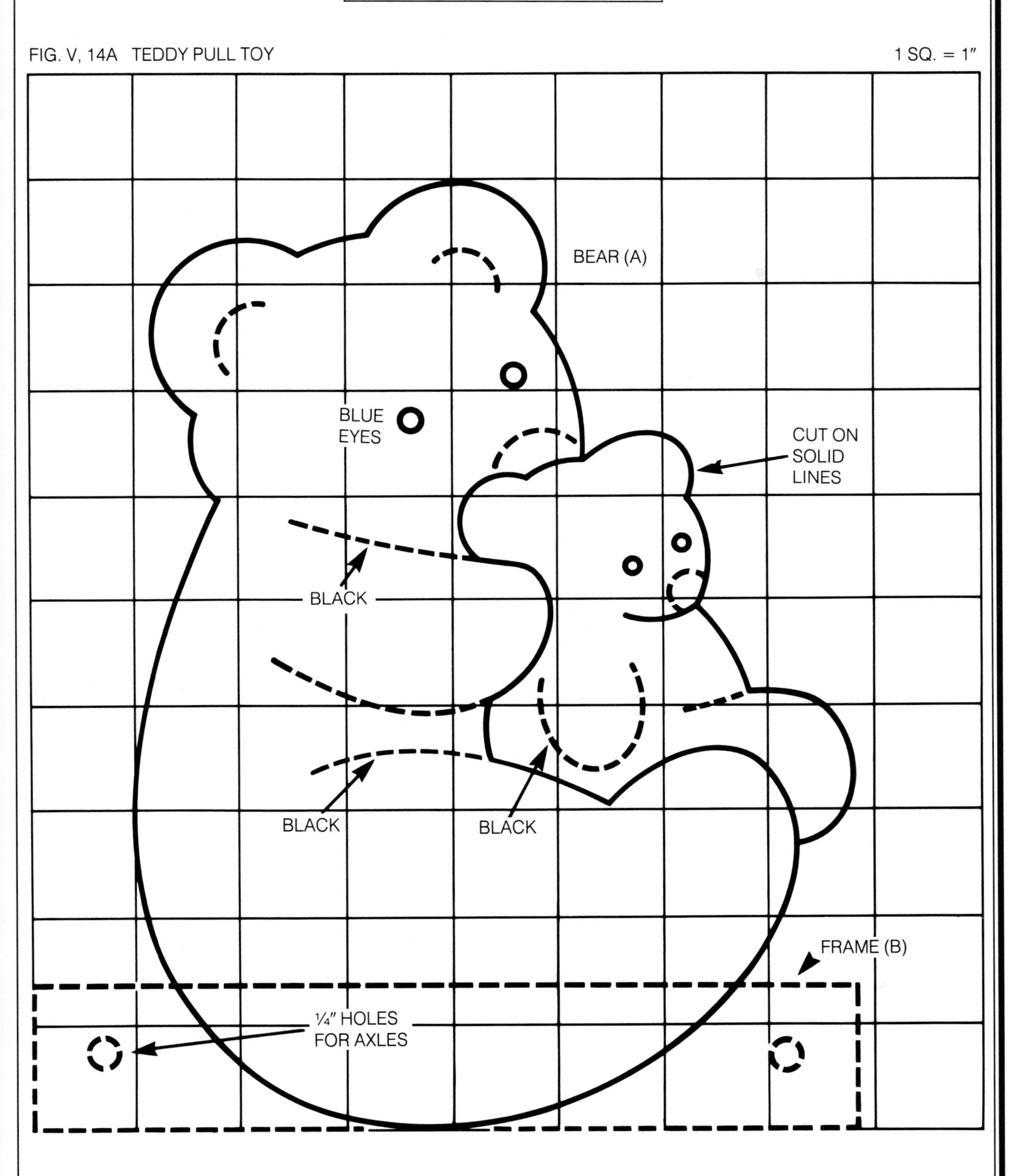

4. Paint the A bears beige. Paint the B frames red. Paint the D flat knob wheels and the round knob blue. Transfer the bear features to both sides of the A bears. Using the artist's paintbrush, and following FIG. V, 14A *(page 149)*, paint the bear features.
5. Place the C axles in the holes of the B frames. Glue the A bears between the B frames centered lengthwise, and flush at the bottom *(see* FIG. V, 14A*)*. Clamp all the pieces to hold them in place, making sure the C axles are straight and square. Let the glue dry completely.
6. Glue a D flat knob wheel on each end of the C axles. Feed one end of the cord into the hole in the round knob, and glue the end in place. Tie the other end of the cord around the front C axle.

FIG. V, 14B ASSEMBLY DIAGRAM

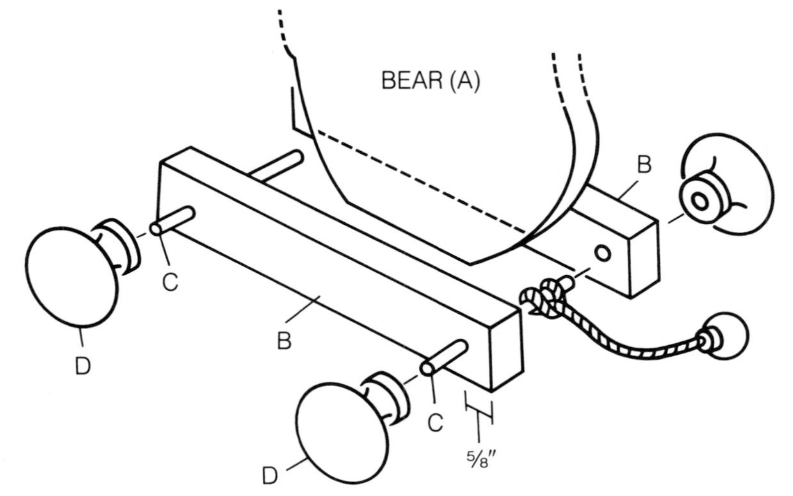

FIG. V, 14C BABY BEAR PUZZLE FULL SIZE

BEAR FAMILY PUZZLES
Materials: 3/4 x 10 x 24 inches of birch plywood; wood glue; graphite paper; stylus or dry ballpoint pen; sandpaper; tack cloth; butcher's wax; clean cloth; jigsaw, or sabre saw; drill with 1/4-inch bit; tracing paper.
Directions:
1. Cut the plywood into four 5 x 7½-inch pieces, and two 4 x 5-inch pieces. Glue together pairs of the same size pieces to form two pieces measuring 1½ x 5 x 7½ inches, and one piece measuring 1½ x 4 x 5 inches.
2. Trace the full-size baby bear pattern in FIG. V, 14C onto tracing paper. Trace the full-size mama bear and papa bear half patterns in FIG. V, 14D onto folded sheets of tracing paper. Trace the patterns onto the other halves of the papers, and open the papers for the full patterns. Using the graphite paper and stylus or dry ballpoint pen, transfer all the patterns to the plywood.
3. Cut out the bear shapes. Cut the puzzle lines. Cut out the papa bear's bow tie by drilling through the center of the tie, putting the saw blade in the hole, and cutting. Drill the eye holes to the depth of the bit angle.
4. Sand the puzzle pieces smooth, and wipe off all the sawdust with the tack cloth. Coat the puzzle pieces with the butcher's wax.

FIG. V, 14D MAMA & PAPA BEAR PUZZLES

FULL SIZE

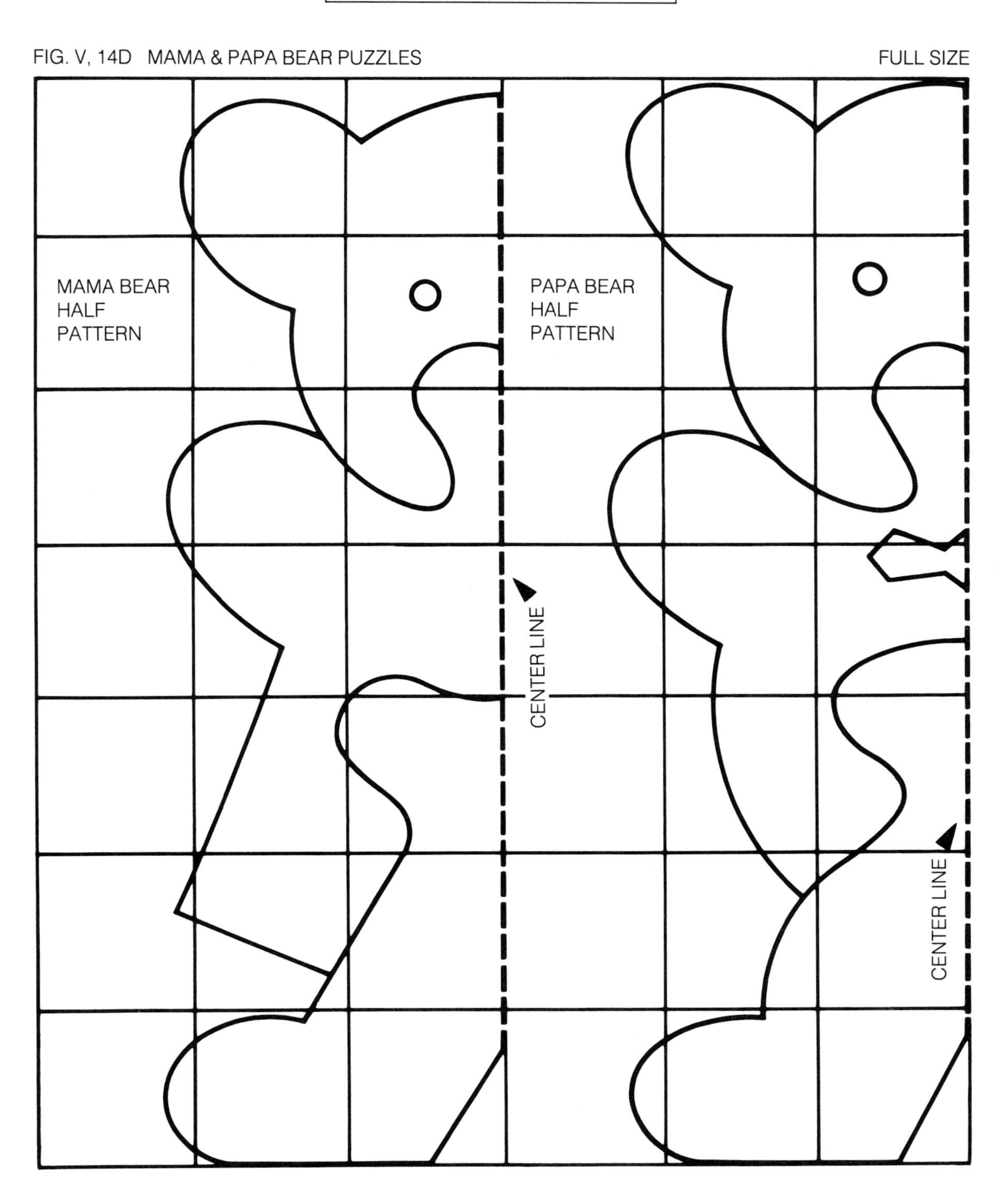

TIPS FOR A "GREEN" CHRISTMAS

Pooling Your Resources

During the Christmas shopping season, you and every one of your friends are bound to make one trip to the mall. Why not join forces and car pool?

Car pooling is a wonderful idea any time of year, but especially during the busy holiday season. By taking one car at a time, you'll all save on fuel. Plus, you'll have an easier time parking one car in the crowded mall parking lot.

Try organizing a neighborhood "pooling" system to take some of the bother out of holiday trips to the mall, post office, supermarket, and even to pick up the kids at school.

BEAR CLOTHES RACK

Materials: 14 inches of 1 x 10 pine lumber; two 2-inch-diameter wooden door pulls; graphite paper; stylus or dry ballpoint pen; sandpaper; tack cloth; red, blue, yellow, green, beige and black acrylic paints; paintbrush; artist's paintbrushes; jigsaw, or sabre saw; drill with small bit; 2 sawtooth hangers; paper for pattern.

Directions:

1. Enlarge the bears pattern in Fig. V, 14E onto paper, following the directions on page 271. Using the graphite paper and stylus or dry ballpoint pen, transfer the solid pattern line to the pine. Cut out the bears. Do not cut between the bears; the rack is one piece joined at the bears' feet.

2. Sand the rack and door pulls smooth, and wipe off all the sawdust with the tack cloth.

3. Paint the rack beige. Transfer the bear features to the rack, and the ball designs to the door pulls. Using the artist's paintbrushes, and following Fig. V, 14E, paint the bear features and ball designs. Let dry completely.

4. Drill shallow starter holes in the rack where indicated in Fig. V, 14E for the door pulls. Screw the door pulls in place.

5. Attach a sawtooth hanger to the back of each bear's head, making sure the hangers are level.

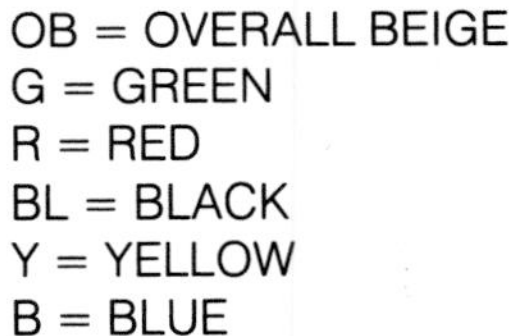

FIG. V, 14E BEAR CLOTHES RACK

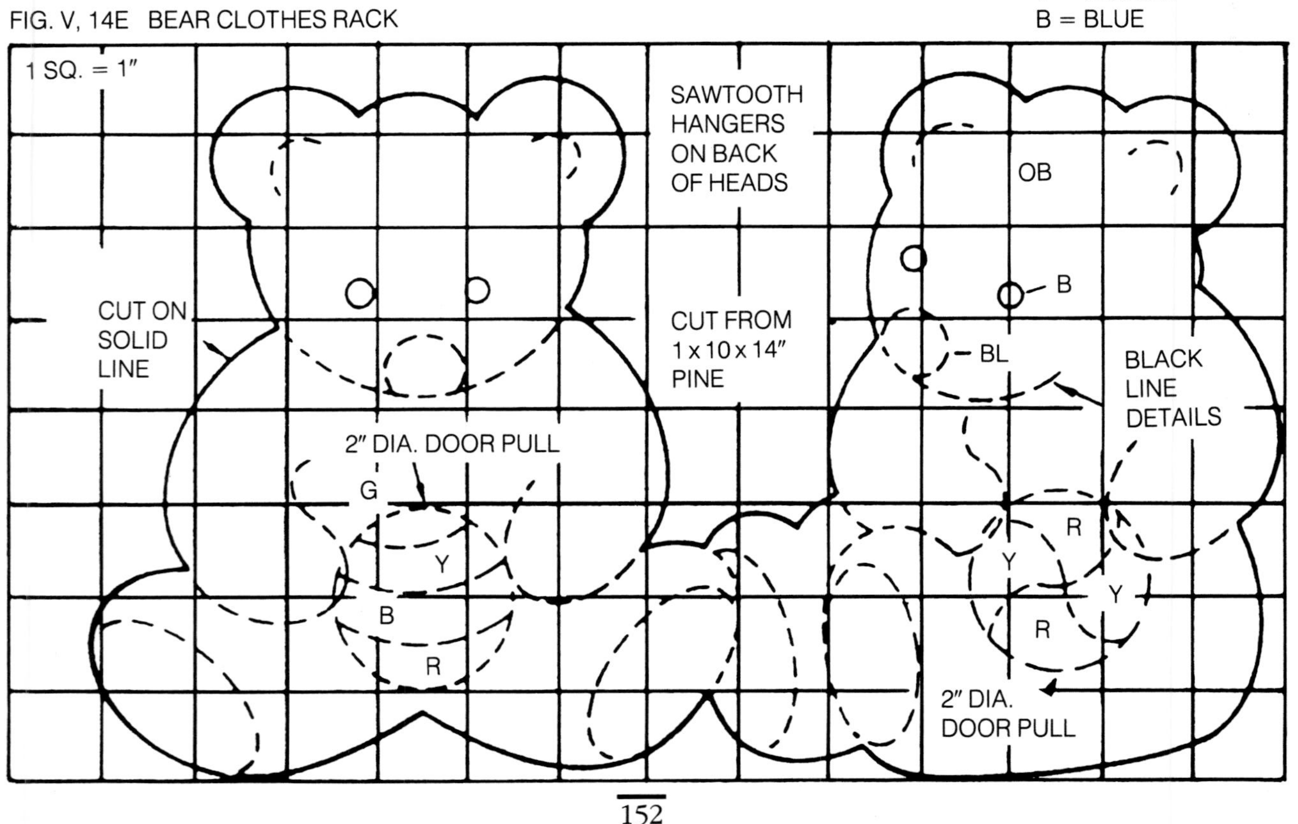

PULL-ALONG DINOSAUR

Average: For those with some experience in woodworking.

Materials: 3 feet of 6-inch-wide, ½-inch-thick clear pine or hardwood; ¼-inch- and 1½-inch-diameter wooden dowels; large wooden bead; two 72-inch-long rawhide shoestrings; white glue; graphite paper; stylus or dry ballpoint pen; sandpaper; tack cloth; jigsaw, or coping saw; drill with assorted bits; paper for pattern.

Directions:

1. Enlarge the dinosaur pattern in Fig. V, 15 *(page 154)* onto paper, following the directions on page 271. Using the graphite paper and stylus or dry ballpoint pen, transfer the pattern pieces to the pine or hardwood, laying the pieces so the wood grain runs up and down the dinosaur body. Transfer two hind legs, two front legs, and one each of the body pieces.

2. Cut out the dinosaur parts. From the 1½-inch-diameter dowel, cut four ½-inch-thick circles for wheels. From the ¼-inch-diameter dowel, cut two 4-inch lengths for axles, and two 2½-inch lengths for pegs.

3. Drill 5/16-inch-diameter holes through the feet on the front and hind legs so the axles will revolve freely. Drill ¼-inch-diameter holes through the tops of the front and hind legs, and through the body pieces where the legs will be attached *(see circles on pattern in* Fig. V, 15*)*. Drill ¼-inch-diameter holes through the centers of the wheels. Drill small holes, just enough for the rawhide shoestring to slip through easily, where the body pieces will be connected, and at the dinosaur's mouth and eye *(see dots on pattern in* Fig. V, 15*)*. Sand the pieces smooth, and wipe off all the sawdust with the tack cloth.

4. Using one rawhide shoestring, cut and thread a length of rawhide through each small hole where the body pieces will be connected. Tie the body pieces together with the rawhide, tying each pair of lengths into a square knot on each side of the body. Trim the rawhide ends, and place a dot of glue on each end to prevent the rawhide from untying.

5. Place generous amounts of glue around the ¼-inch-diameter body and leg holes. Slip the pegs into the body holes, and attach the legs to the ends of the pegs, making sure the peg ends are flush with the legs' outside

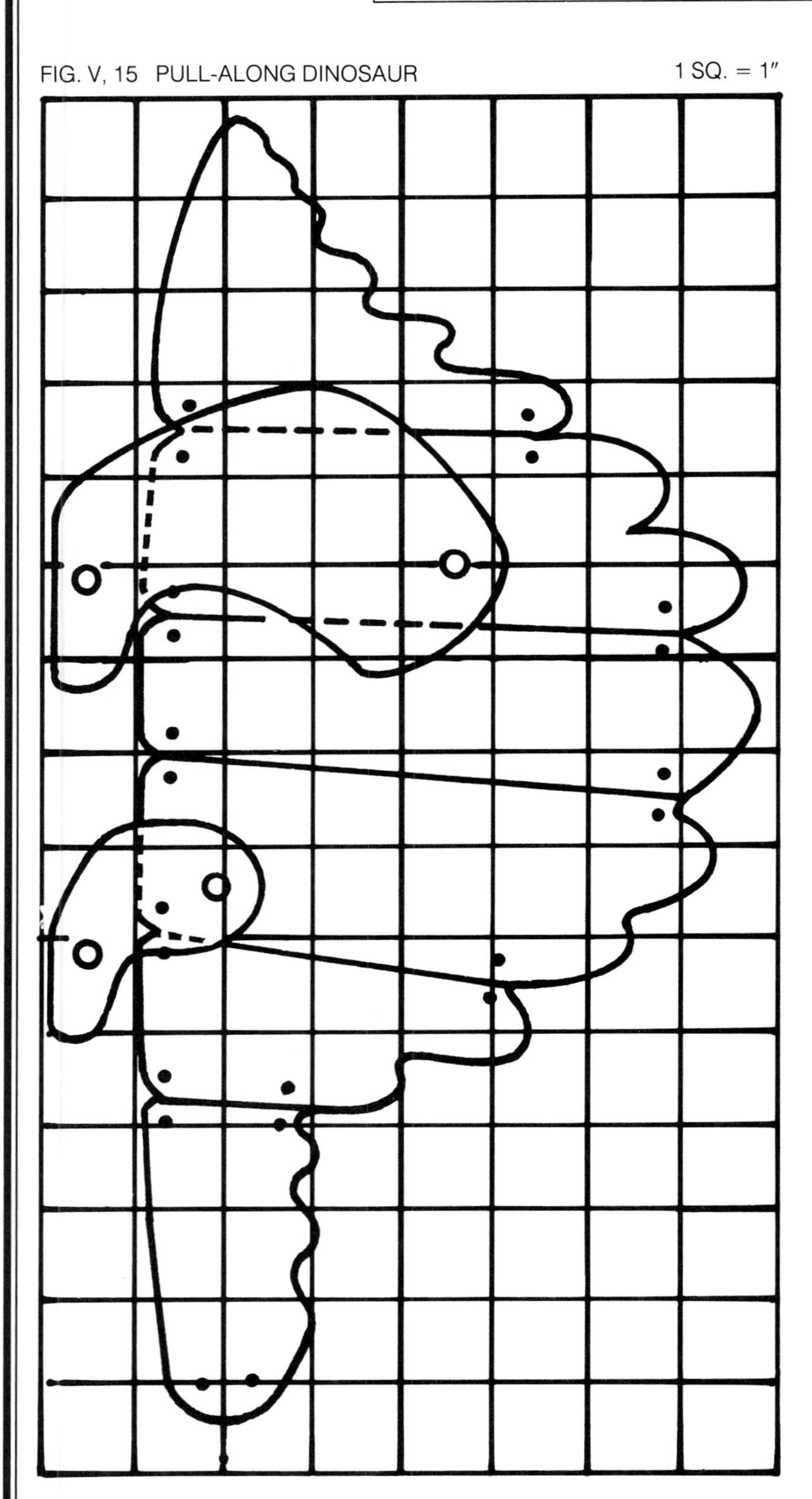

edges. Slip the axles through the holes in the feet, and glue a wheel flush on each end. Before the glue dries, angle the legs properly so all the wheels touch the ground. Let the glue dry completely.

6. Sand the ends of the pegs and axles. Thread and tie one end of the remaining rawhide shoestring through the hole at the dinosaur's mouth. Tie the wooden bead to the other end of the shoestring for a pull.

SIT-ON LOCOMOTIVE

(8 x 11 x 22 inches)

Challenging: Requires more experience in woodworking.

Materials: 48 inches of 5/4 x 6 pine lumber; 5 feet of 1 x 8 pine lumber; 7 feet of 1/4 x 1-inch, and 12 feet of 1/4 x 5/8-inch lattice; 1 1/4-inch-diameter clothes pole dowel; 1-inch-, 7/8-inch-, 1/2-inch- and 3/8-inch-diameter wooden dowels; 3 1/2-inch-long common nail; 3/4-inch wire brads; 4d and 6d finishing nails; four 3/4-inch No. 10 panhead sheet metal screws; two 3/4-inch No. 8 panhead sheet metal screws; four 3/4-inch No. 6 panhead sheet metal screws; two 1 1/2-inch No. 8 flathead wood screws; three 1 1/4-inch No. 8 flathead wood screws; two 7/8-inch I.D. washers; ten 1/2-inch I.D. washers; four 3/4-inch O.D. washers; six 3/8-inch O.D. washers; 1 1/2-inch-long, 1-inch-diameter brass bell; wood glue; graphite paper; stylus or dry ballpoint pen; sandpaper; tack cloth; red, green, light blue, royal blue, silver and black glossy paints, or colors desired; clear gloss polyurethane; paintbrushes; saw; backsaw; miter box; drill with assorted bits; screwdriver; hammer; paper for pattern.

Directions:

1. Trace the full-size cab patterns in FIGS. V, 16B and 16C onto paper. Using the graphite paper and stylus or

dry ballpoint pen, transfer the pattern pieces to 1 x 8 pine. Cut out the D cab front, D1 cab sides, and D2 cab back.

2. Refer to the Cutting Directions to cut the C engine ribs, J cowcatcher and A engine bottom pieces. Shape them following the measurements in FIG. V, 16A. Cut the other locomotive parts to size.

3. Sand the locomotive parts smooth, and wipe off all the sawdust with the tack cloth. Following the diagrams in FIG. V, 16D, and using glue and nails or screws, assemble the cab, engine, chimney/handle, and cowcatcher.

4. Using the photo as a color guide, paint the cab, engine, pistons, chimney/handle, cowcatcher, wheels and wheel shafts. Apply a coat of polyurethane to the seat. Let the paint and polyurethane dry completely.

5. Finish assembling the locomotive. Shape the common nail into the K bell support, slide the bell onto it, and attach it to the C3 engine front *(see photo and* FIG. V, 16D*)*.

Cutting Directions

Code	***Pieces***	***Size***
A (PINE)	1	1¼" x 2½" x 20" Engine bottom
B (PINE)	2	¾" x 3⅝" x 17" Engine sides
C (PINE)	3	¾" x 3½" x 5¼" Engine ribs
C1 (PINE)	1	1¼" x 1½" x 3½" Handle support
C2 (PINE)	1	¾" x 2½" x 2½" Engine rib
C3 (PINE)	1	1¼" x 4" dia. Engine front
C4 (LAT)	2	¼" x ⅞" x 11¾" Engine rails
C5 (LAT)	8	¼" x ⅝" x 11¾" Engine top
D (PINE)	1	¾" x 5" x 7" Cab front
D1 (PINE)	2	¾" x 4" x 6" Cab sides
D2 (PINE)	1	¾" x 2" x 6½" Cab back
D3 (LAT)	8	¼" x 1" x 6¼" Cab roof
E (PINE)	1	¾" x 5½" x 5¾" Seat
F (DOW)	2	1¼" dia. x 4" Pistons
G (DOW)	4	½"dia. x 3" Axles
G1 (PINE)	4	1¼" x 5¼" dia. Wheels
G2 (DOW)	4	⅜" dia. x ⅜" Spacers
G3 (LAT)	2	¼" x ⅝" x 7" Wheel shafts
H (DOW)	1	1¼" dia. x 4" Front axle support
H1 (DOW)	2	⅜" dia. x 3" Front axles
H2 (DOW)	1	⅞" dia. x 11" Chimney
H3 (DOW)	1	1" dia. x 4½" Handle
H4 (PINE)	2	¾" x 1¾" dia. Wheels
J (PINE)	2	¾" x 3½" x 5½" Cowcatcher
K	1	3½" Bell support

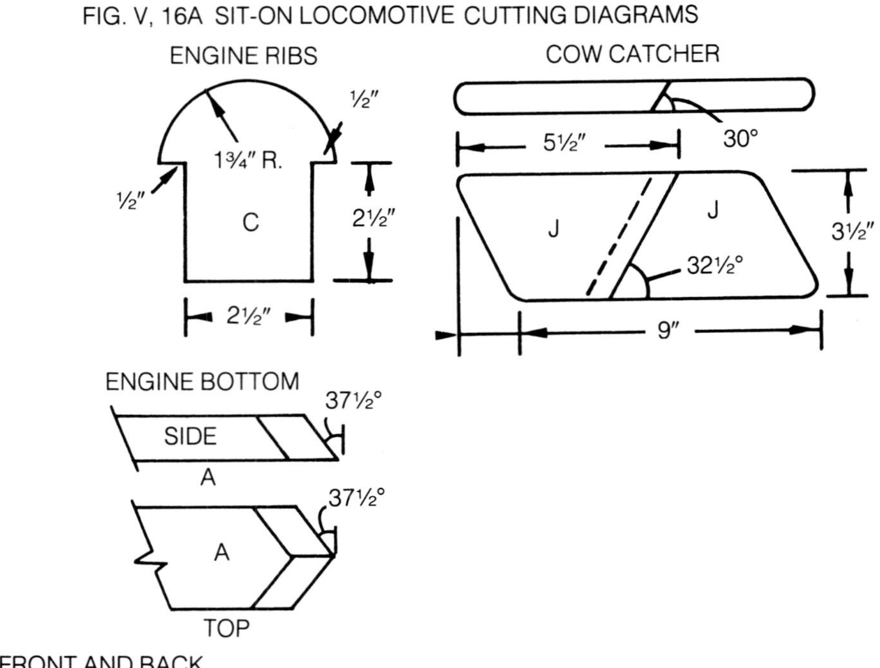

FIG. V, 16B CAB FRONT AND BACK

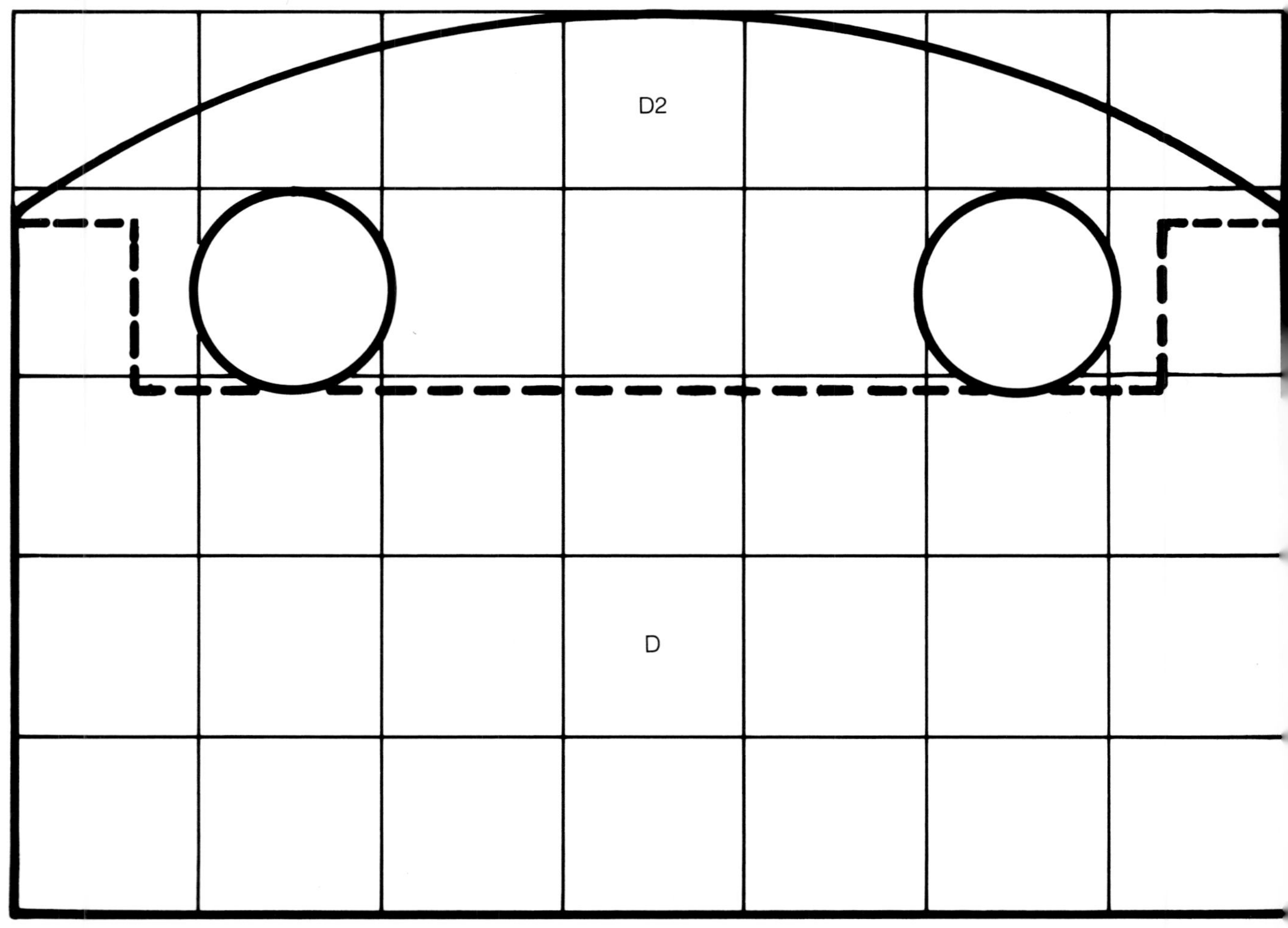

FIG. V, 16D ASSEMBLY DIAGRAMS

D3
D2
D1
D
D1
E
C2
B
C5
H3
H2
C
C
C1
B
G
G
C4
K
C3
1″ DIA. x 1/4″
DOWEL
C
A
F
G1
G3
G2
1 1/4″
H
J
J
H1
H4

FRONT VIEW

D3
C5
D
C4
C
G1
B
A
B

ENGINE SIDES (B)

17″
5 1/2″
5″
3 5/8″
3 3/4″
6″
1/2″ DIA. DOWELS

FIG. V, 16C CAB SIDE

FULL SIZE

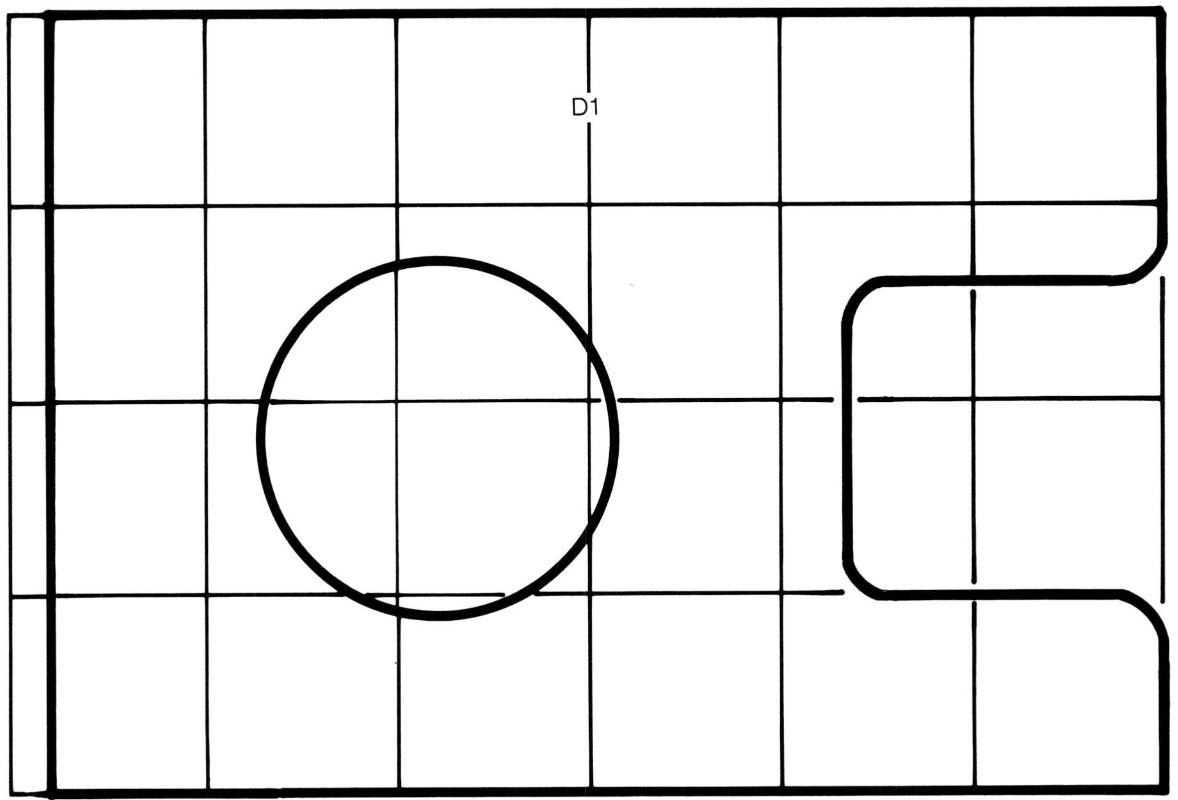

CHRISTMAS COOKING

Now
thrice welcome Christmas
Which brings us good cheer,
Minced pies and plum porridge.
Peace and plenty for many a Christmas to come.
—Irish Christmas Blessing

Some of the most wonderful memories of the holiday season are made in the kitchen, whether you're creating a sumptuous feast for Christmas Eve or baking cookies with the kids.

In this chapter, we've created a "mini cookbook" to help and inspire you throughout the holiday season. Delightful punches and drinks, tantalizing hors d'oeuvres, perfect side dishes, a potpourri of cookie recipes, luscious desserts, tasty breads and muffins—and two complete Christmas dinners, including menus and preparation countdowns to make your celebration deliciously simple.

There are two great joys in cooking: the satisfaction of creating wonderful food, and the pleasure in serving family and friends the best your kitchen can offer.

MENU MAGIC

Christmas Morning Brunch

Menu for 8 to 12

Eggs Benedict
Pumpkin Spice Bread (recipe, page 244)
Whole Wheat Molasses Muffins (recipe, page 246)
Cranberry Almond Muffins (recipe, page 243)
Broiled Pink Grapefruit Halves Sprinkled with Brown Sugar and Cinnamon
Sparkling Citrus Punch (recipe, page 167)
Hot-Blooded Mary (recipe, page 163)
Coffee, Tea

Just Desserts Party

Menu for 8

Chocolate Date Nut Bread (recipe, page 244)
Christmas Tree Cookies (recipe, page 207)
Tatus (recipe, page 240)
Chocolate Orange Spritz Sandwiches (recipe, page 208)
Spicy Apricot Tea Punch (recipe, page 168)
Café Royale (recipe, page 170)
Chocolate à la Russe (recipe, page 171)

Holiday Hors D'Oeuvres

Menu for 16

Daiquiri Punch (recipe, page 163)
Shrimp Roulade (recipe, page 177)
Smoked Salmon and Caviar Cheese Torte (recipe, page 173)
Goat Cheese and Prosciutto in Phyllo Cups (recipe, page 174)
Assorted Pâtés, Crackers and Breads
Strawberries Dipped in Chocolate

Winterfest Supper

Menu for 12

Fresh Dill Dip with Vegetable Dippers (recipe, page 179)
*Creamy Carrot Soup (recipe, page 190)**
Boneless Pork Loin Stuffed with a Mushroom Duxelle (recipe, page 202)
*Baked Apple Relish (recipe, page 189)**
Lemon Broccoli
Barley Pilaf
Chocolate Chestnut Mousse (recipe, page 223)

*Prepare a double batch

Cocktails & Nibbles

Menu for 16

Mulled Wine or Cider (recipe, page 168)
Della Robbia Fruit Punch (recipe, page 166)
Nacho Mushrooms (recipe, page 175)
Red & Green Pepper Triangles (recipe, page 175)
Cream Cheese & Caviar Tortes (recipe, page 178)
Savory Chicken, Spinach & Tomato Squares (recipe, page 176)
Bacon Cheese Squares (recipe, page 180)
Fruitcake Petit Fours (recipe, page 197)

Christmas Dinner

Menu for 12

Claret Cup (recipe, page 163)
Peppery Almonds (recipe, page 174)
Cream of Broccoli Soup
Roast Turkey, Bread Stuffing with Currants and Almonds (recipe, page 186)
*Baked Vegetables with Cheese Sauce (recipe, page 185)**
*Mushroom-Stuffed Onions (recipe, page 191)**
Orange Cranberry Sauce (recipe, page 185)
Quick Corn Relish (recipe, page 189)
Fresh Herb Muffins (recipe, page 247)
Kiwi Trifle (recipe, page 225)
Kumquat Pecan Pie (recipe, page 233)
*Café Supreme (recipe, page 170)**

*Prepare a double batch

PUNCHES AND DRINKS

A collection of wonderful celebratory concoctions to add just the right touch to your holiday feasts.

CLARET CUP

A variation on the traditional claret cup made with lemon juice, "claret" refers to any dry red wine.

Makes 25 servings.

- 1 *can (46 ounces) orange punch, chilled*
- 1 *bottle (750 ml) dry red wine, chilled*
- 1 *bottle (28 ounces) lemon-lime soda, chilled*
- 1/2 *cup Curaçao OR: other orange-flavored liqueur*
- *Ice ring (see tip, below) OR: ice cubes*
- 1 *orange, thinly sliced, for garnish*

1. Pour the orange punch into a punch bowl. Stir the red wine, lemon-lime soda and Curaçao or other orange-flavored liqueur into the orange punch.
2. Slide the ice ring into the punch bowl, or add the ice cubes. Garnish the claret cup with the orange slices.
Note: *Strawberry or cherry punch may be substituted for the orange punch called for in the recipe. Other varieties of fruit, such as lemon or lime slices or whole strawberries, may be used to garnish the punch.*

HOLIDAY COOKING HELPS

Decorative Ice Ring

Pour water into a fancy ring mold, Bundt® or kugelhopf pan until the pan is about one quarter full. Place the pan in the freezer, and freeze until the water is almost solid. Arrange the fruit of your choice (orange, lemon and lime slices, whole or sliced strawberries, pineapple chunks, maraschino cherries, red and green seedless grapes, etc.) on the ice. Freeze again just until the fruit is anchored to the ice. Pour very cold water over the fruit to fill the pan, and freeze again until it is solid.

- To unmold the ice ring, briefly dip the mold or pan in a large pan of warm water. Invert the ice ring onto a plate. Slip the ice ring gently into the punch bowl to prevent splashes.
- Before using a mold to make an ice ring, invert the empty mold into your punch bowl to be sure the ring will fit. Remember that the ice ring and garnishes will add volume to the punch.

DAIQUIRI PUNCH

This tasty punch is a breeze to make because you begin with prepared daiquiri mix.

Makes 25 servings.

- 1/2 *cup light corn syrup*
- 2 *cups light rum*
- 2 *cans (6 ounces each) frozen daiquiri mix, thawed*
- 2 *bottles (28 ounces each) club soda, chilled*
- *Ice ring (see tip, below) OR: ice cubes*
- 1 *lime, thinly sliced, for garnish*

1. Combine the corn syrup and the rum in a punch bowl, stirring to blend them. Stir the thawed daiquiri mix into the rum mixture.
2. Add the club soda to the rum mixture. Carefully slide the ice ring into the punch bowl, or add the ice cubes. Garnish the punch with the lime slices.

HOT-BLOODED MARY

A soul-warming punch for cold winter nights.

Makes 15 servings.

- 1 *can (46 ounces) tomato juice*
- 1 *tablespoon Worcestershire sauce*
- 1 *2-inch-long cinnamon stick*
- 1/8 *teaspoon whole cloves*
- *Salt and freshly ground black pepper, to taste*
- *Lemon juice, to taste*
- 2 *cups vodka*

1. Combine the tomato juice, Worcestershire sauce, cinnamon stick and cloves in a large saucepan. Cook the mixture over low heat for 15 minutes. Season the mixture with the salt and pepper, and the lemon juice.
2. Add the vodka to the hot tomato juice mixture. Serve the punch in heatproof old-fashioned glasses or demitasse cups.

FRUIT OF THE VINE: A MINI-GUIDE TO WINE

The Wine Cellar

Wine can be served before meals, with them and after — or savored by itself, just like any other beverage. Before a meal, many people prefer a dry to medium-sweet wine, such as sherry, vermouth or an aperitif wine. All of these can be served chilled, on the rocks or with soda. Champagne and other dry to semi-dry sparkling wines also make excellent before-dinner drinks. A very sweet wine should not be served before the meal, because the aperitif should lead into the first course, which is not sweet. Thus, serving a very sweet before-dinner drink is similar to beginning the meal with dessert.

For an informal occasion or an everyday-type meal, try a modest, inexpensive wine, known in France and Italy as *vin ordinaire* and *vino da tavola* (meaning "plain" and "table" wine). Serve one of the many white, rosé, blush or red wines available, choosing the variety that best complements the main dish. Better quality wines, and the unusually fine wines called "great," should be reserved for special occasions. At some formal meals, a different wine may be served with each course. Generally, a semi-dry white wine is served with a first dish of fish or seafood, and a more robust red wine with the meat. But, even on formal occasions, it also is appropriate to serve only one wine throughout the meal.

The Wine Service

To bring out their full flavor, white wines should be served chilled and red wines at room temperature. But this rule needs some clarification: "Chilled" means cool in the mouth — slightly chilled, but not icy, with a temperature of around 45° to 50°. If a white wine is chilled too much, or placed in the freezer to chill too quickly, the flavor often is destroyed. White wines, sparkling wines, champagnes and rosés can be chilled properly by refrigerating them for one to two hours — never put wine in the freezer! The only exceptions to this rule are white aperitif or dessert wines, which often are served on the rocks. If time is a problem, place the bottle of wine in an ice bucket or large pot filled with water and ice, and leave the bottle in it for about 20 minutes. This also is a good method to use when serving a crowd.

Red wines should be served at "room temperature," a range between 60° and 68°. If the wine is very warm, stand the bottle near an open window for 10 to 15 minutes to bring down the temperature, or place the wine in the refrigerator for five minutes before serving it. *Never* heat a chilled bottle of wine; this ruins the wine. Let an over-chilled bottle of wine stand until it has returned to the proper temperature.

A bottle of red wine should be uncorked one to two hours before it is consumed. This is called "letting the wine breathe," and allows the full flavor of the wine to develop. This is especially important for older, and more full-bodied, wines. Many of the table wines appropriate for everyday dining do not require anything beyond pouring, but all varieties of wine should be served at the right temperature to best enhance the meal. Just remember this rule: Extremes of heat or cold destroy the flavor of wine.

The Wine List

Dinner Wines: Primarily served with meals, these wines may be white or red, dry or semi-sweet. Dinner wines account for the majority of all wines produced in the world, and are available in an enormous range of flavors and qualities.

Sparkling Wines: These wines usually are reserved for festive occasions. Traditionally, only sparkling wines produced in the Champagne region of France were called "champagne." Recently, however, many countries have begun to label their sparkling wines as champagne. Although white sparkling wines are the best known, there also are rosé, blush, and even red sparkling wines.

Fortified Wines: These wines have been made stronger and longer-lasting by the addition of brandy. Sherry, port and Madeira are the best known varieties. Fortified wines can be sweet or dry; the sweet varieties generally are served with dessert, and the dry as aperitifs.

Aromatized Wines: These wines are fortified and flavored with herbs, seeds and/or spices; vermouth is the best known variety. Aromatic wines can be combined with liquors for cocktails, or served straight as an aperitif.

The Wine Selection

Selecting the best wine to serve with a meal can be a confusing operation. To discover which wine best complements which food, begin with the more traditional food and wine combinations, then try experimenting to your own taste. A clerk in a good wine store often can make suggestions of appropriate or lesser known vintages to try with a particular meal. There also are many books and magazines dealing specifically with wine.

The basic rule of order is white before red and dry before sweet. But you also can follow a dry red dinner wine with a sweet white wine for dessert. The following are some basic guidelines for matching wine with food.

Hors d'Oeuvres and Soup: Serve the same wine selected for the entrée.
Fish: Dry white wine or dry sherry.
Shellfish: Dry or semi-dry white wine, or a light red wine.
Poultry: Either a light or full white wine or red wine. The dish determines the wine selection: The richer the dish, the more robust the flavor of the wine. Cold chicken is best with a light white wine; chicken in a cream sauce is good with a full white wine; roast chicken, duck or goose can be served with a full white wine, or a light or medium-full red wine. Poultry prepared with wine, such as *coq au vin*, should be served with the same wine.
Veal and Pork: Full white wine, light red wine or a rosé.
Beef and Lamb: Full red wine.
Ham: Full white wine, medium-full red wine or a good quality rosé.
Venison and Game: Full red wine is good with venison. For the more delicate game birds, such as pheasant, dove and quail, choose a full white wine. For wild duck, choose a medium-full red wine.
Dessert: Sweet white, rosé and blush wines go well with most cakes, puddings and fruits. There also are sweet red wines that may be served with dessert. Another good choice is a semi-sweet champagne.
Nuts and Cheese: Port, sweet sherry or Madeira.

Do not serve wine with highly spiced foods such as curry or Mexican food—beer is a better choice—or with vinegary foods, such as salads, which can make the wine taste sour. Cheese and wine are a wonderful combination, but be sure to match the strength of the cheese to the robustness of the wine.

The Wine Store

Always lay down wine bottles on their sides to store them; this keeps the cork moist. If the cork dries out, air will get into the bottle and spoil the wine.

Wine should be stored in a cool, dark place. The ideal temperature is about 55° to 60°. It is important to maintain a fairly constant temperature year round, never varying more than a few degrees. Unless you are equipped with good storage conditions, don't buy more wine than you will drink within a reasonable time period—wine doesn't keep well in warm or sunny conditions.

A WINE GUIDE

No. Of Guests	Bottles White (750 ml)	Bottles Red (750 ml)
4	2	1
6	2	2
10	4	2
12	5	3
30	11	7
40	14	10

Note: *If serving wine coolers, plan on two to three 6-packs for 8 to 12 guests, and about 1 pound of ice per person.*

DELLA ROBBIA FRUIT PUNCH

Luca della Robbia, a 15th-century Florentine sculptor and painter, sculpted exquisite wreaths of birds and fruit. Our punch is chilled by a fruit-filled ice ring.

Makes 14 servings.

Ice Ring:
- 1 *bunch seedless green grapes*
- 1 *can (8 ounces) apricot halves, well drained*
- 1 *lime, thinly sliced*
- 1 *navel orange, thinly sliced*
- ½ *pint fresh strawberries OR: dry-pack frozen strawberries*
- *Fresh sprigs of mint*
- 2½ *cups ginger ale*
- ½ *cup fresh lemon juice, strained*

Punch:
- 2 *packages (10 ounces each) frozen strawberries in syrup, thawed*
- 3 *cups apricot nectar, chilled*
- 3 *cups club soda, chilled*
- 1 *cup fresh lemon juice, chilled*
- 1 *can (6 ounces) orange juice concentrate, thawed*
- 1 *cup sugar*
- 1 *bottle (28 ounces) ginger ale, chilled*
- *Mint leaves, for garnish (optional)*

1. Prepare the Ice Ring: Make a pleasing arrangement of green grape clusters, apricot halves, lime and orange slices, fresh or frozen strawberries and mint sprigs in a 1¼-quart, 8-inch-diameter ring mold. Combine the 2½ cups of ginger ale and the ½ cup of lemon juice in a measuring cup. Gradually pour the ginger ale mixture into the mold. Freeze the Ice Ring until it is firm.
2. Prepare the Punch: Just before you are ready to serve the Punch, combine the thawed frozen strawberries, apricot nectar, club soda, 1 cup of lemon juice, orange juice concentrate and the sugar in a large punch bowl. Stir the mixture until the sugar is dissolved. Stir in the bottle of ginger ale.
3. Remove the Ice Ring from the freezer and let it stand for 3 or 4 minutes, or until the Ice Ring is slightly melted and can be easily removed from the mold. Slide the Ice Ring into the punch bowl. Garnish the Punch with the mint leaves, if you wish.

PLANTER'S PUNCH

This eye opening punch will add a flaming touch to your holiday celebrations!

Makes 12 servings.

- 6 *limes*
- ¾ *cup superfine sugar*
- 2 *cups dark rum*
- ¼ *teaspoon bottled aromatic bitters*
- *Club soda (about 48 ounces), chilled*
- 6 *sugar cubes, halved*

1. Cut a ¾-inch slice off each end of all the limes. Scoop out the pulp from the lime ends, and set aside the ends.
2. Squeeze the juice from the rest of the limes into a small pitcher. Add the sugar to the lime juice and stir until the sugar is dissolved. Stir in the rum and the bitters. Let the mixture stand for at least 2 hours to allow the flavors to blend.
3. For each drink, pour ¼ cup of the lime mixture into a small, heatproof stemmed glass. Add club soda to the glass until the liquid is within 1 inch of the rim. Place a sugar cube half in a reserved lime end and drizzle a little rum over the sugar cube. Float the lime end in the drink and light the sugar cube. Lower the lights in the room before serving the punch.

ORANGE BLOSSOMS

Makes 8 servings.

1 quart orange juice, chilled
1½ cups gin OR: vodka
½ cup triple sec
1 can (12 ounces) club soda
Ice cubes
1 orange, thinly sliced, for garnish

1. Combine the orange juice, gin or vodka, triple sec and club soda in a large glass pitcher. Gently stir until the mixture is well blended.
2. Divide the chilled juice mixture among 8 glasses. Add 2 or 3 ice cubes to each glass. Garnish each drink with an orange slice.

HOLIDAY COOKING HELPS

Slim Sipping

- Stick to unsweetened fruit juice-based punches, and avoid eggnogs and other cream-based drinks.
- Unsweetened fruit juices and juice blends are sweet enough to hold their own in most punch recipes. For an extra boost of sweetness, add thawed frozen juice concentrate without diluting it.
- To cut calories when making cold punches, substitute seltzer, club soda or diet soda for some or all of the regular soda called for in the recipe.
- Make an "unspiked" version of your favorite punch in addition to the alcoholic original. Alcohol usually is the most caloric component of punch.

SPARKLING CITRUS PUNCH

Makes 8 servings

1 cup sugar
1 cup water
Zest of 1 orange (orange part of rind only), cut into wide strips
Zest of 1 lemon (yellow part of rind only), cut into wide strips
3 cups water
2 cups orange juice
¾ cup club soda
¼ cup lemon juice
Ice cubes

1. Combine the sugar, the 1 cup of water and the orange and lemon zests in a small saucepan. Bring the mixture to boiling, and boil until the sugar dissolves and the mixture is syrupy, for 8 to 10 minutes. Remove and discard the orange and lemon zests. Let the syrup cool until it is room temperature.
2. Pour the cooled syrup into a large glass pitcher. Stir in the 3 cups of water, the orange juice, club soda and lemon juice. Stir until the mixture is well blended. Add the ice cubes.

HOLIDAY COOKING HELPS

Spirit Safety

Whether hosting or attending parties, bear in mind these important facts about alcohol.

- The alcohol content of 1¼ ounces of 80-proof spirits—a "shot" of liquor—is the same as 12 ounces of beer, 4 ounces of wine and 3 ounces of sherry.
- Light beers and wines have a slightly lower alcohol content than the full-strength variety, but they still are intoxicating. Read the labels carefully.
- The faster you drink, the more concentrated the impact of the alcohol.
- Alcohol consumed on an empty stomach is absorbed readily. Before imbibing, eat a fiber-rich food, such as whole wheat bread, or a protein, such as cheese.
- Always have a "designated driver:" someone in your group who agrees to abstain from alcohol for the evening.
- When hosting, don't rush to refill empty glasses. And never serve "one for the road." Instead, replace alcohol with coffee and sweet snacks an hour or two before you expect the party to end.

SPICY APRICOT TEA PUNCH

Makes 16 servings.

1 *quart water*
23 *ounces (half a 46-ounce can) apricot nectar*
6 *tea bags*
12 *whole allspice*
4 *whole cloves*
4 *cinnamon sticks*
1 *lemon, halved*
1 *cup firmly packed light brown sugar*
1 *cup apricot brandy OR: orange-flavored liqueur*
2 *tablespoons lemon juice*

1. Combine the water, apricot nectar, tea bags, allspice, cloves, cinnamon sticks and lemon halves in a large saucepan. Bring the mixture to boiling, cover the saucepan and steep the mixture for 5 minutes. Remove the tea bags. Let the tea mixture steep for 10 minutes more. Strain the tea mixture, discard the solids and return the liquid to the saucepan.
2. Reheat the tea mixture over low heat. Add the sugar to the tea mixture and stir until the sugar dissolves. Stir in the apricot brandy or orange-flavored liqueur and the lemon juice. Serve the punch warm.

MULLED CRANBERRY JUICE

Makes 12 generous servings.

3 *quarts cranberry juice*
1 *cup sugar*
1 *cup water*
3 *tablespoons lemon juice*
9 *whole cloves*
½ *teaspoon ground cinnamon*
3 *oranges, sliced*

Combine the cranberry juice, sugar, water, lemon juice, cloves, cinnamon and orange slices in a nonaluminum saucepan. Bring the mixture to boiling, stirring to dissolve the sugar. Lower the heat, cover the saucepan and simmer the mixture for 5 minutes. Serve hot.

MULLED WINE OR CIDER

Makes 22 servings.

¾ *cup water*
¾ *cup firmly packed light brown sugar*
¾ *cup golden raisins*
4 *cinnamon sticks*
8 *whole cloves*
8 *whole allspice*
Zest of 1 lemon (yellow part of rind only)
Zest of 1 orange (orange part of rind only)
1 *thinly sliced lemon, seeds removed*
3 *bottles (750 ml each) dry red wine*
OR: 2½ quarts apple cider

1. Combine the water, brown sugar, golden raisins, cinnamon sticks, cloves, allspice, lemon and orange zests, and the lemon slices in a 4-quart stainless steel or enamel saucepan. Bring the mixture to boiling over medium heat. Lower the heat, cover the saucepan and simmer the mixture for 5 minutes. Turn off the heat. Add the wine or the cider and stir well.
2. To serve immediately, heat the mixture gently (do not boil the mixture once the wine or cider has been added). Transfer the mixture to a heatproof punch bowl. To serve the next day, store the mixture overnight in a cool place or in the refrigerator, and heat gently before serving.

MULLED CIDER WITH APPLE BRANDY

Makes 16 servings.

- 6 *cardamom pods, crushed*
- 12 *whole allspice, crushed*
- 3 *½-inch-thick slices fresh gingerroot*
- 1 *small orange*
- 24 *whole cloves*
- 12 *2-inch cinnamon sticks*
- 8 *cups apple cider*
- ¼ *cup firmly packed dark brown sugar*
- 1 *teaspoon ground nutmeg*
- 1 *cup apple brandy (Calvados or apple jack)*

1. Tie the cardamom, allspice and gingerroot slices in a cheesecloth bag. Stud the orange with the cloves, spacing them evenly over the entire orange. Slice the orange into 6 thin "rounds." Insert 2 cinnamon sticks in the center of each slice.

2. Combine the cider, brown sugar, nutmeg, cheesecloth bag and orange slices with cinnamon in a large stainless steel or enamel saucepan. Bring the mixture to boiling over medium heat. Lower the heat and simmer the mixture for 10 minutes. Add the apple brandy and simmer the mixture for 3 minutes more. Discard the cheesecloth bag. Transfer the mulled cider to a heatproof punch bowl. If serving in fine glassware, ladle the hot cider down the side of a teaspoon into the glass to prevent the glass from cracking.

HOLIDAY COOKING HELPS

Pretty Punches — Pronto!

- Instead of blending juices to make a fruit punch, start with a refrigerated or frozen prepared fruit juice medley.
- Use frozen drink mixes, such as daiquiri or piña colada, as the base for your own punch blend. Add wine or champagne, or use club soda or seltzer for a non-alcoholic sipper.
- Since eggs should never be used or eaten raw, prepared eggnog is not only faster, but safer than the homemade variety. For a change of taste, flavor eggnog with a little sherry, rum or triple-strength iced coffee.
- Ice rings *(see tip, page 163)* and ice cubes filled with mint sprigs, lemon zest twirls or fruit can be prepared at your convenience, well ahead of the party. They instantly add a festive touch to any punch bowl, or to individual glasses.
- Mulled wine and cider can warm carolers and couch potatoes alike. Make the spice base ahead, then store the base in a tightly covered container in the refrigerator. At serving time, reheat the spice base, then add the wine or cider.
- Make a hot chocolate base ahead of time by cooking the cocoa and sugar in a little bit of water. Store the cocoa base in the refrigerator. At serving time, add the base to milk, and heat gently.

IRISH COFFEE

Makes 1 serving.

1 *teaspoon sugar*
1 *jigger (1½ ounces) Irish whiskey*
1 *cup strong hot coffee*
1 *tablespoon lightly whipped cream*
Colored coffee sugar (optional; available in coffee specialty shops

Combine the sugar with the whiskey in a heatproof mug, and stir until the sugar is dissolved. Add the hot coffee to the whiskey; do not stir. Top the Irish coffee with the whipped cream and, if you wish, the colored coffee sugar.

CAFÉ ROYALE

Makes 1 serving.

1 *sugar cube*
1 *jigger (1½ ounces) orange-flavored liqueur*
1 *cup strong hot coffee*
Lemon twist (yellow part of rind only)
1 *whole clove*
1 *cinnamon stick*

Combine the sugar and the orange-flavored liqueur in a heatproof mug, and stir until the sugar is dissolved. Stud the lemon twist with the clove. Add the coffee, lemon twist and cinnamon stick to the liqueur mixture.

CHRISTMAS COFFEE

A sweet and spirited finish to a holiday meal.

Makes 1 serving.

1 *cup strong hot coffee*
½ *jigger (¾ ounce) white crème de menthe*
½ *jigger (¾ ounce) dark crème de cacao*
1 *tablespoon lightly whipped cream*
1 *small peppermint stick*

Combine the coffee, crème de menthe and crème de cacao in a heatproof mug. Top the coffee with the whipped cream and the peppermint stick.

CAFÉ SUPREME

Makes 8 to 10 servings.

12 *whole cloves*
1¼ *teaspoons aniseed, crushed*
1 *2-inch-long vanilla bean, split lengthwise*
2 *cinnamon sticks*
6 *cups hot, freshly brewed, strong coffee*
Hot milk OR: whipped cream, for garnish
Natural or light brown sugar, for garnish

1. Tie the cloves, aniseed and vanilla bean in a small cheesecloth bag. Add the bag and the cinnamon sticks to the coffee in a large saucepan. Let the spices steep in the coffee over low heat for 15 minutes. Or pour the coffee into a thermos jug, add the spice bag and the cinnamon sticks, and allow the coffee to steep for at least 15 minutes.
2. Serve the coffee in small mugs or cups. Garnish each serving with hot milk or whipped cream and the natural or light brown sugar.

CAFÉ JAMAICA

Makes 1 serving.

- 1 *jigger (1½ ounces) dark rum*
- 1 *cup strong hot coffee*
- *Pinch ground cinnamon*
- 1 *tablespoon whipped cream*
- *Semisweet chocolate curls**
- 1 *cinnamon stick*

Combine the rum with the coffee in a heatproof mug. Whisk the ground cinnamon into the whipped cream. Top the coffee with the whipped cream and a few chocolate curls. Stand the cinnamon stick in the mug.
***Note:** Use a swivel-bladed vegetable peeler to scrape lengthwise across a bar of slightly softened, semisweet chocolate. As the chocolate curls form, carefully lift them off with a wooden pick, and set them on baking sheets lined with wax paper. Refrigerate the curls for at least 30 minutes before using them. If the bar of chocolate becomes too soft to work with, place it in the refrigerator to chill until it is firm enough to handle. Wipe the peeler blade occasionally to prevent the curls from sticking.*

CHOCOLATE À LA RUSSE

A deliciously adult version of a childhood favorite.

Makes 1 serving.

- 1 *cup prepared hot chocolate*
- 1 *jigger (1½ ounces) peppermint schnapps*
- ½ *jigger (¾ ounce) vodka*
- *Whipped cream*
- *Milk and white chocolate curls (see Note, above)*
- 1 *small peppermint stick*

Combine the hot chocolate, peppermint schnapps and vodka in a large, heatproof mug. Top the chocolate mixture with the whipped cream, milk and white chocolate curls and the peppermint stick.

HOLIDAY COOKING HELPS

Jazz up the Java

Coffee, an American staple, can contribute its own particular cheer to your Christmas celebration when laced with a little liquor or liqueur, or garnished to suit the season.

From the traditional Irish Coffee to the deliciously different taste of Café Royale, our spirited recipes provide a selection of bracing brews for a holiday brunch or fancy finishes for a special dinner.

Of course, adding alcohol is only one way to perk up your coffee. Cinnamon, nutmeg and mace, for instance, all give a wonderful boost to coffee when you add a pinch per cup to the grounds before brewing. A teaspoon of sweetened cocoa powder per brewed quart imparts a faint chocolate flavor to coffee. Add a dollop of whipped cream and a chocolate-dipped candy cane to the mug and you have a cup of true Christmas cheer. For a hint of citrus, add a pinch of dried orange or lemon zest (use the orange or yellow part of the rind only) to the coffee grounds before brewing and float a twist of fresh zest in each cup.

Whether or not you flavor the brew, keep your coffee maker scrupulously clean to avoid a buildup of oils that can affect taste. Start with fresh, cold water and use the correct grind of bean for your coffee maker. Grinding your own coffee beans provides even more fresh flavor. And remember that coffee always tastes best right after it is brewed.

APPETIZERS AND HORS D'OEUVRES

A sensational selection of snackables: Smoked Salmon and Caviar Cheese Torte (recipe, page 173); Flatbread Canapés (recipe, page 178); Shrimp Roulade (recipe, page 177); Goat Cheese and Prosciutto in Phyllo Cups (recipe, page 174); Nacho Mushrooms (recipe, page 175); Red & Green Pepper Triangles (recipe, page 175); Savory Chicken, Spinach & Tomato Squares (recipe, page 176)

NORWEGIAN SEAFOOD DIP

Makes about 3 cups of dip.

2 *packages (8 ounces each) cream cheese, softened*
1 *can (6½ ounces) solid white tuna packed in oil, drained and flaked*
1 *tablespoon grated lemon zest (yellow part of rind only)*
2 *tablespoons lemon juice*
1 *medium-size red onion, chopped*
1 *medium-size tomato, chopped*
1 *can (3¾ ounces) Norwegian brisling sardines packed in oil, well drained*
½ *cup sliced, pitted black olives*
1 *tablespoon drained capers*
Parsley sprigs, for garnish (optional)
Flatbread (optional)

1. Beat the cream cheese in a small bowl with an electric mixer until it is light and fluffy. Add the tuna, lemon zest and lemon juice, and beat until all the ingredients are blended. Spoon the mixture into a 1-quart glass soufflé dish.
2. Sprinkle the chopped onion evenly over the cream cheese mixture. Sprinkle the tomato evenly over the onion layer. Arrange the sardines in a star design on top of the tomato layer *(see photo, page 180)*. Sprinkle the sliced olives and the capers over the sardines. Garnish with the parsley sprigs, and serve the dip with flatbread, if you wish.

SMOKED SALMON AND CAVIAR CHEESE TORTE

A layered cheese dome, perfect for spreading on flatbread. Or, serve with crunchy vegetables.

Makes 16 servings.

2 *packages (8 ounces each) cream cheese, softened*
½ *pound (2 sticks) unsalted butter, softened*
1 *tablespoon grated lemon zest (yellow part of rind only)*
1 *tablespoon lemon juice*
½ *cup finely chopped fresh dill*
¼ *pound smoked salmon, finely chopped*
½ *cup red lumpfish caviar*
Sprigs of fresh dill, for garnish
Flatbread OR: snow peas, zucchini slices and Belgian endive leaves

1. Combine the cream cheese and the butter in a small bowl, and beat with an electric mixer until the mixture is light and fluffy. Add the lemon zest and the lemon juice. Place one-third of the cream cheese mixture in a small bowl. Place the remaining cream cheese mixture in a medium-size bowl. Add the chopped dill to the cream cheese mixture in the small bowl, and blend well. Add the chopped salmon to the cream cheese mixture in the medium-size bowl, and blend well.
2. Line a 2½-cup bowl with plastic wrap, leaving a 2-inch overhang.
3. Spoon the salmon-cream cheese mixture into the lined bowl, and pack it down firmly. Spread ¼ cup of the caviar evenly over the salmon mixture.
4. Spoon the dill-cream cheese mixture over the caviar layer, spreading the mixture evenly, and packing the layers down firmly. Cover the top of the torte with the plastic wrap overhang. Refrigerate the torte until it is firm, for 2 to 3 hours.
5. To serve the torte, fold back the plastic wrap overhang. Unmold the torte onto a serving platter, and carefully remove the plastic wrap. Garnish the top of the torte with the remaining caviar and the dill sprigs. Serve the torte with flatbread for spreading, or with snow peas, zucchini slices and Belgian endive leaves for dipping.

PEPPERY ALMONDS

Four kinds of pepper—cayenne, white, black and paprika—add a real punch to almonds. The amount of spice used in this recipe will produce quite a hot mixture; adjust the seasonings to taste.

Bake at 250° for 35 minutes.
Makes 2 pounds.

- 2 *pounds natural almonds*
- ½ *cup (1 stick) butter*
- 1 *tablespoon sugar*
- 1 *teaspoon salt*
- ½ *teaspoon cayenne pepper*
- ½ *teaspoon freshly ground white pepper*
- ½ *teaspoon freshly ground black pepper*
- *Paprika, to taste*

1. Preheat the oven to very slow (250°).
2. Sauté the almonds in the butter in a large skillet over medium-high heat for 5 minutes, or until the nuts are coated with the melted butter. If you wish, the almonds can be sautéed a part at a time. Transfer the coated almonds and the butter remaining in the skillet to a jelly-roll pan.
3. Combine the sugar, salt, cayenne, white and black peppers in a small measuring cup. Sprinkle the spice mixture over the almonds. Stir the almonds with a wooden spoon to distribute the spice mixture evenly.
4. Bake the almonds in the preheated very slow oven (250°) for 35 minutes, stirring the nuts every 10 minutes, until the almonds are toasted. Check the almonds frequently to prevent burning.
5. Sprinkle the almonds with the paprika. If you wish, place the almonds on paper toweling to drain. Store the almonds in a container with a tight-fitting lid.

GOAT CHEESE AND PROSCIUTTO IN PHYLLO CUPS

Bake at 350° for 20 minutes.
Makes 40 appetizer cups.

- 8 *ounces phyllo dough, thawed if frozen*
- ½ *cup (1 stick) butter, melted*
- 12 *ounces mild-flavored goat cheese, at room temperature*
- 2 *eggs*
- 1 *cup heavy cream*
- 1 *teaspoon dried thyme, crumbled*
- ½ *pound thinly sliced prosciutto*
- *Parsley sprigs, for garnish*

1. Preheat the oven to moderate (350°).
2. Lay the phyllo dough flat on a smooth work surface. Cover the phyllo with plastic wrap, then with a damp kitchen towel, to prevent the dough from drying out.
3. Cut the phyllo sheets into 4-inch squares. Brush 8 phyllo squares with the melted butter. Place 4 of the buttered phyllo squares in a mini muffin-pan cup. Place another buttered phyllo square in the cup at a right angle to the first 4 squares. Repeat with 3 more buttered phyllo squares, placing each square at a right angle to the previous square. The combined phyllo squares should form a tulip shape in the muffin-pan cup. Repeat with the remaining phyllo squares to make 40 phyllo cups.
3. Combine the goat cheese, eggs, cream and thyme in a large bowl. Beat the mixture until it is well blended.
4. Set aside 3 slices of the prosciutto. Finely chop the remaining prosciutto. Stir the chopped prosciutto into the cheese mixture. Spoon the combined mixture into the phyllo cups.
5. Bake the filled cups in the preheated moderate oven (350°) until the phyllo is golden brown and the cheese filling is slightly puffed, for 20 minutes. Remove the cups from the oven and let them stand for 5 minutes. Carefully remove the cups from the pans.
6. Remove any excess fat from the reserved prosciutto slices. Cut the slices into 3-inch-long, ½-inch-wide strips. Roll the strips tightly, and place a prosciutto roll on top of each cup. Garnish each phyllo cup with a small parsley sprig.

RED & GREEN PEPPER TRIANGLES

Bake at 350° for 30 minutes.
Makes 48 triangles.

Red Pepper Purée:

3 *large sweet red peppers, halved, seeded and cut into 1-inch strips*
1 *clove garlic, finely chopped*
1 *tablespoon olive oil*
½ *teaspoon crushed red pepper flakes*

Green Pepper Purée:

3 *large sweet green peppers, halved, seeded and cut into 1-inch strips*
1 *clove garlic, finely chopped*
1 *tablespoon olive oil*
1 *teaspoon dried basil, crumbled*

Phyllo Triangles:

1 *cup (2 sticks) unsalted butter, melted*
1 *package (1 pound) phyllo dough, thawed if frozen*
1 *cup grated Parmesan cheese*
1 *container (15 ounces) ricotta cheese*
1 *pound mozzarella cheese, thinly sliced*

1. Prepare the Red Pepper Purée: Place the red pepper strips in the container of a food processor, and whirl until the peppers are puréed. Sauté the red pepper purée with the garlic in the oil in a large skillet over medium-high heat until most of the liquid has evaporated. Stir in the red pepper flakes, and sauté for 5 minutes more. Place the red pepper purée in a bowl.
2. Prepare the Green Pepper Purée: Place the green pepper strips in the container of the food processor, and whirl until the peppers are puréed. Sauté the green pepper purée with the garlic in the oil in the skillet over medium-high heat until most of the liquid has evaporated. Stir in the basil, and sauté for 5 minutes more. Place the green pepper purée in a second bowl.
3. Prepare the Phyllo Triangles: Brush a 13 x 9 x 2-inch baking pan with some of the melted butter. Lay the phyllo dough flat on a smooth surface. Cover the phyllo with plastic wrap, then with a damp kitchen towel to prevent the dough from drying out. Brush 2 phyllo sheets with melted butter. Place the phyllo sheets in the bottom of the prepared baking pan, and sprinkle them with 1 tablespoon of the Parmesan cheese. Repeat with 6 more phyllo sheets, layering them with the Parmesan cheese. Spread the green pepper purée over the top phyllo sheet. Spread half of the ricotta cheese and half of the mozzarella slices over the green pepper purée.
4. Brush another 8 phyllo sheets with melted butter. Repeat the layering of the buttered phyllo and the Parmesan cheese. Spread the red pepper purée over the top sheet of the second layering of phyllo. Spread the remaining ricotta cheese and mozzarella slices over the red pepper purée. Butter the remaining phyllo sheets, and layer them with the remaining Parmesan cheese. Brush the top phyllo sheet with a generous amount of butter. Using a sharp knife, cut the top phyllo layer into 48 triangles.
5. Preheat the oven to moderate (350°).
6. Bake in the preheated moderate oven (350°) until the top phyllo layer is golden brown, for 30 minutes. Cool the layers slightly.
7. Using the sharp knife, and following the triangles on the top layer, cut through all the phyllo layers. Serve the triangles warm or at room temperature.

NACHO MUSHROOMS

Broil for about 2 minutes.
Makes 24 stuffed mushrooms.

24 *large fresh mushrooms, stems removed*
½ *cup (1 stick) butter, melted*
¼ *pound thinly sliced pepperoni*
½ *pound Monterey Jack cheese with jalapeño peppers, shredded (about 2 cups)*
⅓ *cup chopped green onions*
1 *jar (4 ounces) pimiento, drained and cut into strips*

1. Preheat the broiler.
2. Place the mushrooms, round side up, in a broiler pan. Brush the mushrooms with some of the butter.
3. Broil the mushrooms 6 inches from the heat for 1 minute. Remove the pan from the broiler. Turn over the mushrooms.
4. Tuck a pepperoni slice in each mushroom. Top the pepperoni with some of the shredded cheese and brush with the remaining butter.
6. Broil the mushrooms until the cheese melts. Garnish the mushrooms with the green onions and pimiento.

SAVORY CHICKEN, SPINACH & TOMATO SQUARES

The colors of Christmas captured in a tasty hors d'oeuvre. Each square is topped with a bright cherry tomato half.

Makes 64 squares.

Spinach Layer:
1 *envelope unflavored gelatin*
1/4 *cup cold water*
2 *packages (10 ounces each) frozen chopped spinach, thawed and drained*
1/2 *cup chopped green onions*
1/2 *teaspoon ground nutmeg*

Chicken Layer:
1/2 *cup chopped onion (1 medium-size)*
1 *cup chopped mushrooms (1/4 pound)*
1 *pound boneless chicken breasts, cut into 1/2-inch cubes*
1 *tablespoon butter*
2 *teaspoons dry sherry*
1/2 *teaspoon dried basil, crumbled*
1 *envelope unflavored gelatin*
1/4 *cup cold water*

Tomato Layer:
1 *envelope unflavored gelatin*
1/4 *cup cold water*
2 *cups tomato juice*
1/2 *cup chopped onion (1 medium-size)*
1 *sweet red pepper, halved, seeded and chopped*
1 *whole canned green chili, seeded and chopped*
3 *cloves garlic, finely chopped*
1 *teaspoon prepared horseradish*
2 *tablespoons lime juice*
2 *tablespoons red wine vinegar*
1/4 *teaspoon salt*
1/4 *teaspoon freshly ground pepper*

32 *cherry tomatoes, halved*

1. Line a 9-inch-square baking pan with aluminum foil.
2. Prepare the Spinach Layer: Sprinkle the gelatin over the water in a measuring cup. Let the gelatin stand for 5 minutes to soften. Combine the spinach, green onions and nutmeg in a bowl, and stir until the ingredients are well blended. Set the cup with the gelatin in a small saucepan of simmering water. Heat the gelatin over medium heat, stirring until the gelatin dissolves completely. Stir the gelatin into the spinach mixture. Spread the spinach mixture evenly in the prepared baking pan. Place the pan in the refrigerator.
3. Prepare the Chicken Layer: Sauté the onion, mushrooms and chicken in the butter in a medium-size skillet just until the chicken is tender. Add the sherry and the basil, and cook the mixture for 5 minutes. Sprinkle the gelatin over the water in the measuring cup. Let the gelatin stand for 5 minutes to soften. Set the cup with the gelatin in the small saucepan of simmering water. Heat the gelatin over medium heat, stirring until the gelatin dissolves completely. Stir the gelatin into the chicken mixture. Spread the chicken mixture evenly over the spinach layer in the baking pan. Refrigerate the layers until they are chilled.
4. Prepare the Tomato Layer: Sprinkle the gelatin over the water in the measuring cup. Let the gelatin stand for 5 minutes to soften. Combine the tomato juice, onion, sweet red pepper, green chili pepper, garlic, horseradish, lime juice, vinegar, salt and pepper in a medium-size bowl. Stir until all the ingredients are well blended. Set the cup with the gelatin in the small saucepan of simmering water. Heat the gelatin over medium heat, stirring until the gelatin dissolves completely. Stir the gelatin into the tomato mixture. Pour the tomato mixture over the chicken layer in the baking pan. Place the pan in the refrigerator until the tomato mixture is slightly firm.
5. Place the cherry tomato halves cut side down on top of the tomato layer, arranging the tomato halves in 8 even rows. Refrigerate the mixture until it is firm, for about 4 hours.
6. To serve, cut the mixture into 64 squares, with a cherry tomato half in the center of each square. Using a small spatula, carefully transfer the squares from the baking pan to a serving platter.

SHRIMP ROULADE

A creamy shrimp and mushroom mixture wrapped in a Swiss cheese-flavored savory cake.

Bake at 400° for 30 minutes; reheat at 250°.
Makes 2 roulades (16 servings).

Roulade:
- 1/4 *cup (1/2 stick) butter*
- 1/2 *cup sifted all-purpose flour*
- 1/2 *teaspoon salt*
- 1/4 *teaspoon freshly ground pepper*
- 2 *cups milk*
- 1/4 *cup shredded Swiss cheese*
- 4 *eggs, separated*
- 1/4 *teaspoon cream of tartar*
- *Fine dry bread crumbs*

Shrimp Filling:
- 1/3 *cup chopped onion*
- 3 *tablespoons butter*
- 1 *cup finely chopped mushrooms (1/4 pound)*
- 1 *package (10 ounces) frozen chopped spinach, thawed and drained*
- 1 *cup chopped, shelled and deveined cooked shrimp (3/4 pound)*
- 1 *tablespoon Dijon-style mustard*
- 1/2 *teaspoon dillweed*
- 2 *packages (3 ounces each) cream cheese, softened*
- 1/4 *cup dairy sour cream*

1. Preheat the oven to hot (400°). Butter the bottom of two 15 x 10 x 1-inch jelly-roll pans. Line the bottoms of the pans with wax paper. Butter and flour the paper.
2. Prepare the Roulade: Melt the 1/4 cup of butter in a medium-size saucepan. Stir in the flour, salt and pepper until the mixture is smooth. Cook the mixture, stirring, until it is golden brown, for about 3 minutes. Gradually stir in the milk. Cook the mixture over medium heat, stirring constantly, until it is thick and bubbly. Add the cheese and stir until it is melted.
3. Beat the egg yolks in a small bowl. Stir a little of the hot cheese mixture into the egg yolks. Stir the egg yolk mixture back into the saucepan. Cook the combined mixture over very low heat, stirring constantly, until the mixture is thickened, for about 2 minutes. Do not let the mixture boil. Remove the saucepan from the heat.
4. Beat the egg whites in a small bowl until they are frothy. Add the cream of tartar, and beat the mixture until it forms stiff, but not dry, peaks. Stir a little of the beaten egg whites into the cheese mixture. Gently fold in the remaining egg whites. Divide the batter equally between the prepared pans, spreading the batter evenly in each pan.
5. Bake the cakes in the preheated hot oven (400°) until they are lightly browned, for 30 minutes. Sprinkle two kitchen towels with the bread crumbs. Invert the cakes onto the towels and carefully remove the wax paper.
6. Meanwhile, prepare the Shrimp Filling: Sauté the onion in the 3 tablespoons of butter in a large skillet until the onion is golden brown, for 4 minutes. Add the mushrooms, and cook until the mushrooms are lightly browned, for 5 minutes more. Add the spinach and the shrimp. Cook the mixture, stirring frequently, until the shrimp turns pink, for 2 to 3 minutes. Stir in the mustard, dill, cream cheese and sour cream.
7. Divide the Shrimp Filling in half. Spread half the Shrimp Filling over one of the warm cakes. Gently roll up the cake from a long side, using the towel to help roll. Repeat with the second cake and remaining Shrimp Filling. Let the roulades cool completely.
8. At serving time, preheat the oven to slow (250°).
9. To serve, cut the roulades crosswise into 1-inch-thick slices. Place the slices on a baking sheet. Heat the roulade slices in the preheated slow oven (250°) just until they are warm. Serve the roulade slices warm.
Note: *To prepare ahead, bake, fill and roll the cakes. Wrap the roulades tightly in plastic wrap and refrigerate them. To serve, slice and heat following the directions in Step 9, above.*

FLATBREAD CANAPÉS

Let your imagination — and the photo on page 172 — inspire your culinary creativity when topping flatbread-based canapés. The following is a list of ingredients to try mixing and matching for your next party.

Flatbread
Softened butter
Softened cream cheese
Thin cucumber slices
Hard-cooked egg slices
Sieved hard-cooked egg yolks
Red lumpfish caviar
Norwegian brisling OR: other sardines, packed in oil, drained
Cherry tomato halves
Fresh dill sprigs
Drained capers
Smoked salmon, cut into thin strips
Thin lemon slices
Cooked small shrimp

HOLIDAY COOKING HELPS

Nibble Nomenclature

What's the difference between an hors d'oeuvre and an appetizer? The answer is: not much; the terms basically are interchangeable. By definition, an appetizer is a dish served before a meal to stimulate the appetite. An hors d'oeuvre can be an appetizer, but it also can be served with cocktails or as a snack. Most appetizers can be converted into bite-sized finger food to serve as party nibbles. For example, pâté usually is served by the slice, garnished with tiny pickles and a dollop of mustard. To serve it as an hors d'oeuvre, cut the pâté into small squares, place each square on a small piece of mustard-coated rye bread, and top with a slice of pickle.

By the same token, many hors d'oeuvres can be served as a first course, especially if several are combined. A plate with baby Mozzarella cheese, stuffed mushrooms and sun-dried tomatoes makes a wonderfully easy opener to an Italian feast.

CREAM CHEESE & CAVIAR TORTES

Makes eight 6-ounce tortes.

2 *packages (8 ounces each) cream cheese, softened*
2 *cups (4 sticks) unsalted butter*
4 *hard-cooked egg yolks*
2 *tablespoons drained chopped capers*
2 *tablespoons mayonnaise*
1 *teaspoon dried basil, crumbled*
1/2 *cup chopped parsley*
1/4 *cup finely chopped pine nuts*
2 *tablespoons grated Parmesan cheese*
2 *tablespoons olive oil*
1 *clove garlic, crushed*
1/4 *teaspoon salt*
1/8 *teaspoon freshly ground pepper*
1 *jar (3 1/2 ounces) red lumpfish caviar*
Fresh fruit wedges OR: assorted crackers

1. Line eight 6-ounce custard cups with a double thickness of dampened cheesecloth. The cheesecloth should overhang the sides of the custard cups.
2. Beat together the cream cheese and butter in a large bowl until fluffy. Set aside the cream cheese mixture.
3. Stir together the egg yolks, capers and mayonnaise in a small bowl. Set aside the egg mixture.
4. Stir together the basil, parsley, pine nuts, Parmesan cheese, olive oil, garlic, salt and pepper in a second small bowl. Set aside the basil mixture.
5. Press a small amount of the cream cheese mixture into the bottom of each prepared custard cup. Spoon the caviar over the cream cheese, dividing the caviar equally among the cups. Top the caviar with another layer of the cream cheese mixture, spreading the mixture evenly. Spoon the egg mixture over the second cream cheese layer, dividing the egg mixture equally among the cups. Spread another cream cheese layer over the egg layer. Spoon the basil mixture over the third cream cheese layer, dividing the basil mixture equally among the cups. Top the basil layer with a final cream cheese layer, smoothing the tops. Cover the tortes with the cheesecloth overhangs. Refrigerate the tortes until they are firm, for about 3 hours.
6. To serve, unmold the tortes onto individual serving plates and remove the cheesecloth. Serve the tortes with fruit wedges or crackers.

FRESH DILL DIP WITH VEGETABLE DIPPERS

A tangy combination of yogurt, mayonnaise and fresh dill is a perfect foil for crisp vegetable dippers.

Makes about 1½ cups of dip.

- *¾ cup lowfat plain yogurt*
- *¾ cup mayonnaise*
- *¾ cup chopped fresh dill*
- *1 tablespoon lemon juice*
- *1½ teaspoons Dijon-style mustard*
- *Pinch salt*
- *Pinch freshly ground pepper*
- *1 large head broccoli*
- *2 bunches green onions*
- *1 bunch carrots*
- *1 head celery*

1. Combine the yogurt, mayonnaise, dill, lemon juice, mustard, salt and pepper in a small bowl, and stir until the mixture is thoroughly blended. Cover the bowl and refrigerate the dip until serving time.
2. Trim the broccoli, and separate it into flowerets. Trim the green onions. Peel the carrots. Cut the carrots and the celery into thin sticks.
3. To serve, place the bowl of dip in the center of a serving platter. Place the vegetables around the bowl in a pleasing arrangement.

CURRIED CHICKEN PÂTÉ

For a different taste, substitute cooked turkey for the chicken in this recipe.

Makes about 4 cups.

- *1 medium-size onion, chopped (about ½ cup)*
- *1 green apple, peeled, quartered, cored and coarsely chopped*
- *1 can (4 ounces) slivered blanched almonds*
- *¼ cup (½ stick) butter*
- *2 to 3 teaspoons curry powder*
- *1 teaspoon salt*
- *1 package (8 ounces) cream cheese, softened*
- *4 cups chopped cooked chicken*
- *¼ cup heavy cream*
- *1 tablespoon prepared chutney*
- *2 green onions, trimmed and sliced*
- *Wheat crackers*

1. Sauté the chopped onion, apple and nuts in the butter in a small saucepan over medium heat, until the onion and apple are tender.
2. Add the curry powder and salt to the saucepan, and sauté for 1 minute more, stirring with a wooden spoon to prevent the mixture from burning. Remove the saucepan from the heat and cool the mixture slightly.
3. Whirl the cream cheese in the container of a food processor fitted with a metal blade until the cream cheese is light and fluffy. Add the chicken, heavy cream, chutney, onion-apple mixture and sliced green onions. Continue whirling until the mixture is smooth and well blended. Taste the mixture and adjust the seasonings.
4. Transfer the pâté to decorative crocks. Cover the pâté with plastic wrap and refrigerate it until serving time. Serve the pâté with wheat crackers.

CURRIED MIXED NUTS

These piquant nuts make a delicious accompaniment to cocktails.

Bake at 350° for 5 minutes.
Makes 3 cups.

2 tablespoons vegetable oil
2 teaspoons curry powder
1/8 teaspoon sugar
1/8 teaspoon garlic powder
1 1/3 cups whole cashews (about 7 ounces)
1 1/4 cups pecan halves (about 5 ounces)
3/4 cup walnut halves (about 4 ounces)
1/4 teaspoon salt OR: to taste

1. Preheat the oven to moderate (350°).
2. Combine the oil, curry powder, sugar and garlic powder in a large bowl, and stir until the mixture is well blended. Add the cashews, pecans and walnuts, and stir to coat the nuts completely. Spread the nuts in a single layer on a baking sheet.
3. Bake the nuts in the preheated moderate oven (350°) for 5 minutes. Remove the baking sheet from the oven, sprinkle the salt over the nuts and let them cool completely. Store the nuts in an airtight metal container at room temperature.

Microwave Instructions

(for a 650-watt variable power microwave oven)

Ingredient Changes: Reduce the oil to 1 tablespoon.
Directions: Combine the oil, curry powder, sugar and garlic powder in a microwave-safe 10-inch pie plate. Stir until the mixture is well blended. Add the cashews, pecans and walnuts, and stir until the nuts are completely coated. Microwave, uncovered, at full power for 4½ to 5 minutes, stirring twice during the cooking time. Stir in the salt and let the nuts cool completely in the pie plate.

BACON CHEESE SQUARES

Bake at 400° for 10 minutes, then at 325° for 10 minutes.
Makes 64 squares.

6 eggs
1 teaspoon Dijon-style mustard
1/4 teaspoon salt
1/4 teaspoon freshly ground white pepper
1/4 cup unsifted all-purpose flour
1/4 teaspoon baking powder
2 cups Cheddar cheese, shredded (8 ounces)
2 strips bacon, crisply cooked and finely crumbled
3 tablespoons chopped green onion

1. Preheat the oven to hot (400°).
2. Line a 9 x 9 x 2-inch-square baking pan with aluminum foil; the foil should extend over the edges of the pan. Generously grease the aluminum foil.
3. Beat together the eggs, mustard, salt and pepper in a large bowl until the mixture is foamy. Add the flour and the baking powder. Beat the mixture until it is smooth and no lumps remain.
4. Add the Cheddar cheese, bacon and green onion to the bowl, and stir until all the ingredients are well mixed. Pour the cheese mixture into the prepared pan.
5. Bake the cheese mixture in the preheated hot oven (400°) for 10 minutes. Reduce the oven temperature to slow (325°). Bake the mixture for 10 minutes more.
6. Cool the cheese mixture in the pan on a wire rack for 10 to 20 minutes. Using the aluminum foil overhangs, carefully lift the cheese mixture out of the pan to a cutting board. Peel the aluminum foil down off the sides of the cheese mixture. Cut the cheese mixture into sixty-four 1-inch squares. Serve the squares warm or at room temperature.

RED PEPPER & FETA PHYLLO ROLLS

Broil red pepper for 15 minutes; bake rolls at 400° for 10 to 12 minutes.
Makes 18 appetizers.

- 1 *extra-large sweet red pepper*
- 1/4 *cup coarsely chopped flat-leaf Italian parsley*
- 1/4 *pound feta cheese, crumbled*
- 1 *tablespoon red onion, very finely chopped*
- 2 *cloves garlic, very finely chopped*
- 1/8 *teaspoon freshly ground pepper*
- 1/8 *teaspoon dried oregano, crumbled*
- 4 *sheets (17 x 12 inches) phyllo dough (from 1-pound package)*
- 4 *teaspoons olive oil*
- *Aromatic bitters (optional)*

1. Preheat the broiler. Lay the red pepper on a small baking sheet. Broil the red pepper 2 inches from the heat source, turning over the pepper frequently, until it is blackened all over, for about 15 minutes.
2. When the red pepper is cool enough to handle, run it under cool water. Remove the blackened skin from the red pepper with a sharp knife. Core and seed the red pepper, and cut it into 2-inch-wide strips.
3. Transfer the red pepper to the container of a food processor. Whirl until the pepper is finely chopped. Transfer the red pepper to a small bowl. Stir in the parsley, feta cheese, onion, garlic, pepper and oregano.
4. Preheat the oven to hot (400°).
5. Unfold the phyllo. While working, keep the unused phyllo covered with a damp towel to prevent it from drying out. Place 1 phyllo sheet on the work surface so the short side is facing you. Rub about 1 teaspoon of the oil over the top of the sheet. Lay a second sheet of phyllo on top of the oiled one.
6. Spoon half the red pepper filling across the phyllo short end nearest you, forming a narrow rectangle and leaving a 1-inch border at the sides and bottom.
7. Gently bring the phyllo edge nearest you up and slightly over the filling. Continue to roll up the phyllo, jelly-roll style. Rub about 1 teaspoon of the oil on the bottom seam and top of the roll. Place the roll, seam side down, on a nonstick baking sheet.
8. Repeat with the remaining phyllo, filling and oil. Place the second roll on the baking sheet. If you wish, brush the tops of the rolls with aromatic bitters for a more golden crust.
9. Bake the rolls in the preheated hot oven (400°) for 10 to 12 minutes, or until the tops of the rolls are crisp. Let the rolls cool slightly. Transfer the rolls with a metal spatula to the work surface. Using a very sharp knife, cut each roll crosswise into 9 equal pieces. Arrange the rolls on a serving plate, and serve them warm.

HOLIDAY COOKING HELPS

Guide to a Beautiful Buffet

- When setting up the table, place it with plenty of room to spare. Guests should be able to move around the table easily.
- Arrange the table for easy self-serving and to facilitate traffic flow: first the plates, then the entrées and accompaniments, and last of all, the tableware and napkins.
- Wrap tableware in napkins for easy carrying.
- The bread basket and butter plate should be placed side by side, either at the end of the buffet table, or on an adjoining table. Bring the butter to room temperature for easy spreading.
- Place the correct serving utensils either in or next to each dish.
- Be sure there is plenty of table and seating space for each guest. Card tables and tray tables work very well; disguise them with holiday linens.
- If you choose to seat guests at the dining table, set the table with napkins, tableware and glassware so your guests won't have to pick them up at the buffet.

CRISP PARMESAN PITA WEDGES

Pita wedges are a crunchy snack to serve at a party, or to enjoy with the family at home. These can be made ahead and stored in an airtight container.

Bake at 350° for 10 to 12 minutes.
Makes 48 wedges.

- 6 *tablespoons butter or margarine*
- 4 *tablespoons vegetable oil*
- 2 *cloves garlic, crushed or very finely chopped*
- 1/2 *teaspoon cayenne pepper*
- 1/4 *teaspoon freshly ground black pepper*
- 6 *large pita breads OR: 12 small pita breads*
- 1 *cup grated Parmesan cheese*
- 1/4 *cup chopped fresh parsley (optional)*

1. Preheat the oven to moderate (350°).
2. Melt the butter with the oil in a small saucepan over low heat. Add the garlic, cayenne pepper and black pepper. Simmer the mixture over low heat until it is frothy, for about 2 minutes. Remove the saucepan from the heat.
3. Carefully separate each pita bread into two circles. Lightly brush the "inside" of the pita breads with the butter mixture. Cut each pita bread circle into 4 wedges. (If using small pita breads, cut each pita bread circle into 2 wedges.) Place the wedges, buttered side up, on an ungreased baking sheet. Sprinkle the wedges with the Parmesan cheese and, if you wish, the parsley.
4. Bake the wedges in the preheated moderate oven (350°) for 10 to 12 minutes, or until the wedges are lightly browned. Cool the wedges on the baking sheet on a wire rack. Serve the wedges warm or at room temperature.

HOLIDAY COOKING HELPS

The Calorie/Fat Low-Down: Appetizers and Hors d'Oeuvres

The following tips can help you avoid the post-holiday bulge by skimming off extra calories and fats from your favorite finger foods.
Diet-Friendly Dips: Replace the sour cream in a dip recipe with plain lowfat yogurt, and regular mayonnaise with the reduced-calorie version. The ratio of yogurt to mayonnaise usually can be increased as well. Remember to stick to fresh vegetable dippers to serve with the dips.
Beat-the-Meatballs: Substitute ground turkey or chicken for the ground beef in your favorite meatball recipe. Replace the whole eggs called for with egg whites — usually 2 egg whites replaces each whole egg.
Cheese Savvy: In recipes for nibbles flavored with cheese, halve the amount of cheese called for and, for a cheesy burst of flavor, try sprinkling part of it on top of each hors d'oeuvre instead. Lowfat cheeses can pinch-hit for their higher fat cousins. Invest in a cheese plane — a tool that will enable you to cut off paper-thin slices of cheese.
Cracker Stand-Ins: Use melba toast, Scandinavian flatbread or wedges of split pita bread instead of high-fat crackers for spread or canapé bases. Or make your own toasts: Remove the crusts from whole wheat and rye bread slices. Place the bread slices in a single layer on a baking sheet and bake in a slow (300°) oven until the slices are golden brown and dried out. To add extra flavor, as soon as you remove the toasts from the oven, gently rub them with a cut clove of garlic.
Trot Out the Turkey: Select cold cuts from the large variety of turkey products. They usually are lower in fat than the pork and beef varieties, and taste just as satisfying.
Baked is Better: Avoid deep-fried hors d'oeuvres and concentrate on those that are baked instead.
Low-Cal Kebabs: Kebabs are an easy way to make tantalizing lowfat hors d'oeuvres. For example, try marinating shrimp or scallops in lemon juice, Dijon mustard, garlic, parsley and red pepper flakes. Thread the marinated shrimp or scallops on skewers and broil them.

HOT SPINACH BALLS

You probably have all the ingredients on hand for these savory appetizers. Perfect for impromptu parties—just make the sauce the night before the get-together.

Bake at 375° for 10 minutes.
Makes 40 balls.

- *2 packages (10 ounces each) frozen chopped spinach, thawed and squeezed dry*
- *2 cups herb-flavored stuffing mix, crushed*
- *1 cup firmly packed grated Parmesan cheese*
- *½ cup (1 stick) butter or margarine, melted*
- *¼ cup finely chopped green onions*
- *3 eggs, slightly beaten*
- *Dash grated nutmeg*
- *Mustard Sauce (recipe follows)*

1. Preheat the oven to moderate (375°).
2. Combine the spinach with the stuffing mix, Parmesan cheese, butter or margarine, green onions, eggs and nutmeg in a large bowl. Stir until all the ingredients are well blended. Shape the spinach mixture into 1-inch-diameter balls, and place the balls on a baking sheet. If making ahead, cover the baking sheet with plastic wrap and refrigerate the balls.
3. Bake the spinach balls in the preheated moderate oven (375°) for 10 minutes, or until the balls are slightly brown. Serve the spinach balls hot with the Mustard Sauce.

Mustard Sauce: Combine ¼ cup of dry mustard and ½ cup of white vinegar in a small bowl. Cover the bowl with plastic wrap and let the mixture stand at room temperature for 4 hours. Combine ¼ cup of sugar and 1 egg yolk in a small saucepan. Stir in the mustard-vinegar mixture. Cook the combined mixture over low heat, stirring constantly, until the sauce is thick and smooth. Cover the saucepan and refrigerate the sauce. *Makes 1 cup.*

HAM & CHEESE BALL

This recipe goes together fast, but the cheese ball must be made ahead to allow time for chilling. This makes it a perfect choice for the host or hostess who wants to avoid last-minute fuss.

Makes 1 large ball.

- *1 can (4½ ounces) deviled ham*
- *4 packages (8 ounces each) cream cheese, softened*
- *4 cups sharp Cheddar cheese, grated (1 pound)*
- *1 tablespoon grated onion*
- *1 tablespoon Worcestershire sauce*
- *2 teaspoons lemon juice*
- *2 teaspoons dry mustard*
- *1 teaspoon paprika*
- *1 teaspoon seasoned salt*
- *1 tablespoon chopped parsley*
- *1 tablespoon chopped pimiento*
- *1 cup chopped toasted almonds*
- *Assorted crackers*

1. Combine the deviled ham, cream cheese, Cheddar cheese, onion, Worcestershire sauce, lemon juice, dry mustard, paprika, seasoned salt, parsley and pimiento in a very large bowl. Stir until the mixture is well blended. Cover the bowl and refrigerate the cheese mixture for 1 hour.
2. Shape the chilled cheese mixture into a ball. Roll the cheese ball in the toasted almonds until it is covered with the nuts. Cover the cheese ball with plastic wrap and refrigerate it until 15 minutes before serving. Serve the cheese ball with assorted crackers.

SIDE DISHES

All the extras that make a holiday dinner special:
Orange Cranberry Sauce and Baked Vegetables with Cheese Sauce (recipes, page 185);
Bread Stuffing with Currants and Almonds (recipe, page 186)

BAKED VEGETABLES WITH CHEESE SAUCE

Bake at 325° for 20 to 25 minutes.
Makes 8 servings.

1 *small head cauliflower, stems trimmed and head cut into flowerets (about 4 cups)*
1 *small head broccoli, stems trimmed and head cut into flowerets (about 4 cups)*
6 *large carrots, trimmed, peeled, halved and cut lengthwise into thick sticks (about 2½ cups)*

Cheese Sauce:
¼ *cup (½ stick) butter*
1 *clove garlic, crushed but left whole*
¼ *cup all-purpose flour*
2½ *cups milk*
½ *cup dry white wine*
1 *tablespoon kirsch OR: brandy (optional)*
¼ *teaspoon freshly ground white pepper*
⅛ *teaspoon grated nutmeg*
2½ *cups shredded Gruyère cheese (about 10 ounces)*
⅛ *teaspoon ground hot red pepper*

1. Steam the cauliflower in a large pot just until it is tender, for about 4 minutes. Remove the cauliflower with a slotted spoon to a bowl of ice water to stop the cooking. Then remove the cauliflower with the slotted spoon to paper toweling. Repeat with the broccoli, steaming it for about 4 minutes, and with the carrots, steaming them for about 4 minutes.
2. Prepare the Cheese Sauce: Melt the butter in a medium-size saucepan over medium heat. Sauté the garlic in the butter for 30 seconds, then remove and discard the garlic. Whisk the flour into the butter until they are well mixed. Cook the flour mixture, whisking continually, for 1 minute. Slowly whisk in the milk until it is combined. Whisk in the wine, and the kirsch or brandy if you wish. Bring the mixture to boiling. Lower the heat to medium and continue to cook, whisking occasionally, until the mixture is smooth and thick, for 3 to 4 minutes. Whisk in the white pepper and the nutmeg. Reduce the heat to low. Gradually whisk in the Gruyère cheese and the ground hot red pepper until the cheese is completely melted and the ingredients are well combined; do not let the sauce boil.
The vegetables and the cheese sauce can be prepared ahead up to this point, and refrigerated separately.
3. When ready to bake, preheat the oven to slow (325°).
4. Arrange the vegetables in a 13 x 9 x 2-inch baking dish. Pour the cheese sauce over the vegetables to cover them.
5. Bake in the preheated slow oven (325°) until the vegetables and sauce are heated through, for 20 to 25 minutes. (If the vegetables and the sauce have been made ahead and refrigerated, add 10 to 15 minutes to the heating time).

ORANGE CRANBERRY SAUCE

Makes about 5 cups.

1 *pound whole cranberries*
2 *cups orange juice*
1¼ *cups sugar*
1 *tablespoon grated orange zest (orange part of rind only)*
Strips of orange zest (orange part of rind only), for garnish

1. Rinse the cranberries and drain them. Pick over the cranberries, discarding any stones or grit.
2. Combine the cranberries, orange juice and sugar in a medium-size, nonaluminum saucepan. Bring the mixture to boiling, stirring to combine the ingredients thoroughly. Cook until the cranberry skins pop, for about 5 minutes. Remove the saucepan from the heat. Skim and discard any froth from the top of the sauce. Stir in the orange zest. Cool the sauce and refrigerate it, covered, until serving time. To serve, garnish the sauce with the strips of orange zest.

BREAD STUFFING WITH CURRANTS AND ALMONDS

Makes 10 cups (enough to stuff a 14-pound turkey).

- 1 *large onion, chopped (1 cup)*
- 1 *cup finely chopped celery (3 to 4 stalks)*
- ½ *cup (1 stick) butter*
- 1 *loaf (16 ounces) bread, preferably homemade, cut into ½- to ¾-inch cubes (about 12 cups)*
- ½ *teaspoon dried thyme, crumbled*
- ½ *teaspoon dried rosemary, crumbled*
- *Pinch dried sage*
- ½ *teaspoon salt*
- ¼ *teaspoon freshly ground pepper*
- 1 *cup chicken broth OR: giblet stock, as needed*
- 1 *cup currants*
- 1 *cup slivered almonds (4 ounces), toasted**
- 1 *tart apple, peeled, cored and chopped (1½ cups)*

1. Sauté the onion and the celery in the butter in a large skillet over medium heat until the vegetables are softened, for about 10 minutes.
2. Combine the onion mixture with the bread cubes in a large bowl. Add the thyme, rosemary, sage, salt, pepper and broth or stock. Toss the ingredients together until the bread cubes are evenly moistened. Add the currants, almonds and apple, and toss until the ingredients are well mixed.
3. Stuff the turkey and roast it immediately. Or place the stuffing in a 13 x 9 x 2-inch baking pan and bake, uncovered, in a preheated moderate oven (350°) until the stuffing is crispy and browned on top, and moist underneath, for about 45 minutes.
***Note:** To oven toast almonds, spread the nuts in a shallow baking pan or baking sheet. Bake the almonds in a preheated moderate oven (350°), for 10 minutes, or until the almonds are golden in color, shaking the pan occasionally to redistribute the nuts. To skillet toast almonds, dry sauté the almonds in a large skillet until they are golden in color, shaking the skillet constantly to prevent the nuts from burning.*

OLD-FASHIONED BREAD STUFFING

Makes about 16 servings.

- 1 *large onion, chopped (1 cup)*
- 1 *cup (2 sticks) butter or margarine*
- 1 *cup finely chopped celery*
- 2 *teaspoons poultry seasoning*
- ½ *teaspoon salt*
- ¼ *teaspoon freshly ground pepper*
- 1 *can (13¾ ounces) chicken broth (1¾ cups)*
- 14 *cups cubed white bread (28 slices)*
- ½ *cup chopped fresh parsley*

Sauté the onion in the butter or margarine in a large skillet until the onion is soft but not brown. Stir in the celery, poultry seasoning, salt, pepper and chicken broth. Bring the mixture to boiling. Pour the hot onion mixture over the bread cubes and the parsley in a large bowl. Toss the ingredients together lightly until the bread cubes are evenly moistened. Stuff the turkey and roast it immediately.

HOLIDAY COOKING HELPS

Turkey Stuffing Tips

- Allow ¾ cup of stuffing per pound of bird for turkeys weighing more than 10 pounds, ½ cup of stuffing per pound for smaller turkeys.
- Stuff the turkey just before roasting it. *Never* stuff a turkey ahead of time—you run a very high risk of food poisoning if stuffing sits in an uncooked turkey for any amount of time, even if the turkey is refrigerated or frozen.
- After the turkey is roasted, immediately remove *all* the stuffing from the bird. Serve the stuffing in a separate bowl. Leftover turkey and stuffing should be wrapped separately, and refrigerated.

ORANGE PECAN STUFFING

Makes 12 servings (6 cups).

- 2 *large navel oranges*
- 1 *large onion, finely chopped (1 cup)*
- 1 *cup chopped celery*
- ½ *cup (1 stick) butter or margarine*
- 1 *tablespoon grated orange zest (orange part of rind only)*
- 4 *cups cubed white bread (12 slices)*
- 1 *cup chopped pecans*
- ¼ *cup chopped fresh parsley*
- 1 *teaspoon salt*
- ¼ *teaspoon freshly ground pepper*
- ¼ *teaspoon dried thyme, crumbled*

1. Peel the oranges and separate them into sections over a large bowl to catch any juice. You should have about 1 cup of orange sections. Set aside the orange sections with their juice.
2. Sauté the onion and the celery in the butter or margarine in a large skillet over medium heat until the vegetables are softened, for about 10 minutes. Add the orange sections with any accumulated juice, the orange zest, bread cubes, pecans, parsley, salt, pepper and thyme. Toss lightly until all the ingredients are well mixed and the bread cubes are evenly moistened.
3. Stuff the turkey and roast it immediately. Or place the stuffing in a greased 2-quart baking dish, cover the dish and bake in a preheated slow oven (325°) during the last 30 minutes of roasting time for the turkey.

CORN SAUSAGE STUFFING

Makes 20 servings (10 cups).

- 1 *pound bulk sausage*
- 3 *medium-size onions, chopped (1½ cups)*
- 8 *cups day-old bread cubes (16 slices)*
- 1 *tablespoon dried parsley*
- 1½ *teaspoons poultry seasoning*
- 1 *teaspoon salt*
- ¼ *teaspoon freshly ground pepper*
- 1 *can (about 17 ounces) cream-style corn*

1. Sauté the sausage in a large skillet, stirring to break up the sausage, until the sausage is browned and no pink remains. Using a slotted spoon, remove the sausage from the skillet to a small bowl and set aside the sausage. Pour off all but ¼ cup of the sausage fat. Add the onion to the skillet, and sauté the onion in the ¼ cup of sausage fat until the onion is softened.
2. Combine the bread cubes, parsley, poultry seasoning, salt and pepper in a large bowl. Add the sautéed onion, the sausage and the corn. Toss all the ingredients until they are well mixed and the bread cubes are evenly moistened. Stuff the turkey and roast it immediately.
Note: *If there is any stuffing left over after filling the turkey, refrigerate the leftover stuffing until it is chilled and slightly firm. Form the leftover stuffing into 2-inch-diameter balls. Place the stuffing balls around the turkey in the roasting pan during the last 30 minutes of roasting time.*

TALKING ABOUT TURKEY

CONVENTIONAL OVEN:
Timetable for Roasting Turkey (325°)

Weight (pounds)	**Stuffed** (hours)	**Unstuffed** (hours)
6 to 8	3 to 3½	2½ to 3½
8 to 12	3½ to 4½	3 to 4
12 to 16	4 to 5	3½ to 4½
16 to 20	4½ to 5½	4 to 5
20 to 24	5 to 6½	4½ to 5½

Testing for Doneness

- A meat thermometer inserted in the meatiest part of the thigh, without touching the bone, reads 180° to 185°F. If the thermometer is inserted in the center of the stuffing, it reads 160° to 165°F.
- The turkey juices run clear.
- The drumsticks move up and down easily

Resting Period

Let the cooked turkey stand at room temperature for 15 to 30 minutes. This allows the juices to settle and the meat to firm up for easier carving.

Storing Uncooked Turkey

Fresh Turkey: Keep refrigerated at all times. Cook fresh turkey within 1 to 2 days of purchase.
Frozen Whole Turkey: Store frozen turkey in its original wrapper for up to 12 months at 0°F or lower.

Thawing Frozen Turkey

Note: *Never thaw a turkey at room temperature. Once thawed, the turkey should be cooked as soon as possible.*

Conventional (long) Method

Thawing time—3 to 4 days, or about 24 hours for each 5 pounds of whole frozen turkey.

- Leave the turkey in its original wrapper.
- Place the frozen turkey on a tray in the refrigerator.

Cold Water (short) Method

Thawing time—about 30 minutes per pound of whole frozen turkey.

- Leave the turkey in its original wrapper.
- Place the turkey in a sink or large pan.
- Cover the turkey completely with *cold* water.
- Change the cold water every 30 minutes. Refill the sink or pan immediately when changing the water so the turkey is immersed continuously.

Turkey Hotlines

U.S.D.A. Meat and Poultry Hotline (1-800-535-4555) will answer questions about turkey (and other meat and poultry products) from 10 A.M. to 4 P.M. (EST) Monday through Friday, no weekends or holidays.

The Butterball Turkey Talk-Line (1-800-323-4848) will answer questions about preparing turkey and trimmings. It will be open beginning October 29, 1991 and operate throughout the holidays.

QUICK CORN RELISH

Makes 10 servings.

- 2 *cans (12 ounces each) whole kernel corn*
- ⅔ *cup finely chopped onion*
- ⅔ *cup finely chopped sweet green pepper*
- ⅔ *cup finely chopped pimiento*
- ½ *cup white vinegar*
- 2 *tablespoons vegetable oil*
- ¼ *cup sugar*
- 2 *teaspoons dry mustard*
- ½ *teaspoon salt*
- ½ *teaspoon freshly ground pepper*

1. Drain the corn, reserving ½ cup of the liquid. Combine the drained corn with the onion, green pepper and pimiento in a large bowl.
2. Combine the reserved corn liquid, vinegar, vegetable oil, sugar, dry mustard, salt and pepper in a small saucepan. Bring the mixture to boiling. Pour the hot liquid over the vegetable mixture. Cover the bowl with plastic wrap and refrigerate the relish, stirring occasionally, for 8 hours or overnight.

HOLIDAY COOKING HELPS

Roux Dos and Don'ts

A mixture of flour and melted butter or other fat, roux is used to thicken sauces, soups and gravies.
- Do stir the melted fat (butter or pan drippings) and flour over medium heat until they are thoroughly combined and the mixture is smooth.
- Do cook the roux long enough to dispel the taste of uncooked flour, for 1 to 2 minutes.
- Do constantly stir the roux while it is cooking. This evenly distributes the heat, and enables the starch granules in the flour to swell evenly. The starch in the flour absorbs liquid in a recipe, which causes the liquid to thicken.
- Don't cook roux over too high heat or the flour will burn. This makes the roux taste bitter and the starch granules shrink so the liquid won't thicken.

BAKED APPLE RELISH

Bake at 350° for 25 minutes.
Makes 6 servings.

- 6 *small baking apples*
- 2 *tablespoons butter or margarine*
- 1 *large onion, finely chopped (1 cup)*
- 1 *large tomato, peeled and chopped (1 cup)*
- ¼ *cup raisins*
- 1 *tablespoon finely chopped crystallized ginger*
- ¼ *teaspoon crushed red pepper flakes*
- ¼ *teaspoon dry mustard*
- 4 *tablespoons red currant jelly*
- 4 *tablespoons cider vinegar*

1. Preheat the oven to moderate (350°).
2. Cut a slice from the top of each apple. Core the apple and discard the apple cores. Scoop out the apple flesh with the tip of a small spoon, leaving a shell about ½- to ¾-inch thick. Chop the apple flesh and set it aside. You should have about 1 cup of chopped apple.
3. Heat the butter or margarine in a large skillet. Add the onion and sauté for 5 minutes. Stir in the reserved chopped apple, the tomato, raisins, crystallized ginger, red pepper flakes, mustard, 1 tablespoon of the currant jelly and 1 tablespoon of the vinegar. Cook the mixture, stirring often, for 5 minutes more, or until the mixture is slightly thickened.
4. Place the apple shells in a shallow baking pan. Spoon the apple mixture into the apple shells. Add the remaining 3 tablespoons of currant jelly and vinegar to the skillet. Heat the jelly mixture just until the jelly is melted. Spoon the jelly sauce over and around the stuffed apples.
5. Bake the stuffed apples in the preheated moderate oven (350°), basting once or twice with the jelly sauce, until the apples are glazed and tender, for 25 minutes. Let the stuffed apples cool for 15 minutes, basting them with the juices in the pan. Serve the apple relish warm.

HOLIDAY COOKING HELPS

Tasty Ways to Skim Calories & Fat

Vegetables are full of nutrients and dietary fiber, and naturally low in calories and fat. But what you put on them, or the way in which they are prepared, can turn them into high-calorie, high cholesterol dishes. The following are tips for keeping even the most festive vegetable dishes good to the taste *and* good to the waist.

- Make creamed spinach (and other creamy dishes) with lowfat milk instead of whole milk or cream.
- Top baked potatoes with a mixture of plain lowfat yogurt, cooled sautéed onions, chopped green onions and chives. Season with cracked pepper.
- Add caraway seeds and finely chopped garlic to plain lowfat yogurt. Toss with steamed potatoes.
- Top baked sweet potatoes or yams with lowfat lemon yogurt.
- Instead of the traditional mixture of sweet potatoes, marshmallows, sugar and butter, try this recipe instead. Bake, peel and slice the sweet potatoes. Layer the potato slices in a shallow baking dish with sliced apples and a little cinnamon sugar. Top the mixture with a tablespoon or two of finely chopped pecans, a little more cinnamon sugar and 1 tablespoon of butter cut into tiny pieces. Bake until apples are tender and dish is heated through.
- Instead of haphazardly topping cooked vegetables with globs of butter, melt just 1 tablespoon of butter and mix it with a lower calorie flavor booster, such as lemon or orange juice, defatted chicken broth, tomato juice or prepared mustard. Toss the butter mixture with the vegetables.
- Sauté vegetables in a wok or nonstick skillet to minimize the need for added fat.
- Try adding a little nonfat plain yogurt or buttermilk to mashed potatoes instead of butter or milk. Leave the potato skins on for extra flavor, texture and nutrients.
- To make great sauces for vegetables, start with other vegetables. Purée cooked vegetables, add a little defatted chicken broth and season to taste. Try cauliflower with broccoli or carrot sauce, or zucchini with tomato sauce.
- Toss quartered potatoes with a little olive oil, rosemary, salt and pepper. Roast the potatoes in a hot oven (400°) until they are tender on the inside, golden and crisp on the outside.

CREAMY CARROT SOUP

For the best flavor, make this creamy soup a day ahead. Gently reheat the soup before serving it.

Makes 8 servings.

5 *tablespoons butter or margarine*
1 *pound carrots, peeled, trimmed and thinly sliced*
2 *large onions, chopped*
1 *cup chopped celery*
8 *cups hot homemade chicken stock OR: hot canned chicken broth*
3 *tablespoons all-purpose flour*
1½ *cups heavy cream*
Salt, to taste
1 *teaspoon ground nutmeg*
Carrot curls, for garnish

1. Melt 2 tablespoons of the butter or margarine in a large heavy skillet over medium-high heat. Add the sliced carrots, onions and celery, and cook the mixture, stirring occasionally, until the onion is softened, for about 5 minutes.
2. Add 2 cups of the stock or broth. Bring the mixture to boiling. Cover the skillet and simmer the mixture over medium-low heat until the carrots are tender, for about 6 minutes. Stir in 1 cup of the stock or broth until it is well combined.
3. Working in batches if necessary, transfer the vegetables and the liquid to the container of a food processor or electric blender. Whirl until the vegetable mixture is puréed.
4. Melt the remaining 3 tablespoons of butter in a large, heavy saucepan. Add the flour and cook over medium-low heat, whisking constantly, until the mixture is smooth and well combined, for about 2 minutes. Gradually whisk in the remaining 5 cups of hot stock or broth. Bring the mixture to boiling, whisking until the broth is smooth and just slightly thickened. Reduce the heat and simmer the broth for 2 minutes. Add the vegetable purée and the heavy cream. Cook the soup over low heat, stirring constantly, until all the ingredients are well blended; do not let the soup boil. Add the salt to taste and the nutmeg. Garnish each serving with a few carrot curls.

MUSHROOM-STUFFED ONIONS

Bake at 350° for 45 minutes.
Makes 8 servings.

8 *medium-size onions, outer skin removed*
Boiling salted water
1/4 *cup (1/2 stick) butter or margarine*
1/4 *pound bulk sausage*
1/4 *pound mushrooms, chopped*
2 *cups fresh whole wheat bread crumbs (4 slices)*
1/4 *cup nonfat OR: lowfat milk*
1/4 *cup chopped fresh parsley*
1/4 *teaspoon dried thyme, crumbled*
1/8 *teaspoon salt*
1/8 *teaspoon freshly ground pepper*
Additional butter or margarine (optional)
1/2 *cup homemade beef stock OR: canned beef broth*
1/2 *cup dry white wine*
Additional chopped fresh parsley, for garnish (optional)

1. Cut off the top quarter of each onion, and reserve the onion quarters for another use. Using a sharp paring knife, cut out the centers of the onions leaving a shell with about 1/4-inch-thick sides and a 1-inch-deep cavity. Finely chop the cut out onion centers, and set the chopped onion aside; you should have about 2 cups of chopped onion.
2. Preheat the oven to moderate (350°). Grease a flameproof shallow baking pan large enough to hold the onion shells.
3. Cook the onion shells in the boiling salted water in a large saucepan for 5 minutes. Remove the onion shells with a slotted spoon to paper toweling and place the shells upside down to drain.
4. Sauté the reserved 2 cups of chopped onion in the 1/4 cup of butter or margarine in a large skillet. Crumble the sausage into the skillet and sauté until the sausage is no longer pink. Add the mushrooms and sauté until they are soft.
5. Meanwhile, soak the bread crumbs in the milk in a small bowl. Squeeze the bread crumbs dry and add them to the sausage-mushroom mixture. Cook the mixture, stirring constantly, for 5 minutes. Season the mixture with the parsley, thyme, salt and pepper.
6. Arrange the onion shells in the prepared baking pan, placing the shells close together. If necessary, slice a thin layer off the bottoms of the onion shells, so they can stand upright.
7. Fill the onion shells with the mushroom stuffing, mounding the stuffing high in the shells. If you wish, dot the tops of the stuffed onions with additional pats of butter or margarine. Pour the stock or broth and the wine into the baking pan. Place the baking pan on top of the stove and bring the liquid mixture to boiling.
8. Bake the stuffed onions in the preheated moderate oven (350°) for 10 minutes, basting the onions occasionally. Cover the pan and bake the stuffed onions for 35 minutes more.
9. Transfer the stuffed onions to a serving platter. Boil the liquid in the baking pan to reduce it by half, for about 5 minutes. Pour the thickened liquid over the stuffed onions on the platter. Garnish the tops of the onions with the chopped parsley, if you wish.

HOLIDAY COOKING HELPS

Speedy Sides

- Winter squash needs just a dot of butter or margarine and a pinch each of nutmeg and sugar to make a deliciously easy side dish. Squash cooks quickly in the microwave.
- Fill hollowed-out tomatoes with thawed frozen spinach soufflé or blanched broccoli flowerets. Bake the stuffed tomatoes until the filling is cooked and the tomatoes are tender but still hold their shape.
- Sauté leftover rice with green onions and red pepper strips in a skillet over medium heat. Stir in a dollop of sour cream or plain yogurt before serving.
- Add the juice and zest of one lemon (yellow part of the rind only) to rice as it is cooking. Before serving, season the rice with a little butter or margarine, salt and pepper.
- Toss steamed broccoli with lightly toasted sesame seeds, melted butter or margarine, chopped green onion and a few drops of Oriental sesame oil.
- Cook sliced carrots in a mixture of apple juice and sweet sherry. Add a little butter or margarine, raisins and cinnamon toward the end of the cooking time.
- Shredded zucchini and carrots makes a colorful side dish to accompany the holiday roast.

CHRISTMAS DINNER

Two fabulous meals for your celebration. The first, a sumptuous feast: Spinach, Mushroom and Carrot Pâté (recipe, page 195); Roast Turkey with Bread & Butter Stuffing and Green Beans Amandine (recipe, page 196); Fruitcake Petit Fours (recipe, page 197); Glazed Stuffed Acorn Squash (recipe, page 196); Consommé with Madeira and Lemon (recipe, page 194); Cranberry Orange Mold (recipe, page 197)

Christmas Celebration Dinner

Menu for 8

Consommé with Madeira and Lemon *
Spinach, Mushroom and Carrot Pâté *
Roast Turkey with
Bread & Butter Stuffing *
Glazed Stuffed Acorn Squash *
Green Beans Amandine *
Cranberry Orange Mold *
Fruitcake Petit Fours *
Coffee and Tea

*Recipe follows

CHRISTMAS CELEBRATION DINNER COUNTDOWN

UP TO ONE MONTH AHEAD:
—Prepare, but do not glaze, the Fruitcake Petit Fours. Cover the Fruitcake Petit Fours tightly with plastic wrap and freeze them.
—Prepare and freeze the consommé base for Consommé with Madeira and Lemon.

UP TO SEVERAL DAYS AHEAD:
—Prepare and refrigerate the Spinach, Mushroom and Carrot Pâté.
—Prepare and refrigerate the Cranberry Orange Mold.
—Prepare, but do not glaze, the Fruitcake Petit Fours, if they were not prepared ahead and frozen. Refrigerate the petit fours in an airtight container for up to 3 days.
—Prepare and refrigerate the consommé base for Consommé with Madeira and Lemon, if it was not prepared ahead and frozen. The consommé base may be refrigerated for up to 2 days.

THE DAY BEFORE:
—Prepare and refrigerate the Bread & Butter Stuffing; do *not* stuff the turkey until just before roasting it.
—Thaw the Fruitcake Petit Fours, if they were prepared ahead and frozen. Glaze the thawed or refrigerated Fruitcake Petit Fours.

THE MORNING BEFORE:
—Cut up the green beans for Green Beans Amandine and refrigerate them. Cut up the acorn squash and prepare the stuffing for Glazed Stuffed Acorn Squash; refrigerate the acorn squash halves and the stuffing separately.

SEVERAL HOURS BEFORE:
—Stuff the turkey and *immediately* begin roasting it.

ONE HOUR BEFORE:
—Finish preparing the Glazed Stuffed Acorn Squash.
—Unmold and garnish the Cranberry Orange Mold.
—Slice the Spinach, Mushroom and Carrot Pâté, and place the slices on individual serving plates.

JUST BEFORE SERVING:
—Finish preparing the Consommé with Madeira and Lemon.
—Prepare the Green Beans Amandine.

DURING DINNER:
—Prepare the coffee and tea.

CONSOMMÉ WITH MADEIRA AND LEMON

Makes 8 servings.

3 quarts homemade beef consommé
OR: canned beef consommé
1/2 cup Madeira wine
1/3 cup freshly squeezed lemon juice
Lemon slices and chopped fresh parsley, for garnish

1. Simmer the homemade or canned consommé in a large saucepan until the consommé is hot. Remove the saucepan from the heat, and stir in the Madeira wine and the lemon juice.
2. Ladle the consommé into individual soup bowls. Float a lemon slice and a sprinkling of parsley on top of each serving. Serve the consommé immediately.

SPINACH, MUSHROOM AND CARROT PÂTÉ

Bake at 350° for 1½ hours.
Makes 8 generous servings.

Spinach Layer:
- 2 *packages (10 ounces each) frozen chopped spinach, thawed*
- 2 *eggs*
- ½ *cup heavy cream*
- ⅓ *cup grated Parmesan cheese*
- ¼ *cup dry bread crumbs*
- 1 *clove garlic, very finely chopped*
- 1 *teaspoon dried basil, crumbled*
- ½ *teaspoon salt*
- *Large pinch cayenne pepper*

Mushroom Layer:
- 1 *pound mushrooms, wiped clean*
- ⅓ *cup finely chopped shallots OR: onion*
- 2 *tablespoons butter*
- 2 *eggs*
- ¼ *cup heavy cream*
- ⅓ *cup dry bread crumbs*
- ½ *teaspoon salt*
- ⅛ *teaspoon freshly ground pepper*
- *Pinch grated or ground nutmeg*

Carrot Layer:
- 1 *pound carrots, peeled and sliced*
- 2 *eggs*
- ¼ *cup heavy cream*
- 1 *tablespoon maple syrup*
- ½ *teaspoon salt*
- ½ *teaspoon ground cinnamon*
- *Large pinch cayenne pepper*
- ½ *cup dry bread crumbs*

1. Preheat the oven to moderate (350°). Grease a 9x5x3-inch loaf pan. Line the bottom and the sides of the loaf pan with wax paper, leaving a wax paper overhang on the long sides of the pan. Set aside the prepared loaf pan.
2. Prepare the Spinach Layer: Place the spinach in a colander in the sink. Place paper toweling over the spinach and press out as much liquid as possible.
3. Beat the eggs in a medium-size bowl. Add the spinach, heavy cream, Parmesan cheese, bread crumbs, garlic, basil, salt and cayenne pepper, and beat until the mixture is well blended. Spoon the spinach mixture into the prepared loaf pan and smooth the top of the spinach mixture.
4. Prepare the Mushroom Layer: Set aside enough large mushrooms to line up end to end the length of the loaf pan. Place the remaining mushrooms in the container of a food processor, and process until the mushrooms are finely chopped. Set aside the chopped mushrooms.
5. Sauté the shallots or onion in the butter in a small skillet over medium heat. Remove the skillet from the heat. Combine the chopped mushrooms, shallot or onion mixture, eggs, heavy cream, bread crumbs, salt, the ⅛ teaspoon of pepper and the nutmeg in a large bowl, and stir until the mixture is well blended. Spoon half of the mushroom mixture on top of the spinach layer in the loaf pan. Place the reserved mushrooms, caps down, in a line down the center of the pan, pressing them gently into the mushroom layer. Spoon the remaining mushroom mixture into the pan, and smooth the top.
6. Prepare the Carrot Layer: Steam the carrots until they are tender. Drain the carrots and cool them completely.
7. Place the carrots in the clean container of the food processor. Add the eggs, heavy cream, maple syrup, salt, cinnamon and cayenne pepper. Process the carrot mixture until it is smooth. Add the bread crumbs. Process just until all the ingredients are blended. Spoon the carrot mixture on top of the mushroom layer, and smooth the top of the carrot mixture.
8. Grease the inner side of the wax paper overhang. Fold the greased wax paper overhang over the pâté. Cover the top of the pan with aluminum foil. Set the loaf pan in a larger roasting pan and place both pans in the oven. Pour hot water into the roasting pan until the water is halfway up the sides of the loaf pan.
9. Bake in the preheated moderate oven (350°) until the pâté is firm and a knife inserted in the center comes out clean, for 1½ hours. Set the loaf pan on a wire rack. Remove the aluminum foil and let the pâté cool in the pan for 1 hour. Carefully invert the loaf pan onto the wire rack. Remove the loaf pan and the wax paper, and let the pâté cool to room temperature. Place the pâté on a serving platter (the carrot layer is the bottom of the pâté), cover the pâté and refrigerate it for at least 4 hours, or for up to 2 days.

GLAZED STUFFED ACORN SQUASH

The delightful, crunchy filling bakes right in this popular winter squash.

Bake at 350° for 55 minutes.
Makes 8 servings.

4 *acorn squash, halved and seeded*
Salt and freshly ground pepper, to taste
1/2 *cup honey*
1/4 *cup (1/2 stick) butter, softened*
2 *tablespoons Worcestershire sauce*
1/2 *cup chopped walnuts OR: pecans*
1/2 *cup dark seedless raisins*

1. Preheat the oven to moderate (350°).
2. Place the acorn squash halves, cut side down, in a shallow baking pan. Pour hot water into the pan to a depth of ½ inch.
3. Bake in the preheated moderate oven (350°) until the acorn squash is almost tender, for 40 minutes.
4. Turn over the acorn squash halves, and season them with the salt and pepper. Combine the honey, butter and Worcestershire sauce, and stir until the mixture is well blended. Stir in the walnuts or pecans and the raisins. Spoon the stuffing into the acorn squash halves.
5. Bake the stuffed acorn squash halves in the preheated moderate oven (350°) until the stuffing is heated through, for 15 minutes.

BREAD & BUTTER STUFFING

Makes enough stuffing for a 12-pound bird.

1 *medium-size onion, chopped (1/2 cup)*
1/2 *cup chopped celery*
2 *tablespoons butter*
1/2 *pound sliced white bread, cubed and dried**
1 1/2 *teaspoons dried basil, crumbled*
1/2 *cup homemade chicken stock OR: 1 1/2 teaspoons chicken boullion and 1/2 cup boiling water*

1. Sauté the onion and celery in the butter in a large saucepan for 5 minutes. Add the bread cubes and basil, and toss until the ingredients are well mixed.
2. Pour the chicken stock or chicken boullion dissolved in boiling water over the bread cube mixture, and toss until the bread cubes are evenly moistened. Stuff the turkey and immediately start roasting it.
Note: To dry bread cubes, spread the cubes in a single layer in a jelly-roll pan. Bake in a slow oven (325°) until the bread cubes are dry, for 15 minutes.

GREEN BEANS AMANDINE

Makes 8 servings.

2 *pounds green beans, trimmed and cut into 3-inch-long pieces*
1 *cup water*
1/2 *cup (1 stick) butter*
1/2 *cup sliced almonds*
Salt and freshly ground pepper, to taste

1. Combine the green beans and water in a saucepan. Cover the saucepan and bring the water to boiling. Lower the heat and simmer the green beans until they are crisply tender, for 10 to 15 minutes. Drain the green beans, and return them to the saucepan.
2. Meanwhile, melt the butter in a small skillet. Add the almonds and sauté them, stirring often, until the almonds are golden, for 3 minutes.
3. Pour the almond mixture over the green beans. Add the salt and pepper, and gently toss to combine the ingredients. Serve the green beans immediately.

FRUITCAKE PETIT FOURS

Bake at 300° for 50 minutes.
Makes twenty-five 1½-inch square petit fours.

- 1 *cup dried apricots, finely chopped*
- 1 *cup dried pineapple, finely chopped*
- 1 *cup dark seedless raisins*
- ¾ *cup candied red cherries, halved*
- ⅓ *cup plus 1 tablespoon brandy OR: orange juice*
- 1½ *cups all-purpose flour*
- ¾ *teaspoon baking powder*
- ½ *teaspoon salt*
- ¾ *cup (1½ sticks) butter*
- ¾ *cup firmly packed brown sugar*
- 3 *eggs*
- 1½ *teaspoons almond extract*
- 1½ *cups blanched whole almonds*
- 1 *tablespoon light corn syrup*
- *Sugar Glaze (recipe follows)*
- 25 *candied red cherry halves*

1. Combine the apricots, pineapple, raisins and cherries in a bowl. Stir in the ⅓ cup of brandy. Let the fruits stand for 15 minutes, stirring once.
2. Preheat the oven to slow (300°). Grease a 9 x 13 x 2-inch baking pan.
3. Combine the flour, baking powder and salt on a piece of wax paper. Set aside the flour mixture.
4. Beat together the butter and brown sugar in a large bowl until the mixture is fluffy. Beat in the eggs, one at a time. Beat in the almond extract.
5. Add the flour mixture and the fruit mixture, and stir until all the ingredients are well blended. Stir in the almonds. Pour the batter into the prepared baking pan.
6. Bake the fruitcake in the preheated slow oven (300°) until a wooden pick inserted in the center comes out clean, for 50 minutes. Remove the pan to a wire rack.
7. Combine the corn syrup with the 1 tablespoon of brandy. Brush the mixture over the warm fruitcake.
8. Cut the fruitcake into 25 equal squares. Remove the squares to the wire rack set over a piece of wax paper.
9. Spoon some of the Sugar Glaze over each fruitcake petit four, and let the glaze set. Place a candied red cherry half in the center of each fruitcake petit four.

Sugar Glaze: Beat together 2 cups of sifted 10X (confectioners' powdered) sugar and ¼ cup of lemon juice. Gradually beat in milk until the glaze is the consistency of thick cream. *Makes 2⅓ cups.*

CRANBERRY ORANGE MOLD

Makes 8 servings.

- 2 *envelopes unflavored gelatin*
- 2 *cups orange juice*
- 3 *cups fresh cranberries OR: thawed frozen cranberries*
- 1½ *cups sugar*
- 1 *can (11 ounces) mandarin orange segments, drained*
- 1 *tablespoon lemon juice*
- *Nonstick vegetable cooking spray*
- *Strips of orange zest (orange part of rind only)*

1. Sprinkle the gelatin over the juice in a 1½-quart saucepan. Let the gelatin stand for 5 minutes to soften. Cook over low heat, stirring constantly, until the gelatin dissolves completely. Set aside the gelatin mixture.
2. Combine the cranberries, sugar and mandarin orange segments in a 2-quart saucepan. Heat the mixture to boiling over medium heat. Lower the heat and simmer the mixture for 10 minutes. Stir in the gelatin mixture and the lemon juice. Refrigerate the cranberry mixture until it is slightly thickened, stirring the mixture occasionally.
3. Spray a 4-cup fancy mold with the nonstick vegetable cooking spray. Pour in the cranberry mixture and cover the mold. Refrigerate the cranberry mixture until it is firm, for 4 hours.
4. To unmold, carefully loosen the cranberry mixture around the edges with a sharp knife. Dip the mold into a pan of hot water for 30 seconds. Invert the mold onto a serving platter. Garnish the Cranberry Orange Mold with the strips of orange zest.

Light & Delicious 900-Calorie Christmas Feast

Menu for 8

Cranberry Coulis *
Zucchini Chicken Soup *
Winter Greens and Pink Grapefruit with Warm Balsamic Dressing *
Boneless Pork Loin Stuffed with a Mushroom Duxelle *
OR: Turkey Breast with Thickened Pan Juices *
Maple Lime Sweet Potatoes *
Roasted Yellow Peppers *
Cardamom Bread Wreaths *
Choice of One Dessert:
Strawberry Layer Cake with Fluffy Frosting *
OR: Pumpkin Cheesecake *

*Recipe follows

LIGHT & DELICIOUS 900-CALORIE CHRISTMAS FEAST COUNTDOWN

3 WEEKS BEFORE:
—Prepare the Cardamom Bread Wreaths. Freeze the breads for up to 3 weeks.
—Prepare the cake layers for the Strawberry Layer Cake with Fluffy Frosting. Wrap each cake layer tightly and freeze the cake layers for up to 3 weeks.

1 WEEK BEFORE:
—Prepare and refrigerate the Cranberry Coulis.
—Prepare and refrigerate the Balsamic Dressing.

3 DAYS BEFORE:
—If you are serving the Boneless Pork Loin, prepare and refrigerate the Mushroom Duxelle.

2 DAYS BEFORE:
—Bake the sweet potatoes for the Maple Lime Sweet Potatoes. Slice the baked potatoes, arrange the slices in a shallow baking dish and refrigerate the dish. Prepare the maple lime syrup; refrigerate the syrup separately.
—Prepare the Roasted Yellow Peppers; do not drizzle with the olive oil. Wrap the yellow peppers tightly and refrigerate them.

1 DAY BEFORE:
—Prepare the Zucchini Chicken Soup through Step 3, reducing the cooking time by 10 minutes. Refrigerate the soup.
—Prepare and refrigerate the Pumpkin Cheesecake.
—Prepare the cake layers for Strawberry Layer Cake with Fluffy Frosting, if they were not prepared ahead and frozen.
—Prepare the Cardamom Bread Wreaths, if they were not prepared ahead and frozen.
—Wash, dry and tear the lettuce for Winter Greens and Pink Grapefruit. Wrap the prepared lettuce in paper toweling, place the wrapped lettuce in a plastic bag and refrigerate it. Section the pink grapefruits and refrigerate the grapefruit sections.
—Thaw the cake layers for Strawberry Layer Cake with Fluffy Frosting, if they were prepared ahead and frozen.
—Thaw the Cardamom Bread Wreaths, if they were prepared ahead and frozen.

EARLY IN THE DAY:
—Finish preparing the Strawberry Layer Cake with Fluffy Frosting.
—Arrange the prepared lettuce and the endive for Winter Greens and Pink Grapefruit in a salad bowl. Cover the bowl with damp paper toweling and refrigerate it.
—Bring the prepared sweet potatoes for Maple Lime Sweet Potatoes to room temperature, if they were prepared ahead and refrigerated. Finish preparing the Maple Lime Sweet Potatoes, increasing the baking time by 10 minutes, until the potatoes are warmed through.

SEVERAL HOURS BEFORE:
—If you are serving Boneless Pork Loin, prepare the Mushroom Duxelle, if it was not prepared ahead and refrigerated. Stuff the pork loin and start roasting it.
—If you are serving Turkey Breast with Thickened Pan Juices, prepare and start roasting the turkey breast.
—Prepare the Maple Lime Sweet Potatoes, if they were not prepared ahead and refrigerated.
—Prepare the Zucchini Chicken Soup, if it was not prepared ahead and refrigerated.

JUST BEFORE SERVING TIME:
—Finish preparing the Zucchini Chicken Soup. Cook the soup for the time indicated in Step 3, and continue with Step 4.
—Finish preparing the Winter Greens and Pink Grapefruit with Warm Balsamic Dressing.
—If you are serving Turkey Breast with Thickened Pan Juices, prepare the thickened pan juices.

CRANBERRY COULIS

Makes 2½ cups; 32 calories per 2 tablespoons of sauce.

1 *cup water*
½ *cup plus 2 tablespoons sugar*
1 *bag (12 ounces) fresh cranberries*
OR: thawed frozen cranberries

1. Combine the water, sugar and cranberries in a medium-size saucepan. Bring the mixture to boiling. Boil, uncovered, stirring occasionally, until the berries pop and the mixture thickens slightly, for 5 minutes.
2. Transfer the mixture to a small serving bowl and cool the mixture slightly. Cover the bowl with plastic wrap and refrigerate the coulis for several hours, or until it is cold.

ZUCCHINI CHICKEN SOUP

Makes 8 servings (6 cups); 40 calories per serving.

1½ *pounds zucchini, sliced into ⅛-inch-thick rounds*
½ *teaspoon salt*
2 *medium-size onions, coarsely chopped*
½ *to 1 teaspoon reduced-calorie margarine*
1 *quart homemade chicken stock*
OR: canned chicken broth, defatted
½ *cup chopped seeded tomatoes*
2 *teaspoons lemon juice*
½ *teaspoon dried tarragon, crumbled*
¼ *teaspoon dried basil, crumbled*

1. Place the zucchini in a colander in the sink. Sprinkle the zucchini with the salt, and toss the zucchini. Let the zucchini stand for 20 minutes. Dry the zucchini with paper toweling.
2. Sauté the zucchini and the onion in ½ teaspoon of the margarine in a large, nonstick saucepan over medium-high heat for 5 minutes. If necessary, add the remaining ½ teaspoon of margarine to prevent the vegetables from sticking.
3. Add the chicken stock or broth and the tomatoes. Bring the mixture to boiling. Lower the heat and simmer the mixture until the vegetables soften, for 10 to 15 minutes.
4. Stir in the lemon juice, tarragon and basil. Serve the soup hot.

WINTER GREENS AND PINK GRAPEFRUIT WITH WARM BALSAMIC DRESSING

Makes 8 servings; 76 calories per serving.

16 *cups torn assorted lettuce leaves, including red leaf and romaine*
1 *to 2 Belgian endive, ends trimmed and leaves separated*
2 *medium-size pink grapefruit, sectioned*

Warm Balsamic Dressing:
½ *cup pink grapefruit juice*
2 *tablespoons balsamic vinegar*
¼ *teaspoon salt*
2 *cloves garlic, pressed or crushed*
2 *tablespoons olive oil*

1. Arrange the lettuce and the endive in a large serving bowl. Set aside the grapefruit sections.
2. Prepare the Warm Balsamic Dressing: Combine the grapefruit juice, vinegar and salt in a 2-cup measure.
3. Sauté the garlic in the oil in a small skillet for 1 to 2 minutes, or until the garlic is golden. Let the oil cool to lukewarm.
4. Strain the oil into the grapefruit juice mixture and discard the garlic.
5. Arrange the grapefruit sections over the greens. Pour the dressing over, toss the salad and serve.

THE LIGHTER SIDE OF FEASTING

• Instead of basting turkey with butter, stuffing it with a sausage mixture and serving it with a cream gravy, try roasting an all-white-meat turkey breast. Remove the skin before serving the turkey breast to ensure moist meat but less fat. Prepare homemade bread crumbs and combine them with dried mixed fruit or fresh herbs to make stuffing. Moisten the stuffing with a little defatted chicken broth. To make gravy, use defatted chicken broth and lowfat milk instead of half-and-half or heavy cream. Add more body to gravy with puréed cooked onions or several cooked chicken livers, stirring them into the gravy thoroughly.
• Instead of prime rib with Yorkshire pudding, serve leaner beef tenderloin with parslied new potatoes and plain baked apples. Another tasty alternative is mustard-glazed pork tenderloin with whole wheat bread and raisin stuffing on the side.
• For a simply wonderful substitute for candied yams, bake the yams, cut them into cubes, and drizzle the yam cubes sparingly with maple syrup. Or top yam cubes with a small spoonful of brown sugar or naturally sweet crushed pineapple in pineapple juice.
• Acorn squash is a deliciously low-calorie vegetable, and so easy to prepare! Cut an acorn squash into rings, place the squash rings in a baking pan with a little water, cover the pan and bake until the squash is tender. Serve the squash rings topped with a dollop of cranberry relish or fruit chutney.
• Instead of serving heavy creamed soups, such as oyster stew, New England clam chowder, cream of broccoli, potato or pumpkin, base soups on defatted beef or chicken stock, or vegetable purées. Some luscious lighter variety soups include Manhattan clam chowder (tomato-based), escarole, Greek-style lemon, vegetable or even quick-to-put-together egg drop soup. Another alternative is preparing cream soups without the cream: Use whole or lowfat milk thickened with several tablespoons of flour. Thick vegetable purée soups can be thinned out with a little skim milk. Use a light touch with garnishes: slivered green onions, vegetable or fruit slices and fresh herbs all make tasty toppings for soup.
• For before-dinner snacking, set out crisp tender asparagus spears, either fresh or thawed frozen, with a mustard vinaigrette—go easy on the oil! Shrimp and scallops make perfect appetizers when poached in lemon. And even "imitation" crabmeat is a good light choice, served with homemade mild chili sauce, salsa or cocktail sauce. These all are healthier alternatives to salted nuts, assorted cheeses or smoked meats.
• For lusciously light desserts, try a rolled sponge cake filled with liqueur-flavored whipped cream. Or an open-faced apple tart glazed with strained apricot preserves. Fill cream puffs with lowfat frozen yogurt or chocolate pudding made with skim milk, then dust the tops with 10X (confectioners' powdered) sugar.

CARVING THE TURKEY

1. Place the turkey, breast side up, on a cutting board. Steady the bird with the back of the carving fork to avoid sticking the tines into the meat and releasing the juices. Slice through the skin between the breast and thigh. Pull the leg back to locate the joint. Cut through the joint to remove the leg.
2. Gently stretch apart the drumstick and thigh, and find the joint. With a firm downward movement of the knife, cut through the joint.
3. Carve the thigh and wing: Moving parallel to the bone, cut slices from the thigh. To remove the wing, cut through the skin at the corner of the breast around the wing. Move the wing to locate the joint. Cut through the joint to remove the wing with a small part of the breast.
4. Starting at the outside of the breast, cut diagonally downward through the breast to produce thin slices. Steady the turkey with the back of the carving fork to avoid sticking the tines into the meat. When ready to refill the serving platter, repeat all the carving steps on the other side of the turkey.

BONELESS PORK LOIN STUFFED WITH A MUSHROOM DUXELLE

Roast at 400° for 30 minutes; then at 350° for 30 to 40 minutes.
Makes 16 servings; 208 calories per serving.

½ cup very finely chopped shallots (3½ ounces)
2½ pounds mushrooms, very finely chopped
¼ teaspoon reduced-calorie margarine
2 tablespoons Madeira OR: dry white wine
1 tablespoon lemon juice
1 teaspoon dried thyme, crumbled
1 teaspoon salt
½ teaspoon freshly ground pepper
1 trimmed boneless center-cut pork loin, untied (4 pounds)
2 ounces jarred red pimientos, drained and sliced into ⅛-inch-wide strips (scant ½ cup)
1½ cups plus 2 tablespoons water
2 tablespoons cornstarch OR: all-purpose flour

1. Prepare the Mushroom Duxelle: Sauté the shallots and as much of the mushrooms as will fit, in the margarine in a large nonstick skillet. As the mixture cooks down, add the remaining mushrooms. Cook the mixture, stirring, for 20 minutes. Stir in the Madeira or white wine, the lemon juice, thyme, ½ teaspoon of the salt and the pepper. Cook the mixture, stirring, for 10 to 20 minutes, or until the liquid has evaporated. Watch carefully toward the end; the mushroom duxelle should be almost dry.
2. Preheat the oven to hot (400°).
3. Place the loin boned side up, fat-trimmed side down, on a work surface. Place a knife to one side on top of the loin and cut down two-thirds of the way through the meat. With the knife still in the meat, turn the side of the knife parallel to the work surface and cut across, but not all the way through the meat, to form a pocket. Open up the pocket.
4. Season the pocket with the remaining ½ teaspoon of salt. Pat the mushroom duxelle evenly over the bottom part of the pocket. Arrange the pimiento strips, slightly overlapping, on the duxelle in 3 long rows down the length of the roast.
5. Roll up the pork from the long side to enclose the duxelle. Turn the stuffed roast seam side up and tie it at 1½-inch intervals with kitchen twine. Insert 3 wooden picks through each end to hold in the duxelle. Place the roast, seam side down, on a rack in a large roasting pan. Add 1½ cups of water to the pan.
6. Roast the pork loin in the preheated hot oven (400°) for 30 minutes. Reduce the heat to moderate (350°). Roast for 30 to 40 minutes more, or until a meat thermometer inserted in the thickest portion of the meat, without touching the duxelle, registers 160°.
7. Remove the pork loin from the pan and let it stand for 10 minutes before slicing.
8. Transfer the pan juices to a saucepan; you should have about 2 cups. Stir the cornstarch or flour into the remaining 2 tablespoons of water in a cup until the mixture is smooth. Add the cornstarch mixture to the saucepan, and bring the mixture to boiling. Lower the heat and simmer the gravy, stirring, until it has thickened, for 1 minute. Serve the gravy with the pork.

MAPLE LIME SWEET POTATOES

Bake at 350° for about 50 minutes.
Makes 8 servings; 159 calories per serving.

3 pounds sweet potatoes, scrubbed
½ cup reduced-calorie imitation maple syrup
4 teaspoons fresh lime juice

1. Preheat the oven to moderate (350°).
2. Bake the sweet potatoes in the preheated moderate oven (350°) until the potatoes are tender, for about 45 minutes.
3. Meanwhile, stir together the maple syrup and the lime juice in a 1-cup glass measure. Set aside the syrup mixture, but do not refrigerate it.
4. Remove the potatoes from the oven, but do not turn off the oven. When the potatoes are cool enough to handle, peel them. Cut the potatoes in half lengthwise. Slice each half lengthwise into ½-inch-wide slices. Layer the slices in an ovenproof 2-quart baking dish. Pour about three-quarters of the syrup mixture over the potatoes.
5. Bake the sweet potatoes at 350° until they are warm, for 5 minutes. Pour the remaining syrup over the potatoes, and serve.

ROASTED YELLOW PEPPERS

Broil for 15 minutes.
Makes 8 servings; 7 calories per serving.

4 *medium-size sweet yellow peppers (about 1¼ pounds)*
Olive oil (optional)

1. Preheat the broiler. Lay the yellow peppers in a single layer on the broiler pan.
2. Broil the yellow peppers 2 inches from the heat source, turning them frequently, until they are blackened, for 15 minutes. Cool the yellow peppers under cold water. Remove the blackened skin with a sharp knife, but leave the stems intact. Slice the yellow peppers in half through the stems, and core and seed the peppers. Blot the yellow peppers dry with paper toweling. Serve the yellow peppers immediately, or refrigerate them until serving time. Bring the yellow peppers to room temperature before serving them.
3. At serving time, drizzle the roasted yellow peppers with olive oil, if you wish.

TURKEY BREAST WITH THICKENED PAN JUICES

Bake at 325° for about 2½ hours.
Makes 16 servings; 148 calories per serving.

2 *large carrots, peeled and cut into thick slices*
1 *celery stalk, cut into thick slices*
1 *large onion, coarsely chopped*
¾ *cup dry white wine*
½ *cup water*
½ *teaspoon dried thyme, crumbled*
1 *small bay leaf*
6 *pounds turkey breast on bone, thawed if frozen*
1 *to 3 cups homemade chicken stock OR: canned chicken broth, chilled and all fat skimmed off*
2 *to 3 tablespoons all-purpose flour*
½ *teaspoon salt*
¼ *teaspoon freshly ground pepper*

1. Preheat the oven to slow (325°).
2. Place the carrots, celery and onion in the center of a large roasting pan. Add the wine, water, thyme and bay leaf. Set the turkey breast, skin side up, on top of the vegetables. Cover the turkey breast and the baking pan completely with heavy-duty aluminum foil.
3. Bake the turkey breast in the preheated slow oven (325°) for 1 hour. Remove the aluminum foil. Bake the turkey breast for 1 hour and 15 minutes to 1 hour and 30 minutes more, or until a meat thermometer inserted in the thickest portion of the breast, without touching the bone, registers 180°.
4. Remove the turkey breast to a large serving platter, cover the turkey with aluminum foil and keep it warm.
5. Strain the liquid left in the roasting pan into a 4-cup glass measure, discarding the vegetables. Allow the pan juices to stand a few minutes until the fat rises to the top. Skim off and discard all the fat using a bulb baster.
5. Add enough defatted chicken stock or broth to the pan juices to make 3 cups. Pour the pan juices into a medium-size saucepan. Stir together ½ cup of additional chicken stock or broth and 2 tablespoons of the flour in a small bowl until the mixture is smooth. Add the remaining tablespoon of flour if thicker pan juices are desired. Stir the flour mixture into the pan juices. Bring the pan juices to boiling, stirring constantly. Cook the pan juices until they thicken slightly, for 3 to 5 minutes. Season the thickened pan juices with the salt and pepper. To serve, pour the thicken pan juices into a gravy boat.
6. Slice the turkey breast and pass the gravy boat.

CARDAMOM BREAD WREATHS

Bake at 350° for 25 minutes.
Makes 2 bread wreaths (14 servings each);
110 calories per serving.

*1/4 cup warm water (105° to 115°)**
1/4 cup sugar
1 envelope active dry yeast
2 eggs, slightly beaten
1/4 cup reduced-calorie margarine
1 cup plus 2 tablespoons canned evaporated skim milk
1/2 teaspoon salt
1/2 teaspoon ground cardamom
4 1/2 to 5 1/2 cups all-purpose flour
1 egg white

1. Combine the water, 1 tablespoon of the sugar and the yeast in a large bowl. Stir until the yeast is dissolved. Let the yeast mixture stand until it is bubbly, for about 10 minutes.
2. Beat in the remaining sugar, the eggs, margarine, 1 cup of the evaporated skim milk, the salt and cardamom. Beat in 3 cups of the flour until the mixture is smooth. Gradually add enough of the remaining flour to form a soft dough. Let the dough stand, covered, for 30 minutes.
3. Turn out the dough onto a heavily floured surface. Knead until the dough is smooth and elastic, for about 8 to 10 minutes. Press the dough into a greased large bowl and turn the greased side up. Cover the bowl and let the dough rise in a warm place, away from drafts, until it is doubled in size, for about 1 hour.
4. Divide the dough in half, and work with one half at a time. Divide the half into thirds. Roll each third between your palms and a lightly oiled surface into a 22-inch rope. Braid the 3 ropes together, starting from the center and working to the ends. Trim the ends of the dough braids to be even.
5. Place a 3 1/2- to 4-inch-diameter soufflé dish or metal bowl in the center of a baking sheet. Grease the outside of the dish. Wrap the dough braid around the dish to form a wreath. Bring the ends of the braid together and trim the excess dough. Pinch the ends to seal them.
6. Roll the dough trimmings into an 11-inch-long rope. Shape the rope into a bow without knotting it, keeping the trailing ends of the dough parallel to each other. Place the bow over the sealed portion of the wreath. Repeat with the remaining half of the dough to make a second wreath.
7. Beat the remaining 2 tablespoons of evaporated milk with the egg white in a cup. Brush the wreaths with the egg wash. Lightly cover the wreaths with plastic wrap and let them rise in a warm place, away from drafts, until they are doubled in size, for 45 minutes to 1 hour. Brush the wreaths again with the egg wash.
8. Meanwhile, preheat the oven to moderate (350°).
9. Bake the bread wreaths, one at a time, in the middle of the preheated moderate oven (350°) for 25 minutes, or until each wreath is golden brown and sounds hollow when lightly tapped with your fingertips. Cool the bread wreaths on wire racks.
***Note:** *Warm water should feel tepid when dropped on your wrist.*

STRAWBERRY LAYER CAKE WITH FLUFFY FROSTING

This cake is a bit tricky to make, so let the experienced baker in the house try it first.

Bake cake layers at 400° for 5 minutes.
Makes 8 servings; 190 calories per serving.

Cake Layers:
2/3 cup sifted cake flour (not self-rising)
1 1/2 teaspoons baking powder
1/4 cup sugar
1 teaspoon grated orange or lemon zest (orange or yellow part of rind only)
4 eggs, separated
1/8 teaspoon salt

Strawberry Filling:
1 envelope whipped topping mix
1/2 cup cold skim milk
1/4 cup reduced-sugar strawberry spread

Fluffy Frosting:
1/3 cup sugar
2 tablespoons dark corn syrup
3 tablespoons water
2 egg whites

1. Preheat the oven to hot (400°). Grease three 8 x 1½-inch round nonstick layer cake pans. Line the bottoms of the pans with aluminum foil and grease the foil.
2. Prepare the Cake Layers: Sift together the cake flour and the baking powder onto a piece of wax paper. Combine the sugar with the orange or lemon zest on a second piece of wax paper. Beat together the sugar mixture and the egg yolks in a small bowl with an electric mixer at high speed for 7 minutes. Beat in the flour mixture; the combined mixture will be very thick and sticky.
3. Beat the egg whites and the salt in a clean bowl with clean beaters until soft peaks form. Stir one-third of the egg whites into the egg yolk mixture. Fold in the remaining egg whites. Divide the batter evenly among the prepared pans.
4. Bake the cake layers in the preheated hot oven (400°) for 5 minutes, or until the layers pull away from the sides of the pans and spring back when lightly touched with your fingertip. Loosen the layers around the edges with a thin knife. Invert the layers onto wire racks and peel off the aluminum foil. Cool the cake layers completely.
5. Prepare the Strawberry Filling: Prepare the whipped topping mix following the package directions, using the skim milk instead of whole milk. Fold in the strawberry spread. Refrigerate the filling for 10 minutes to firm it up, if necessary.
6. Set one cake layer on a cake plate. Spread the layer with half the filling and top it with the second cake layer. Spread the second layer with the remaining filling and top it with the third cake layer. Refrigerate the cake for 1 hour before frosting it.
7. Prepare the Fluffy Frosting: Combine the sugar, corn syrup and water in a very small, heavy saucepan.
8. Beat the egg whites in a small bowl with an electric mixer until firm peaks form. Bring the corn syrup mixture to boiling. Continue boiling, without stirring, until the syrup mixture registers 242° on a candy thermometer. With the electric mixer running, very slowly pour the hot syrup in a thin stream into the egg whites, beating constantly (the hot syrup mixture will cook the egg whites sufficiently to avoid the risk of infection from salmonella bacteria sometimes found in raw eggs). Continue beating at high speed until stiff, glossy peaks form. Frost the cake, and serve it.

PUMPKIN CHEESECAKE

Bake at 350° for 45 minutes.
Makes 10 servings; 133 calories per serving.

Nonstick vegetable cooking spray
3 *tablespoons finely crushed zwieback biscuit crumbs*
1½ *cups lowfat cottage cheese*
1½ *cups canned pumpkin purée (not pie filling)*
½ *cup granulated sugar*
¼ *cup firmly packed dark brown sugar*
3 *tablespoons all-purpose flour*
2 *eggs, slightly beaten*
¾ *cup skim milk*
2 *teaspoons fresh lemon juice*
1 *teaspoon ground cinnamon*
½ *teaspoon ground ginger*
½ *teaspoon salt*
⅛ *teaspoon ground nutmeg*

1. Preheat the oven to moderate (350°).
2. Spray the sides and bottom of an 8-inch springform pan, with a tight-fitting bottom, with the nonstick vegetable cooking spray. Sprinkle the biscuit crumbs over the bottom of the pan.
3. Place the cottage cheese in the container of a food processor. Whirl until the cheese is very smooth (there should be no lumps), scraping down the sides of the container once or twice.
4. Add the pumpkin purée, granulated and brown sugars, flour, eggs, milk, lemon juice, cinnamon, ginger, salt and nutmeg to the processor container. Whirl until the pumpkin mixture is smooth. Let the pumpkin mixture stand for 5 minutes. Ladle the pumpkin mixture into the prepared springform pan.
5. Bake the cheesecake in the preheated moderate oven (350°) for 45 minutes; the outer edge of the cheesecake will be set but the center still will be soft. Turn off the oven. Leave the cheesecake in the oven for 30 minutes more.
6. Cool the cheesecake slightly in the pan on a wire rack. Lightly cover the cheesecake and refrigerate it overnight, or until the cheesecake is well chilled. To serve, run a thin knife around the outer edge of the cheesecake, and remove the pan side.

COOKIES

A bakeshop collection of cookies: Cookie Tiers (recipe, page 209); Chocolate Orange Spritz Sandwiches (recipe, page 208); Chocolate Pistachio Meringues (recipe, page 211); Raspberry Almond Sandwich Cookies (recipe, page 207); Raspberry Thumbprints (recipe, page 209); Sprinkled Stars (recipe, page 208); Christmas Tree Cookies (recipe, page 207); Grand Marnier Wreaths (recipe, page 210).

RASPBERRY ALMOND SANDWICH COOKIES

Bake at 350° for 8 to 10 minutes.
Makes about 2 dozen sandwich cookies.

- ¾ *cup (1½ sticks) unsalted butter or margarine, softened*
- ¼ *cup sugar*
- 1 *teaspoon almond extract*
- 2 *cups sifted all-purpose flour*
- 1 *egg white, slightly beaten*
- 1 *tablespoon finely chopped almonds*
- 1½ *teaspoons sugar*
- ½ *cup seedless red raspberry preserves*

1. Beat together the butter or margarine, the ¼ cup of sugar and the almond extract in a large bowl until it is light and fluffy. Beat in the flour until it is well blended. Shape the dough into a ball, wrap it in plastic wrap and refrigerate until the dough is chilled, for about 1 hour.
2. Place a piece of wax paper on top of a slightly damp baking sheet, and lightly flour the wax paper. Divide the dough into thirds. Roll out one-third of the dough on the prepared baking sheet to a ⅛-inch thickness. Cut out the dough with a lightly floured, 2-inch hexagonal or round cookie cutter; do not lift the dough off the baking sheet. For half the cookies, cut out the centers with a floured, ¾-inch cookie cutter. Place the baking sheet in the freezer for 5 minutes to stiffen the dough.
3. Remove the excess dough from around the cookies, gather it together and set it aside. Using a spatula, carefully remove the cookies from the baking sheet. Place the cookies on an ungreased baking sheet, leaving about 1½ inches between the cookies. Remove the center cutouts from the cookies and add them to the excess dough.
4. Preheat the oven to moderate (350°).
5. Repeat the rolling and cutting with the remaining two-thirds of the dough, one-third at a time. Continue to gather together the excess dough, roll it and cut it out until all the dough has been used.
6. Brush only the cookie rings with the egg white. Combine the almonds with the 1½ teaspoons of sugar, and sprinkle the mixture over the cookie rings.
7. Bake in the preheated moderate oven (350°) until the cookies are a light golden brown, for 8 to 10 minutes. Remove the cookies to wire racks to cool. Spread the bottom of each whole cookie with some of the raspberry preserves. Place a cookie ring on top of the preserves to make a sandwich.

CHRISTMAS TREE COOKIES

Bake at 375° for 9 to 10 minutes.
Makes about 2½ dozen 4-inch cookies.

- 2½ *cups sifted all-purpose flour*
- 1 *teaspoon baking powder*
- ⅛ *teaspoon salt*
- ½ *cup (1 stick) butter or margarine, softened*
- 1 *cup sugar*
- 1 *egg*
- 1 *teaspoon vanilla*
- ½ *teaspoon almond extract*
- *Tube of green decorator icing*
- *Silver dragées*

1. Sift together the flour, baking powder and salt onto a piece of wax paper. Grease 2 baking sheets and set them aside.
2. Beat together the butter or margarine and the sugar in a large bowl until it is light and fluffy. Beat in the egg, vanilla and almond extract. Gradually stir in the flour mixture to make a stiff dough; if the dough becomes too dry, add 1 to 2 tablespoons of milk. Shape the dough into a ball, wrap it in wax paper and refrigerate the dough until it is chilled, for about 30 minutes.
3. Preheat the oven to moderate (375°).
4. Divide the dough into thirds. Roll out the dough, one-third at a time, on a lightly floured surface to a ⅜-inch thickness. Cut out the dough with a floured, 4-inch Christmas tree-shaped cookie cutter. Place the cookies on the prepared baking sheets, leaving about 2 inches between each cookie.
5. Bake in the preheated moderate oven (375°) until the cookies are lightly browned around the edges, for 9 to 10 minutes. Remove the cookies to wire racks to cool.
6. Using the photo on page 206 as a guide, decorate the cookies with the green icing and the silver candy balls.

CHOCOLATE ORANGE SPRITZ SANDWICHES

Bake at 350° for 10 to 12 minutes.
Makes about 3½ dozen sandwich cookies.

4 cups sifted all-purpose flour
1 teaspoon baking powder
1 teaspoon salt
1½ cups (3 sticks) unsalted butter or margarine, softened
1 cup sugar
1 egg
1 teaspoon vanilla
1 tablespoon grated orange zest (orange part of rind only)
2 tablespoons unsweetened cocoa powder
Orange Butter Cream and Chocolate Orange Butter Cream (recipes follow)

1. Preheat the oven to moderate (350°).
2. Sift together the flour, baking powder and salt onto a piece of wax paper.
3. Beat together the butter or margarine and the sugar in a large bowl until it is light and fluffy. Beat in the egg and the vanilla. Stir in the flour mixture until it is well blended. Divide the dough in half. Stir the orange zest into one half of the dough. Stir the cocoa powder into the second half of the dough.
4. Fill a cookie press with the orange-flavored dough. Press out the dough into the shape desired, onto an ungreased baking sheet, leaving about 2 inches between each cookie.
5. Bake in the preheated moderate oven (350°) until the cookies are lightly browned around the edges, for 10 to 12 minutes. Transfer the cookies to wire racks and let the cookies cool completely.
6. Fill the clean cookie press with the chocolate dough. Press out the chocolate cookies in the same shape following Step 4. Bake and cool the cookies following the directions in Step 5.
7. Spread Orange Butter Cream or Chocolate Orange Butter Cream over the flat sides of the orange cookies. Top each orange cookie with a chocolate cookie to make a sandwich. If you wish, use additional Butter Cream to pipe designs on the sandwiches.

Orange Butter Cream: Beat together ¼ cup (½ stick) of butter and ½ teaspoon of grated orange zest (orange part of rind only) in a bowl until it is light and fluffy. Beat in 2 cups of unsifted 10X (confectioners' powdered) sugar and 1 to 2 tablespoons of orange juice until it is a good spreading consistency.
Chocolate Orange Butter Cream: Remove half the Orange Butter Cream to another bowl. Blend in 2 teaspoons of unsweetened cocoa powder.
Makes enough to fill 3½ dozen sandwich cookies.

SPRINKLED STARS

Bake at 350° for 15 to 17 minutes for 3-inch cookies; 10 to 12 minutes for 2½-inch cookies.
Makes 16 large cookies or 30 small cookies.

½ cup (1 stick) butter, softened
½ cup (1 stick) margarine, softened
1 cup sugar
6 egg yolks
1 teaspoon vanilla
4 cups sifted all-purpose flour
1 egg, slightly beaten
Colored nonpareils

1. Beat together the butter, margarine and sugar in a large bowl until it is light and fluffy. Beat in the egg yolks and the vanilla until they are combined. Stir in the flour until well blended. Shape the dough into a ball, wrap it in wax paper and refrigerate for 15 minutes.
2. Meanwhile, preheat the oven to moderate (350°). Lightly grease 2 baking sheets.
3. Divide the dough into thirds. Roll out the dough, one-third at a time, on a floured surface to a ¼-inch thickness. Cut out the dough with a 2½- or 3-inch star-shaped cookie cutter. Transfer the cookies to the prepared baking sheets, leaving 2 inches between the cookies. Brush the cookies with the beaten egg, and sprinkle with the nonpareils. Gather the excess dough, reroll and cut out until all the dough has been used.
4. Bake in the preheated moderate oven (350°) for 15 to 17 minutes for 3-inch cookies, and 10 to 12 minutes for 2½-inch cookies. Remove the cookies to wire racks to cool completely.

COOKIE TIERS

Bake at 350° for 10 to 12 minutes for 2-inch cookies;
8 to 10 minutes for 1- and 1½-inch cookies.
Makes 2½ dozen cookie tiers.

- ¾ *cup (1½ sticks) unsalted butter*
- ¾ *cup sugar*
- 4 *hard-cooked egg yolks*
- 2 *tablespoons white rum*
- 2 *cups sifted all-purpose flour*
- ¼ *teaspoon salt*
- ⅓ *cup currant jelly*
- *Sifted 10X (confectioners' powdered) sugar*
- *Candied cherry halves (optional)*

1. Beat together the butter and the sugar in a large bowl until it is light and fluffy. Press the hard-cooked egg yolks through a sieve into the butter mixture. Stir in the rum until it is combined. Stir in the flour and the salt until the mixture is well blended. Shape the dough into a ball, wrap it in plastic wrap and refrigerate the dough overnight.
2. When ready to bake the cookies, preheat the oven to moderate (350°).
3. Divide the dough into thirds. Roll out the chilled dough, one-third at a time, between pieces of wax paper to a ⅛-inch thickness. Carefully peel off the top piece of wax paper. Cut out the dough with plain or scalloped-edged cookie cutters in three sizes: 2-inch, 1½-inch and 1-inch. Transfer the cookies to ungreased baking sheets, placing the 2-inch cookies on one sheet and the 1½- and 1-inch cookies on a second sheet. Gather together the excess dough, reroll and cut out cookies until all the dough has been used.
4. Bake in the preheated moderate oven (350°) for 10 to 12 minutes for 2-inch cookies, and 8 to 10 minutes for 1½- and 1-inch cookies, or until the edges of the cookies are lightly browned. Remove the cookies to wire racks to cool completely.
5. Spread the flat sides of the 1½-inch cookies with a thin layer of jelly. Place the 1½-inch cookies, jellied side down, on top of the 2-inch cookies. Repeat with the 1-inch cookies, placing them on top of the 1½-inch cookies to make three-tiered cookies. Dust with the 10X (confectioners' powdered) sugar. If you wish, place a candied cherry half on top of each cookie.

RASPBERRY THUMBPRINTS

Bake at 400° for 12 to 14 minutes.
Makes about 8 dozen cookies.

- 1 *container (16 ounces) cottage cheese*
- 1 *pound (4 sticks) unsalted butter or margarine, softened*
- 1 *teaspoon vanilla*
- 4 *cups unsifted all-purpose flour*
- ½ *teaspoon salt*
- *Nonstick vegetable cooking spray*
- *Granulated sugar*
- 1 *cup seedless raspberry preserves*

1. Press the cottage cheese through a sieve into a large bowl, or whirl the cottage cheese in the container of a food processor until it is puréed, and place it in a large bowl. Add the butter and the vanilla to the cottage cheese, and beat until the mixture is light and fluffy. Stir in the flour and the salt until they are well blended. Shape the dough into a ball, wrap it in wax paper and refrigerate the dough for 30 minutes, until it is firm.
2. Meanwhile, preheat the oven to hot (400°). Lightly grease several baking sheets with the nonstick vegetable cooking spray.
3. Break off walnut-sized pieces of the chilled dough, and roll them into small balls. Roll the dough balls in the sugar. Place the dough balls on the prepared baking sheets, leaving about 2 inches between the cookies. Make an indentation in the middle of each cookie with your thumb. Fill each indentation with ½ teaspoon of the raspberry preserves.
4. Bake the cookies in the preheated hot oven (400°) until they are lightly browned and crispy, for 12 to 14 minutes. Remove the cookies to wire racks to cool completely.

GRAND MARNIER WREATHS

Bake at 350° for 10 to 12 minutes.
Makes about 3 dozen cookies.

- 2¼ *cups unsifted all-purpose flour*
- 1 *teaspoon ground nutmeg*
- ¼ *teaspoon salt*
- ⅔ *cup unsalted butter or margarine, softened*
- ⅓ *cup sugar*
- 2 *tablespoons grated orange zest (orange part of rind only)*
- 1 *egg*
- 2 *tablespoons Grand Marnier*
- ½ *cup candied red cherries, chopped*
- *Grand Marnier Glaze (recipe follows)*
- *Candied red cherry halves, for garnish*
- *Candied green cherries, cut into wedges, for garnish*

1. Preheat the oven to moderate (350°). Grease several baking sheets and set them aside.
2. Sift together the flour, nutmeg and salt onto a piece of wax paper.
3. Beat together the butter or margarine, sugar and orange zest in a large bowl until it is light and fluffy. Beat in the egg and the Grand Marnier. Add the flour mixture to the butter mixture until they are well blended. Gently fold in the ½ cup of candied red cherries. Roll 1 tablespoon of the dough into a 5-inch-long rope. Shape the rope into a wreath, pinching the ends together to seal them. Repeat with the remaining dough. Place the wreaths on the prepared baking sheets, leaving about 2 inches between each cookie.
4. Bake in the preheated moderate oven (350°) until the wreaths are lightly browned around the edges, for 10 to 12 minutes. Transfer the wreaths to wire racks to cool completely. Spread some of the Glaze over the top of each wreath. Garnish the wreaths with a candied red cherry half and 2 candied green cherry wedges.

Grand Marnier Glaze: Stir together 1¼ cups of sifted 10X (confectioners' powdered) sugar, 1 tablespoon of Grand Marnier, ⅛ teaspoon of ground nutmeg and 1 tablespoon of milk until the glaze is smooth and a good spreading consistency. If the glaze is too thick, add additional milk as needed.

HOLIDAY COOKING HELPS

The Great Christmas Cookie Swap

A cookie swap is a wonderful way to make the most of your Christmas baking — and have a good time with friends too! Here are some simple guidelines to making this year's cookie swap the best ever.
1. Limit the guest list to 10 or fewer; more than 10 people can be overwhelming.
2. Schedule the swap for the second week in December — early enough, but not too early! The date should be far enough ahead of Christmas so that it won't overlap hectic last-minute shopping time, but close enough to Christmas so the cookies don't become stale before holiday entertaining.
3. Ask each guest to bring three or four dozen cookies. Everyone should take home the same number of cookies they brought to the swap.
4. Remind guests to bring empty containers for their "swap" cookies. Have a few sturdy paper plates on hand for those who forget!
5. Ask the guest to include their favorite cookie recipes on 3 x 5-inch file cards. Most people enjoy exchanging the recipes along with the cookies.

CHOCOLATE PISTACHIO MERINGUES

Bake at 250° for 30 minutes.
Makes about 3 dozen cookies.

- 1/3 *cup pistachio nuts*
- 1/4 *cup semisweet chocolate pieces*
- 2 *egg whites*
- 1/8 *teaspoon cream of tartar*
- 2/3 *cup superfine sugar*
- 1/2 *teaspoon vanilla*

1. Preheat the oven to slow (250°). Grease, flour and set aside 2 baking sheets.
2. Combine the pistachios and the chocolate pieces in the container of an electric blender or food processor. Whirl until the chocolate and nuts are very finely chopped. Set aside the chocolate-pistachio mixture.
3. Beat together the egg whites and the cream of tartar in a small bowl with an electric mixer until the mixture forms soft peaks. Gradually add the superfine sugar, 1 tablespoon at a time, beating constantly until the mixture forms very stiff peaks. Fold in the chocolate-pistachio mixture and the vanilla. Using a teaspoon, drop small mounds of the meringue onto the prepared baking sheets, leaving 1 inch between each cookie.
4. Bake the cookies in the preheated slow oven (250°) for 30 minutes, or until the cookies are firm but not browned. Let the cookies stand for several minutes on the baking sheets. Loosen the cookies carefully with a thin spatula or knife, and transfer the cookies to a wire rack to cool completely. Store the cookies in a tightly covered container in a dry place.

HOLIDAY COOKING HELPS

Baking the Best Cookies

1. Carefully measure the amounts called for in a recipe, and follow the recipe directions exactly.
2. When working with a soft dough, try to avoid extremes in kitchen temperatures. If the room is too cool, the dough will become too stiff to work with; if the room is too hot, the dough will become too soft.
3. If a recipe calls for firm, chilled dough, keep the bowl of dough in the refrigerator and remove only the amount needed to roll or cut out.
4. Don't use baking sheets that touch the sides of the oven. This prevents the necessary circulation of heat for even baking.
5. To grease baking sheets, use nonstick vegetable cooking spray or a very thin layer of vegetable shortening.
6. Leave plenty of room between the cookies on the baking sheet so they won't spread out and merge when baking.
7. Invest in an oven thermometer. An oven's actual temperature may vary from the temperature indicated on its dial; a good oven thermometer is the most accurate way to gauge oven temperature.
8. Position the oven racks in the center of the oven for evenly baked cookies.
9. Check the cookies for doneness at the minimum baking time. The maximum baking time may be too long, and the cookies may burn.

BUTTERY ALMOND COOKIES

Bake at 375° for 8 to 10 minutes.
Makes about 8 dozen cookies.

- 3 *cups sifted all-purpose flour*
- 4 *teaspoons baking powder*
- 1 *teaspoon salt*
- 1 *cup (2 sticks) unsalted butter, at room temperature, cut into tablespoons*
- 2 *cups sugar*
- 2 *eggs, slightly beaten*
- ½ *cup finely ground blanched almonds*
- 1 *teaspoon almond extract*
- *Shiny Chocolate Glaze (recipe, page 214)*

1. Sift together the flour, baking powder and salt onto a piece of wax paper.
2. Beat the butter in a large bowl until it is light. Gradually add the sugar, beating until the mixture is fluffy. Stir in the eggs, almonds and almond extract. Stir in the flour mixture until the dough is well blended.
3. Divide the dough in half. If the dough is too sticky to work with, wrap both halves in plastic wrap and refrigerate the dough for 30 minutes to 1 hour. Or place the dough in the freezer until it is firm, for 5 to 15 minutes.
4. Roll one dough half into a 12-inch-long log. Repeat with the other dough half to make a second log. Wrap both dough logs in wax paper and twist the ends of the paper to seal them. Freeze the logs for 1 to 1½ hours, or until the dough is frozen solid. Or place the wrapped logs in plastic bags and freeze the dough for up to 1 month.
5. When ready to bake, preheat the oven to moderate (375°). Cut each log into ¼-inch-thick slices. Arrange the slices on ungreased baking sheets, leaving 2 inches between each cookie.
6. Bake in the preheated moderate oven (375°) until the edges of the cookies are lightly browned, for 8 to 10 minutes.
7. Transfer the cookies to a wire rack with a spatula. Allow the cookies to cool completely; the cooled cookies will be crisp.
8. Spread the Shiny Chocolate Glaze on half of each cookie, and let the glaze set. Or drizzle the Shiny Chocolate Glaze from a teaspoon over the cookies in a zigzag or crisscross pattern, and let the glaze set.

LEMON SUNSHINE COOKIES

Bake at 375° for 8 to 10 minutes.
Makes about 8 dozen cookies.

- 3 *cups sifted all-purpose flour*
- 4 *teaspoons baking powder*
- 1 *teaspoon salt*
- 1 *cup (2 sticks) unsalted butter, at room temperature, cut into tablespoons*
- 2 *cups sugar*
- 2 *eggs, slightly beaten*
- ½ *cup finely ground blanched almonds*
- 1 *tablespoon lemon juice*
- 1 *tablespoon grated lemon zest (yellow part of rind only)*
- 8 *to 10 drops yellow food coloring*
- *Sugar Glaze (recipe, page 214)*
- *Chopped pistachio nuts OR: thin strips of lemon zest (yellow part of rind only), for garnish*

1. Prepare the cookie dough following Steps 1 through 7 of the Buttery Almond Cookies *(recipe, at left)*, adding the lemon juice, grated lemon zest and yellow food coloring to the butter mixture in Step 2 before adding the flour mixture.
2. Spread the Sugar Glaze over the tops of the Lemon Sunshine Cookies, and sprinkle them with the chopped pistachio nuts. Or spread the tops of the cookies with the Sugar Glaze and lightly press a strip of lemon zest on top of the glaze. Let the glaze set.

CHOCOLATE SNOWFLAKES

Bake at 375° for 8 to 10 minutes.
Makes about 8 dozen cookies.

- 3 *cups sifted all-purpose flour*
- 4 *teaspoons baking powder*
- 1 *teaspoon salt*
- 1 *cup (2 sticks) unsalted butter, at room temperature, cut into tablespoons*
- 2 *cups sugar*
- 2 *eggs, slightly beaten*
- 1/2 *cup finely ground blanched almonds*
- 4 *squares (1 ounce each) unsweetened chocolate, melted and cooled slightly*
- *Shiny Chocolate Glaze (recipe, page 214)*
- *Sugar Glaze (recipe, page 214)*

1. Prepare the cookie dough following Steps 1 through 7 of the Buttery Almond Cookies *(recipe, page 212)*, adding the melted chocolate to the butter mixture in Step 2 before adding the flour mixture.
2. Drizzle the Shiny Chocolate Glaze from the tip of a teaspoon over the tops of the cookies in a rough star pattern; let the glaze set. Drizzle the Sugar Glaze from the tip of another teaspoon over the Shiny Chocolate Glaze in a different rough star pattern. Let both glazes set completely.

GINGER ORANGE ORNAMENTS

Bake at 375° for 8 to 10 minutes.
Makes about 8 dozen cookies.

- 3 *cups sifted all-purpose flour*
- 4 *teaspoons baking powder*
- 1 *teaspoon salt*
- 1 *cup (2 sticks) unsalted butter, at room temperature, cut into tablespoons*
- 2 *cups sugar*
- 2 *eggs, slightly beaten*
- 1/2 *cup finely ground blanched almonds*
- 1 *teaspoon grated orange zest (orange part of rind only)*
- 1/8 *to 1/4 teaspoon orange food coloring paste*
- 1 *tablespoon crystallized ginger, very finely chopped*
- *Sugar Glaze (recipe, page 214)*
- *Candied orange slices, cut into wedges, for garnish*
- *Slivered almonds OR: chopped pecans and silver dragées, for garnish*

1. Prepare the cookie dough following Steps 1 through 7 of the Buttery Almond Cookies *(recipe, page 212)*, adding the orange zest, orange food coloring paste and ginger to the butter mixture in Step 2 before adding the flour mixture.
2. Spread the Sugar Glaze in the center of each cookie. Press four candied orange wedges, pointed ends out, on top of the glaze, and an almond sliver between each wedge. Or press three candied orange wedges, pointed ends in, on top of the glaze and sprinkle the chopped pecans and silver dragées over the orange wedges and glaze. Let the glaze set completely.

SUGAR GLAZE

Makes 1 cup (enough to decorate 8 dozen cookies).

2 *cups sifted 10X (confectioners' powdered) sugar*
2 *to 4 tablespoons milk*

Whisk together the 10X (confectioners' powdered) sugar and 2 tablespoons of the milk until the mixture is blended. Whisk in enough of the remaining milk to make the glaze a good drizzling consistency.

SHINY CHOCOLATE GLAZE

Makes about 1 cup (enough to decorate about 8 dozen cookies).

8 *squares (1 ounce each) semisweet chocolate*
4 *tablespoons vegetable shortening*

Place the chocolate and the shortening in a small saucepan and melt them over very low heat, stirring occasionally. Cool the mixture slightly before using it.

HOLIDAY COOKING HELPS

No-Bake Mint Julep Cups

Crush enough vanilla wafer cookies to make 2½ cups of crumbs. Combine the cookie crumbs with 1 cup of sifted 10X (confectioners' powdered) sugar, 1 cup of finely chopped walnuts or pecans, 3 tablespoons of light corn syrup, 3 tablespoons of bourbon and 1 tablespoon of white crème de menthe in a large bowl. Stir until the mixture is well blended. Drop a teaspoon of the mixture into a miniature muffin-pan liner cup. Drop a second teaspoonful of the mixture on top of the first. Repeat with the remaining liner cups until all the mixture has been used. Let the cups set at room temperature for 24 hours. Store in an airtight container.

HOLIDAY COOKING HELPS

Baking with Kids

Kids love to work in the kitchen—and Christmas is a great time to teach them many cooking techniques that will be helpful in years to come. But they must learn that safety always comes first when cooking.

- An adult must be present. Young children must never begin a cooking project unless an adult, who can give them undivided attention, is present.
- Cleanliness and cooking go hand in hand. Wash hands with soap and hot water, and wear aprons when cooking.
- Only an adult may turn on the oven. Never allow a child to open the oven without adult supervision. Extra care must be taken around a hot oven at all times to prevent burns.
- Use thick oven mitts or pot holders when removing baking sheets from the oven. Place hot baking sheets on wire racks, never on the countertop. Also wear mitts while removing baked cookies from hot sheets.
- Keep sharp knives away from young children, and allow older children to use them only under the supervision of an adult.
- Store all cookies in metal or plastic containers with tight-fitting covers to keep the cookies fresh and insects out.
- Cleaning up afterwards is part of cooking. Wash all utensils and work surfaces with hot sudsy water. Leave the kitchen as you found it.

GINGER-SPICED COOKIE DOUGH

Use Ginger-Spiced Cookie Dough to make the cookies on pages 215 and 216. Makes enough dough for about 6½ dozen small cookies.

- 2½ *cups all-purpose flour*
- 2½ *teaspoons ground ginger*
- 2 *teaspoons baking powder*
- 1 *teaspoon ground cinnamon*
- ½ *to ¾ teaspoon freshly ground black pepper*
- ½ *teaspoon ground allspice*
- ½ *cup (1 stick) unsalted butter, softened*
- 1 *cup sugar*
- 1 *egg*
- 1 *tablespoon vanilla*

1. Combine the flour, ginger, baking powder, cinnamon, pepper and allspice in a medium-size bowl.
2. Beat together the butter and the sugar in a large bowl with an electric mixer until the mixture is light-colored and fluffy. Beat in the egg and the vanilla until they are well blended.
3. Reduce the mixer speed to low. Gradually beat the flour mixture into the butter mixture until they are well combined.
4. Divide the dough in half. Shape each half into a thick disk. Refrigerate the dough, wrapped in plastic wrap, for 1 to 2 hours.

GRADUATED STARS

Bake at 375° for 8 to 10 minutes.
Makes 27 stars.

- 1 *recipe Ginger-Spiced Cookie Dough (recipe, at left)*
- *Decorating Frosting (recipe, page 217)*
- *Red and green paste food colorings*
- *Red, green and white sugar crystals*
- *Red, green and white nonpareils*
- *Small red cinnamon candies*

1. Prepare the Ginger-Spiced Cookie Dough through Step 3. Divide the dough into thirds. Wrap the dough in plastic wrap and refrigerate it following Step 4.
2. When ready to make the cookies, preheat the oven to moderate (375°).
3. Roll out one-third of the dough on a lightly floured surface to ⅛-inch thickness. Cut out the dough with lightly floured 2¾-, 2½- and 2-inch star-shaped cookie cutters. Reroll and cut out the scraps 2 times. Place the cookies on ungreased large baking sheets, leaving 1½ inches between each cookie.
4. Bake the cookies in the preheated moderate oven (375°) for about 8 to 10 minutes. Cool the cookies on the baking sheets on wire racks for 1 minute. Transfer the cookies to the wire racks to cool completely.
5. Repeat the rolling, cutting and baking with the remaining dough.
6. Divide the Decorating Frosting into thirds. Tint one-third of the frosting red, one-third of the frosting green and leave the remaining one-third of the frosting white. Frost the cookies as desired, cover and set aside any remaining frosting. Decorate the cookies with the red, green and white sugar crystals, red, green and white nonpareils and small red cinnamon candies. Let the frosting dry.
7. Place a 2-inch star on top of a 2½-inch star, and place both of the smaller stars on top of a 2⅔-inch cookie. Attach the stars with dabs of the reserved frosting. Arrange the stacked stars so the points are staggered. Repeat with the remaining cookies.

CHRISTMAS PACKAGES

Bake at 375° for 8 to 10 minutes.
Makes 4½ dozen cookies.

1 *recipe Ginger-Spiced Cookie Dough (recipe, page 215)*
Decorating Frosting (recipe, page 217)
Red and green paste food colorings
Red, green and white sugar crystals
Red, green and white nonpareils
Small red cinnamon candies

1. Prepare the Ginger-Spiced Cookie Dough through Step 3. Divide the dough into thirds. Wrap the dough in plastic wrap and refrigerate the dough following Step 4.
2. When ready to make the cookies, preheat the oven to moderate (375°).
3. Roll out one-third of the dough on a lightly floured surface to a 12 x 8-inch rectangle. Cut the large rectangle into 3 x 2-inch rectangles. Place the cookies on ungreased large baking sheets, leaving 1½ inches between the cookies.
4. Bake the cookies in the preheated moderate oven (375°) for 8 to 10 minutes. Cool the cookies on the baking sheets on wire racks for 1 minute. Transfer the cookies to the wire racks to cool completely.
5. Repeat the rolling, cutting and baking with the remaining dough.
6. Divide the Decorating Frosting into thirds. Tint one-third of the frosting red, one-third of the frosting green, and leave the remaining one-third of the frosting white. Frost the cookies as desired to make them look like Christmas packages. Decorate the cookies with the red, green and white sugar crystals, red, green and white nonpareils and small red cinnamon candies. Let the frosting dry completely.

SNOWMEN

Bake at 375° for 8 to 10 minutes.
Makes 1½ dozen cookies.

1 *recipe Ginger-Spiced Cookie Dough (recipe, page 215)*
Decorating Frosting (recipe, page 217)
Red, green and black paste food colorings
Red, green and white sugar crystals
Red, green and white nonpareils
Small red cinnamon candies
Red and green plain chocolate candies
Red shoestring licorice

1. Prepare the Ginger-Spiced Cookie Dough.
2. When ready to make the cookies, preheat the oven to moderate (375°).
3. If necessary, let the dough soften at room temperature before rolling it. Roll out half the dough on a lightly floured surface to a ⅛-inch thickness. Cut out the dough with lightly floured 3-, 2- and 1-inch-diameter round cookie cutters. Reroll and cut out the scraps once.
4. Place one 3-inch cookie on an ungreased baking sheet. Place one 2-inch cookie next to and touching the 3-inch cookie. Pinch the cookies together slightly to seal them. Place a 1-inch cookie next to the 2-inch cookie to make a snowman head, and pinch to seal them. Repeat with the remaining cookies, leaving 1½ inches between the snowmen.
4. Bake the snowmen in the preheated moderate oven (375°) for 8 to 10 minutes. Cool the snowmen on the baking sheets on wire racks for 1 minute. Transfer the snowmen to the wire racks to cool completely.
5. Repeat the rolling, cutting and shaping with the remaining dough, and bake the snowmen.
6. Divide the Decorating Frosting in half. Leave half the frosting white. Divide the remaining half into thirds. Tint one-third of the frosting red, one-third of the frosting green and the remaining third of the frosting black. Frost the snowmen as desired. Decorate the snowmen with the red, green and white sugar crystals, red, green and white nonpareils, small red cinnamon candies, red and green plain chocolate candies, and red shoestring licorice.

HOLIDAY COOKING HELPS

Quick Cookie Tips

- Skip a step in cookie-making and start with purchased, refrigerated cookie dough. Personalize the cookies by adding your own decorations, such as Decorating Frosting (recipe, at right), nonpareils and colored sugar.
- If you're really pressed for time, don't make cookies that require you to chill the dough in the refrigerator or freezer, or those that call for elaborate decorations. Choose drop, press or bar cookies, and use simple garnishes such as whole, pre-sliced or pre-chopped nuts, colored sugar or nonpareils, dried fruits and purchased, tinted frosting in a tube.
- Make your own refrigerated cookie dough to freeze and have on hand when you need it. Remove the ends of large juice cans, wash the cans in hot water and dry them thoroughly. Shape the cookie dough into logs and pack the logs in the juice cans. Wrap the cans tightly in aluminum foil, then overwrap the cans with plastic wrap and freeze them. When ready to bake the cookies, push out the cookie dough logs and slice off rounds as you go. Place the cookies, still frozen, on baking sheets and bake the cookies following the individual recipe directions (you may have to increase the baking time slightly).
- Convert your favorite drop cookie recipe into bar cookies: For thin bar cookies, press the dough into a greased jelly-roll pan; for thicker bar cookies, press the dough into a greased 9 x 13-inch baking pan. Bake the cookies until they are firm to the touch.
- Use packaged brownie mix to make brownie drop cookies: Prepare the brownies following the package directions. If you wish, stir in semisweet chocolate pieces and chopped walnuts. Drop the batter, a tablespoon at a time, onto greased baking sheets, leaving about 2 inches between the cookies. Bake the cookies for 8 to 10 minutes, or until the cookies spring back when lightly touched with your fingertip.

DECORATING FROSTING

Makes 3 cups.

*Packaged meringue powder**

Prepare 1 recipe of Royal Icing following the directions on a package of meringue powder. One tablespoon of the frosting will frost one 4 x 3-inch cookie, and 1 teaspoon will frost one 3 x 2-inch cookie.
Note: *We recommend using dried meringue powder for uncooked frosting, instead of making meringue from raw egg whites. Recent reports have indicated the presence of salmonella bacteria in raw eggs. To avoid this potential health risk, substitute meringue powder, which is available in stores where baking and cake decorating supplies are sold. Or see the tip below to order meringue powder by mail.*

HOLIDAY COOKING HELPS

A Buyer's Guide to Meringue Powder

Meringue powder is available from:
- Galloway's Cake and Party Supply Co., 2208 Church Ave., Brooklyn, NY 11226; 718-462-8728.
- Maid of Scandinavia, 3244 Raleigh Ave., Minneapolis, MN 55416; 1-800-328-6722.
- Wilton Enterprises, Inc., 2240 W. 75th St., Woodbridge, IL 60517; 312-963-7100.

PEANUT BUTTER COOKIE DOUGH

Use Peanut Butter Cookie Dough to make the cookies on pages 218-221.

Makes enough dough for about 6½ dozen small cookies.

- *2½ cups all-purpose flour*
- *1 teaspoon baking powder*
- *¼ teaspoon salt*
- *¾ cup (1½ sticks) unsalted butter, at room temperature*
- *¾ cup smooth peanut butter*
- *¾ cup sugar*
- *1 egg*
- *1 teaspoon vanilla*

1. Combine the flour, baking powder and salt in a medium-size bowl.
2. Beat together the butter, peanut butter and sugar in a large bowl with an electric mixer at medium speed until the mixture is light-colored and fluffy. Beat in the egg and the vanilla until they are well blended.
3. Reduce the mixer speed to low. Gradually beat the flour mixture into the butter mixture until they are well combined.
4. Divide the dough in half. Shape each half into a thick disk and wrap the disks in plastic wrap. Refrigerate the dough overnight.

CHRISTMAS CUTOUT COOKIES

Bake at 375° for 8 to 10 minutes.
Makes about 6 dozen small cookies.

- *1 recipe Peanut Butter Cookie Dough (recipe, at left)*
- *Cookie decorations as desired*

1. Prepare the Peanut Butter Cookie Dough.
2. When ready to bake the cookies, preheat the oven to moderate (375°).
3. If the dough is too hard to work with, let it soften at room temperature before rolling it. Roll out half the dough on a lightly floured surface to a ⅛-inch thickness. Cut out the dough with lightly floured holiday cookie cutters. Reroll and cut out the scraps 2 times. To hang the cookies, make a hole with a wooden pick in the top of each cookie. Place the cookies on an ungreased large baking sheet, leaving 1½ inches between the cookies.
4. Bake the cookies in the preheated moderate oven (375°) for 8 to 10 minutes, or until the cookies are browned around the edges. If the hanging holes seal, reopen them with a wooden pick while the cookies are still soft. Cool the cookies on the baking sheets on wire racks for 1 minute. Transfer the cookies to the wire racks to cool completely.
5. Repeat the rolling, cutting and baking with the remaining dough.
6. Decorate the cookies as desired.

CHRISTMAS CANES AND WREATHS

These treats may double as ornaments, but handle them gently since they're fragile.

Bake at 375° for 8 to 10 minutes.
Makes about 3 dozen cookies.

Peanut Butter Cookie Dough (recipe, page 218)
Red and/or green paste food coloring

1. Prepare the Peanut Butter Cookie Dough through Step 3.
2. Divide the dough in half. Color the dough halves with the desired amount of red or green food coloring, or leave one half of the dough plain, depending on the color of cookies desired. Shape each dough half into a thick disk. Wrap the disks in plastic wrap, and refrigerate them overnight.
3. When ready to make the cookies, preheat the oven to moderate (375°).
4. Cut each half of the dough into quarters. Rewrap and refrigerate the unused dough. If necessary, let the dough soften slightly at room temperature before shaping it.
5. Roll out 2 different-colored 6-inch-long strips of dough on a lightly floured surface, using 1½ teaspoons of dough for each strip. Lay the strips side by side. Twist the strips together beginning at the middle and working to each end. Pinch the ends to seal them; the dough tends to crack, but can be pinched back together easily. Transfer the twisted strips to an ungreased baking sheet, leaving about 1½ inches between the cookies. Form the twisted strips into either a cane shape or a wreath, pinching the ends together to seal the wreaths. Repeat with the remaining dough. If the dough softens too much, wrap it in plastic wrap, and return the dough to the refrigerator for a few minutes to firm up.
6. Bake the cookies in the preheated moderate oven (375°) for 8 to 10 minutes. Cool the cookies on the baking sheets on wire racks for 1 minute. Transfer the cookies to the wire racks to cool completely.

MARBLE CHOCOLATE RIBBONS

Bake at 375° for 5 to 7 minutes.
Makes 8 dozen cookies.

Peanut Butter Cookie Dough (recipe, page 218)
3 squares (1 ounce each) semisweet chocolate, melted and cooled
1 package (6 ounces) chocolate melting wafers
4 teaspoons vegetable shortening
1 package (6 ounces) creamy white chocolate melting wafers

1. Prepare the Peanut Butter Cookie Dough through Step 1. In Step 2, add the semisweet chocolate to the butter mixture. Continue through Step 3.
2. Preheat the oven to moderate (375°).
3. Spoon a portion of the dough into a cookie press fitted with the plate for ribbon strips. Press the dough into 3-inch-long ribbons on large ungreased baking sheets, leaving 2 inches between the cookies.
4. Bake in the preheated moderate oven (375°) until the ribbons are lightly browned, for 5 to 7 minutes. Cool the ribbons on the baking sheets on wire racks for 1 minute. Transfer the ribbons to the wire racks to cool completely. Repeat with the remaining dough.
5. Combine the chocolate melting wafers and 2 teaspoons of the shortening in a small saucepan. Cook the mixture over low heat, stirring, until it is melted and smooth. Cool the mixture, stirring occasionally, until the mixture registers 88° on a candy thermometer, for about 20 minutes. Repeat with the white chocolate melting wafers and the remaining shortening, cooling the mixture to 84°, for about 20 minutes.
6. Line the cooled baking sheets with aluminum foil.
7. Pour the cooled white and dark chocolate mixtures into the same bowl, pouring each mixture from the opposite side. Gently swirl a thin metal spatula through the white and dark chocolate mixtures to marbleize them slightly. Carefully dip a cookie ribbon straight down into the chocolate marble mixture, lifting the ribbon straight up and out of the bowl. Let the excess chocolate drip off the ribbons, and place the cookies on the prepared baking sheets. If you wish, dip the opposite ends of the ribbons into the chocolate marble mixture. When the chocolate marble is set, loosen the ribbons from the baking sheet with a spatula.

CHOCOLATE NUT COOKIES

Bake at 375° for 10 to 12 minutes.
Makes 8 dozen cookies.

Peanut Butter Cookie Dough (recipe, page 218)
1 *package (12 ounces) semisweet chocolate pieces*
1/4 *cup dark corn syrup*
2 *teaspoons instant espresso powder*
2 *cups finely chopped walnuts OR: pecans*

1. Prepare the Peanut Butter Cookie Dough.
2. At least 4 hours before baking the cookies, combine the chocolate pieces, corn syrup and espresso powder in the top of a double boiler set over hot, not boiling, water. Cook the mixture, stirring occasionally, until the chocolate is melted and the espresso powder is completely dissolved. Remove the double boiler top from the heat and stir in the walnuts or pecans. Pour the mixture into a medium-size bowl. Cover the bowl with plastic wrap and refrigerate the chocolate mixture for 1 hour, or until it is firm enough to work with.
3. Divide the chocolate mixture in half. Roll each half into a 1-inch-diameter, 12-inch-long log. Cover the chocolate logs with plastic wrap and refrigerate them for 15 minutes.
4. If necessary, let the Peanut Butter Cookie Dough soften at room temperature before rolling it.
5. Roll out half the dough on a lightly floured surface to a 12½ x 5-inch rectangle. Place a chocolate log lengthwise down the center of the rectangle, and wrap the dough around the chocolate log. Repeat with the remaining dough and chocolate log. Refrigerate both logs until they are firm enough to cut, for several hours or overnight.
6. When ready to make the cookies, preheat the oven to moderate (375°).
7. Cut each log into ¼-inch-thick slices, and place the slices on ungreased large baking sheets, leaving 1½ inches between the cookies.*
8. Bake the cookies in the preheated moderate oven (375°) for 10 to 12 minutes. Cool the cookies on the baking sheets on wire racks for 1 minute. Transfer the cookies to the wire racks to cool completely.
***Note:** The dough may separate from the chocolate when you slice the log, but you can easily mold the log back into shape.*

PEANUT BUTTER 'N JAM TARTS

Bake at 375° for 7 minutes.
Makes 7 dozen tarts.

Peanut Butter Cookie Dough (recipe, page 218)
1¾ *cups smooth OR: chunky peanut butter*
1¾ *cups raspberry jam OR: strawberry jam*
Red or green candied cherries, halved (optional)

1. Prepare the Peanut Butter Cookie Dough through Step 3.
2. When ready to make the tarts, preheat the oven to moderate (375°).
3. Shape 2 level teaspoons of the dough into a ball for each tart shell. Press the balls into greased gem-size (1¾-inch) muffin-pan cups.
4. Bake the tart shells in the preheated moderate oven (375°) for 7 minutes, or until they are lightly golden around the edges. Cool the tart shells in the pans on wire racks for 5 minutes. Using a thin spatula, carefully remove the tart shells to wire racks to cool completely.
5. Place 1 teaspoon of the peanut butter in each tart shell. Top with 1 teaspoon of the raspberry or strawberry jam. If you wish, garnish each tart with a red or green candied cherry half.

HOLIDAY COOKING HELPS

Mailing Cookies

- Choose the right cookies: Soft drop, bar and fruit cookies all mail well.
- Place pairs of cookies flat sides together, wrap them in aluminum foil and seal with tape.
- Use clean large coffee cans, or decorative tins to pack cookies for mailing.
- Line the container with wax paper, and tuck crumpled wax paper into any empty spaces.
- Place the container in a corrugated cardboard box, and tuck crumpled newspaper or plain popcorn into any empty spaces in the box. Seal the box with filament tape. Use a waterproof marker to write "Perishable" above the address, below the postage and on the underside of the box.

CHRISTMAS BELLS

Bake at 375° for 5 to 8 minutes.
Makes 8 dozen cookies.

Peanut Butter Cookie Dough (recipe, page 218)
Red or green plain chocolate candies
Cookie decorations as desired

1. Prepare the Peanut Butter Cookie Dough.
2. When ready to make the cookies, preheat the oven to moderate (375°).
3. Divide the dough in half. Roll out half the dough on a lightly floured surface to a ⅛-inch thickness. Cut out the dough with a lightly floured 2-inch bell-shaped cookie cutter. Reroll and cut out the scraps 2 times. Place the cookies on ungreased large baking sheets, leaving 1½ inches between the cookies. To hang the cookies, make a hole with a wooden pick in the top of each cookie. Press a red or green plain chocolate candy at the bottom of each bell cookie for the clapper.
4. Bake in the preheated moderate oven (375°) until the cookies are lightly browned around the edges, for 5 to 8 minutes. If the hanging holes seal, reopen them with a wooden pick while the cookies are still soft. Cool the cookies on the baking sheets on wire racks for 1 minute. Transfer the cookies to the wire racks to cool completely.
5. Repeat the rolling, cutting and baking with the remaining dough.
6. Decorate the cookies as desired.

HOLIDAY COOKING HELPS

The Cookie Low Down: Lowering Calories and Fat in Cookie Recipes

- Meringue cookies made with egg whites are virtually fat free. Add a tablespoon or two of chopped nuts, chopped chocolate or cocoa powder, or small amounts of crisp cereal flakes for extra flavor and texture.
- Miniature cookies are perfect for the holidays. Just halve the size of the cookie called for in the recipes. Small bar cookies are great to serve with special coffees and teas. Button-sized drop cookies are an ideal accompaniment to sorbets and fruit desserts.
- Use nonstick vegetable cooking spray instead of butter, margarine or vegetable shortening to grease baking sheets; you'll need less shortening to coat the sheets.
- Try reducing the amount of sugar called for in cookie recipes. The sugar content of most cookie recipes usually can be reduced by a third without a noticeable change in the taste of the cookie.
- Use reduced-sugar jams, jellies or preserves for sandwich cookie fillings.
- Try substituting natural-style peanut butter for the standard peanut butter. In addition to less added salt and sugar, your cookies will taste more peanutty!

CAKES, PIES AND OTHER DESSERTS

The crowning glory of your holiday feast: Kiwi Trifle (recipe, page 225); Croquembouche (recipe, page 229); Cranberry Snow (recipe, page 224); Chocolate Chestnut Mousse (recipe, page 223); Gingerbread Cookies (recipe, page 227); Bûche de Noël (recipe, page 226); Ginger Pumpkin Cheesecake (recipe, page 228).

CHOCOLATE CHESTNUT MOUSSE

Chestnut purée gives this rich chocolate mousse extra texture and flavor. Prepare the mousse a day ahead and garnish with whipped cream just before serving.

Makes 16 servings.

- 1 *package (12 ounces) semisweet chocolate pieces*
- 1/2 *cup (1 stick) unsalted butter*
- 4 *egg yolks*
- 2/3 *cup granulated sugar*
- 1/4 *teaspoon salt*
- 1 *can (15 1/2 ounces) chestnut purée*
- 1 *tablespoon rum*
- 1/2 *teaspoon vanilla*
- 2 1/2 *cups heavy cream*
- 1 *tablespoon 10X (confectioners' powdered) sugar*
- *Red and green candied cherries, for garnish (optional)*

1. Combine the chocolate and the butter in the top of a double boiler set over simmering water. Cook, stirring occasionally, until the chocolate is melted and the mixture is smooth.

2. Stir the egg yolks into the chocolate mixture one at a time, beating well after each addition. Cook the mixture, beating constantly with a wire whisk, for 2 minutes. Add the granulated sugar and the salt, beating constantly, and cook the mixture for 2 minutes more, or until the mixture is hot. Remove the pan from the heat. Stir in the chestnut purée, a little at a time, breaking up any large pieces of the purée with the back of a wooden spoon. The purée should not be smoothed completely; small bits of the purée add texture to the mousse. Add the rum and the vanilla, and stir until they are combined.

3. Beat 2 cups of the heavy cream in a medium-size bowl with an electric mixer until it is stiff. Fold the whipped cream into the chocolate mixture.
4. Pour the chocolate chestnut cream into a decorative 1¾- to 2-quart serving bowl. Cover the bowl with plastic wrap and refrigerate the mousse for 4 hours, or overnight.
5. To serve, beat the remaining ½ cup of heavy cream with the 10X (confectioners' powdered) sugar. Spoon the whipped cream into a pastry bag fitted with a medium-size star tip. Pipe a whipped cream lattice over the top of the mousse, then pipe whipped cream around the edges of the bowl. Garnish the mousse with the red and green candied cherries, if you wish.

CRANBERRY SNOW

This make-ahead dessert is a sweet, frothy cranberry cream mixture served with a cranberry sauce.

Makes 8 servings.

1½ cups water
1 cup sugar
5 cups cranberries from two 12-ounce bags; reserve the remaining cranberries to use in Cranberry Sauce (recipe follows)
3 envelopes unflavored gelatin
2 tablespoons lemon juice
2 cups heavy cream
Nonstick vegetable cooking spray
Cranberry Sauce (recipe follows)

1. Combine 1 cup of the water and ¾ cup of the sugar in a medium-size saucepan. Bring the mixture to boiling over high heat, stirring to dissolve the sugar. Add the cranberries, and cook until they start to pop, for about 2 minutes. Lower the heat to medium, and simmer the cranberry mixture for 5 minutes.
2. Meanwhile, sprinkle the gelatin over the remaining ½ cup water in a small bowl and let the mixture stand for 5 minutes to soften the gelatin.
3. Pour the hot cranberry mixture into the container of an electric blender or food processor. Whirl until the mixture is puréed, for about 1 minute. Add the gelatin and the lemon juice. Whirl just until the mixture is blended and the gelatin is melted. Strain the mixture into a large bowl, and discard the solids.
4. Fill a second large bowl halfway with ice cubes. Place the bowl with the cranberry mixture on top of the ice. Chill the cranberry mixture, stirring occasionally, until it is the consistency of unbeaten egg whites, for about 15 minutes. Remove the bowl with the cranberry mixture from the bowl of ice.
5. Beat the heavy cream with the remaining ¼ cup of sugar in a third large bowl until the cream is stiff.
6. Gently fold the whipped cream into the cranberry mixture until no white streaks remain. Lightly grease a 6-cup fancy mold with nonstick vegetable cooking spray.* Pour the snow into the mold and refrigerate the snow overnight.
7. Prepare and refrigerate the Cranberry Sauce.
8. To serve, loosen the edge of the snow with a thin knife. Dip the mold quickly in hot water to loosen the snow, then invert the fancy mold onto a serving platter. Remove the mold. Spoon about ¼ cup of the Cranberry Sauce around the bottom edge of the snow. Place the remaining Cranberry Sauce in a small bowl, and serve with the Cranberry Snow.
***Note:** Do not use a tin or tinned mold for this recipe.*

Cranberry Sauce: Combine ⅔ cup of water and ⅔ cup of sugar in a medium-size saucepan. Bring the mixture to boiling over high heat, stirring constantly to dissolve the sugar. Lower the heat to medium. Stir in 2 cups of cranberries. Boil the cranberries gently for 2 minutes. Remove the saucepan from the heat and cool the cranberry sauce to room temperature. Pour the cranberry sauce into a small bowl, cover the bowl with plastic wrap and refrigerate the sauce overnight.

Microwave Instructions

(for a 650-watt variable power microwave oven)

Directions: Stir together the water, sugar and cranberries in a microwave-safe 3-quart casserole dish. Cover the dish. Microwave at full power for 10 minutes, stirring once. Continue with Step 2 above. To make the Cranberry Sauce, combine the ⅔ cup of water and ⅔ cup of sugar in a microwave-safe 4-cup measure. Microwave, uncovered, at full power for 4 minutes. Stir the mixture to dissolve the sugar. Stir in the 2 cups of cranberries. Microwave, uncovered, at full power for 1 minute more.

KIWI TRIFLE

Kiwi makes a delicious and colorful addition to this variation of classic trifle.

Makes 10 servings.

Custard:
- 2 *tablespoons cornstarch*
- 1/4 *cup sugar*
- 3 1/2 *cups milk*
- 4 *egg yolks*
- 2 *tablespoons cream sherry*

Sherry Syrup:
- 1/3 *cup water*
- 3 *tablespoons sugar*
- 2 *tablespoons cream sherry*

- 2 *frozen poundcakes (10 3/4 ounces each), thawed*
- 5 *kiwifruits, peeled and cut crosswise in 1/4-inch-thick slices*
- 2 *tablespoons seedless raspberry jam*
- 1/2 *cup heavy cream whipped with 1 tablespoon 10X (confectioners' powdered) sugar, for garnish*
- 2 *tablespoons seedless raspberry jam, for garnish (optional)*

1. Prepare the Custard: Combine the cornstarch and the 1/4 cup of sugar in a medium-size saucepan. Stir in 3 cups of the milk. Cook over medium heat, stirring gently with a wooden spoon, until the mixture comes to a boil and thickens slightly. Remove the saucepan from the heat.
2. Combine the egg yolks and the remaining 1/2 cup of milk in a small bowl. Slowly stir 1 cup of the hot milk mixture into the egg yolk mixture, then stir all the egg yolk mixture into the saucepan. Return the saucepan to medium heat and cook, stirring, until the custard thickens, for 1 minute more; do not allow the custard to boil. Remove the saucepan from the heat and stir in the 2 tablespoons of cream sherry. Strain the custard into a medium-size bowl. Cover the surface of the custard with plastic wrap, and refrigerate the custard until it is chilled, for 2 hours.
3. Prepare the Sherry Syrup: Combine the water and the 3 tablespoons of sugar in a small saucepan. Bring the mixture to boiling over high heat, stirring constantly to dissolve the sugar. Lower the heat to medium, and boil the mixture gently for 2 minutes more. Remove the saucepan from the heat and stir in the 2 tablespoons of cream sherry. Let the syrup cool for about 1 hour, or until it is room temperature.
4. To assemble the trifle, cut 1 poundcake in half horizontally, placing the halves side by side on a cutting board. Measure the diameter of a straight-sided, 2 3/4- to 3-quart glass serving bowl. (The bowl should be about 7 inches in diameter and 4 inches tall.) Trace the top edge of the bowl onto a piece of wax paper for a pattern. Cut out the wax paper pattern and place it on top of the poundcake halves. Using the paper pattern, cut out the poundcake halves to make a round cake layer; use the trimmings to make a full circle of poundcake. Repeat with the second poundcake.
5. Cut 4 of the kiwi slices in half. Place the kiwi half slices, rounded edges up, around the base of the serving bowl, spacing the slices evenly and pressing the kiwi firmly against the side of the bowl. Spoon one-third of the custard (about 1 1/3 cups) into the bottom of the bowl. Carefully transfer the first poundcake layer to the bowl, placing it on top of the custard. Brush half of the Sherry Syrup over the first poundcake layer. Stir the 2 tablespoons raspberry jam until it is smooth, and brush 1 tablespoon of the raspberry jam over the Sherry Syrup.
6. Set aside 6 to 8 kiwi slices for garnish. Layer the remaining kiwi slices in an overlapping spiral on top of the first poundcake layer. Spoon another third of the custard over the kiwi slices. Carefully transfer the second poundcake layer to the bowl, placing it on top of the second custard layer. Brush the second poundcake layer with the remaining Sherry Syrup, then with the remaining tablespoon of raspberry jam. Spoon the remaining custard on top of the second poundcake layer. Cover the bowl with plastic wrap, and refrigerate the trifle for 4 hours, or overnight.
7. Garnish the top of the trifle with the whipped cream and the reserved kiwi slices. If you wish, spoon the 2 tablespoons of raspberry jam around the outside edge of the bowl.

BÛCHE DE NOËL

Bake at 375° for 14 to 16 minutes.
Makes 12 servings.

- 1/4 *cup unsweetened cocoa powder*
- 1/4 *cup all-purpose flour*
- 1/2 *teaspoon ground cinnamon*
- 1/4 *teaspoon ground ginger*
- 1/8 *teaspoon ground cardamom*
- 6 *eggs, separated, at room temperature*
- 1/4 *teaspoon cream of tartar*
- 3/4 *cup granulated sugar*
- 1/4 *teaspoon vanilla*
- *10X (confectioners' powdered) sugar*
- *Coffee Cream Frosting and Filling (recipe follows)*
- *Holly Leaves (recipe follows)*
- *Chocolate Mushrooms (recipe follows)*

1. Preheat the oven to moderate (375°). Grease a 15 x 10 x 1-inch jelly-roll pan. Line the pan with a piece of wax paper.
2. Sift together the cocoa powder, flour, cinnamon, ginger and cardamom into a small bowl.
3. Beat the egg whites with the cream of tartar in a large bowl with an electric mixer until the mixture is frothy. Gradually beat in 1/4 cup of the granulated sugar, beating well after each addition. Continue beating the egg white mixture until it forms stiff peaks. Set aside the egg whites.
4. Beat the egg yolks with the remaining 1/2 cup of granulated sugar in a medium-size bowl with the electric mixer at high speed until the mixture is thick and lemon-colored, for about 5 minutes. Beat in the vanilla. Fold the cocoa mixture into the yolk mixture.
5. Gently fold the chocolate mixture into the egg white mixture until no white streaks remain. Pour the batter into the prepared jelly-roll pan, spreading it evenly.
6. Bake the cake in the preheated moderate oven (375°) for 14 to 16 minutes, or until the top springs back when lightly pressed with your fingertip.
7. Remove the pan from the oven. Loosen the cake around the edges of the pan with a thin knife. Sprinkle the top of the cake with the 10X (confectioners' powdered) sugar. Cover the cake with a clean, lint-free tea towel. Invert the cake, and carefully peel off the wax paper. Starting at a long end, roll up the cake and towel together. Place the cake, seam side down, on a wire rack to cool completely.
8. Meanwhile, prepare the Coffee Cream Frosting and Filling.
9. When the cake has cooled completely, carefully unroll it; the cake will remain slightly curled. Spoon and gently spread one-third of the Coffee Cream Filling over the inside of the cake. Carefully roll up the cake again without the towel.
10. Using a very sharp serrated knife, cut off each end of the rolled cake, making parallel diagonal cuts. Set aside the cut-off cake ends. Carefully transfer the rolled cake to a large serving platter, placing the cake seam side down. Place one of the reserved cake ends against the cake, with the diagonal cut facing the cake; use a little Coffee Cream Frosting to "glue" the end in place. Repeat on the opposite side and end of the cake *(see photo, page 222)*. Frost the cake and the "knots" with the remaining Coffee Cream Frosting; leave the rolled ends of the cake and the knots unfrosted. To create a bark effect, dip the tines of a fork into hot water and run the tines gently over the frosting.
11. Garnish the cake with the Holly Leaves and the Chocolate Mushrooms.

Coffee Cream Frosting and Filling: Stir 2 teaspoons of instant coffee granules into 1 tablespoon of boiling water until the coffee is dissolved. Let the coffee cool. Combine 2 1/2 cups of 10X (confectioners' powdered) sugar, 1 cup (2 sticks) of unsalted butter, softened, and the coffee in a large bowl. Beat the mixture until it is light and fluffy, for 3 minutes.

Holly Leaves: Separate candied angelica to make a single thickness. Cut out six 1-inch-long holly leaves from the candied angelica sheets. Place the 3 angelica leaves on the cake at the base of a knot. Place 3 small red cinnamon candies in the center of the leaf group for holly berries. Repeat with the remaining angelica leaves and cinnamon candies at the base of the second knot. If candied angelica is not available, substitute spearmint leaf jelly candies, halved.

Chocolate Mushrooms: Melt 1 chocolate kiss candy in a small cup over hot water. Dip the point of a second chocolate kiss candy into the melted chocolate, and press a nonpareil chocolate candy on the tip of the chocolate kiss. Repeat to make 6 chocolate mushrooms.

GINGERBREAD COOKIES

An old-fashioned holiday cookie favorite for the young and young-at-heart alike.

Bake at 375° for 6 to 7 minutes.
Makes about sixty-four 3-inch cookies.

- 5 *cups all-purpose flour*
- 1½ *tablespoons baking soda*
- 1 *tablespoon ground ginger*
- 2 *teaspoons ground cinnamon*
- ½ *teaspoon ground cloves*
- ½ *cup vegetable shortening*
- ½ *cup (1 stick) butter, softened*
- 1 *cup firmly packed light brown sugar*
- 1 *egg*
- ¾ *cup molasses*
- 1 *tablespoon distilled white vinegar*
- 1 *recipe Decorating Frosting (recipe, page 217)*
- *Colored sugar sprinkles*
- *Silver dragées*
- *Small red cinnamon candies*
- *Red and green paste food colorings*

1. Sift together the flour, baking soda, ginger, cinnamon and cloves into a medium-size bowl.
2. Beat together the shortening and the butter in a large bowl with an electric mixer at high speed until the mixture is creamy. Add the brown sugar and the egg, and beat until the mixture is fluffy. Add the molasses and the vinegar, beating just until all the ingredients are combined.
3. Reduce the mixer speed to low. Beat in 3 cups of the flour mixture just until it is combined. Stir in the remaining flour mixture with a wooden spoon.
4. Divide the dough into 4 equal parts. Shape each dough quarter into a ball and press the ball to flatten it slightly. Wrap each ball of dough in plastic wrap. Refrigerate the dough until it is firm, for 4 hours or overnight.
5. When ready to bake the cookies, preheat the oven to moderate (375°). Lightly grease several baking sheets.
6. Roll out one ball of dough on a lightly floured surface to a ⅛-inch thickness. Cut out the dough using lightly floured 3-inch holiday cookie cutters. Transfer the dough cutouts to the prepared baking sheets. Gather together the excess dough, and repeat the rolling and cutting until all the dough has been used.
7. Bake in the preheated moderate oven (375°) until the cookies are lightly browned around the edges, for 6 to 7 minutes. Transfer the cookies to wire racks to cool completely. Repeat the rolling, cutting and baking until the remaining dough balls have been used.
8. Prepare the Decorating Frosting.
9. Divide the frosting in half. Place one half in a large bowl and leave this frosting white. Divide the second half of the frosting into thirds. Leave one-third white, and tint one-third red and one-third green with the paste food coloring; keep all the frosting covered with damp paper toweling to prevent it from drying out while you work.
10. Spread a thin layer of the white frosting from the large bowl over some of the cookies. Decorate the frosted cookies with the colored sugar sprinkles, silver dragées and small red cinnamon candies; the decorating must be done immediately as the frosting dries very quickly.
11. Spoon the small portion of white frosting into a pastry bag fitted with a medium-size writing tip. Pipe the white frosting onto the cookies to decorate them. Repeat with the red- and green-tinted frostings, using a clean pastry bag and writing tip for each color of frosting. Immediately decorate the cookies with the sugar sprinkles, silver dragées and cinnamon candies.

HOLIDAY COOKING HELPS

Cookie Care

- Store crisp cookies in a container with a loose-fitting lid. Place pieces of wax paper between the cookie layers. If the cookies begin to soften, place them on a baking sheet in a slow oven (300°) for 3 to 5 minutes to make them crisp again.
- Store soft cookies in an airtight container with a slice of apple on a piece of wax paper to keep the cookies soft and moist. To freshen soft cookies, place them in a casserole dish with a snug-fitting cover. Place the covered casserole dish in a slow oven (300°) for 8 to 10 minutes.

GINGER PUMPKIN CHEESECAKE

Makes 12 servings.

Gingersnap Crust:

1 *cup plus 3 tablespoons gingersnap cookie crumbs (about 24 packaged gingersnap cookies)*
4 *tablespoons butter, melted*
1 *tablespoon light brown sugar*

Cheesecake Filling:

2 *envelopes unflavored gelatin*
1/3 *cup cool water*
1 *cup (1/2 pint) heavy cream*
2 *packages (8 ounces each) cream cheese, softened*
2/3 *cup granulated sugar*
1 *can (1 pound) pumpkin purée*
1/2 *teaspoon ground ginger*
1/2 *teaspoon ground cinnamon*
1/8 *teaspoon ground cloves*

Garnish (optional):

Gingersnap cookie pieces
1 *sheet strawberry-flavored fruit roll-up*
Red and green plain chocolate candies

1. Prepare the Gingersnap Crust: Combine 1 cup of the gingersnap cookie crumbs, 3 tablespoons of the melted butter and the light brown sugar in a small bowl.
2. Brush the sides of an 8-inch springform pan with the remaining tablespoon of melted butter. Sprinkle the greased pan sides with the remaining 3 tablespoons crumbs, rotating the pan to coat the sides.
3. Pour the gingersnap crumb mixture into the springform pan. Using your fingertips, press the crumb mixture firmly and evenly over the bottom of the pan. Place the springform pan in the refrigerator until the gingersnap crust has set.
4. Prepare the Cheesecake Filling: Sprinkle the gelatin over the water in a 1-cup glass measure. Let the gelatin mixture stand until it has softened, for 5 minutes. Fill a small saucepan with hot water to reach 1 inch up the sides of the measuring cup. Set the measuring cup in the saucepan, and cook over medium heat until the gelatin dissolves, for about 1 minute. Remove the measuring cup from the saucepan, and set the gelatin mixture aside to cool slightly.
5. Beat the heavy cream in a medium-size bowl with an electric mixer until the whipped cream forms stiff peaks. Set aside the whipped cream. Beat together the cream cheese and the granulated sugar in a large bowl until the mixture is smooth, for 2 minutes. Add the pumpkin purée, the ginger, cinnamon and cloves, beating until the ingredients are combined, for 1 minute. Stir in the gelatin mixture. Gently fold the whipped cream into the pumpkin mixture. Pour the cheesecake filling into the prepared springform pan. Refrigerate the cheesecake for 4 hours, or overnight.
6. Place the cheesecake on a serving platter, and remove the pan sides. Garnish the cheesecake, if you wish, by arranging the gingersnap cookie pieces on top of the cheesecake in the shape of a wreath. Make a bow from the fruit roll-up and place it at the top of the "wreath." Scatter the red and green plain chocolate candies around the gingersnap wreath.

HOLIDAY COOKING HELPS

Baking Pan Substitutions

- **For a 4-cup baking dish:** one 9-inch pie plate; or one 7 3/8 x 3 5/8 x 2 5/8-inch loaf pan; or one 8 x 1 1/4-inch round layer cake pan.
- **For a 6-cup baking dish:** one 10-inch pie plate; or one 8- or 9 x 1 1/2-inch round layer cake pan; or one 8 1/2 x 3 5/8 x 2 5/8-inch loaf pan.
- **For an 8-cup baking dish:** one 8 x 8 x 2-inch square pan; or one 11 x 7 x 1 1/2-inch baking pan; or one 9 x 5 x 3-inch loaf pan.
- **For a 10-cup baking dish:** one 9 x 9 x 2-inch square pan; or one 11 3/4 x 7 1/2 x 1 3/4-inch baking pan; or one 15 1/2 x 10 3/4 x 1-inch jelly-roll pan.
- **For three 8-inch round layer cake pans:** two 9 x 9 x 2-inch square pans.
- **For two 9-inch round layer cake pans:** two 8 x 8 x 2-inch square pans; or one 13 x 9 x 2-inch baking pan.
- **For one 9 x 5 x 3-inch loaf pan:** one 9 x 9 x 2-inch square pan.
- **For one 9-inch angel cake tube pan:** one 10 x 3 3/4-inch Bundt® pan; or one 9 x 3 1/2-inch fancy tube pan.

Note: *If a shallow pan is substituted, decrease the baking time slightly. If a deeper pan is substituted, increase the baking time slightly.*

CROQUEMBOUCHE

This dazzling dessert is pretty enough to use as your holiday table centerpiece!

Bake at 400° for 35 minutes.
Makes 20 servings (3 puffs each).

Puffs:
1½ cups water
¾ cup (1½ sticks) unsalted butter
2 teaspoons sugar
¼ teaspoon salt
1½ cups unsifted all-purpose flour
6 eggs

Caramelized Sugar:
1½ cups sugar
2 tablespoons lemon juice
8 red candied cherries, halved
8 green candied cherries, halved

1. Preheat the oven to hot (400°).
2. Prepare the Puffs: Combine the water, butter, 2 teaspoons of sugar and salt in a large saucepan. Bring the mixture to a rolling boil over medium-high heat.
3. Add the flour all at once to the boiling butter mixture. Stir vigorously with a wooden spoon until the mixture forms a thick, smooth ball that leaves the sides of the saucepan clean. Remove the saucepan from the heat.
4. Beat the eggs into the flour mixture, one at a time, using the wooden spoon or an electric mixer, until the paste is shiny and smooth.
5. Drop the paste by well-rounded teaspoonfuls onto 2 ungreased large baking sheets, leaving 1½ inches between the puffs. You should have about 60 puffs.
6. Bake the puffs in the preheated hot oven (400°) for 35 minutes, or until they are puffed and golden brown. Carefully transfer the puffs to a wire rack and cool them completely.
7. Prepare the Caramelized Sugar: Combine the 1½ cups of sugar and the lemon juice in a heavy, medium-size skillet, and cook the mixture over medium-high heat, stirring occasionally with a wooden spoon, until the sugar is dissolved and the syrup is light golden in color; do not let the syrup burn. Remove the saucepan from the heat.
8. Place 14 of the puffs in a 9-inch circle on a serving platter. Place about 5 more puffs in the center of the circle. Working quickly and carefully (do not let the hot syrup touch your skin), dip the bottom of one of the remaining puffs in the caramelized sugar, and place it on the circle of base puffs. Repeat to make a slightly smaller circle of puffs on top of the first puff circle. Fill the center of the second ring with more puffs dipped in the caramelized sugar.* Continue to make increasingly smaller puff circles on top of each other, forming a tree shape with the puff circles. Drizzle any remaining caramelized sugar over the puff tree. Garnish the croquembouche with the candied cherry halves. Refrigerate the croquembouche for up to 1 or 2 days.
***Note:** *If the caramelized sugar begins to thicken while you are working, warm it slightly over very low heat.*

HONEYED DOUGHNUT HOLES

This holiday treat can be made several days ahead and refrigerated until ready to serve.

Makes 12 servings (5 balls per serving).

Vegetable oil for deep-fat frying

Doughnut Holes:
- 2½ *cups unsifted all-purpose flour*
- 1 *teaspoon baking powder*
- 1 *teaspoon ground cinnamon*
- 1 *teaspoon grated lemon zest (yellow part of rind only)*
- 4 *eggs, slightly beaten*
- 1 *tablespoon vegetable oil*

Honey Syrup:
- 1 *cup honey*
- ¼ *cup water*
- 3 *tablespoons lemon juice*
- *Zest of 1 lemon (yellow part of rind only), cut into 3 x ⅛-inch strips*
- *Whipped cream (optional)*

1. Heat the vegetable oil in a deep-fat fryer until it is very hot (400°).
2. Prepare the Doughnut Holes: Sift together the flour, baking powder and cinnamon into a large bowl. Add the grated lemon zest, eggs and the 1 tablespoon of vegetable oil. Stir the mixture until it is thoroughly blended. If necessary, add enough additional flour to make a soft dough.
3. Knead the dough on a lightly floured surface until it is smooth. Divide the dough into 4 equal pieces. Roll each piece into a ¾-inch-thick rope. Cut each rope crosswise into ¾-inch pieces; you should have about 60 dough balls.
4. Deep-fry the dough balls, a few at a time, in the preheated oil until the doughnut holes are golden brown, for about 3 minutes. Using a slotted spoon, carefully remove the doughnut holes from the hot oil and place them on several thicknesses of paper toweling to drain. When the doughnut holes are cool, place them in a heatproof large bowl.
5. Prepare the Honey Syrup: Combine the honey, water, lemon juice and strips of lemon zest in a medium-size saucepan. Bring the mixture to boiling over high heat. Lower the heat and simmer the syrup, stirring occasionally, for 10 minutes.
6. Pour the Honey Syrup over the doughnut holes. Stir gently until all of the doughnut holes are thoroughly coated with the syrup. Cover the bowl with plastic wrap. Refrigerate the doughnut holes overnight or for up to 1 week, stirring the doughnuts periodically to coat them with the syrup. Serve the doughnut holes with a dollop of whipped cream, if you wish.

HOLIDAY COOKING HELPS

Speedy Sweets, Quick Treats

- To make Grasshopper Parfaits, layer vanilla ice cream and crushed chocolate cookies with alternating splashes of green crème de menthe and white crème de menthe. Top with a dollop of whipped cream and crushed peppermint candies.
- Jazz up ready-to-bake frozen pies with a few special touches:
  —Combine ¼ cup (½ stick) of unsalted butter, ¼ cup of sugar, ½ cup of all-purpose flour and ¼ teaspoon of cinnamon in a small bowl until the mixture is crumbly. Sprinkle the mixture over the top crust of a fruit pie before baking.
  —Combine 1 cup of sifted 10X (confectioners' powdered) sugar with ½ teaspoon of vanilla and ½ teaspoon of rum in a small bowl. Slowly stir in about 1 tablespoon of milk until the mixture is a thick, smooth consistency. Drizzle the glaze over the top of a cooled pie.
- Combine 1 cup of semisweet chocolate pieces with 2 tablespoons of smooth peanut butter and 1 tablespoon of milk in a small saucepan. Cook the mixture over low heat, stirring, until the chocolate is melted. Remove the saucepan from the heat and stir in 1 tablespoon of crème de cacao. Serve the sauce over toasted slices of prepared pound cake, topped with a dollop of ice cream or frozen yogurt.
- Hot fruit, fresh, canned or frozen, is always a welcome winter treat. Try sautéed apples with golden raisins, chopped dates and toasted walnuts; bananas sautéed in butter, orange juice and rum; canned apricots or peaches simmered with cinnamon sticks, fresh gingerroot and lemon slices.

MINT BAVARIAN WITH CHOCOLATE SAUCE

This dessert really is an overnight sensation. A wonderful treat for family and friends.

Makes 8 servings.

Nonstick vegetable cooking spray
1 *envelope unflavored gelatin*
1/3 *cup sugar*
1 *cup milk*
2 *egg yolks*
1/4 *cup green crème de menthe*
1 *cup heavy cream*
Whipped cream, for garnish
Fresh mint leaves, for garnish (optional)
Chocolate Sauce (recipe follows)

1. Generously grease a 5-cup decorative mold with the nonstick vegetable cooking spray. Set aside the mold.
2. Stir together the gelatin and the sugar in a small saucepan until they are well combined. Stir in the milk and egg yolks until they are well blended. Let the mixture stand for 1 minute to soften the gelatin. Cook the mixture over low heat, stirring constantly, until the mixture is hot and the gelatin is dissolved, for about 4 minutes; do not let the mixture boil. Remove the saucepan from the heat.
3. Stir in the crème de menthe. Pour the mixture into a medium-size bowl, and place the bowl in a larger bowl of ice and water to speed the setting. Stir the mixture often until it begins to thicken, for about 15 minutes.
4. Meanwhile, beat the heavy cream in a chilled bowl with an electric mixer with chilled beaters until the cream forms soft peaks.
5. Fold the whipped cream into the gelatin mixture. Pour the Bavarian mixture into the prepared mold and refrigerate the Bavarian until it is firm, for at least 5 hours or overnight.
6. To serve, unmold the Bavarian onto a serving platter. Garnish with the additional whipped cream and, if you wish, fresh mint leaves. Serve the Mint Bavarian with the Chocolate Sauce.

Chocolate Sauce: Melt 2 squares (1 ounce each) of semisweet chocolate and 1 tablespoon of butter in the top of a double boiler set over simmering water. Add 3 tablespoons of sugar, 1/8 teaspoon of salt and 1 tablespoon of light corn syrup, and stir until the mixture is well blended. Stir in 1/4 cup of milk and 2 tablespoons of heavy cream. Cook the sauce, stirring occasionally, for 10 minutes, or until the sauce has thickened slightly. Remove the top from the double boiler. Stir in 1/2 teaspoon of vanilla. Cool the Chocolate Sauce to room temperature before serving it.
Makes about 3/4 cup.

HOLIDAY COOKING HELPS

Sweets, Skinny-Style

It actually is possible to shave off calories and fat from desserts without losing your sweet finish.

- Although frozen yogurt often is just as caloric as ice cream, it is almost always lower in fat. Dress up vanilla frozen yogurt with cranberries and raisins simmered in orange juice with a little honey.
- Sponge cake, purchased or homemade, can make a lowfat base for many desserts. Cut a 1-inch slice from the top of the cake, and set it aside. Scoop out enough sponge cake to make a 1-inch shell. Fill the shell with layers of softened frozen yogurt and puréed fruit. Place the cake top over the yogurt filling, lightly pressing the cake top down. Freeze the filled sponge cake until the yogurt is solid.
- Make a fresh fruit cup from as many different varieties of fruit as possible. Serve the fruit cup with one or two cookies for a touch of sweetness.
- Make crêpe batter using lowfat milk, and substitute egg whites for half of the whole eggs in the recipe. Fill the cooked crêpes with a mixture of lightly sweetened, puréed ricotta cheese, chopped candied orange peel and a splash of orange-flavored liqueur. Top with orange slices and a dollop of vanilla yogurt.
- Meringue shells are virtually fat free. Fill them with sorbet and fruit for a colorful dessert.
- Serve freshly ground coffee laced with a shot of liqueur and accompanied by tiny cookies.

HONEY WALNUT PIE

This pie keeps well, either refrigerated or frozen.

Bake at 350° for 50 to 60 minutes.
Makes one 9-inch pie (8 servings).

Pastry for a 9-inch pie shell
- 1/2 *cup (1 stick) butter, at room temperature*
- 1/4 *cup firmly packed light brown sugar*
- 1/4 *cup granulated sugar*
- 1/2 *cup honey*
- 1/2 *cup light corn syrup*
- 3 *eggs, slightly beaten*
- 2 *tablespoons dark rum*
- *Juice and grated zest of 1/2 lemon (yellow part of rind only)*
- 1 *teaspoon vanilla*
- 1 *teaspoon ground cinnamon*
- 1/8 *teaspoon salt*
- 1 1/2 *cups chopped walnuts*
- 1 *cup walnut halves*

1. Preheat the oven to moderate (350°).
2. Roll out the pastry to an 11-inch-diameter circle on a lightly floured surface. Fit the pastry into a 9-inch pie pan. Fold over the excess dough and crimp the edge of the pie crust.
3. Beat together the butter, brown sugar and granulated sugar in a small bowl with an electric mixer at high speed until the mixture is creamy. Beat in the honey and corn syrup, then the eggs and the rum. Add the lemon juice drop by drop, beating constantly. If the mixture curdles, add 1 tablespoon of flour. When all the lemon juice has been added, beat in the lemon zest, the vanilla, cinnamon, salt and the chopped walnuts. Pour the filling into the pie crust. Place the walnut halves on top of the filling.
4. Bake the pie in the preheated moderate oven (350°) for 50 to 60 minutes, or until the filling is firm and the top of the pie is golden brown. There may be some cracks in the filling; this is normal. Serve the pie warm. If you make the pie ahead, cool the pie, cover it with plastic wrap and refrigerate or freeze it. At serving time, reheat the pie at 300° for about 20 minutes.

HOLIDAY COOKING HELPS

Doughs and Don'ts

Here are a few tips to help make your pastry flaky, light and picture-perfect.
- Handle pastry dough as little as possible; unlike bread dough, pastry dough that is overhandled will become tough. As soon as the dough holds together, form a ball, divide it in half and shape one half into a round about 1 inch high on a lightly floured pastry cloth. Roll out the round to the size specified in the recipe. Repeat with the remaining dough.
- Always roll pie dough from the center out to the edge so that the crust will be even in size and thickness. As you roll out the dough, turn it gently to prevent sticking.
- Use the pie plate as a size guide. Turn it upside-down on the rolled dough and check the dough size for additional rolling needed. As a general rule, it's best to roll out the dough 2 inches larger than the pie plate.
- Fold the rolled pastry in half over the rolling pin, lay one half over the pie plate to help center it and flip the other half over the rest of the pie plate.
- Be sure to fit the dough loosely in the pie plate. If the dough is stretched taut, it will shrink and break during baking.
- For lattice pies as well as pastry shells, turn under the edges of the dough and pinch them to form a stand-up edge. There is no need to seal in the juices as there is with most two-crust pies.
- The trimmings from pie pastry can be used to make an extra treat. Gather together the scraps, roll them out, cut them into strips and sprinkle the strips with sugar and cinnamon. Bake the pastry strips in a moderate oven (350°) until they are golden.
- To catch runovers during baking, place a sheet of aluminum foil on the oven rack below the pie.

KUMQUAT PECAN PIE

Look for fresh kumquats, since they really make a difference in this recipe. If they're not available, use prepared kumquats and omit the sugar in the recipe.

Bake at 375° for 45 minutes.
Makes 8 servings.

Butter Crust (recipe, at right)
1/2 *pound fresh kumquats, halved, pitted and chopped OR: 1 jar (8 ounces) kumquats, drained, halved, pitted and chopped*
2 *cups golden raisins*
1/2 *cup Grand Marnier OR: other orange-flavored liqueur*
1/2 *cup dark rum*
Grated zest of 1 orange (orange part of rind only)
2 *Granny Smith apples (about 1/2 pound)*
1/4 *cup sugar (omit if using prepared kumquats)*
1/2 *cup orange juice*
2 *tablespoons cornstarch*
2 *cups chopped toasted pecans* *
1 *egg*
1 *tablespoon water*

1. Prepare the Butter Crust. Wrap the crust in plastic wrap and refrigerate it for 4 hours.
2. Combine the fresh or prepared kumquats, the raisins, Grand Marnier or other orange-flavored liqueur, the rum and the orange zest in a medium-size saucepan. Toss to blend all the ingredients. Cover the saucepan with plastic wrap and let the mixture stand for 4 hours, stirring occasionally.
3. Halve, core, peel and chop the apples. Stir the chopped apples into the kumquat mixture. If using fresh kumquats, stir in the sugar. Add the orange juice and the cornstarch. Cook the mixture over medium heat, stirring constantly, until the mixture thickens and bubbles. Remove the saucepan from the heat and let the mixture cool completely.
4. When ready to bake the pie, preheat the oven to moderate (375°). Roll out half of the pastry to an 11-inch-diameter circle on a lightly floured surface. Transfer the pastry circle to a 9-inch pie pan, and gently press the pastry into the pan. Trim the pastry overhang to 1-inch.
5. Stir the toasted pecans into the cooled pie filling. Pour the filling into the pie crust, spreading the filling evenly over the pastry.
6. Roll out the remaining pastry to a 1/8-inch thickness. Cut the pastry into 1/2-inch-wide strips. Place the pastry strips in a lattice pattern over the top of the pie filling. Trim the ends of the pastry strips flush with the edge of the pie crust. Fold the pie crust overhang over the ends of the strips, and crimp all the pastry together around the edge of the pie.
7. Beat together the egg and the water, and brush the mixture over the top of the pie crust and pastry lattice.
8. Bake the pie in the preheated moderate oven (375°) for 45 minutes, or until the filling bubbles up and the pie crust is golden brown.
***Note:** *To oven toast pecans, spread the nuts in a single layer in a shallow baking pan. Bake the pecans in a preheated slow oven (300°) for 10 to 15 minutes, stirring occasionally, or until the nuts are fragrant and golden in color. Cool the pecans completely before adding them to the pie filling.*

BUTTER CRUST

Makes enough pastry for one double-crust pie.

2 1/2 *cups all-purpose unbleached flour*
1/3 *cup sugar*
Pinch salt
3/4 *cup (1 1/2 sticks) frozen unsalted butter, cut into 1/2-inch pieces*
5 *to 6 tablespoons ice water*

1. Place the flour, sugar and salt in the container of a food processor. Add the butter and whirl until the mixture resembles coarse crumbs.
2. With the motor running, pour the ice water through the feed tube. Continue pulse-processing for 30 seconds, or just until the mixture forms a ball. Do not overprocess the pastry.
3. Remove the dough from the processor. Flatten the dough ball into a disk, wrap the disk in plastic wrap and refrigerate the dough for at least 3 hours.
Note: *For Cinnamon Butter Crust, add 2 teaspoons ground cinnamon to the flour and sugar.*

CONFECTIONS

Spectacular sweets for special occasions. A treat that's certain to please: Amaretto Bon Bons (recipe, page 235)

AMARETTO BON BONS

A delicate blend of chocolate, espresso coffee and the popular almond-flavored liqueur.

Makes about 24 one-inch balls.

- 1 *package (6 ounces) semisweet chocolate pieces*
- 3 *tablespoons corn syrup*
- 1/4 *cup superfine granulated sugar*
- 2 *teaspoons instant espresso coffee powder*
- 1 *teaspoon boiling water*
- 1/4 *cup Amaretto liqueur*
- 1 *cup (approximately 24 cookies) crushed almond-flavored cookies OR: shortbread cookies*
- 1/2 *cup chopped toasted almonds*
- *Unsweetened cocoa powder*

1. Combine the semisweet chocolate pieces, corn syrup, superfine sugar, instant espresso and water in the top of a double boiler. Cook the mixture over barely simmering water just until the chocolate is melted. Remove the double boiler from the heat.
2. Add the Amaretto liqueur, almond-flavored or shortbread cookie crumbs and the almonds to the chocolate mixture, and stir until all the ingredients are blended. Cool the mixture to room temperature. Place the mixture in the refrigerator to chill.
3. Using two teaspoons and your hands, shape the chocolate into 1-inch-diameter balls. Roll each chocolate ball in the cocoa powder until it is completely coated with the cocoa. Keep the bon bons in a tightly covered container in the refrigerator.

SPICED PECANS

For a change of taste, substitute walnuts or almonds for the pecans in this recipe. These spicy nuts are a bazaar best-seller.

Bake at 300° for 25 minutes.
Makes 2 cups.

- 1 *egg*
- 2 *tablespoons water*
- 2 *cups (1/2 pound) pecan halves*
- 1/2 *cup sugar*
- 1 *teaspoon ground cinnamon*
- 3/4 *teaspoon salt*
- 1/4 *teaspoon ground cloves*
- 1/4 *teaspoon ground nutmeg*

1. Preheat the oven to slow (300°).
2. Beat together the egg and water with a fork in a medium-size bowl until they are well blended. Add the pecans to the bowl, and stir until all the nuts are coated with the egg mixture. Remove the pecans from the bowl with a fork and arrange them in an 8-inch square baking pan.
3. Combine the sugar, cinnamon, salt, cloves and nutmeg in a small bowl. Sprinkle the spice mixture over the pecans in the baking pan. Toss the pecans gently until they are thoroughly coated with the spice mixture. Spread the coated pecans on an ungreased baking sheet.
4. Bake the coated pecans in the preheated slow oven (300°), shaking the baking sheet several times to rearrange the nuts, for 25 minutes, or until the pecans are golden brown in color. Check the pecans frequently to avoid burning them.
5. Cool the pecans on the baking sheet. Store the spiced pecans in an airtight metal container.

CREAMY MINT LOGS

Makes three 12-inch logs.

- 1/2 *cup (1 stick) butter, softened*
- 1 *box (16 ounces) 10X (confectioners' powdered) sugar, sifted*
- 3 *tablespoons green crème de menthe*
- 1/4 *teaspoon almond extract*
- 1 *ounce (1 square) semisweet chocolate, finely grated*

1. Beat the butter in a large bowl with an electric mixer until it is creamy. With the mixer on low speed, gradually add the sugar to the butter. Add the crème de menthe and the almond extract. Chill the mixture for 30 minutes.
2. Divide the mixture into thirds. Place a 12-inch piece of wax paper on a flat surface. Sprinkle a third of the grated chocolate over the surface of the wax paper. Mold one part of the mint mixture into a 12-inch log along an edge of the wax paper. Roll the log back and forth over the surface of the wax paper, coating the log with the grated chocolate as you roll. Continue rolling until the entire surface of the log is coated with the chocolate. Wrap the wax paper around the log. Repeat with the remaining mint mixture and grated chocolate to make two more logs. Refrigerate the logs for several hours or overnight.
3. Remove the logs from the refrigerator and let them stand at room temperature for 10 minutes. Unwrap the logs and carefully cut them into 1/4-inch slices. Layer the log slices on a plate, placing wax paper between each layer. Cover the plate loosely and place it in the refrigerator for 24 hours to allow the slices to harden.

ALMOND NUT BRITTLE

Makes about 24 pieces.

- 2 *cups whole blanched almonds* *
- 2 *cups firmly packed light brown sugar*
- 1/2 *cup water*
- 1/2 *cup light corn syrup*
- 1/4 *cup (1/2 stick) butter*
- 1/4 *teaspoon baking soda*
- 1/2 *teaspoon vanilla*

1. Toast the almonds in a heavy skillet over low heat for 5 to 7 minutes, stirring them or shaking the skillet to keep the almonds from over-browning. Keep the almonds warm in a slow oven (250°).
2. Combine the brown sugar, water and corn syrup in a medium-size heavy saucepan. Heat the mixture, stirring, until the sugar is completely dissolved. Insert a candy thermometer into the mixture, and continue cooking the mixture until the thermometer reaches 310°, or until a small amount of the mixture hardens when dropped into cold water. Do not stir the mixture while it is cooking, but use a wooden spoon to test it occasionally.
3. Remove the saucepan from the heat. Quickly stir in the toasted almonds, the butter, baking soda and vanilla, until the mixture is thoroughly blended. Let the mixture stand until the bubbles subside. Meanwhile, butter a baking sheet and a spatula. Pour the mixture onto the baking sheet, using the spatula to spread the mixture over the baking sheet thinly and fairly evenly.
4. Let the brittle cool at room temperature. Break the brittle into 2-inch pieces, and store the pieces in an airtight container, placing wax paper between the layers of brittle. Store the container in the refrigerator or other cool place. Allow the brittle to ripen for 24 hours before serving. The brittle will keep for 1 month.
***Note:** If you wish, substitute 2 cups of dry roasted peanuts for the almonds in the recipe above. Do not toast the peanuts; begin with Step 2.*

PECAN NOUGAT LOGS

These nut-covered nougat logs are a chewy delight coated with rich caramel.

Makes 22 rolls.

Nougat Base 1:
- 3/4 *cup sugar*
- 2/3 *cup light corn syrup*
- 2 *tablespoons water*
- 1/4 *cup egg whites (2 eggs), at room temperature*

Nougat Base 2:
- 2 *cups sugar*
- 1/2 *cups light corn syrup*
- 1/2 *cup hot water*

- 1/4 *cup (1/2 stick) butter, melted*
- 1 *teaspoon vanilla*
- 1/8 *teaspoon salt*

Dipping Caramel:
- 2 1/2 *cups sugar*
- 1 3/4 *cups light corn syrup*
- 2 *cups half and half*
- 1 *teaspoon vanilla*
- 1/2 *teaspoon salt*
- 6 *cans (6 ounces each) pecan halves*

1. Prepare Nougat Base 1: Combine the ¾ cup of sugar, ⅔ cup of corn syrup and 2 tablespoons of water in a medium-size saucepan. Bring the mixture to boiling over medium-high heat until the syrup registers 238°, or "soft ball" stage, on a candy thermometer. Remove the saucepan from the heat. Meanwhile, beat the egg whites with an electric mixer until they form stiff peaks. Gradually pour the hot syrup over the beaten egg whites, beating constantly. It is important to add the syrup to the egg whites while it is very hot to eliminate the risk of salmonella. Continue to beat the mixture until it is lukewarm and thickened, for about 5 minutes. Transfer the nougat base to a large bowl. Do not let the nougat base stand for more than 1 hour.
2. Butter an 8 x 8 x 2-inch baking pan. Line the pan with wax paper, and butter the wax paper generously.
3. Prepare Nougat Base 2: Combine the 2 cups of sugar, ½ cup of corn syrup and ½ cup of hot water in a medium-size saucepan. Bring the mixture to boiling over medium-high heat until the syrup registers 258°, or "hard ball" stage, on a candy thermometer. Remove the saucepan from the heat, and let the mixture stand for 2 minutes.
4. Pour Nougat Base 2 into the center of Nougat Base 1 in the large bowl. Beat the combined Bases with a wooden spoon until the mixture is thick and well blended. Gradually add the melted butter to the combined Nougat Bases, and beat until all the ingredients are well blended. Beat in the vanilla and the salt.
5. Pour the nougat mixture into the prepared baking pan. Set aside the baking pan and allow the nougat to harden slightly.
6. Prepare the Dipping Caramel: Combine the 2½ cups of sugar, 1¾ cups of corn syrup and ½ cup of the half and half in a large heavy saucepan. Cook the mixture until it registers 238°, or "soft ball" stage, on a candy thermometer. Gradually add another ½ cup of the half and half to the saucepan, stirring constantly, and cook the mixture for 10 minutes. Gradually add the remaining 1 cup of half and half. Continue to cook the mixture until the caramel registers 242°, or "firm ball" stage, on a candy thermometer. As the temperature of the caramel rises, gradually lower the heat to prevent scorching. Remove the saucepan from the heat and stir in the vanilla and the salt. Pour the caramel into the top of a double boiler set over hot water.
7. Remove the hardened nougat from the baking pan and remove the wax paper. Cut the nougat in half and cut each half crosswise into 11 equal strips.
8. Spread the pecans on a flat tray or platter. Using tongs or a fork, dip each nougat strip into the warm caramel. Roll each caramel-coated nougat strip in the pecans and place it on a wire rack to allow the caramel to set. Store the nougat logs in plastic wrap or between layers of wax paper in plastic bags.

SPICY ORANGE WALNUTS

A combination of spices and the tang of orange make these crunchy walnuts a special treat indeed.

Bake at 250° for 1 hour.
Makes 2 cups.

- 1½ *cups 10X (confectioners' powdered) sugar*
- 2 *tablespoons cornstarch*
- 1 *teaspoon ground cinnamon*
- ¼ *teaspoon ground cloves*
- ¼ *teaspoon ground allspice*
- ⅛ *teaspoon salt*
- 1 *tablespoon grated orange zest (orange part of rind only)*
- 1 *egg white*
- 1 *tablespoon orange juice*
- 2 *cups whole walnuts*

1. Preheat the oven to slow (250°).
2. Sift together the 10X (confectioners' powdered) sugar, cornstarch, cinnamon, cloves, allspice and salt into a medium-size bowl. Stir in the orange zest.
3. Beat the egg white and the orange juice with an electric mixer until the mixture is slightly foamy. Add the walnuts and toss them until they are coated thoroughly with the egg white mixture. Drain the walnuts completely.
4. Roll the damp walnuts, one third at a time, in the sugar mixture until the walnuts are evenly coated. Spread the coated walnuts over two jelly-roll pans, making sure the nuts do not touch.
5. Bake the walnuts in the preheated slow oven (250°) for 1 hour, or until the nuts are dry. Cool the walnuts completely before storing them in an airtight container. The walnuts will keep for up to 1 month.

PEANUT BUTTER CHOCOLATE FUDGE

Makes about 2 pounds.

- 1 *package (8 ounces) semisweet chocolate squares*
- 1 *can (14 ounces) sweetened condensed milk (not evaporated milk)*
- ½ *cup coarsely chopped dry roasted peanuts*
- 1 *cup peanut butter chips (½ of a 12-ounce bag)*
- 1 *teaspoon butter*

1. Line an 8-inch square baking pan with wax paper, and set it aside. Combine 7 squares of the semisweet chocolate with ⅔ cup of the sweetened condensed milk in a small saucepan, and cook over low heat until the chocolate is melted. Stir the peanuts into the chocolate mixture. Quickly pour the mixture into the prepared baking pan, spreading the mixture evenly over the bottom of the pan.
2. Combine the peanut butter chips with the remaining ⅓ cup of sweetened condensed milk in a second small saucepan, and cook over low heat until the peanut butter chips are melted. Spread the peanut butter mixture over the chocolate mixture in the baking pan.
3. Combine the remaining square of chocolate with the butter in a third small saucepan, and cook over low heat until the chocolate is melted. Using a spoon or a wax paper cone, drizzle the melted chocolate over the peanut butter layer in the baking pan. Place the fudge in the refrigerator to chill for 2 hours, or until the fudge is firm. Turn out the fudge onto a cutting board and peel off the wax paper. Cut the fudge into squares. Store the fudge in a tightly covered container in the refrigerator. The fudge will keep for up to 3 weeks.

CANDIED ORANGE PEEL

Makes 3 cups of strips (about 5 ounces).

4 *large navel oranges*
Cold water
2 *cups sugar*
1 *cup hot water*
1/4 *cup light corn syrup*
Few drops yellow food coloring
1/3 *cup sugar*

1. Cut the peel on each orange into quarters; remove the peel in sections using a swivel-bladed vegetable peeler. Place the peels in a large saucepan and add enough cold water to cover the peels. Bring the water to boiling, and boil the peels for 2 minutes. Drain the peels, and repeat the boiling 3 times, using fresh cold water each time.
2. Combine the 2 cups of sugar, 1 cup of hot water and corn syrup in a medium-size heavy saucepan. Cook the mixture over medium-high heat, stirring the mixture until the sugar is dissolved. Add the drained orange peels and the yellow food coloring to the saucepan. Lower the heat and cook for about 25 minutes, or until the peels are translucent and tender. Let the peels cool in the syrup for 30 minutes. Drain the peels in a colander, reserving the syrup if you wish.*
3. Place the remaining ⅓ cup of sugar in a large plastic bag. Add the drained orange peels, a few at a time, and shake the bag to coat the peels completely with the sugar. Remove the coated peels from the bag and place them on a wire rack to dry. Repeat with the remaining peels until they are all coated with sugar. Store the orange peels in an airtight container for up to 1 month.
***Note:** *Leftover syrup can be used to sweeten tea. The syrup is also excellent for poaching pears, apples, prunes or apricots.*

CHOCOLATE ALMOND TRUFFLES

This recipe makes two kinds of treats—truffle logs that you can slice, and bite-size truffle nuggets.

Makes 4 truffle logs and 24 truffle nuggets.

1 *pound semisweet chocolate OR: bittersweet chocolate, chopped**
1 *can (8 ounces) almond paste*
2 *tablespoons unsalted butter*
1 *cup 10X (confectioners' powdered) sugar, sifted*
2 *tablespoons rum OR: brandy*
1 *cup cocoa powder*

1. Place the chopped semisweet or bittersweet chocolate in the container of a food processor fitted with a metal blade. Cover the processor, and grind the chocolate by pulsing the processor on and off.
2. Add the almond paste, butter, sifted 10X (confectioners' powdered) sugar and the rum or brandy to the ground chocolate. Cover, and process until the mixture is smooth and well blended, stopping the processor once or twice to scrape down the sides of the container.
3. Divide the mixture in half, and set aside one half. Shape the first half of the mixture into twenty-four 1-inch-diameter balls. Divide the reserved half of the mixture into quarters, and roll each quarter into a 1-inch-diameter log.
4. Sift the cocoa powder onto a sheet of wax paper. Carefully roll the four logs and the 24 nuggets in the cocoa powder. Place the coated nuggets on a baking sheet lined with wax paper, and let the nuggets stand for 30 minutes. Roll the nuggets again in additional cocoa powder, if necessary.
5. Pack the logs and the nuggets in a doily-lined container with a lid, and cover the truffles with plastic wrap. The truffles may be stored in the refrigerator, but they should be brought back to room temperature before serving.
***Note:** *If you are using blocks of chocolate, cut it into small pieces with a sharp knife. If you are using 3-ounce bars of chocolate, break them directly into the container of the food processor. If you are using semisweet chocolate pieces, they may be poured directly into the processor.*

TATUS

Chocolate fudge balls flavored with orange and spices, tatus are a popular treat in Italy.

Bake at 375° for 12 minutes.
Makes about 5 dozen tatus.

- 3½ *cups all-purpose flour*
- ½ *cup cocoa powder*
- 2 *teaspoons baking powder*
- 2 *teaspoons ground cinnamon*
- 1 *teaspoon ground allspice*
- ½ *teaspoon ground nutmeg*
- ½ *cup vegetable shortening*
- ¾ *cup sugar*
- 2 *eggs*
- 1 *teaspoon vanilla*
- *Grated zest of 1 orange (orange part of rind only)*
- *Juice of 1 orange*
- ¼ *cup milk*
- ½ *cup finely chopped walnuts*
- *Cocoa Glaze (recipe follows)*
- *Prepared white icing (from a 4¼-ounce tube)*

1. Sift together the flour, cocoa powder, baking powder, cinnamon, allspice and nutmeg onto a piece of wax paper.
2. Combine the shortening and the sugar in a large bowl, and beat with an electric mixer at high speed until the mixture is light and fluffy. Add the eggs and beat until they are incorporated. Beat in the vanilla, orange zest, orange juice and milk.
3. Gradually add the sifted flour mixture to the egg mixture, beating after each addition. Add the chopped nuts. Wrap the dough in wax paper and place it in the refrigerator until the dough is easy to handle.
4. Preheat the oven to moderate (375°). Lightly grease several baking sheets.
5. Shape the dough into 1-inch-diameter balls. Place the dough balls, spacing them 2 inches apart, on the prepared baking sheets.
6. Bake the dough balls in the preheated moderate oven (375°) for 12 minutes, or until the tatus are firm. Remove the tatus from the baking sheets to wire racks to cool.
7. When the tatus are completely cool, frost them with the Cocoa Glaze. Let the tatus stand until the glaze has hardened, then decorate the top of each candy with a spiral of the prepared white icing.

Cocoa Glaze: Combine 1 box (1 pound) of sifted 10X (confectioners' powdered) sugar with ½ cup of cocoa powder and 1 tablespoon of softened butter in a large bowl. Stir with a wooden spoon until all the ingredients are well blended. Beat in ¼ to ½ cup of milk, until the glaze is the consistency of thick cream.
Makes enough glaze to frost 1 batch of tatus.

HONEY ALMOND MOUNDS

Just two ingredients—almonds and honey—go into these Italian Christmas candies.

Bake at 300° for 20 minutes.
Makes 12 candies.

- 4 *cups (1 pound) slivered almonds*
- ½ *cup honey*
- *Multi-colored sprinkles, for garnish (optional)*

1. Preheat the oven to slow (300°).
2. Spread the almonds in a single layer in an ungreased 15 x 10 x 1-inch jelly-roll pan.
3. Bake the almonds in the preheated slow oven (300°), shaking the pan several times, until the almonds are a rich golden color, for 20 minutes.
4. Bring the honey to boiling in a large heavy skillet. Add the almonds to the skillet. Reduce the heat to low and cook the mixture, stirring constantly, for 2 minutes, or just until the almonds begin sticking together. Remove the skillet from the heat.
5. Dampen a wooden board. Spoon the almond mixture into 24 equal mounds on the board. Sprinkle each mound with multi-colored sprinkles, if you wish.
6. Let the almond mounds cool and harden on the wooden board for at least an hour. Wrap the mounds in wax paper or plastic wrap.

GOLDEN FIG CUPS

Makes 20 candies.

- 1/4 *cup (1/2 stick) butter or margarine, softened*
- 1/4 *cup firmly packed brown sugar*
- 1 *teaspoon grated lemon zest (yellow part of rind only)*
- 1 *cup graham cracker crumbs (7 whole crackers, crushed)*
- 1 *cup finely chopped dried figs, stems removed*
- 1/4 *cup honey*
- 2 *tablespoons grated orange zest (orange part of rind only)*
- 1/4 *cup orange juice*

1. Generously grease 20 miniature (1¾ inches) muffin-pan cups. Press a 3-inch square of wax paper into each muffin-pan cup.
2. Beat together the butter or margarine, brown sugar and lemon zest in a large bowl with an electric mixer on high speed until the mixture is creamy. Add the graham cracker crumbs and stir until the mixture is thoroughly combined.
3. Press a rounded tablespoon of the crumb mixture firmly into the bottom and partly up the side of each lined muffin-pan cup. Refrigerate the pans for about 1 hour, or until the graham cracker cups are firm.
4. Combine the figs, honey, orange zest and orange juice in a small saucepan. Bring the mixture to boiling. Reduce the heat to low and cook the mixture, stirring constantly, for about 2 minutes, or until the mixture thickens. Cool the fig mixture.
5. Spoon a rounded teaspoon of the fig mixture into each graham cracker cup. Remove the fig cups from the muffin-pans by gently pulling up the wax paper liners. Serve the fig cups in miniature muffin-pan liners. Store the fig cups, covered, in the refrigerator.

CHINESE CHOCOLATE DROPS

Makes 1½ dozen candies.

- 1/4 *cup (1/2 stick) butter or margarine*
- 6 *squares (1 ounce each) semisweet chocolate*
- 1 *tablespoon light corn syrup*
- 1/4 *teaspoon almond extract*
- 1 *can (3 ounces) chow mein noodles, crumbled*
- 3/4 *cup sliced blanched almonds*
- 18 *whole blanched almonds*

1. Combine the butter and the chocolate in a medium-size heavy saucepan, and cook the mixture over low heat until the chocolate is melted. Remove the saucepan from the heat. Stir in the corn syrup and the almond extract.
2. Combine the chow mein noodles and the sliced almonds in a large bowl. Add the chocolate mixture to the bowl and stir until all the ingredients are thoroughly combined.
3. Line a baking sheet with wax paper. Drop the chocolate-almond mixture by rounded tablespoonfuls onto the prepared baking sheet. Press a whole almond onto the top of each mound. Refrigerate the chocolate drops for about 30 minutes, or until they are firm.

BREADS AND GINGERBREADS

A taste-tempting array of breads and muffins: Pumpkin Spice Bread (recipe, page 244); Chocolate Orange Bread (recipe, page 245); Cranberry Almond Muffins (recipe, page 243); Chocolate Date Nut Bread (recipe, page 244); Banana Nut Muffins (recipe, page 243); Confetti Muffins (recipe, page 246); Fresh Herb Muffins (recipe, page 247); Whole Wheat Molasses Muffins (recipe, page 246)

BANANA NUT MUFFINS

An all-time family favorite.

Bake at 425° for 40 minutes.
Makes 12 muffins.

- 1 *egg, well beaten*
- 1 *cup milk*
- 1/4 *cup (1/2 stick) butter, melted and cooled*
- 1/3 *cup sugar*
- 1 *tablespoon baking powder*
- 2 *cups all-purpose flour*
- 1/2 *cup coarsely chopped pecans*
- 1 *banana, mashed*
- 1 *teaspoon grated lemon zest (yellow part of rind only)*
- 1 *teaspoon sugar*

1. Preheat the oven to hot (425°). Grease twelve 2½-inch muffin-pan cups, and set them aside.
2. Combine the egg, milk, butter, ⅓ cup of sugar, baking powder, flour and pecans in a large bowl, and beat until the mixture is thoroughly blended. Add the banana, and beat just until it is combined. Do not overmix; the batter will look lumpy.
3. Using a large spoon and rubber spatula, fill each prepared muffin-pan cup three-quarters full of batter. Sprinkle the tops evenly with the lemon zest and the 1 teaspoon of sugar.
4. Bake in the preheated hot oven (425°) until the muffins are golden brown, for 40 minutes. Serve the muffins warm.

CRANBERRY ALMOND MUFFINS

These berry-good muffins, boasting a seasonal fruit, are a treat all year long.

Bake at 425° for 45 minutes.
Makes 12 muffins.

- 3 *cups all-purpose flour*
- 1/2 *cup sugar*
- 2 *teaspoons baking powder*
- 1 *teaspoon baking soda*
- 1/2 *teaspoon salt*
- 1 *container (16 ounces) dairy sour cream*
- 1/3 *cup milk*
- 1/2 *cup vegetable oil*
- 1/2 *teaspoon almond extract*
- 2 *eggs*
- 1 1/2 *cups fresh or frozen cranberries, coarsely chopped*
- 2/3 *cup sliced blanched almonds*

1. Preheat the oven to hot (425°). Grease twelve 2½-inch muffin-pan cups, and set them aside.
2. Combine the flour, sugar, baking powder, baking soda and salt in a large bowl, and stir until they are well mixed.
3. Combine the sour cream, milk, oil, almond extract, eggs and cranberries in medium-size bowl, and stir until they are blended. Add the cranberry mixture to the flour mixture, stirring just until they are blended. Do not overmix; the batter will look lumpy. Stir in half of the almonds.
4. Using a large spoon and a rubber spatula, fill each prepared muffin-pan cup two-thirds full of batter. Sprinkle the tops with the remaining almonds.
5. Bake the muffins in the preheated hot oven (425°) for 45 minutes, or until the muffins are golden brown on top and a wooden pick inserted in the centers of the muffins comes out clean. Serve the muffins warm.

CHOCOLATE DATE NUT BREAD

Bake at 350° for 1 hour and 10 minutes.
Makes 1 loaf.

- 3/4 *cup boiling water*
- 1 *cup sliced pitted dates*
- 1 *package (6 ounces) semisweet chocolate pieces*
- 1/4 *cup (1/2 stick) unsalted butter*
- 1 *egg*
- 3/4 *cup milk*
- 1 *teaspoon vanilla*
- 2 1/2 *cups all-purpose flour*
- 1/3 *cup sugar*
- 1 *teaspoon baking powder*
- 1 *teaspoon baking soda*
- 1/2 *teaspoon salt*
- 1 *cup coarsely chopped walnuts*
- *10X (confectioners' powdered) sugar*

1. Preheat the oven to moderate (350°). Grease a 9 x 5-inch loaf pan, and set it aside.
2. Pour boiling water over the dates in a small bowl, and set it aside. Melt the chocolate pieces with the butter in a heavy 1-quart saucepan over low heat. Beat together the egg, milk and vanilla in a second small bowl, just until they are mixed.
3. Stir together the flour, sugar, baking powder, baking soda, salt and walnuts in a large bowl. Add the dates with their liquid, the chocolate mixture and the egg mixture to the flour mixture. Stir until all the ingredients are well blended. Scrape the batter into the prepared pan, and smooth the top with a spatula.
4. Bake the bread in the preheated moderate oven (350°) for 1 hour and 10 minutes, or until a wooden pick inserted in the center of the bread comes out clean. Cool the bread in the pan on a wire rack for 10 minutes. Remove the bread from the pan and let it cool completely on the wire rack. To serve, dust the bread with the 10X (confectioners' powdered) sugar.

PUMPKIN SPICE BREAD

Raisins, pecans and maple syrup make this bread perfect for a holiday brunch.

Bake at 325° for 1 hour and 15 minutes.
Makes 1 loaf.

- 3 *cups all-purpose flour*
- 2 *teaspoons baking powder*
- 1 *teaspoon baking soda*
- 1 *teaspoon ground cinnamon*
- 1/2 *teaspoon salt*
- 1/2 *teaspoon allspice*
- 2 *eggs*
- 1 *can (16 ounces) solid-pack pumpkin purée (not pumpkin pie filling)*
- 1 *cup firmly packed light brown sugar*
- 1/2 *cup maple syrup*
- 1/2 *cup vegetable oil*
- 1/2 *cup golden raisins*
- 1/2 *cup chopped pecans*

1. Preheat the oven to slow (325°). Grease a 9 x 5-inch loaf pan, and set it aside.
2. Stir together the flour, baking powder, baking soda, cinnamon, salt and allspice in a large bowl.
3. Beat together the eggs, pumpkin purée, brown sugar, maple syrup and oil in a medium-size bowl. Add the pumpkin mixture to the flour mixture, and stir just until the ingredients are moistened. Fold in the raisins and pecans. Scrape the batter into the prepared pan.
4. Bake the bread in the preheated slow oven (325°) for 1 hour and 15 minutes, or until a wooden pick inserted in the center of the bread comes out clean. Cool the bread in the pan on a wire rack for 10 minutes. Remove the bread from the pan, and let it cool completely on the wire rack.

CHOCOLATE ORANGE BREAD

A delicious combination of flavors make this quick bread a rich treat.

Bake at 300° for 1 hour and 15 minutes.
Makes 1 loaf.

- 3 *cups sifted all-purpose flour*
- 1 *cup sugar*
- 4 *teaspoons baking powder*
- 1 *teaspoon ground cinnamon*
- 1 *teaspoon ground nutmeg*
- ½ *teaspoon salt*
- ½ *cup chopped walnuts*
- 3 *tablespoons grated orange zest (orange part of rind only)*
- 1 *package (6 ounces) semisweet chocolate pieces*
- 1 *egg, beaten*
- 1½ *cups orange juice*
- 2 *tablespoons vegetable oil*
- *Orange Glaze (recipe follows)*
- *Zest of 1 orange (orange part of rind only), cut into julienne strips (optional)*

1. Preheat the oven to slow (300°). Grease a 9 x 5-inch loaf pan, and set it aside.
2. Sift together the flour, sugar, baking powder, cinnamon, nutmeg and salt into a large bowl. Stir in the walnuts, grated orange zest and chocolate pieces.
3. Stir together the egg, orange juice and oil in a small bowl. Add the egg mixture to the flour mixture, and stir just until they are blended. Scrape the batter into the prepared pan.
4. Bake the bread in the preheated slow oven (300°) for 1 hour and 15 minutes, or until a wooden pick inserted in the center of the bread comes out clean. Cool the bread in the pan on a wire rack.
5. Drizzle the Orange Glaze over the top of the cooled bread. If you wish, make knots of the orange zest and garnish the top of the bread with the orange knots.

Orange Glaze: Combine 1 cup of 10X (confectioners' powdered) sugar with 2 tablespoons of orange juice in a small bowl, and stir until the glaze is smooth.
Makes about 1 cup.

HOLIDAY COOKING HELPS

Baking Equivalent Chart

Ingredients	Equivalent
Flour	
Regular, 1 pound	4 cups, sifted
2 pounds	8 cups, sifted
5 pounds	20 cups, sifted
10 pounds	40 cups, sifted
25 pounds	100 cups, sifted
Cake Flour, 1 pound	4½ cups, plus 2 tablespoons, sifted
Crackers and Grains	
Graham crackers, 11 squares	1 cup crumbs
Oatmeal, 18 ounces, quick	7 cups
½ ounce packet, plain	½ cup
Sugar	
Granulated, 1 pound	2 cups
2 pounds	4 cups
5 pounds	10 cups
Brown, 1 pound	2¼ cups, packed
10X (confectioners' powdered), 1 pound	4 cups
Nuts, shelled	
Walnuts, 1 pound, whole	4 cups
10 ounce pack, broken	2½ cups
(home ground)	2⅔ cups
Almonds, 1 pound, whole	3½ cups
¼ pound, whole	7 ounces
6 ounce pack, sliced	2 cups
Filberts, 6 ounce pack, whole	1½ cups
(home ground)	2 cups
Pecans, 1 pound, whole	4 cups
Fruit	
Mixed, candied, 4 ounces chopped	½ cup
Citron, 4 ounces chopped	½ cup
Cherries, candied, 8 ounces whole	1 cup
Raisins, 15 ounces	3 cups

CONFETTI MUFFINS

A savory muffin with sweet red and green peppers and parsley. These muffins may be frozen for up to 1 month.

Bake at 400° for 35 minutes.
Makes 6 muffins.

1	*egg*
1¼	*cups milk*
¼	*cup (½ stick) butter, melted*
2	*cups all-purpose flour*
1	*tablespoon baking powder*
½	*teaspoon salt*
¼	*cup chopped sweet red pepper*
¼	*cup chopped sweet green pepper*
½	*cup shredded Swiss cheese (2 ounces)*
¼	*cup grated Parmesan cheese*
2	*tablespoons chopped green onion including tops*
1	*clove garlic, finely chopped*
2	*tablespoons chopped fresh parsley*

1. Preheat the oven to hot (400°). Grease six 2½-inch muffin-pan cups, and set them aside.
2. Beat the egg in a large bowl. Stir in the milk and the butter. Combine the flour, baking powder, salt, red and green peppers, Swiss and Parmesan cheeses, green onion, garlic and parsley in a medium-size bowl. Add the flour mixture to the egg mixture and stir just until all the ingredients are moistened. Do not overmix; the batter will look lumpy.
3. Using a large spoon and a rubber spatula, fill each prepared muffin-pan cup two-thirds full of batter. Place the muffin-pan cups on a baking sheet.
4. Bake the muffins in the preheated hot oven (400°) for 35 minutes, or until the muffins are golden brown and a wooden pick inserted in the centers comes out clean. Cool the muffins in the muffin pan on a wire rack for 5 minutes. Remove the muffins from the muffin-pan cups. Serve the muffins warm.

WHOLE WHEAT MOLASSES MUFFINS

Bake at 425° for 20 minutes.
Makes 12 muffins.

1	*cup all-purpose flour*
1	*cup whole wheat flour*
2	*teaspoons baking powder*
1	*teaspoon salt*
¼	*cup molasses*
1	*egg, slightly beaten*
1	*cup milk*
½	*cup (1 stick) butter, melted and cooled*

1. Preheat the oven to hot (425°). Grease twelve 2½-inch muffin-pan cups, and set them aside.
2. Combine the all-purpose and whole wheat flours, the baking powder, salt, molasses, egg, milk and butter in a large bowl, and stir just until the ingredients are moistened. Do not overmix; the batter will look lumpy.
3. Using a large spoon and a rubber spatula, fill each prepared muffin-pan cup two-thirds full of batter.
4. Bake the muffins in the preheated hot oven (425°) for 20 minutes, or until a wooden pick inserted in the centers of the muffins comes out clean. Serve the muffins warm.

HOLIDAY COOKING HELPS

Hints for Healthier Breads and Muffins

- Choose recipes for quick breads and muffins that call for oil instead of butter.
- Substitute egg whites for all or part of the whole eggs called for in a recipe. In general, 2 egg whites can be substituted for 1 whole egg.
- Use lowfat or nonfat plain yogurt or buttermilk instead of the sour cream called for in a recipe.
- Reduce the sugar called for in a recipe by a third.
- Grease loaf pans and muffin-pan cups with nonstick vegetable cooking spray.
- Reduce the amount of nuts called for in a recipe.

FRESH HERB MUFFINS

These savory muffins are a perfect accompaniment to soup, chili or a salad.

Bake at 400° for 20 minutes.
Makes 20 muffins.

- *3½ cups all-purpose flour*
- *1 teaspoon salt*
- *¼ cup sugar*
- *4 teaspoons baking powder*
- *4 eggs*
- *1½ cups milk*
- *½ cup (1 stick) butter, melted and cooled*
- *½ cup loosely packed, finely chopped fresh parsley*
- *½ cup loosely packed, finely chopped fresh dill*
- *½ cup loosely packed, finely chopped fresh basil*

1. Preheat the oven to hot (400°). Grease twenty 2½-inch muffin-pan cups, and set them aside.
2. Combine the flour, salt, sugar and baking powder in a large bowl, and set it aside. Beat together the eggs and the milk in a medium-size bowl until they are blended. Stir in the melted butter.
3. Add the egg mixture to the flour mixture, and stir just until the ingredients are moistened. Do not overmix; the batter will look lumpy. Stir in the parsley, dill and basil.
4. Using a large spoon and a rubber spatula, fill each prepared muffin-pan cup three-quarters full of batter.
5. Bake the muffins in the preheated hot oven (400°) for 20 minutes, or until the muffins are lightly browned. Remove the muffins from the muffin-pan cups. Serve the muffins warm.

HOLIDAY COOKING HELPS

A Magic Touch with Mixes

Add your own special touches to quick bread and muffin mixes to add homemade flavor in a snap.
- Add chopped apples or pears to gingerbread mix.
- Add candied ginger to date nut bread mix.
- Spoon prepared batter into muffin-pan cups until they are half full. Add a tablespoon of jam, cranberry relish or chopped dried fruit. Top with the remaining batter and bake as directed.

Frozen bread dough can be used to make wonderfully unique breads. To make swirl bread, roll out the dough to a rectangle as wide as the length of your loaf pan. Spread with one of the following toppings, roll up the dough jelly-roll style and place the roll seam side down in a prepared loaf pan.
- Combine chopped fresh herbs and butter.
- Sprinkle Parmesan cheese and paprika.
- Sauté chopped onions, cool them and combine the onions with poppy seeds.
- Combine cinnamon and sugar, raisins and chopped nuts.

Baking miniature muffins and loaves instead of the regular-size muffins and loaves usually reduces the baking time.

HOLIDAY COOKING HELPS

Hints for Gingerbread Houses

- To preserve a gingerbread house, wrap the house tightly in plastic wrap, and store it in a cool, dry place. Or, if you wish, spray the house with semigloss polyurethane spray. Let the polyurethane dry completely and store the house, tightly covered, in a cool, dark place.
- Let your imagination run wild when designing a gingerbread house. Base your design on a fairy tale, such as the witch's cottage in *Hansel and Gretel*, or Sleeping Beauty's castle. Or use your own home as the inspiration for a gingerbread house.
- Carry a gingerbread theme throughout a holiday home: Hang gingerbread cookies from ribbons in the windows or from chandeliers; group gingerbread men on a mantel; decorate your tree with gingerbread cookies.

GINGERBREAD HOUSE

Materials

1 batch Gingerbread Dough (recipe, page 252)
Paper for patterns
Scissors
Two or more flat baking sheets (without edges)
Aluminum foil
Tape
Rolling pin
All-purpose flour
Very sharp paring knife
Wire racks
1 batch Royal Frosting (recipe, page 252)
Wet cotton cloth
Small spatula
½-inch-thick plywood base, approximately 18x24-inches
Heavy cans or bottles
Pastry bag fitted with ⅛-inch plain round tip
Assorted candies: round white mint candy wafers, small red cinnamon candies, variety of small striped peppermint candy sticks, candy cane wreath with taffeta bow, red and green ball candies, pebble candies, shell candies, miniature nonpareils, 5 small candy canes, 3 larger candy canes, or your own selection
Floral wire (optional)

1. Prepare the Gingerbread Dough. Enlarge the house pattern pieces in Fig. IV, 1 *(page 253)* onto paper, following the directions on page 271. Cut out the paper patterns. Line the baking sheets with aluminum foil and lightly tape the foil in place. Evenly space two racks in the oven, and preheat the oven to moderate (350°).
2. Working with one quarter of the dough at a time, pat out the dough onto one of the baking sheets, flattening the dough slightly. Lightly sprinkle the dough and the rolling pin with flour, and roll out the dough until it is ¼-inch-thick. Using the paper patterns and following Fig. IV, 1, cut out as many house pieces as possible from the dough with the sharp paring knife.

(Continued on page 250)

3. Carefully remove the excess dough from around the gingerbread house pieces. Gather the excess dough into a ball, and set it aside. Repeat with a second quarter of the dough and another baking sheet. Remove and discard the tape.
4. Bake the gingerbread house pieces in the preheated moderate oven (350°) for 15 to 18 minutes, or until the gingerbread pieces are golden brown around the edges and slightly firm. Let the gingerbread house pieces cool completely on the baking sheets; they will harden as they cool. Or slide off the aluminum foil sheets onto a wire rack and let the gingerbread pieces cool on the aluminum foil. When the gingerbread pieces are completely cool, peel off and discard the aluminum foil. Repeat the rolling, cutting and baking with the remaining Gingerbread Dough. If necessary, cool the baking sheets by running cool water over their backs and drying the sheets thoroughly before using them again.
5. Prepare the Royal Frosting. Keep the bowl covered with a wet cloth to prevent the frosting from drying out. Using the spatula, spread a thin layer of the frosting over the top and side edges of the plywood base. Let the frosting dry completely.
6. Spread Royal Frosting along the two side edges and along the bottom edge of the House Back piece. Spread the frosting along the bottom edges of the House Right Side and House Left Side pieces. Place the House Right Side edge at a right angle to the right edge of the House Back piece. Place the House Left Side edge at a right angle with the left edge of the House Back piece. Press the edges gently but firmly together, and place the heavy cans or bottles on either side of the pieces to hold them in place while the frosting dries *(see Step 1, page 251)*. Spread a second line of frosting along all the inside corner and bottom seams to reinforce them.
7. Repeat with the Right Front, Left Front and Left Side Front house pieces, and more frosting. Be sure to work continuously so the frosting does not harden before the house pieces have been glued together. Adjust the wall pieces as necessary, placing more cans or bottles on either side of the walls to hold them in place while the frosting dries. Let the frosting dry completely.
8. Spoon frosting into the pastry bag until it is half full. Using the pastry bag fitted with a plain ⅛-inch tip, make evenly spaced lines on the shutters: 8 lines on the small Shutters, and 10 lines on the Back Shutters. Using the photo on page 249 as a guide, decorate the Front Door with the frosting and candies. Let the Front Door, Shutters and Back Shutters dry completely.
9. Spread frosting on the top edges of the House Back, House Left Side, House Right Side and Left Front pieces. Spread frosting along one long edge of both of the Roof pieces. Place the Roof pieces on top of the house side pieces, pressing the Roof pieces gently and firmly into place *(see Step 2)*. Let the frosting dry completely; the stiffness of the frosting will hold the roof pieces in place. Repeat with the Left Side front, Right Front and Roof Front pieces *(see Step 3)*. Let the frosting dry completely.
10. Spread a small amount of frosting on the back of each Shutter, and press the Shutters gently and firmly to the walls on either side of each window opening on the House Left Side, House Right Side, Left Front and Right Front pieces *(see Step 4)*. Repeat with the Back Shutters on the House Back. Spread a small amount of frosting on the back of the Front Door, and press the door gently and firmly in place on the Right Front house piece *(see Step 5)*.
11. Spread frosting along the long side edges of the four Chimney pieces. Press all the edges together at right angles and let the frosting dry completely. Spread frosting along the chimney bottom edges and, using the photo as a placement guide, gently press the chimney to the top of the roof. Let the frosting dry completely.
12. Using the photo as a guide, decorate the house. Pipe a dot of frosting on the back of a round white mint candy wafer. Starting on the bottom edge of the roof, press the wafer to the roof to make a shingle. Repeat until the entire roof is covered with wafer shingles *(see Step 6)*. Spread a thin layer of frosting around all four sides of the chimney. Press small red cinnamon candies into the frosting. Pipe a line of frosting along the back of two small, thin striped peppermint candy sticks, and press the sticks above and below a window. Repeat on the other windows. Pipe a line of frosting along each outside wall edge, and press small red cinnamon candies into the frosting. Pipe frosting on the back of the candy cane wreath where it rests against the house and window trim, and press the wreath above the top window on the House Left Side. Pipe dots of frosting along the ridge of the main roof, and press a green ball candy into each dot. Repeat along the ridge of the small front roof, pressing red ball candies into the dots of frosting. Pipe frosting around the bottom edge of the house, and press green candies into the frosting.

Step 1 Hold the walls in place with heavy cans or bottles while the frosting dries.

Step 2 Press the Roof pieces gently but firmly in place to make a slanted roof.

Step 3 Press the Roof Front pieces in place as you did in Step 2 for the main roof.

Step 4 Attach the Shutters to the walls with small amounts of frosting.

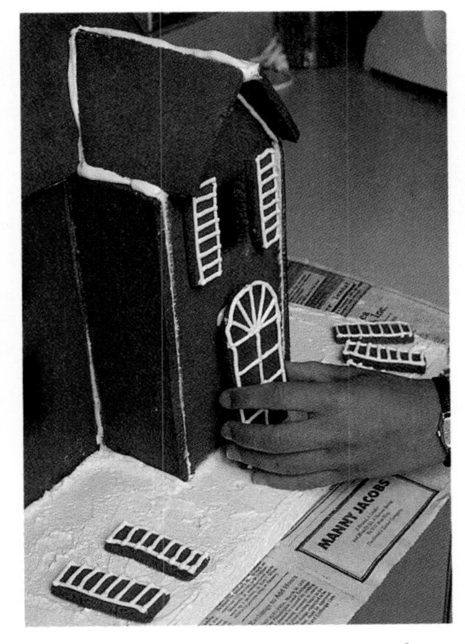

Step 5 Attach the Front Door to the walls as shown.

Step 6 Cover the main roof and the small front roof with white mint candy wafers.

Spread frosting to make a path to the front door, and press pebble and shell candies into the frosting as paving stones. Make a fence around the base using dollops of frosting and thicker, small striped peppermint sticks. Make a ring of 5 frosting dots in the "yard." Press the ends of the 5 small candy canes into the frosting dots, and lean the canes with their backs together. Pipe a large dot in the center of the cane backs and press a red ball candy into the large dot. If you wish, use small lengths of floral wire to hold the candy canes together until the frosting dries. Repeat with the 3 larger candy canes. Sprinkle the miniature nonpareils outside of the "yard." To make icicles, pipe small amounts of frosting onto the edge of the roof, pulling the pastry bag away so the icicles hang down.

GINGERBREAD DOUGH

Sugar, molasses and corn syrup make this dough very strong—perfect for constructing a gingerbread house.

Makes 5 pounds of dough (enough to make the Gingerbread House, photo, page 249).

- 10 *cups all-purpose flour*
- 2 *tablespoons ground cinnamon*
- 1 *teaspoon ground ginger*
- ½ *teaspoon ground cloves*
- 1 *teaspoon salt*
- 1½ *cups vegetable shortening*
- 1½ *cups sugar*
- 1 *cup light corn syrup OR: honey*
- 1 *cup light molasses*
- ¼ *cup warm water*

1. Stir together the flour, cinnamon, ginger, cloves and salt in a large bowl.
2. Combine the shortening and sugar in a second large bowl,* and beat for 1 minute on high speed, or until the mixture is well blended. Add the corn syrup or honey and the molasses, and beat until the mixture is fluffy, for 1 to 2 minutes. Beat in 3 cups of the flour mixture, 1 cup at a time. Beat in the warm water. Gradually beat in the remaining flour mixture until the mixture forms a stiff but not dry dough of a good rolling consistency. Cover the dough with plastic wrap and let it stand for 1 hour. The dough may be made ahead up to this point and refrigerated. Return the dough to room temperature before proceeding.
***Note:** *The volume of the dough in this recipe requires a heavy, upright mixer with a very large bowl. If you do not have an upright mixer, either divide the dough into two batches and use a small mixer, or stir the dough with a heavy-duty wooden spoon.*

ROYAL FROSTING

This frosting holds the gingerbread pieces together and is used for decorating the house. Keep the frosting bowl covered with a wet cloth at all times to prevent the frosting from drying out as you work. If you do not have a heavy, upright mixer, prepare the frosting in two batches.

Makes about 6 cups of frosting (enough to make the Gingerbread House, photo, page 249).

- 6 *large egg whites, at room temperature*
- 2 *pounds sifted 10X (confectioners' powdered) sugar*
- 1 *teaspoon cream of tartar*

Combine the egg whites, 10X (confectioners' powdered) sugar and cream of tartar in a large bowl. Beat the mixture at high speed until the frosting is fluffy and forms stiff peaks, for about 7 minutes. If the frosting becomes too stiff, add a little water and beat until it softens to a spreadable consistency.
Note: *This frosting uses raw eggs. If the Gingerbread House will be eaten, substitute Decorating Frosting (recipe, page 217) to avoid the risk of infection from salmonella bacteria sometimes found in raw eggs.*

FIG. VI, 1
GINGERBREAD
HOUSE

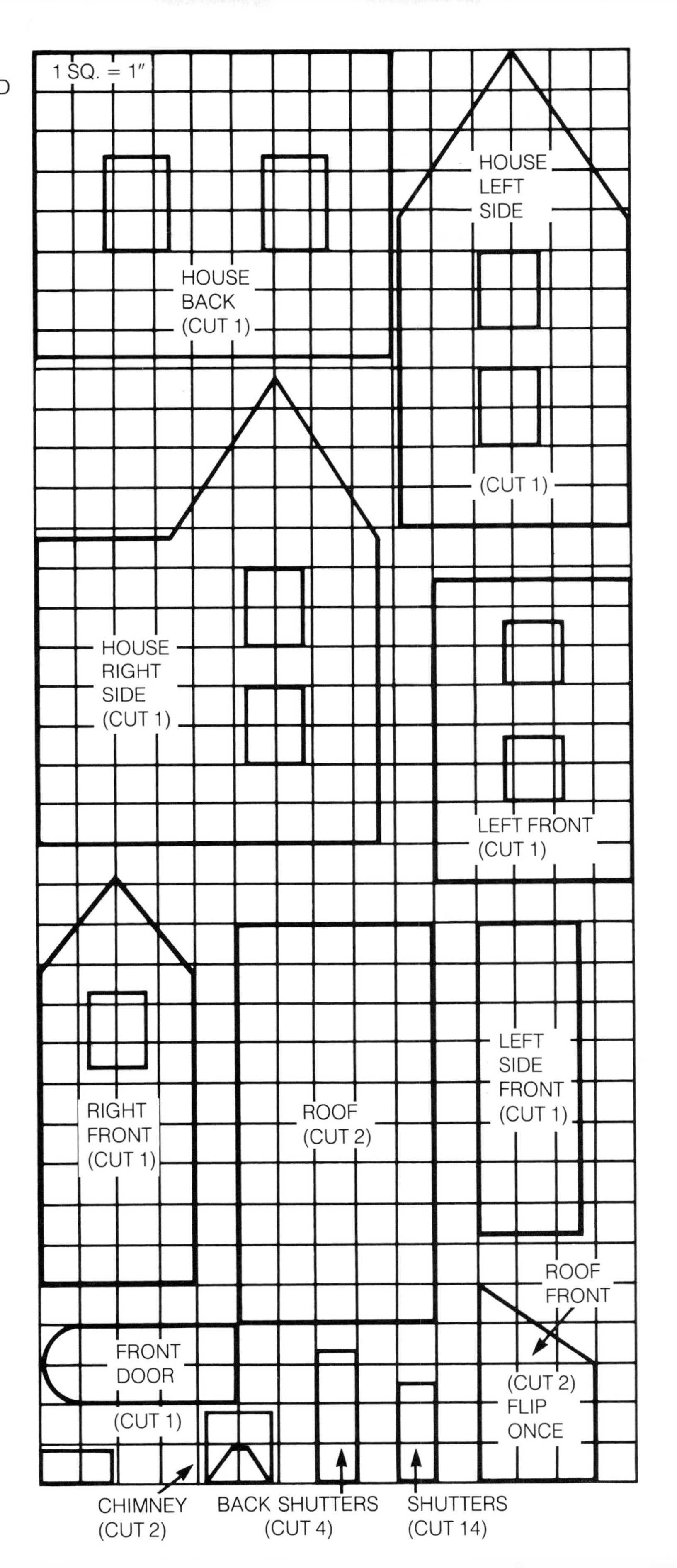

CONDIMENTS, CHUTNEY & JAM

Wonderful relishes, special vinegars, marvelous mustards and other tasty treats to give as gifts or serve at your own holiday meals.

CRANBERRY APRICOT PRUNE RELISH

This relish can perk up poultry, roast pork or leftover ham. Or try a little with morning toast and coffee.

Makes about 6 cups.

- 1 *package (12 ounces) fresh OR: frozen cranberries*
- 1 *package (12 ounces) prunes*
- 1 *package (8 ounces) dried apricots*
- 2 *cups water*
- 2 *cups sugar*
- 1 *tablespoon lemon juice*
- ½ *teaspoon ground cinnamon*
- ⅛ *teaspoon ground cloves*
- 1 *cup coarsely chopped walnuts*

1. Combine the fresh or frozen cranberries, the prunes, apricots, water, sugar, lemon juice, cinnamon and cloves in a medium-size saucepan. Bring the mixture to boiling. Lower the heat and simmer the mixture for about 15 minutes, or until the fruits are tender. Add the walnuts, and simmer for 5 minutes more. Remove the saucepan from the heat and let the mixture cool.
2. Store the relish in a covered container in the refrigerator for 2 to 3 weeks.

CRANBERRY RUM RAISIN RELISH

Makes about 5 cups.

- 2 *cups sugar*
- 1 *cinnamon stick*
- 6 *whole cloves*
- ½ *cup water*
- 1 *medium-size navel orange with peel, chopped and seeded*
- 1 *package (12 ounces) fresh OR: frozen cranberries*
- ½ *cup light rum*
- 1 *package (15 ounces) golden raisins*

1. Combine the sugar, cinnamon stick, cloves, water, orange, fresh or frozen cranberries, rum and raisins in a medium-size saucepan. Bring the mixture to boiling. Lower the heat and simmer the mixture for about 15 minutes, or until the mixture has thickened. Remove the saucepan from the heat and let the relish cool.
2. Store the relish in a covered container in the refrigerator for 2 to 3 weeks.

HONEY TARRAGON MUSTARD

Makes about 2 cups.

- ½ *cup dry mustard, preferably imported*
- ⅓ *cup mustard seeds*
- ⅔ *cup water*
- ¾ *cup white wine vinegar*
- 3 *tablespoons honey*
- 2 *teaspoons salt*
- 2 *teaspoons dried tarragon, crumbled*

1. Combine the dry mustard, mustard seeds and water in the container of an electric blender. Whirl until the mixture is coarsely puréed. Transfer the mustard mixture to a bowl, cover the bowl and let the mixture stand for 8 hours.
2. Add the vinegar, honey, and salt to the bowl, and stir until the mixture is well blended. For a creamier consistency, whirl the mixture again in the electric blender. Stir the tarragon into the mustard.
3. Store the mustard in screw-top jars in the refrigerator for up to several months.

GINGER MADEIRA MUSTARD

A tasty accompaniment to ham, cold chicken and chilled cooked vegetables.

Makes 1¼ cups.

- ¼ *cup mustard seeds*
- ⅓ *cup red wine vinegar*
- ¼ *cup Madeira wine*
- ¼ *cup water*
- 3 *tablespoons chopped fresh dill*
- 2 *teaspoons honey*
- 1 *teaspoon salt*
- ½ *teaspoon ground ginger*
- ¼ *teaspoon freshly ground pepper*

1. Combine the mustard seeds, vinegar and Madeira wine in a small bowl. Let the mixture stand for 3 hours.
2. Combine the mustard seed mixture with the water, dill, honey, salt, ginger and pepper in the container of an electric blender. Whirl until the mixture is smooth.
3. Store the mustard in screw-top jars in the refrigerator for up to several months.

HOT HORSERADISH MUSTARD

Try this spicy mustard with cold roast beef or a platter of luncheon meats.

Makes about 1¾ cups.

- ½ *cup dry mustard*
- ¼ *cup mustard seeds*
- ½ *cup cider vinegar*
- ⅓ *cup white wine vinegar*
- 3 *tablespoons honey*
- 2 *tablespoons drained prepared horseradish*
- 1 *teaspoon red pepper flakes*

1. Combine the dry mustard, mustard seeds, cider and white wine vinegars, honey, horseradish and red pepper flakes in the container of an electric blender. Whirl until the mixture is smooth.
2. Store the mustard in screw-top jars in the refrigerator for up to several months.

HOLIDAY COOKING HELPS

Low-Cal Condiments

- Use homemade or purchased unsweetened applesauce as the base for your own fruity condiments. Add raisins or other dried fruits, grated orange or lemon zest (orange or yellow part of rinds only), and a little "sweet" spice, such as ground cinnamon, cloves and/or ginger.
- Mustards are lower in calories and sugar than most varieties of catsup.
- Prepare sauces for dipping based on low-sodium soy sauce, vinegars, or tomato juice.
- Cook dried fruits in unsweetened fruit juice until they are very tender. Purée the cooked fruits to make low calorie "fruit butters," delicious with roast poultry, pork or ham. Fruit butter also is delightful with Neufchâtel or other lowfat spreadable cheeses.
- Simmer herbs such as parsley and coriander with a little chicken broth. Purée the mixture, and serve it as a condiment to curries or fish dishes.
- Add a little chopped fresh dill to nonfat plain yogurt. This makes a classic partner for poached salmon, or a tasty topping for a baked potato.

CARROT-STUFFED RIPE OLIVES

Makes 3 cups.

- 2 *cans (5.7 ounces each) black pitted olives, drained*
- 1 *whole carrot, peeled and cut into 2½-inch-long julienne sticks*
- ½ *teaspoon dried thyme, crumbled*
- 12 *white peppercorns*
- 1½ *cups olive oil*

1. Place the olives in a strainer and rinse them under cold water. Drain the olives well.
2. Carefully stuff the olives with the carrot sticks. Place the stuffed olives in a large screw-top jar, or several small screw-top jars. Combine the thyme, white peppercorns and olive oil, and pour the mixture over the olives, dividing the mixture evenly if using several jars. Cover the jars tightly.
3. Refrigerate the olives for 5 days to let the flavors develop. Store the olives in the refrigerator for up to several months.

ALMOND-STUFFED GREEN OLIVES

Makes 2 cups.

- 2 *jars (4¾ ounces each) pimiento-stuffed green olives, drained*
- 1 *can (4½ ounces) whole blanched almonds*
- 1 *teaspoon crushed red pepper flakes*
- 1½ *cups olive oil*

1. Place the green olives in a strainer and rinse them under cold water. Drain the green olives well.
2. Stuff a whole almond into the center of each green olive, inserting the almond beside the pimiento. Place the stuffed green olives in a large screw-top jar, or several small screw-top jars. Combine the red pepper flakes and the olive oil. Pour the mixture over the stuffed olives, dividing the mixture evenly if using several jars. Cover the jars tightly.
3. Refrigerate the green olives for 5 days to let the flavors develop. Store the green olives in the refrigerator for up to several months.

GARLIC GREEN OLIVES

Makes 2 cups.

- 2 *cans (7 ounces each) large green olives with pits, drained*
- 3 *cloves garlic*
- 6 *whole peppercorns*
- 1 *teaspoon sesame seeds*
- ½ *teaspoon dried thyme, crumbled*
- 1½ *cups olive oil*

1. Place the green olives in a strainer and rinse them under cold water. Drain the green olives well.
2. Place the green olives in a large screw-top jar, or several small screw-top jars. Combine the garlic cloves, peppercorns, sesame seeds, thyme and olive oil. Pour the mixture over the stuffed olives, dividing it evenly if using several jars. Cover the jars tightly.
3. Refrigerate the green olives for 5 days to let the flavors develop. Store the green olives in the refrigerator for up to several months.

SHALLOT CIDER VINEGAR

Makes 1 quart.

- 3½ *cups cider vinegar*
- 6 *whole shallots, peeled*
- 2 *sprigs fresh parsley*
- 8 *whole peppercorns*
- 1 *bay leaf*

1. Sterilize a 1-quart bottle with a tight-fitting cover. Let the sterilized bottle dry completely.
2. Heat the cider vinegar in a medium-size nonaluminum saucepan just until it is boiling. Remove the saucepan from the heat, and let the cider vinegar cool slightly. Pour the cider vinegar into the prepared bottle. Add the shallots, parsley sprigs, peppercorns and bay leaf to the bottle. Let the vinegar mixture cool completely. Cover the bottle and seal mixture tightly.
3. Let the vinegar stand at room temperature for 2 to 3 weeks, shaking the bottle occasionally, to let the flavors develop.

HERBED WHITE VINEGAR

Makes 1 quart.

3½ cups white vinegar
2 sprigs fresh parsley
2 sprigs fresh dill
1 medium-size red onion, sliced
8 whole peppercorns
2 celery stalks with leaves

1. Sterilize a 1-quart bottle with a tight-fitting cover. Let the sterilized bottle dry completely.
2. Heat the white vinegar in a medium-size nonaluminum saucepan just until it is boiling. Remove the saucepan from the heat, and let the vinegar cool slightly. Pour the vinegar into the prepared bottle. Add the parsley and dill sprigs, the onion slices, peppercorns and celery stalks to the bottle. Let the mixture cool completely. Cover the bottle and seal the mixture tightly.
3. Let the vinegar mixture stand at room temperature for 2 to 3 weeks, shaking the bottle occasionally, to let the flavors develop.

HOLIDAY COOKING HELPS

Instant Flourishes: Condiments in a Flash

- Add a chopped apple to canned whole-berry cranberry sauce. Or stir a few tablespoons of canned whole-berry cranberry sauce into unsweetened applesauce. Sauté sliced apples in a little butter. Season the sautéed apple slices with apple pie spice and a splash of Calvados or apple jack brandy.
- Stir grated lemon zest (yellow part of rind only) and crushed dried rosemary into Dijon mustard to make a zippy canapé spread or condiment for ham.
- Combine Dijon mustard, honey and a pinch of grated or ground nutmeg for a honey-mustard sauce that's great with pork or chicken.
- Combine prepared horseradish, sour cream and applesauce for an accompaniment to potato pancakes, roast pork and lamb chops.

GARLIC RED WINE VINEGAR

Use this vinegar to deglaze a skillet after sautéing hamburgers or chops. Or use it in your favorite salad dressing recipe for a taste twist.

Makes 1 quart.

3½ cups red wine vinegar
6 cloves garlic, peeled
2 sprigs fresh parsley
1 bay leaf
8 whole peppercorns
½ teaspoon crushed red pepper flakes

1. Sterilize a 1-quart bottle with a tight-fitting cover. Let the sterilized bottle dry completely.
2. Heat the red wine vinegar in a medium-size nonaluminum saucepan just until it is boiling. Remove the saucepan from the heat, and let the red wine vinegar cool slightly. Pour the red wine vinegar into the prepared bottle. Add the garlic cloves, parsley sprigs, bay leaf, peppercorns and red pepper flakes to the bottle. Let the mixture cool completely. Cover the bottle and seal the mixture tightly.
3. Let the vinegar mixture stand at room temperature for 2 to 3 weeks, shaking the bottle occasionally, to let the flavors develop.

APRICOT ORANGE CHUTNEY

Made from dried apricots, a whole orange, candied ginger and golden raisins, this chutney is delicious both in sandwiches and as a condiment.

Makes 3 pints.

- 1 *pound dried apricots*
- 1 *large onion (about ½ pound), peeled and cut into eighths*
- 1 *navel orange, washed, cut into eighths and trimmed*
- 2 *cloves garlic, peeled*
- 5 *slices candied ginger*
- 1½ *to 1¾ cups firmly packed light brown sugar*
- 2½ *cups cider vinegar*
- ½ *cup golden raisins*
- 1 *tablespoon salt*
- 1 *teaspoon crushed red pepper flakes*
- 1 *three-inch-long cinnamon stick*

1. Place the dried apricots in the container of a food processor fitted with the metal blade. Process the apricots, pulsing the processor on and off, until the apricots are very finely chopped. Transfer the chopped apricots to a heavy large saucepan.
2. Place the onion, orange, garlic cloves and candied ginger in the container of the food processor. Process the mixture, pulsing the processor on and off, until the mixture is very finely chopped. Add the orange mixture to the apricots in the saucepan. Stir in the sugar, vinegar, raisins, salt, red pepper flakes and the cinnamon stick.
3. Bring the mixture to boiling over medium heat. Lower the heat. Simmer the mixture, stirring often to prevent burning, for 45 minutes to 1 hour, or until the chutney is thickened and clear. Towards the end of the cooking time, the chutney must be stirred almost constantly to prevent it from burning.
4. Transfer the chutney to 3 hot sterilized 1-pint jars. Seal the jars immediately.

SPICED STRAWBERRY JAM

An old favorite, spiced-up. This jam is even more of a treat when you spread it on hot bread.

Makes enough to fill six 8-ounce jars.

- 2 *pints (4 cups) strawberries, washed and hulled*
- 4 *cups sugar*
- ½ *teaspoon ground mace*
- 1 *package (about 2 ounces) powdered fruit pectin*
- ¾ *cup apple juice*

1. Place as many strawberries as will fit on the bottom of a large glass or ceramic bowl. Crush the layer of strawberries. Repeat until all the strawberries have been crushed. (You should have about 2 cups of crushed strawberries.)
2. Add the sugar and the mace to the crushed strawberries, and stir to blend the mixture. Let the mixture stand until the sugar is dissolved, for about 15 minutes.
3. Combine the pectin and the apple juice in a small saucepan, and bring the mixture to boiling. Boil the mixture vigorously for 1 minute. Stir the apple juice mixture into the strawberry mixture and continue stirring for 3 minutes. (Some sugar crystals will remain in the combined mixture.)
4. Ladle the jam quickly into 6 hot sterilized 8-ounce jars. Seal the jars immediately, and let the jam stand at room temperature for 24 hours. Label, date and freeze the jam until ready to give or serve.

CRAFTS BASICS & ABBREVIATIONS

HOW TO KNIT

THE BASIC STITCHES

Get out your needles and yarn, and slowly read your way through this special section. Practice the basic stitches illustrated here as you go along. Once you know them, you're ready to start knitting.

CASTING ON: This puts the first row of stitches on the needle. Measure off about two yards of yarn (or about an inch for each stitch you are going to cast on). Make a slip knot at this point by making a medium-size loop of yarn; then pull another small loop through it. Place the slip knot on one needle and pull one end gently to tighten (FIG. 1).

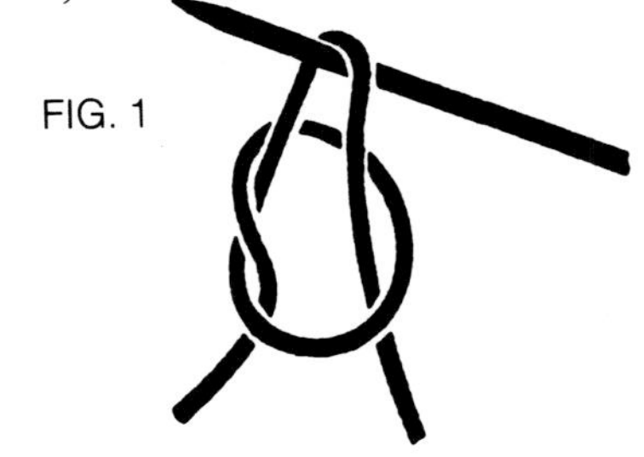
FIG. 1

• Hold the needle in your right hand. Hold both strands of yarn in the palm of your left hand securely but not rigidly. Slide your left thumb and forefinger between the two strands and spread these two fingers out so that you have formed a triangle of yarn.
• Your left thumb should hold the free end of yarn, your forefinger the yarn from the ball. The needle in your right hand holds the first stitch (FIG. 2).

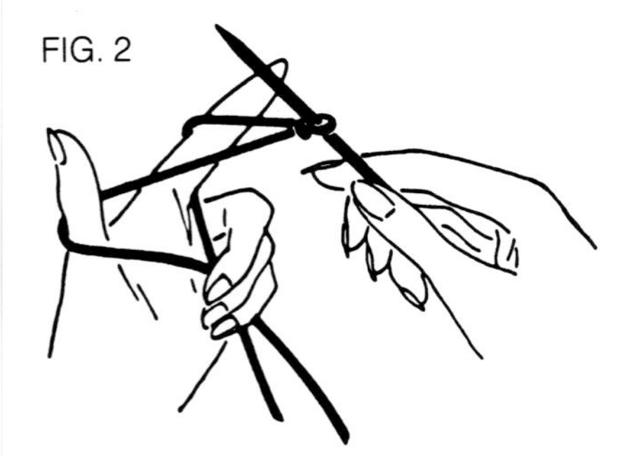
FIG. 2

You are now in position to cast on.
• Bring the needle in your right hand toward you; slip the tip of the needle under the front strand of the loop on your left thumb (FIG. 3).

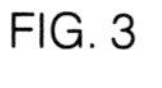
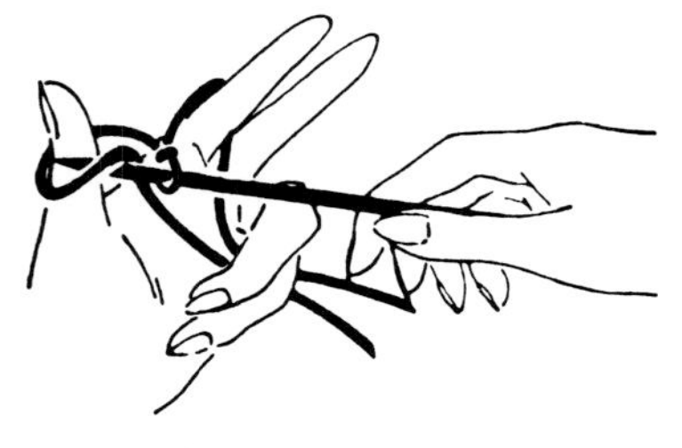
FIG. 3

• Now, with the needle, catch the strand of yarn that is on your left forefinger (FIG. 4).

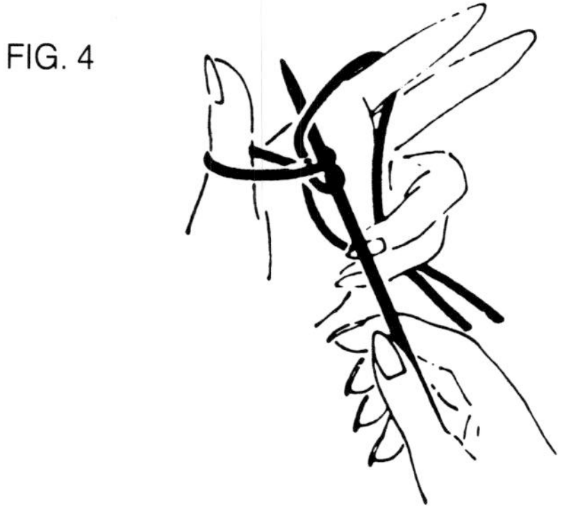
FIG. 4

• Draw it through the thumb loop to form a stitch on the needle (FIG. 5).

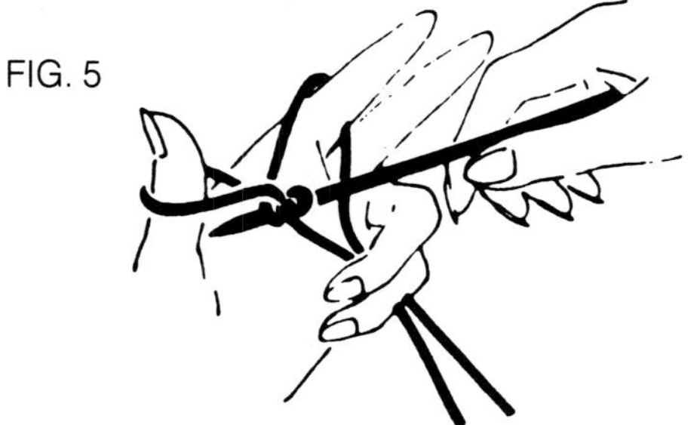
FIG. 5

KNITTING ABBREVIATIONS AND SYMBOLS

Knitting directions are always written in standard abbreviations. Although they may look confusing, with practice you'll soon know them:
beg—beginning; **bet**—between; **bl**—block; **ch**—chain; **CC**—contrasting color; **dec(s)**—decrease(s); **dp**—double-pointed; ″ or **in(s)**—inch(es); **incl**—inclusive; **inc(s)**—increase(s); **k**—knit; **lp(s)**—loop(s); **MC**—main color; **oz(s)**—ounces(s); **psso**—pass slipped stitch over last stitch worked; **pat(s)**—pattern(s); **p**—purl; **rem**—remaining; **rpt**—repeat; **rnd(s)**—round(s); **sk**—skip; **sl**—slip; **sl st**—slip stitch; **sp(s),**—space(s); **st(s)**—stitch(es); **st st**—stockinette stitch; **tog**—together, **yo**—yarn over; **pc**—popcorn stitch.
* **(asterisk)**—directions immediately following * are to be repeated the specified number of times indicated in addition to the first time—i.e. "repeat from * 3 times more" means 4 times in all.
( ) (parentheses)—directions should be worked as often as specified—i.e., "(k 1, k 2 tog, k 3) 5 times" means to work what is in ( ) 5 times in all.

• Holding the stitch on the needle with your right index finger, slip the loop off your left thumb (FIG. 6). Tighten up the stitch on the needle by pulling the freed strand back with your left thumb, bringing the yarn back into position for casting on more stitches (FIG. 2).

FIG. 6

• ***Do not cast on too tightly.*** Stitches should slide easily on the needle. Repeat from * until you have cast on the number of stitches specified in your instructions.

KNIT STITCH (k): Hold the needle with the cast-on stitches in your left hand (FIG. 7).

FIG. 7

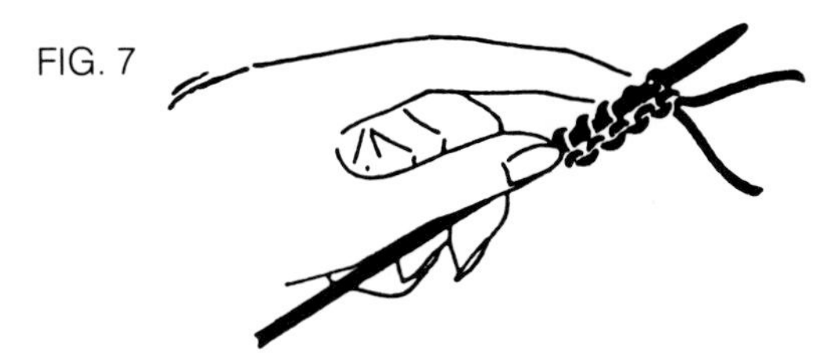

• Pick up the other needle in your right hand. With yarn from the ball in ***back*** (the side farthest away from you) of the work, insert the tip of the right-hand needle from ***left to right*** through the front loop of the first stitch on the left-hand needle (FIG. 8).

FIG. 8

• Holding both needles in this position with your left hand, wrap the yarn over your little finger, under your two middle fingers and over the forefinger of your right hand. Hold the yarn firmly, but loosely enough so that it will slide through your fingers as you knit. Return the right-hand needle to your right hand.
• With your right forefinger, pass the yarn under (from right to left) and then over (from left to right) the tip of the right-hand needle, forming a loop on the needle (FIG. 9).

FIG. 9

• Now draw this loop through the stitch on the left-hand needle (FIG. 10).

FIG. 10

• Slip the original stitch off the left-hand needle, leaving the new stitch on right-hand needle (Fig. 11).

FIG. 11

Note: Keep the stitches loose enough to slide along the needles, but tight enough to maintain their position on the needles until you want them to slide. Continue until you have knitted all the stitches from the left-hand needle onto the right-hand needle.

• To start the next row, pass the needle with stitches on it to your left hand, reversing it, so that it is now the left-hand needle.

PURL STITCH (p): Purling is the reverse of knitting. Again, keep the stitches loose enough to slide, but firm enough to work with. To purl, hold the needle with the stitches in your left hand, with the yarn in ***front*** of your work. Insert the tip of the right-hand needle from ***right to left*** through the front loop of the first stitch on the left-hand needle (Fig. 12).

FIG. 12

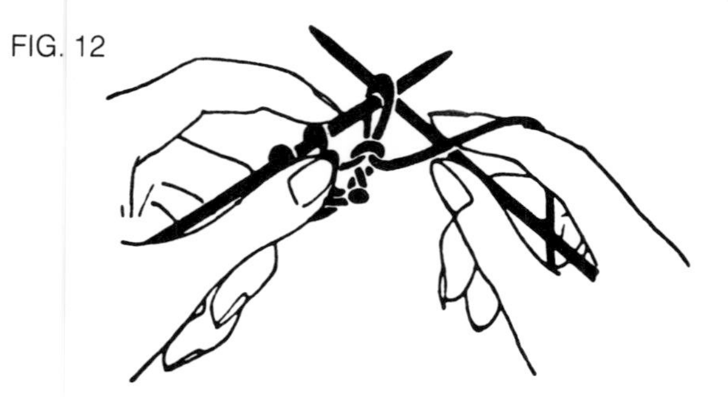

• With your right hand holding the yarn as you would to knit, but in ***front*** of the needles, pass the yarn over the tip of the right-hand needle, then under it, forming a loop on the needle (Fig. 13).

FIG. 13

• Holding the yarn firmly so that it won't slip off, draw this loop through the stitch on the left-hand needle (Fig. 14).

FIG. 14

• Slip the original stitch off of the left-hand needle, leaving the new stitch on the right-hand needle (Fig. 15).

FIG. 15

SLIPSTITCH (sl st): Insert the tip of the right-hand needle into the next stitch on the left-hand needle, as if to purl, unless otherwise directed. Slip this stitch off the left-hand needle onto the right, but ***do not*** work the stitch (Fig. 16).

FIG. 16

BINDING OFF: This makes a finished edge and locks the stitches securely in place. Knit (or purl) two stitches. Then, with the tip of the left-hand needle, lift the first of these two stitches over the second stitch and drop it off the tip of the right-hand needle (FIG. 17).

FIG. 17

One stitch remains on the right-hand needle, and one stitch has been bound off.

- Knit (or purl) the next stitch; lift the first stitch over the last stitch and off the tip of the needle. Again, one stitch remains on the right-hand needle, and another stitch has been bound off. Repeat from * until the required number of stitches have been bound off.
- Remember that you work two stitches to bind off one stitch. If, for example, the directions read, "k 6, bind off the next 4 sts, k 6 . . . " you must knit six stitches, then knit ***two more*** stitches before starting to bind off. Bind off four times. After the four stitches have been bound off, count the last stitch remaining on the right-hand needle as the first stitch of the next six stitches. When binding off, always knit the knitted stitches and purl the purled stitches.
- Be careful not to bind off too tightly or too loosely. The tension should be the same as the rest of the knitting.
- To end off the last stitch on the bound-off edge, if you are ending this piece of work here, cut the yarn leaving a 6-inch end; pass the cut end through the remaining loop on the right-hand needle and pull snugly (FIG. 18).

FIG. 18

SHAPING TECHNIQUES

Now that you are familiar with the basic stitches, you are ready to learn the techniques for shaping your knitting projects.

INCREASING (inc): This means adding stitches in a given area to shape your work. There are several ways to increase.

1. *To increase by knitting twice into the same stitch:* Knit the stitch in the usual way through the front loop (FIG. 19), but ***before*** dropping the stitch from the left-hand needle, knit ***another*** stitch on the same loop by placing the needle into the back of the stitch (FIG. 20). Slip the original stitch off your left-hand needle. You now have made two stitches from one stitch.

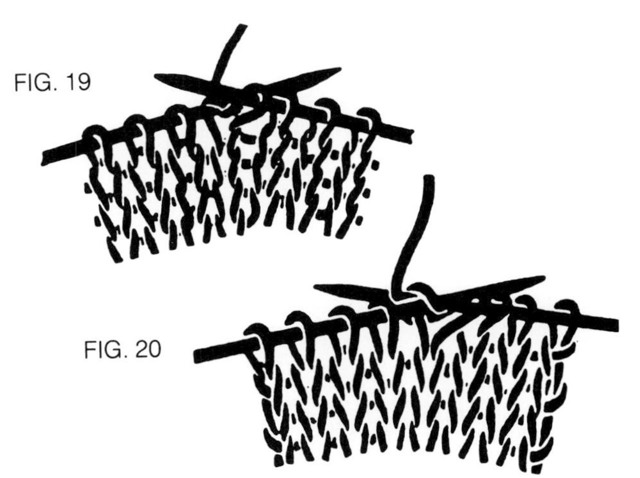

FIG. 19

FIG. 20

2. *To increase by knitting between stitches:* Insert the tip of the right-hand needle under the strand of yarn ***between*** the stitch you've just worked and the following stitch; slip it onto the tip of the left-hand needle (FIG. 21).

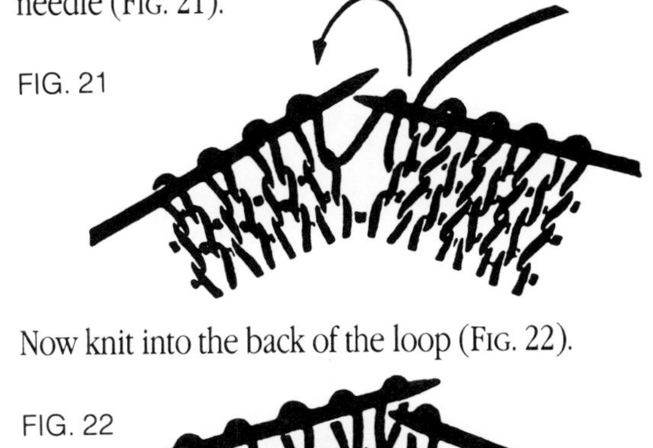

FIG. 21

Now knit into the back of the loop (FIG. 22).

FIG. 22

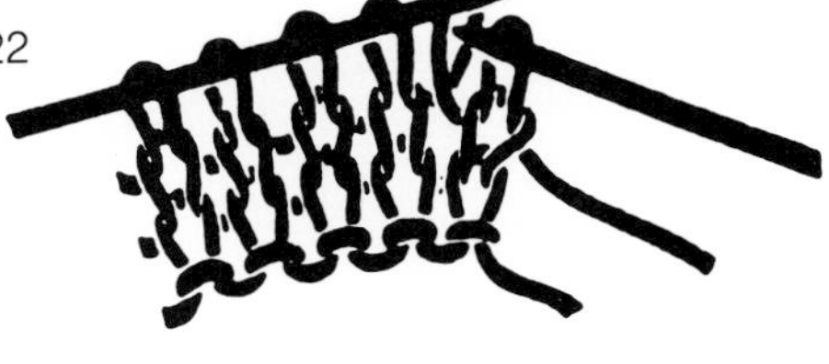

3. *To increase by "yarn-over" (yo):* Pass the yarn ***over*** the right-hand needle after finishing one stitch and before starting the next stitch, making an extra stitch (see the arrow in FIG. 23). If you are knitting, bring the yarn ***under*** the needle to the back. If you are purling, wind the yarn ***around*** the needle once. On the next row, work all yarn-overs as stitches.

FIG. 23

DECREASING (dec): This means reducing the number of stitches in a given area to shape your work. Two methods for decreasing are:
1. *To decrease by knitting* (FIG. 24) *or purling* (FIG. 25) *two stitches together:*

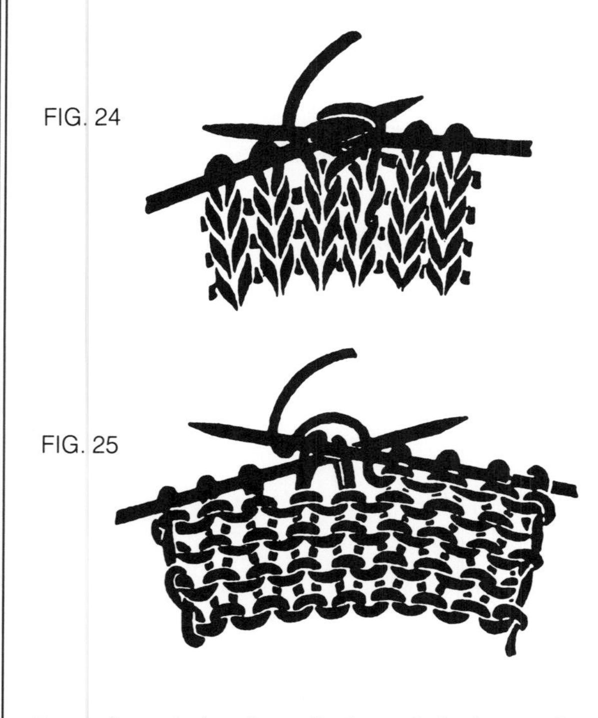

FIG. 24

FIG. 25

Insert the right-hand needle through the loops of two stitches on the left-hand needle at the same time. Complete the stitch. This is written as "k 2 tog" or "p 2 tog."

• If you work through the ***front*** loops of the stitches, your decreasing stitch will slant to the right. If you work through the ***back*** loops of the stitches, your decreasing stitch will slant to the left.
2. *Slip 1 stitch, knit 1 and psso:* Insert the right-hand needle through the stitch on the left-hand needle, but instead of working it, just slip it off onto the right-hand needle (see FIG. 16). Work the next stitch in the usual way. With the tip of the left-hand needle, lift the slipped stitch over the last stitch worked and off the tip of the right-hand needle (FIG. 26).
Your decreasing stitch will slant to the left. This is written as "sl 1, k 1, psso."

FIG. 26

Pass Slipped Stitch Over (psso): Slip one stitch from the left-hand needle to the right-hand needle and, being careful to keep it in position, work the next stitch. Then, with the tip of the left-hand needle, lift the slipped stitch over the last stitch and off the tip of the right-hand needle (FIG. 26).

ATTACHING YARN

When you finish one ball of yarn, or if you wish to change colors, attach the new ball of yarn at the start of a row. Tie the new yarn to an end of the previous yarn, making a secure knot to join the two yarns. Continue to work (FIG. 27).

FIG. 27

HOW TO CROCHET

THE BASIC STITCHES

Most crochet stitches are started from a base of chain stitches. However, our stitches are started from a row of single crochet stitches which gives body to the sample swatches and makes practice work easier to handle. When making a specific item, follow the stitch directions as given.

• Holding the crochet hook properly (Fig. 1), start by practicing the slip knot (Fig. 2A through Fig. 2D) and base chain (Fig. 3A through Fig. 3C).

FIG. 1 HOLDING THE HOOK

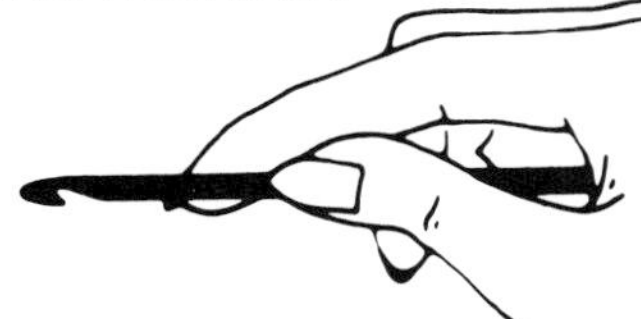

FIG. 2A THE SLIP KNOT (BASIS FOR CHAIN STITCH)

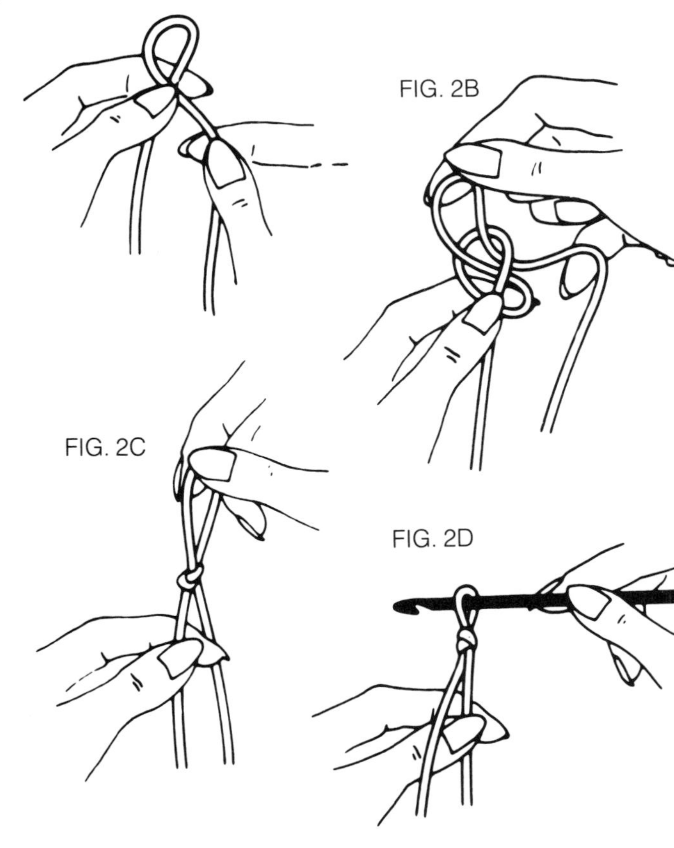

CHAIN STITCH (ch): Follow the steps in Fig. 3A through Fig. 3C. As you make the chain stitch loops, the yarn should slide easily between your index and middle fingers. Make about 15 loops. If they are all the same size, you have maintained even tension. If the stitches are uneven, rip them out by pulling on the long end of the yarn. Practice the chain stitch until you can crochet a perfect chain.

From here on, we won't be showing hands—just the hook and the stitches. ***Note:*** *Left-handed crocheters can use the illustrations for right-handed crocheting by turning the book upside down in front of a free-standing mirror. The reflected illustrations will provide left-handed instructions.*

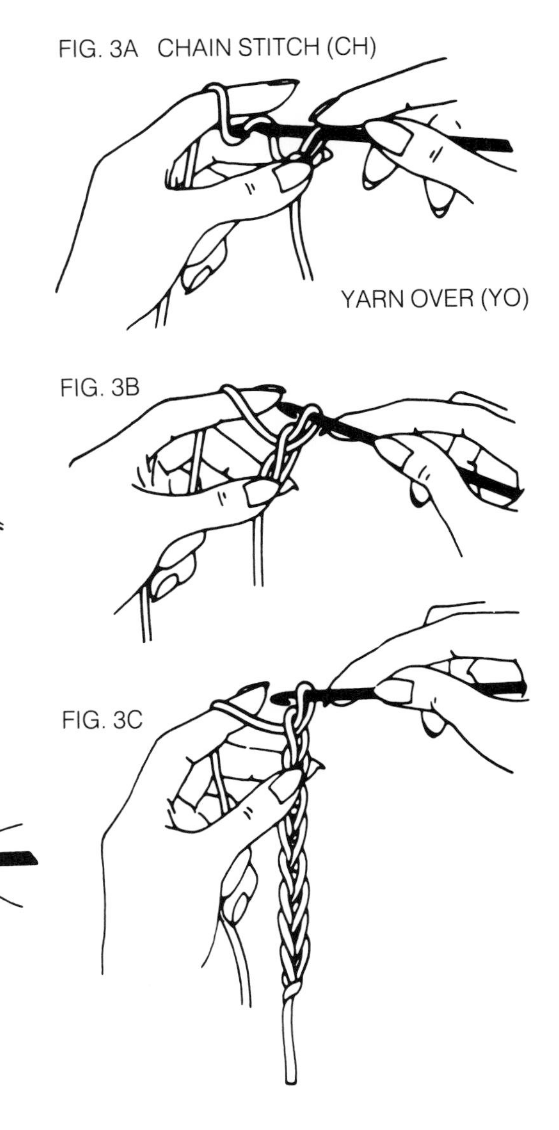

CROCHET ABBREVIATIONS AND SYMBOLS

The following is a list of standard crochet abbreviations with definitions of the terms given. To help you become accustomed to the abbreviations used, we have repeated them throughout our instructions.

beg—begin, beginning; **ch**—chain; **dc**—double crochet; **dec**—decrease; **dtr**—double treble crochet; **hdc**—half double crochet; **in(s)** or "—inch(es); **inc**—increase; **oz(s)**—ounce(s); **pat**—pattern; **pc**—picot; **rem**—remaining; **rnd**—round; **rpt**—repeat; **sc**—single crochet; **skn(s)**—skein(s); **sk**—skip; **sl st**—slip stitch; **sp**—space; **st(s)**—stitch(es); **tog**—together; **tr**—triple crochet; **work even**—continue without further increase or decrease; **yo**—yarn over.

*** (asterisk)**—directions immediately following * are to be repeated the specified number of times indicated in addition to the first time.

( ) (parentheses)—directions should be worked as often as specified.

SINGLE CROCHET (sc): Follow the steps in (FIG. 4A through FIG. 4H). To practice, make a 20-loop chain (this means 20 loops in addition to the slip knot). Turn the chain, as shown, and insert the hook in the second chain from the hook (see arrow) to make the first sc stitch. Yarn over (yo); for the second stitch, see the next arrow. Repeat to the end of the chain. Because you started in the second chain from the hook, you end up with only 19 sc. To add the 20th stitch, ch 1 (called a turning chain) and pull the yarn through. Now turn your work around (the "back" is now facing you) and start the second row of sc in the first stitch of the previous row (at the arrow). Make sure your hook goes under both of the strands at the top of the stitch. Don't forget to make a ch 1 turning chain at the end before turning your work. Keep practicing until your rows are perfect.

ENDING OFF: Follow the steps in (FIG. 5A and FIG. 5B). To finish off your crochet, cut off all but 6-inches of yarn and end off as shown. (To "break off and fasten," follow the same procedure.)

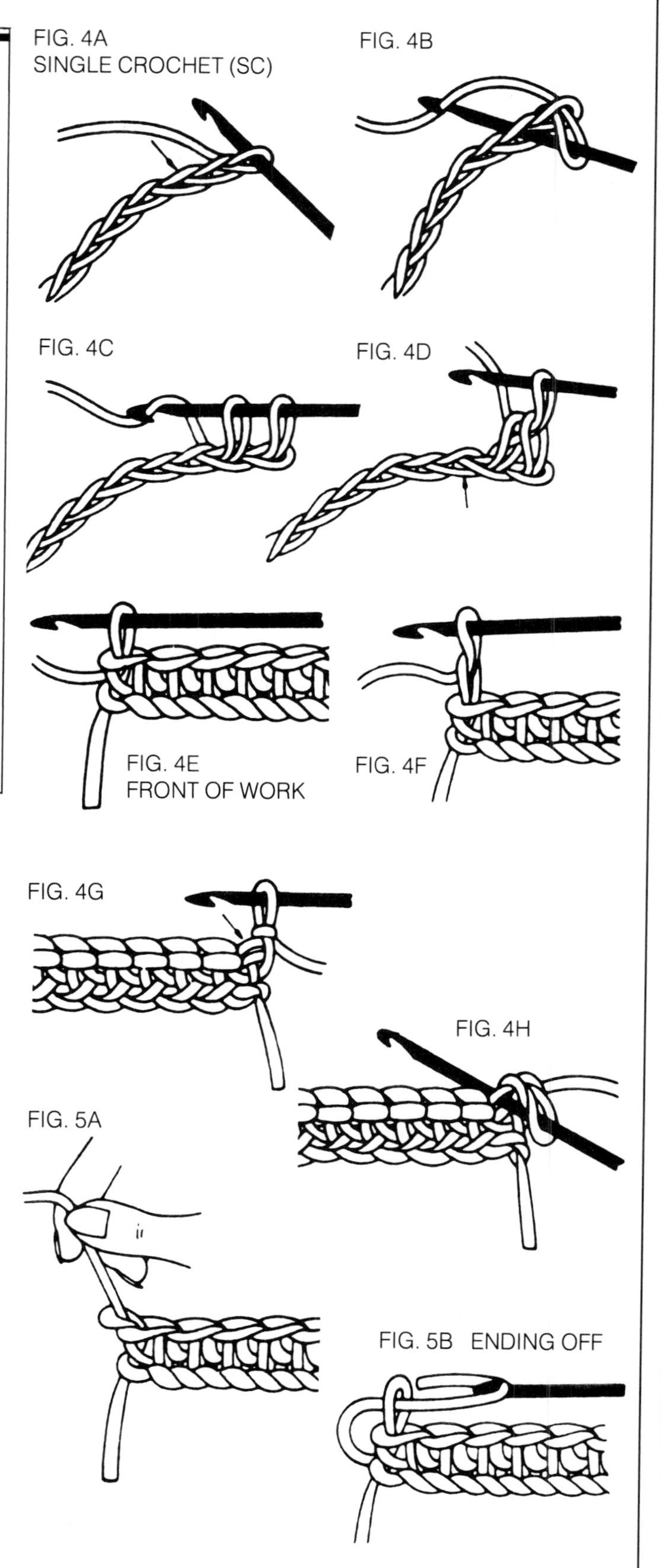

DOUBLE CROCHET (dc): Follow the steps in (Fig. 6A through Fig. 6F). To practice, ch 20, then make a row of 20 sc. Now, instead of a ch 1, you will make a ch 3. Turn your work, yo and insert the hook in the second stitch of the previous row (at the arrow), going under both strands at the top of the stitch. Pull the yarn through. You now have three loops on the hook. Yo and pull through the first two, then yo and pull through the remaining two—one double crochet (dc) made. Continue across the row, making a dc in each stitch (st) across. Dc in the top of the turning chain (see arrow in Fig. 7). Ch 3. Turn work. Dc in second stitch on the previous row and continue as before.

FIG.7

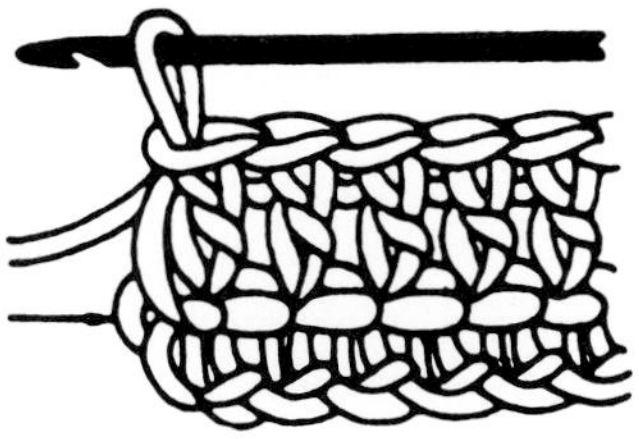

Note: *You may also start a row of dc on a base chain (omitting the sc row). In this case, insert the hook in the fourth chain from the hook, instead of the second (Fig. 8).*

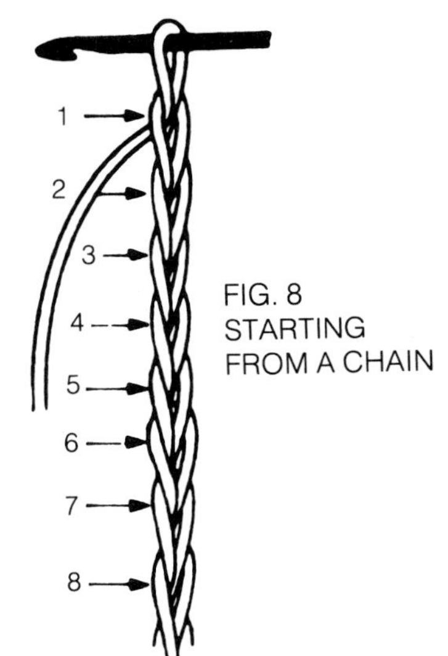

FIG. 8
STARTING
FROM A CHAIN

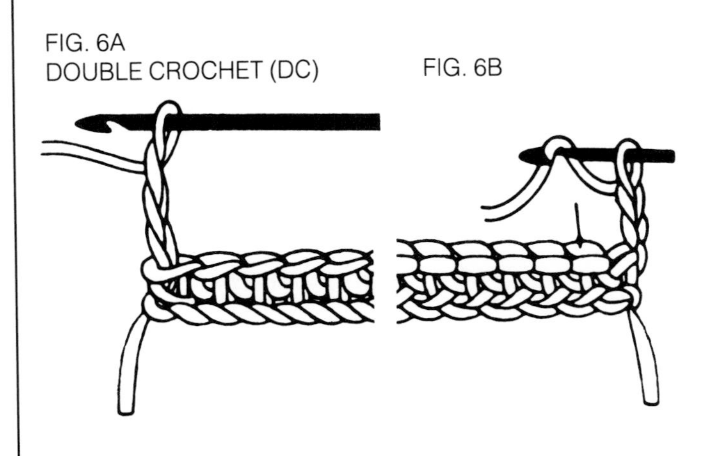

FIG. 6A
DOUBLE CROCHET (DC)

FIG. 6B

FIG. 6C

FIG. 6D

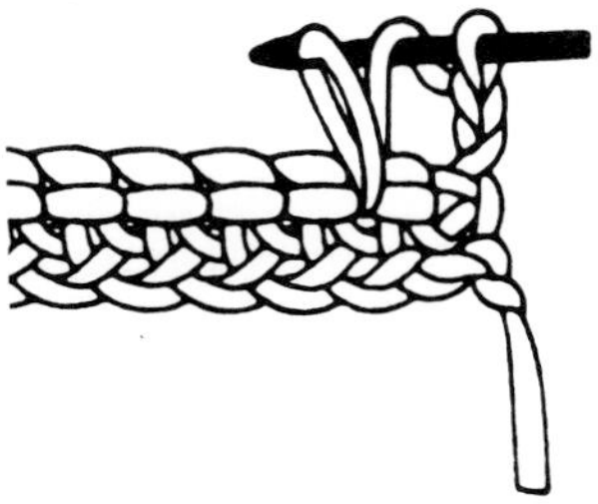

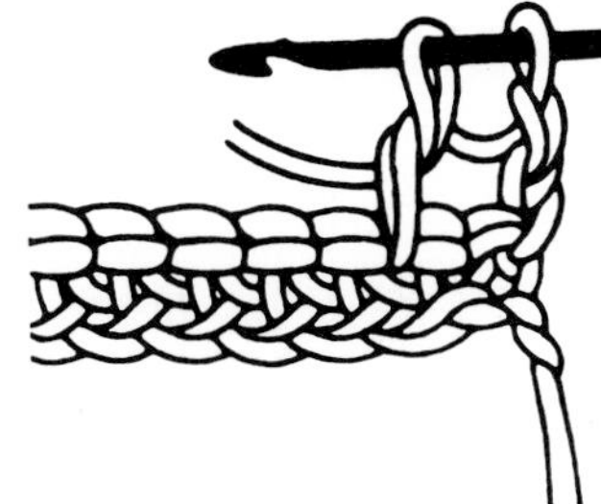

FIG. 6E

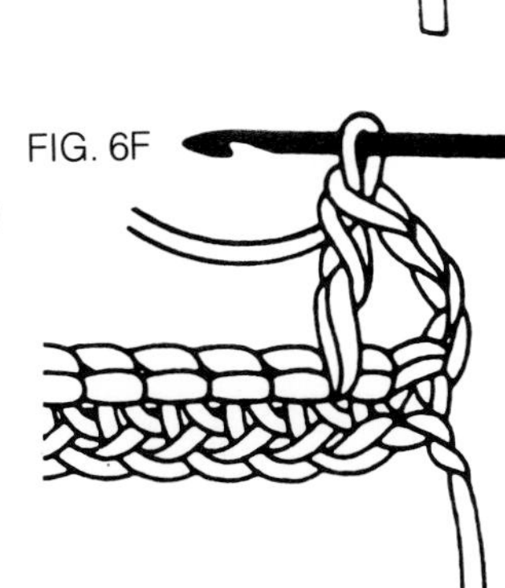

FIG. 6F

SLIP STITCH (sl st): Follow the steps in Fig. 9A. This is the stitch you will use for joining, shaping and ending off. After you chain and turn, ***do not*** yo. Just insert the hook into the ***first*** stitch of the previous row (see Fig. 9A and Fig. 9B), and pull the yarn through the stitch, then through the loop on the hook—the sl st is made.

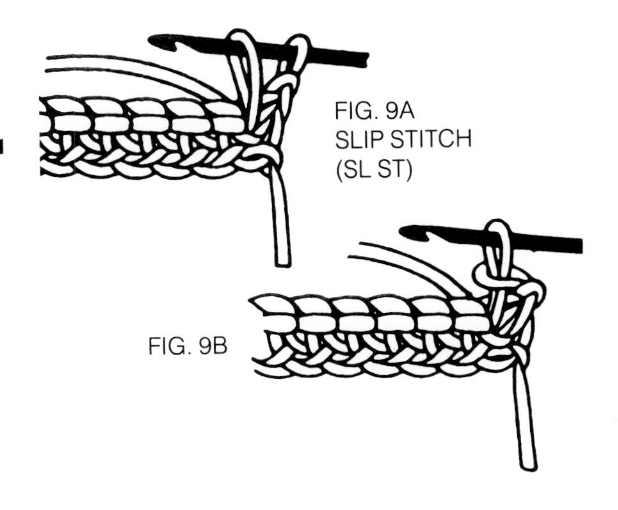

FIG. 9A
SLIP STITCH
(SL ST)

FIG. 9B

HALF DOUBLE CROCHET (hdc): Follow the steps in Figs. 10A and 10B.

To practice, make a chain and a row of sc. Ch 2 and turn; yo. Insert the hook in the second stitch, as shown; yo and pull through to make three loops on the hook. Yo and pull the yarn through *all* three loops at the same time—hdc made. This stitch primarily is used as a transitional stitch from an sc to a dc. Try it and see—starting with sc's, then an hdc and then dc's.

FIG. 10A
HALF DOUBLE CROCHET

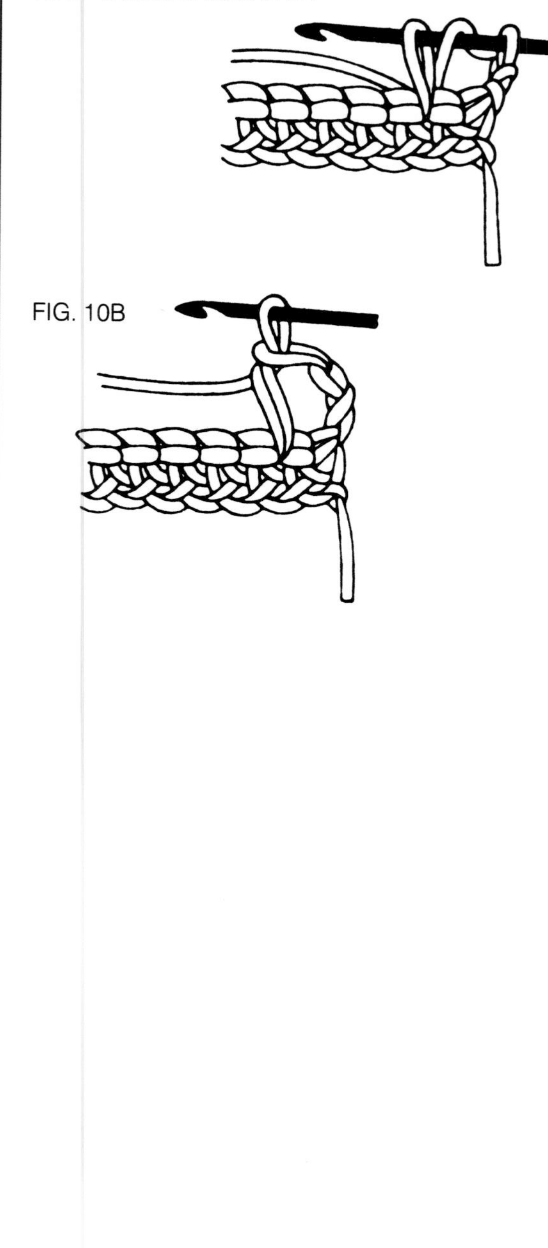

FIG. 10B

SHAPING TECHNIQUES FOR CROCHETING

Now that you have practiced and made sample squares of all the basic stitches, you are ready to learn the adding and subtracting stitches that will shape your project by changing the length of a row as per the instructions. This is done by increasing (inc) and decreasing (dec).

To increase (inc): Just make two stitches in the same stitch in the previous row (see arrow in Fig. 11). The technique is the same for any kind of stitch.

FIG. 11 INCREASING (INC)
FOR SINGLE CROCHET

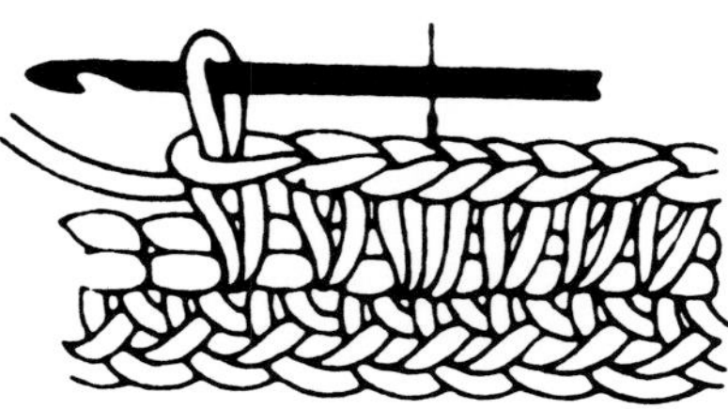

To decrease (dec) for single-crochet (sc): Yo and pull the yarn through two stitches to make three loops on the hook (see steps in Figs. 12A and 12B). Pull the yarn through all the loops at once—dec made. Continue in the stitches called for in the instructions.

FIG. 12A DECREASING (DEC)

FOR SINGLE CROCHET FIG. 12B

To decrease for double crochet (dc): In a dc row, make the next stitch and stop when you have two loops on the hook. Now yo and make a dc in the next stitch. At the point where you have three loops on the hook, pull yarn through all loops at the same time. Finish the row with regular dc.

HOW TO BLOCK LIKE A PRO

These step-by-step instructions for blocking will insure that your needlework has a professional finished look.

MATERIALS:

• ***A Blocking Board*** An absolute *must* for professional-looking blocking. You can usually buy a blocking board at craft and sewing centers.
• ***Rustproof T-pins and Staples*** Used to hold the needlework pieces in place.
• ***Undyed Cotton Cloth*** A dampened cloth covers the needlework while it is being pressed.
• ***Iron*** With a dry setting.
• ***Yellow Soap*** Dels Naptha or Kirkman. For blocking needlepoint. Restores natural sizing to canvas and helps prevent infestations of insects.

KNITTED OR CROCHETED WORK:

The purpose of blocking is to align the stitches, loft the yarn and straighten the knitted or crocheted pieces.
• Pin the work or the pieces, right side down, to the blocking board with the T-pins. Place the pins close together to avoid ripples in the work.
• Dampen a cotton cloth with water and wring it out; the cloth should be moist, not dripping wet. Place the cloth over the work on the board.
• Set the iron on "dry" and select a temperature setting suited to the fibers in the work.
• Gently iron over the cloth in the direction of the stitches. ***Do not*** apply pressure to the iron or iron against the grain. You may need to remoisten the cloth and iron the work several times, until it is moist and warm to the touch.
• Carefully remove the cloth. If the cloth clings, leaving the work damp and rippled, don't panic. This occurs when a synthetic fiber is pressed with steam that is too hot. No permanent damage can be done unless pressure is used and the stitches are flattened. To restore the work to the desired shape, pat the pieces gently with your hands.
• Allow the work to dry on the board in a flat position for at least 24 hours.
• When the work is completely dry, remove the pins; the pieces are ready to be assembled.

Note: *You can ease or stretch pieces a bit to achieve the desired size, but you can't turn a size 10 sweater into a size 16, or shrink a size 40 vest into a size 34.*

NEEDLEPOINT PROJECTS:

Blocking needlepoint realigns the threads of the canvas, lofts the yarn and naturally sets each stitch.
Note: *Check for yarn color fastness before you begin to needlepoint. If you've completed a work, and are unsure of the color fastness,* **do not block.** *Press the work on the wrong side with a warm iron. This won't yield the same results, but avoids color streaking.*
• Place a bar of yellow soap in a bowl of warm water; let it stand until the water is slick to the touch.
• Place the work, right side down, on the blocking board.
• Dip a cotton cloth into the soapy water and wring it out. Place the damp cloth over the needlepoint.
• Set an iron on "dry" with temperature suited to fibers in the work. Lightly iron the cloth; ***do not*** apply pressure.
• Repeat dampening the cloth and pressing until the canvas is very soft and flexible; moist, but not wet.
• Turn the needlepoint right side up on the board.
• Keeping the threads of the canvas parallel to the grid on the blocking board, staple the canvas to the board leaving 1 inch between the staples and the edge of the needlepoint. (Remove tape or selvages before stapling.) The staples should be fairly close together (do not use pins; staples maintain a straight line and even tension across the work).
• Staple along the bottom edge of the canvas, again, maintaining an even tension across the work. Gently pull one side of the canvas to align the fabric grain with the grid lines on the board, and staple along this edge. Repeat on the other side of the canvas. (***Do not*** stretch the canvas; just pull it gently into its original size.) As you are aligning the third and fourth sides, wrinkles may appear in the center of the work; as the fourth side is eased into alignment, these should disappear. If the canvas is pulled off the grain while being blocked, remove the staples and realign the sides. When the grain of the work is perfectly square, the stitching should be aligned; you are not straightening the stitching, you are squaring the threads of the canvas.
• Allow the needlepoint to dry for at least 24 hours.
• When the needlepoint is completely dry, gently pull it up from the board; the staples will pull out easily. Your needlepoint is now ready to be finished.

Note: *If the design becomes distorted, reblock the piece.*

STITCH GUIDE

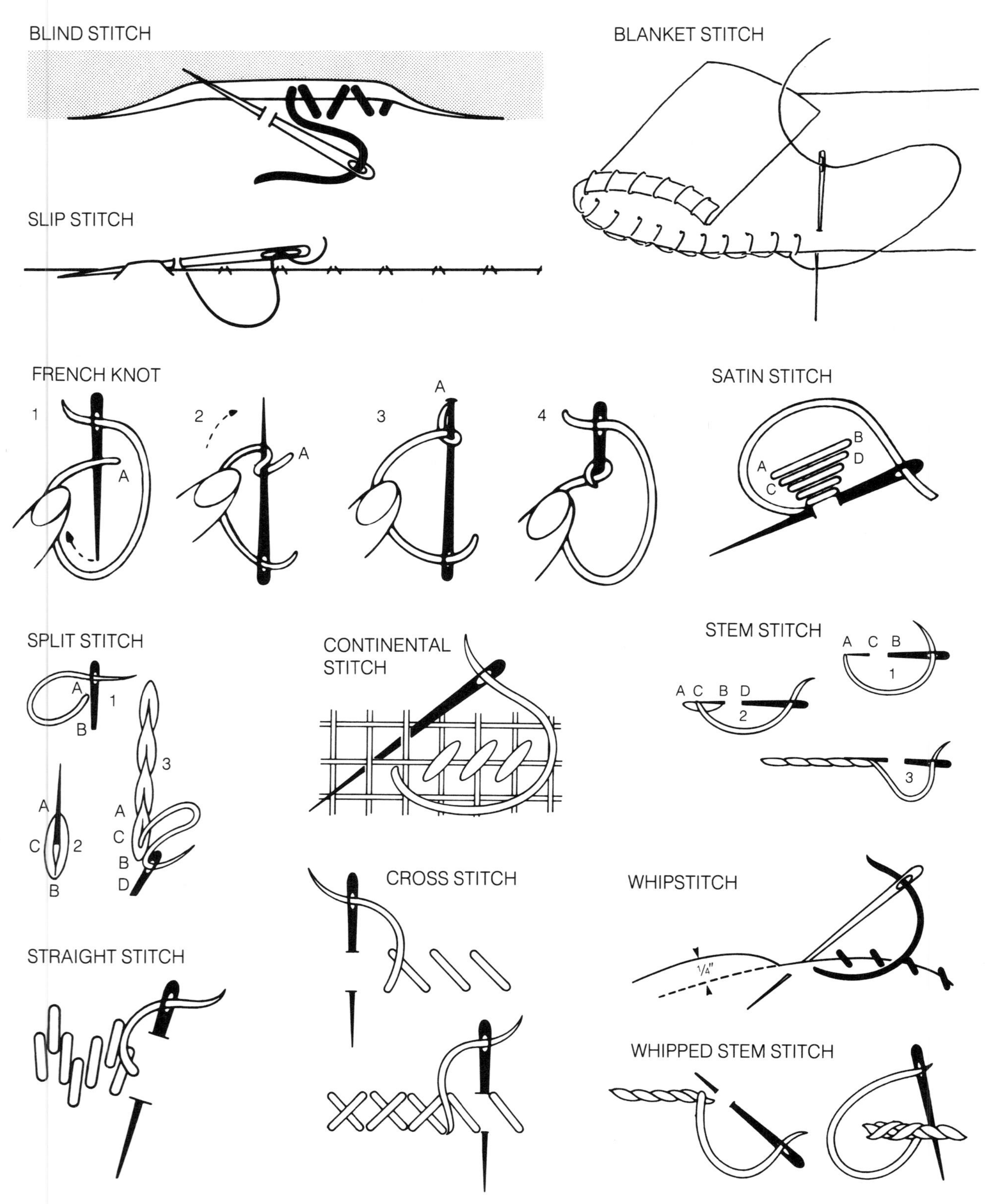

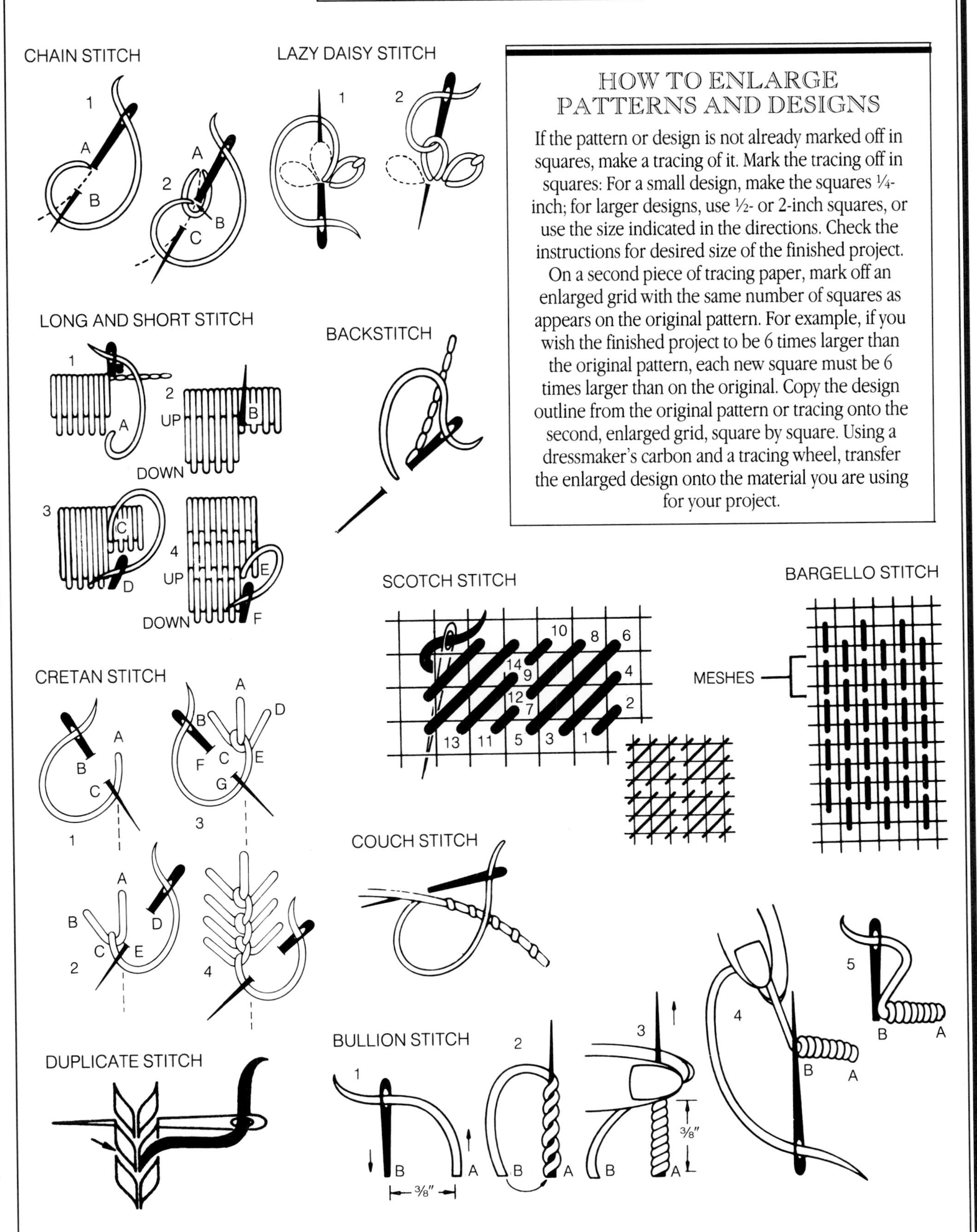

HOW TO ENLARGE PATTERNS AND DESIGNS

If the pattern or design is not already marked off in squares, make a tracing of it. Mark the tracing off in squares: For a small design, make the squares ¼-inch; for larger designs, use ½- or 2-inch squares, or use the size indicated in the directions. Check the instructions for desired size of the finished project.

On a second piece of tracing paper, mark off an enlarged grid with the same number of squares as appears on the original pattern. For example, if you wish the finished project to be 6 times larger than the original pattern, each new square must be 6 times larger than on the original. Copy the design outline from the original pattern or tracing onto the second, enlarged grid, square by square. Using a dressmaker's carbon and a tracing wheel, transfer the enlarged design onto the material you are using for your project.

INDEX

A

B

D

E

F

Q

R

S

T

PHOTOGRAPHERS

Robert Ander: *Page 92.* David Bishop: *Pages 7, 27, 28, 36, 42, 43, 192, 228.*
Richard Blinkoff: *Pages 129, 131.* Leombruno Bodi: *Page 106.* Ralph Bogertman: *Pages 9, 11, 16, 19, 22, 26, 93.*
Richard Cappellutti: *Pages 78, 139.* David Glomb: *Pages 21, 23.* Joshua Green: *Page 220.*
Joseph Heppt: *Pages 129, 131, 144, 153.* Irwin Horowitz: *Pages 242-243.* Elyse Lewin: *Pages 56, 57.*
Taylor Lewis: *Pages 10, 17, 92, 94.* Bill McGinn: *Pages 12, 30-31, 32, 40, 58, 60, 62-63, 72, 74, 80, 81, 82, 83, 84 89, 94, 95, 102, 105, 108, 110, 119, 120, 129, 131, 134, 137, 144, 148, 153, 155, 199, 201, 254.*
Ron Nicolayen: *Page 114.* Jeff Niki: *Pages 117, 122, 126, 141.* Bradley Olman: *Page 10.*
Frances Pellegrini: *Pages 3, 4, 24-25, 48, 50, 51, 100.* Dean Powell: *Pages 35, 45, 61, 96-97.*
Ron Schwerin: *Pages 180, 204.* Michael Skott: *Page 162.* Gordon E. Smith: *Pages 14, 172.*
Michael Soluri: *Pages 47, 53.* Bob Stoller: *Pages 90, 91, 103.* Rene Velez: *Pages 10, 12, 32, 40, 58, 62-63, 68-69, 72, 74, 77, 80, 81, 82, 83, 84, 86, 95, 103, 105, 108, 110, 119, 120, 129, 131, 134, 137, 139, 144, 148, 153, 155, 199, 201.* Elizabeth Zeschin: *Page 55.*

CONTRIBUTING CRAFT EDITORS

Pam Aulson: *Pages 90, 91.* Joanne Beretta: *Pages 14, 30-31.* Michael Cannarozzi: *Page 72.*
Marci Crestani: *Pages 21, 23, 28.* Alexandra Eames: *Pages 16, 19.* Bonnie Egli: *Page 74.*
Vicki Enteen: *Pages 62-63.* Wendy Everett: *Page 141.* Blake Hampton: *Pages 68-69, 78, 80, 81, 82, 83, 84, 86.*
Sang Han: *Page 119.* Priscilla Hauser: *Page 108.* Margot Hotchkiss: *Pages 35, 55, 61, 96-97.*
Alla Ladyzhensky: *Pages 42, 43, 62-63.* Eleanor Lewis: *Pages 30-31.* Steve Levine: *Page 122.*
Patricia Marks: *Page 106.* Buff McAllister: *Page 153.* Cathy Miller: *Page 10.* Jill Morris: *Page 139.*
Josephine Neri: *Page 120.* Niddy Noddy: *Page 126.* Kathy Orr: *Pages 47, 53.* Lillian Pacelli: *Page 32.*
Audrey Peyton: *Page 134.* Robert Pfreundschuh: *Page 95.* Mary Jane Protus (for Paton Yarns): *Page 117.*
Evelyn Rodriguez: *Page 141.* Barbara Schultz: *Page 7.* Jane Slovachek: *Pages 62-63, 105, 137.*
Michelle Slovak: *Pages 60, 94.* Tom Tavernor: *Page 110.* Jean Wilkinson: *Pages 48, 50, 51.*
Doris Wright: *Pages 62-63.* Joanne Young: *Page 92.*

CONTRIBUTING FOOD EDITORS

Joanne Borkoski: *Page 251.* Joanne Brett: *Page 213, 214, 215, 216, 217, 218, 219.* Beatrice Cihak: *Pages 168, 187.*
Lois Cristofano: *Pages 166, 173, 175, 181, 182, 183, 184, 185, 186, 255, 256, 257, 258.*
Susan Ohlson Elo: *Page 222.* Jim Fobel: *Pages 198, 202.* Ceri Hadda: *Pages 177, 182, 187, 252, 253, 259.*
Dora Jonassen: *Page 167.* Barbara Lewis: *Pages 205, 206, 207, 208, 209.*
Diane Mogelever: *Pages 243, 244, 245, 246, 247, 248, 249, 250.*
Veronica Petta: *Pages 210, 211, 212, 235, 236, 238, 239, 240, 241.* David Ricketts: *Page 239.*
Janice Schindeler: *Pages 170, 171.* Andrea Swenson: *Page 173.*